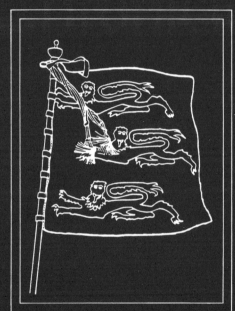

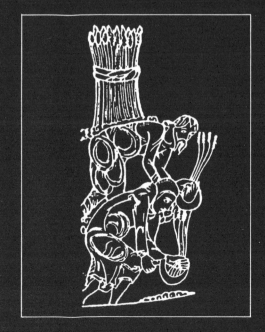

D1143406

The Plantagenet Chronicles

General Editor
Dr Elizabeth Hallam

Weidenfeld and Nicolson
London

Copyright © Phoebe Phillips Editions 1986

First published in 1986 by
George Weidenfeld & Nicolson Ltd
91 Clapham High Street, London SW4 7TA

All rights reserved. No part of this publication may be
reproduced, stored in a retrieval system, or transmitted in any
form or by any means, electronic, mechanical or otherwise,
without prior permission in writing of the copyright owner.

ISBN 0 297 79013 7

Frontispiece *The Plantagenet banner; a*
modern version by Polly Hope, from a 16th-
century engraving. Three gold lions were on
Geoffrey of Anjou's shield, as well as in later
illustrations of Henry II and Richard I.

Created and produced by PHOEBE PHILLIPS EDITIONS

Editorial Director: Tessa Clark

Editorial:
Editor: Cecilia Walters
Fiona St Aubyn
Sheila Mortimer
Joanna Chapman
Fred Gill
R M Healey
Richard Bird
Picture Research: Celestine Dars

Design and Production:
Anthony T Short
Rachael Foster
Tanya A M Hines
Tony Fahy

Specially commissioned photographs:
Marianne Majerus

Maps:
Dennis Curran

Phototypesetting:
Tradespools Ltd, Frome, Somerset

Origination:
Anglia Reproductions, Witham, Essex

Printed and bound in Italy by
Arnoldo Mondadori

General Editor:
Dr Elizabeth Hallam, *Assistant Keeper of Medieval Records at the Public Record Office, London*

Translators:
Editor: Dr Richard Mortimer, *Cambridge University*
Anne Dawtry
Catharine Edwards
Peter Lillington
David Smallwood
Emily Thomas
Brigette Vale
Nicolas Webb
Geoffrey West
Amanda Whitmore

Contributors to illustrated spreads:
Dr David Bates, *Lecturer, Cardiff University*
Jim Bradbury, *Head of History Section, West London Institute of Higher Education*
Dr Trevor Chalmers, *Public Record Office, London*
Dr David Crook, *Public Record Office, London*
R.B. Dobson, *Professor of History, University of York*
Lindy Grant, *Conway Library, Courtauld Institute of Art*
Ruth Harvey, *Lecturer, University of London*
Nicholas Hooper, *Lecturer, University of St Andrews*
Dr J.B. Post, *Public Record Office, London*

Special help from:
Philip Attwood, *British Museum*
Terry Ball
John Hurst
Kensington Central Reference Library
The London Library
Medieval Village Research Group
Keith Miller, *British Museum*
Elizabeth Treip, *Western Manuscripts, Sotheby's*
Philip Escreet, *Keeper of Special Collections, Glasgow University Library*

To all chroniclers of their times,
this book is gratefully dedicated.

'A day will come when some laborious
monk
Will bring to light my zealous,
nameless toil,
Kindle, as I, his lamp, and from
the parchment
Shaking the dust of ages, will transcribe
My chronicles.'

ALEXANDER PUSHKIN
1825

Contents

Introduction

The foundations of Plantagenet success were laid by a line of obscure castellans in the Loire valley who, in the tenth century, rose to become counts of Anjou. Fiery tempered, strong in battle, swift to avenge a wrong, but generous to the Church, these men were highly effective in playing complex political games, and gradually built up a strong power base through a mixture of warfare, diplomacy and good marriage alliances. In 1128 the successful and respected Count Fulk V became king of Jerusalem. The rule in Anjou of his son Geoffrey the Fair (1128–51), who captured Normandy and claimed the throne of England through his wife the Empress Matilda, was of crucial importance to the fortunes of the family in western Europe; and it is appropriate that Geoffrey's descendants bore his surname, Plantagenet, which he earned by wearing a sprig of broom (genêt) in his hat. His son Henry II followed the traditional Angevin recipe of efficacious political manoeuvres, a brilliant marriage and potent aggression, and thereby built up and maintained a vast dominion stretching from the Scottish border to the Pyrenees and encompassing more than half of France. He was succeeded by two of his sons: Richard I (1189–99), a charismatic and effective military leader and crusader, and John (1199–1216), who lost most of his French possessions, including the Plantagenets' ancestral homeland of Anjou, to King Philip II of France, and who almost forfeited his crown to Louis, Philip's son. His extortion and high-handedness towards his barons paradoxically produced a lasting memorial, Magna Carta, in fact little more than a curb on royal misbehaviour forced from the king by duress, but which posterity has hailed as the foundation-stone of our popular rights and liberties.

Left The capital of a column in Notre-Dame-la-Grande, Poitiers. Such polychrome decoration, which remains in only a few places, would have made the entire church brilliant with colour and light.

Until the 13th century, the ability to read and write was the almost exclusive preserve of people in holy orders – whether humble clerks, learned scholars or great archbishops and abbots. Kings and nobles needed clerics to run their governments and their law courts, to collect their taxes and to keep account of their money, and to compose the writs and charters which ordered their will to be done. Although most people spoke to one another, or wrote poetry and songs in their native tongue, the common language of the Church and government throughout medieval Europe was Latin; it formed a bridge between ecclesiastics whatever their place of origin, but it also set them apart from the rest of society, even as they fulfilled their main duty of interceding with God for the spiritual health of mankind.

The majority of medieval chroniclers came from monasteries or cathedral churches, places which were at once the powerhouses of prayer and – usually – well-established institutions with great pride in their own traditions, and a natural concern to safeguard their own properties and independence. The chronicler sought not to produce the rational and detached analyses of the historian today, but to show the working-out of God's purpose in events, beginning with the Creation and leading up to his own time. That could be done through the history of his native land, the triumphs and travails of his monastery or the life history of a saint or ruler.

Although subject to the ordinary preconceptions of their times, chroniclers wrote for diverse reasons – some to glorify a king, a monastery or a saint, others to instruct, to explain or to entertain. But all pointed out moral and religious lessons in some form, and all had their eyes on posterity, nourishing the hope that future generations would laboriously copy and draw upon their chronicles. This actually happened in many cases: Henry of Huntingdon's *History of the English*, for example, was an outstanding success, which was copied many times in the 12th century, turning up in places as far apart as the Norman abbey of Le Bec and Durham Cathedral priory; it remained a standard account of its period until the 17th century. Other works have survived in only one or two early manuscripts, among them *The Life of St Hugh*, which was hardly copied at all in medieval England but which became very popular on the Continent from the 15th century.

Both Henry of Huntingdon's *History* and *The Life of St Hugh* have been previously printed in English, although in the case of the first, not since the 19th century, but almost all the other texts in this book are here translated for the first time. For reasons of space, they are not reproduced in their entirety, but passages have been chosen which describe the principal occurrences in any given year and which illuminate the particular interests and preconceptions of the authors. Within the longer extracts, some passages (and occasionally sentences and phrases) have been deliberately omitted to avoid repetition or to clarify the style of the original.

We have taken full advantage of some of our chroniclers interest in accuracy. Diceto's *Images of History* is written clearly and compactly, and within a tidy and relatively reliable chronological framework. However, some of our other sources, such as the chronicles of the counts of Anjou, contain many unsubstantiated myths, telling tales of dramatic and chivalrous deeds rather than giving a clear narrative of events. Indeed, in some instances the authors clearly fabricate incidents which never happened and which may conflict with other more reliable versions. Even the apparently more soundly-based accounts will not always agree either with one another or still less with modern interpretations of events or identifications of names and places. We have provided some explanatory editorial comments (in the passages printed in italics and in the words and phrases which are in square brackets in the text), but otherwise, apart from occasionally supplying dates and surnames or titles to distinguish certain key participants, we have left the chroniclers to tell their own tales.

The Chroniclers

Gervase, a monk and later sacrist of Canterbury Cathedral priory, and Ralph, abbot of Coggeshall, both set out in the early 13th century to write a history of the English people and their kings. Each explained it very much as it related to the history of his own church, however, and incidentally provided many entertaining stories and much useful material on English politics for the years 1201 to 1210 where other narrative sources are relatively scanty. The 'Barnwell' annalist, an anonymous monk or canon whose work is of great importance as evidence for the last years of John's reign (1210 to 1216), by contrast shows far less local bias (his text was preserved at Barnwell priory but probably not written there) and takes an even-handed approach to the conflict between King John and his barons. He shows sympathy for the rebels but also for John, a figure to be greatly maligned in other, later chronicles.

Some monasteries produced official histories of their royal or noble patrons. For example, at Marmoutier Abbey in the Loire valley between 1164 and 1173 the monk John composed a new version of *The Deeds of the Counts of Anjou*. This stirring and dramatic work had been put together at the abbey and at the counts' court over the previous century by several chroniclers, including Abbot Odo and Thomas of Loches, chaplain to Count Fulk V. Much of it, particularly the material about the early Angevins, was little more than legend, but it was written up and dedicated to the very real Henry II, the greatest of his line, who was also king of England and duke of Normandy and Aquitaine. Shortly after completing it, John continued the story by inscribing a colourful and highly laudatory biography of Geoffrey the Fair, Henry II's father.

John of Marmoutier's lively and often apocryphal tales contrast with the somewhat more measured approach of many 12th-century English chroniclers. Henry, archdeacon of Huntingdon, in his *History of the English*, produced a near-contemporary account of the reign of Stephen which is at once highly readable and full of moral lessons, and which contains factual material which, if idiosyncratically chosen, is carefully deployed. This work was first commissioned by Roger, bishop of Salisbury, a leading ecclesiastic and royal administrator, but was revised and recast by its author as its popularity increased. Far more meticulous in its composition is the *Images of History* by Ralph of Diceto, a canon, archivist and later dean of St Paul's Cathedral in London, who was writing up to 1201, the probable date of his death. Like his contemporary the royal clerk Roger Howden (who certainly penned one major chronicle and who may have been the author of *The Deeds of King Henry II and King Richard I*), Diceto set out to produce an accurate history. Concentrating particularly on the English Church, he drew heavily on many royal documents and letters of his day to tell the story for him. He analyses events, using marginal signs to point out different topics such as the controversies between Church and State, and the quarrels between Henry II and his sons, occurrences which he saw happen. Any writer seeking to give an objective account of his own times is bound to encounter problems: Diceto both admired Henry II and deplored Thomas Becket's martyrdom, an incident for which that king had been indirectly responsible; but this difficulty produced valuable results, for his account of the quarrel of king and archbishop has a remarkable sense of detachment about it.

In his *Life of St Thomas Becket*, composed in the 1170s, not long after its subject's martyrdom, William FitzStephen, formerly a clerk in Becket's household, gives a lively and dramatic account of the archbishop's life and death, which is full of social comment, and which contains an important description of the city of London, Becket's birthplace. It was intended specifically to glorify and magnify its subject, as was also Adam of Eynsham's life of St Hugh of Lincoln, one of the most remarkable figures in the 12th-century English Church. Hugh, like Thomas Becket, fell out with Henry II – and with his sons – over ecclesiastical privileges, but was able to restore royal equanimity with his inimitable sense of humour, a quality which Becket seems to have lacked.

Both biographers are, however, careful not to criticize the king too much, unlike Gerald of Wales in his later years. Gerald, archdeacon of Brecon, was a voluminous and popular writer on subjects like the customs and characteristics of the Welsh and the Irish, but, embittered by his longstanding failure to become bishop of St David's, he penned hostile and vindictive satire on the fate which overcomes the sinful ruler, with particular reference to Henry II.

To put the chronicles into wider historical perspective, our team of scholars has written a series of notes which explain and build upon assertions and comments in the main narrative, whether by describing the characters of the principal protagonists, analysing the framework of political events, tracing social and economic developments, exploring the religious context, or examining some of the artistic and cultural movements and looking at the art and monuments of the day. These notes are illustrated with photographs selected to bring the material vividly to life. Many depict the places mentioned in the text, many others show illuminated and other manuscripts and artefacts of the period. Others still are of somewhat later manuscripts and objects, and have been chosen either to show how certain incidents were viewed later on, or because they give graphic illustrations of relatively unchanging social customs. Full details of the provenance of individual manuscripts are given at the back of this book.

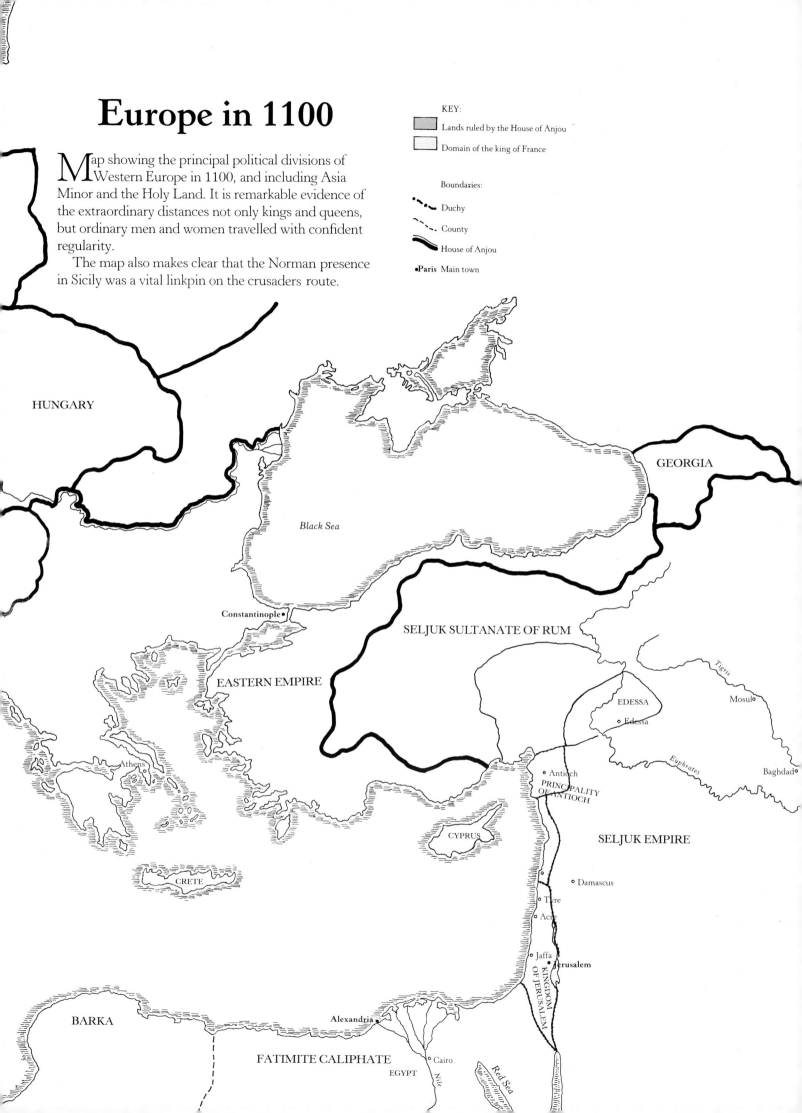

Europe in 1100

Map showing the principal political divisions of Western Europe in 1100, and including Asia Minor and the Holy Land. It is remarkable evidence of the extraordinary distances not only kings and queens, but ordinary men and women travelled with confident regularity.

The map also makes clear that the Norman presence in Sicily was a vital linkpin on the crusaders route.

KEY:

Lands ruled by the House of Anjou

Domain of the king of France

Boundaries:

— · — Duchy

— - — County

～～ House of Anjou

•Paris Main town

HUNGARY

GEORGIA

Black Sea

Constantinople •

SELJUK SULTANATE OF RUM

EASTERN EMPIRE

EDESSA

• Edessa

Mosul ○

Tigris

Euphrates

Baghdad ○

Athens

Antioch •

PRINCIPALITY OF ANTIOCH

SELJUK EMPIRE

CYPRUS

Damascus ○

CRETE

Tyre ○

Acre ○

Jaffa ○

Jerusalem •

KINGDOM OF JERUSALEM

BARKA

Alexandria •

FATIMITE CALIPHATE

Cairo ○

EGYPT

Nile

Red Sea

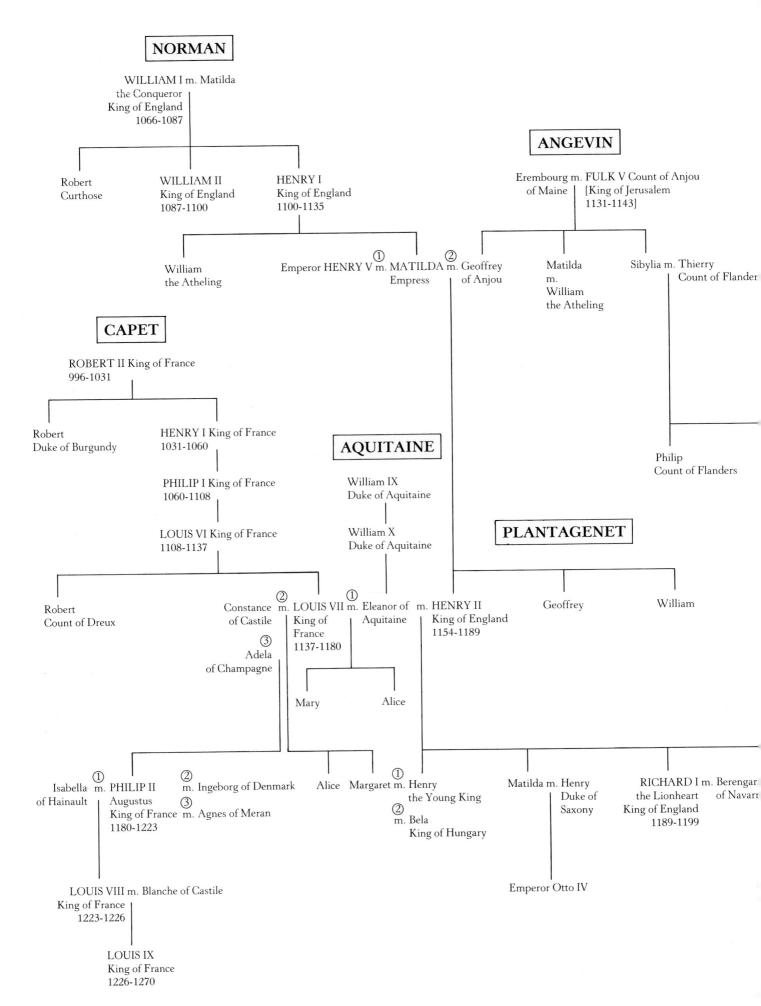

NORMAN

WILLIAM I m. Matilda
the Conqueror
King of England
1066-1087

Robert Curthose

WILLIAM II
King of England
1087-1100

HENRY I
King of England
1100-1135

William
the Atheling

Emperor HENRY V ① m. MATILDA ② m. Geoffrey
Empress   of Anjou

ANGEVIN

Erembourg m. FULK V Count of Anjou
of Maine   [King of Jerusalem
                1131-1143]

Matilda
m.
William
the Atheling

Sibylia m. Thierry
          Count of Flander

Philip
Count of Flanders

CAPET

ROBERT II King of France
996-1031

Robert
Duke of Burgundy

HENRY I King of France
1031-1060

PHILIP I King of France
1060-1108

LOUIS VI King of France
1108-1137

AQUITAINE

William IX
Duke of Aquitaine

William X
Duke of Aquitaine

PLANTAGENET

Robert
Count of Dreux

Constance m. LOUIS VII m. Eleanor of m. HENRY II
of Castile ② King of ① Aquitaine   King of England
              France   1154-1189
Adela ③   1137-1180
of Champagne

Geoffrey

William

Mary   Alice

Isabella ① m. PHILIP II   ② m. Ingeborg of Denmark
of Hainault   Augustus
              King of France ③ m. Agnes of Meran
              1180-1223

Alice Margaret m. ① Henry
                     the Young King
                  ② m. Bela
                     King of Hungary

Matilda m. Henry
           Duke of
           Saxony

RICHARD I m. Berengar
the Lionheart of Navarr
King of England
1189-1199

LOUIS VIII m. Blanche of Castile
King of France
1223-1226

Emperor Otto IV

LOUIS IX
King of France
1226-1270

Kings of England and France

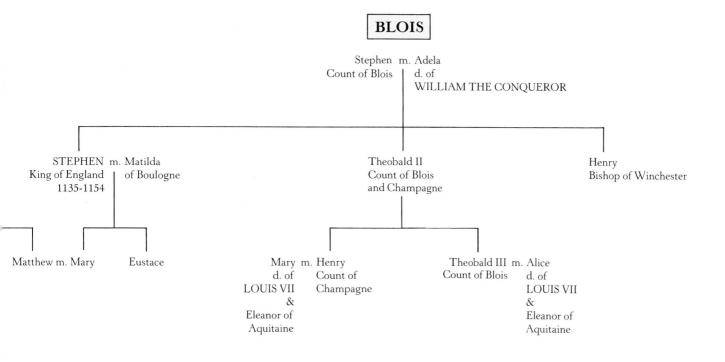

BLOIS

Stephen m. Adela
Count of Blois | d. of
WILLIAM THE CONQUEROR

STEPHEN m. Matilda
King of England | of Boulogne
1135-1154

Theobald II
Count of Blois
and Champagne

Henry
Bishop of Winchester

Matthew m. Mary   Eustace

Mary m. Henry
d. of   Count of
LOUIS VII   Champagne
&
Eleanor of
Aquitaine

Theobald III m. Alice
Count of Blois   d. of
LOUIS VII
&
Eleanor of
Aquitaine

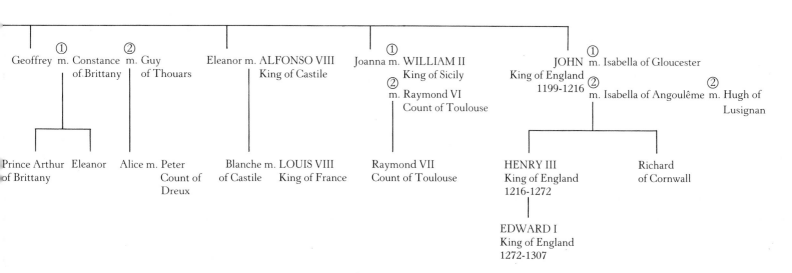

Geoffrey ① m. Constance ② m. Guy
of Brittany   of Thouars

Eleanor m. ALFONSO VIII
King of Castile

Joanna ① m. WILLIAM II
King of Sicily
② m. Raymond VI
Count of Toulouse

JOHN ① m. Isabella of Gloucester
King of England
1199-1216 ② m. Isabella of Angoulême ② m. Hugh of
Lusignan

Prince Arthur Eleanor
of Brittany

Alice m. Peter
Count of
Dreux

Blanche m. LOUIS VIII
of Castile   King of France

Raymond VII
Count of Toulouse

HENRY III
King of England
1216-1272

Richard
of Cornwall

EDWARD I
King of England
1272-1307

17

Part 1

Origins of the Angevin dynasty

The fortunes of the house of Anjou were founded on the prowess of Ingelgar, a semi-legendary soldier of fortune who carved out an estate for himself in the Loire valley. His son, Fulk the Red, built effectively on his foundations and became count of Anjou by 941. Under his grandson, Fulk the Good (941–960) the region enjoyed a time of tranquil prosperity. During the next 170 years Anjou was ruled by some extraordinary men: Geoffrey Greygown (960–987), whose prowess was the stuff of legend, and whose story begins this history of the Plantagenets; Fulk Nerra (987-1040), violent, charismatic and cruel, and a master of strategic castle-building; the more subtle Geoffrey Martel (1040–60); and, after nearly 50 years of disorder, Fulk V (1109–29), who became king of Jerusalem. Their lives and deeds are vividly – if often apocryphally – described in the Chronicle of the Counts of Anjou. *This valuable history, the work of several writers including Thomas of Loches, a chaplain of Count Fulk V, was given its final form in the 1160s by John, a monk of Marmoutier Abbey.*

(Opposite: The castle at Angers)

Fulk the Good had three sons. Geoffrey, the eldest, became count of Anjou, while the second, Guy, became bishop of Le Puy. Drogo, the youngest and Fulk's favourite – he had been conceived when Fulk was past middle age – was educated in literature and the liberal arts and, through the kindness of King Hugh Capet of France, he succeeded his brother as bishop of Le Puy.

960

Count Geoffrey was a skilful soldier in the French manner, stout-hearted and strong and most successful in battle.

At that time Huasten the Dane had been attacking the coast of France for three years, and now he joined his cousins, Edward and Hilduin, who were both counts of Flanders. He had with him a force of fifteen thousand Danes and Saxons, among whom was a warrior of extraordinary stature and courage, Ethelulf. Together the Danes and Swedes were ravaging French lands, plundering and burning towns and villages wherever they could. With the aid of the Flemings, they overran and laid waste with fire and sword almost all of that region of Flanders inhabited by the French, before deciding to advance to Paris and sow fear and terror there.

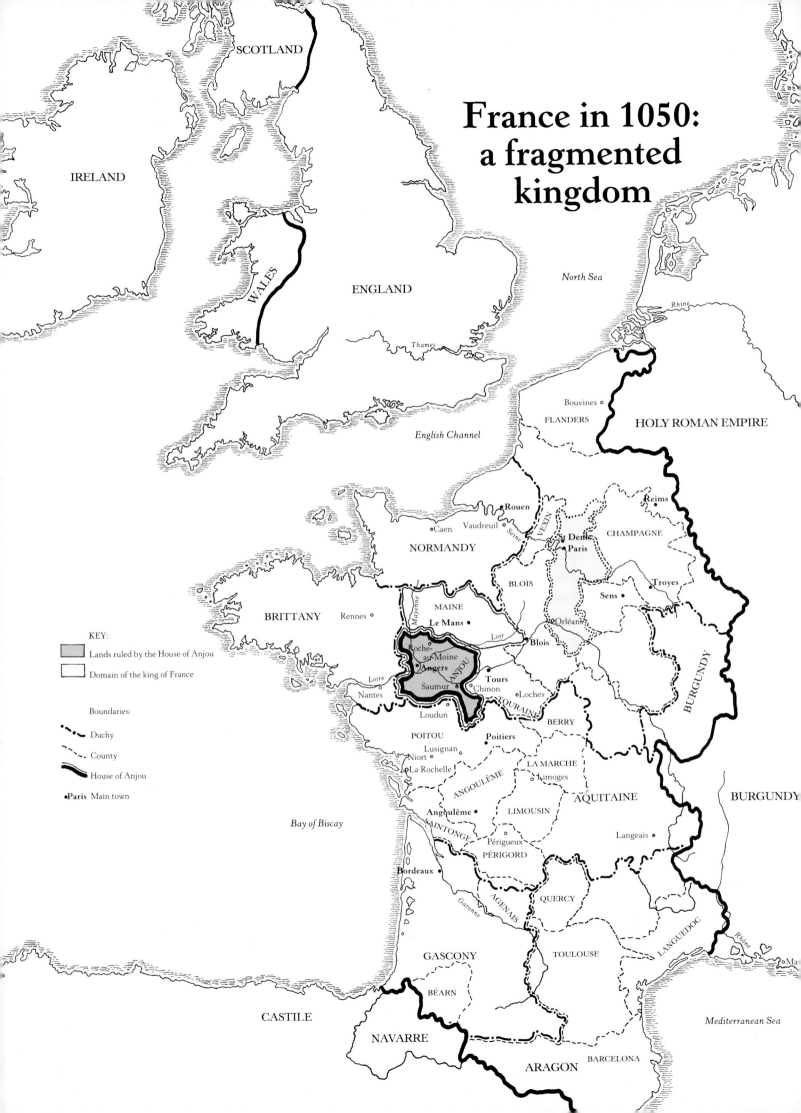

France in 1050: a fragmented kingdom

SCOTLAND

IRELAND

WALES

ENGLAND

North Sea

Thames

English Channel

Rhine

Bouvines

FLANDERS

HOLY ROMAN EMPIRE

•Rouen

Reims

○Caen   Vaudreuil

VEXIN

CHAMPAGNE

St Denis

•Paris

NORMANDY

Seine

BLOIS

Troyes

Sens

MAINE

Rennes •

•**Le Mans** •

Loir

•Orléans

BRITTANY

Mayenne

Blois

Roche-
au-Moine

ANJOU

Tours

BURGUNDY

Angers

Saumur

Chinon

Loches

Loire

TOURAINE

BERRY

Nantes

Loudun

POITOU

Poitiers

BURGUNDY

Lusignan

LA MARCHE

Niort

•Limoges

○La Rochelle

ANGOULÊME

AQUITAINE

Bay of Biscay

LIMOUSIN

Langeais •

Angoulême •

SAINTONGE

Périgueux •

PÉRIGORD

Bordeaux

QUERCY

AGENAIS

Garonne

Rhône

GASCONY

TOULOUSE

LANGUEDOC

Ma

Mediterranean Sea

CASTILE

BÉARN

NAVARRE

ARAGON

BARCELONA

KEY:

Lands ruled by the House of Anjou

Domain of the king of France

Boundaries:

Duchy

County

House of Anjou

•Paris   Main town

In 800 the Emperor Charlemagne was crowned by the Pope as ruler of a massive Empire which encompassed modern France, Italy and most of Germany. In 843 it was divided between his grandsons, West Francia, or France, being given to Charles the Bald. During the next century the authority of the Carolingian rulers in France gradually collapsed, and in 987 they were replaced by Hugh Capet and his line.

In the middle of the 11th century there was little to distinguish the king of France from the count of Anjou or any of the other great vassals. In theory the Capetian kings held sway over the whole country, and they were crowned and annointed by the archbishops of Reims with great solemnity. But in practice the French royal house controlled only a small area around Paris and Orléans known as Ile-de-France. Beyond this 'island' lay a patchwork of duchies, counties, viscounties and castellanies. In some regions anarchy reigned; but others, like Anjou and Blois, and later Normandy, were under the grip of powerful magnates who equalled or surpassed the king in real power. To preserve any credibility the Capetian kings were impelled to join in with the constantly shifting pattern of alliances and power struggles which resembled a vast, savage and protracted game.

The first round finally went to the House of Anjou when in the middle of the 12th century it assembled a collection of duchies and counties which overshadowed the royal lands.

Asia Minor and the Holy Land
c.1100

The First Crusade arrived in a Holy Land which was the principal theatre of war between the Seljuk Turks, centred in Baghdad, and the Fatimid caliphs of Egypt. Profiting from this rivalry the Western army took Jerusalem in 1099 and set up three crusader states: the kingdom of Jerusalem, the county of Tripoli and the principality of Antioch. The last was claimed also by the emperor of Constantinople, who managed to extend his own authority in the wake of the Franks.

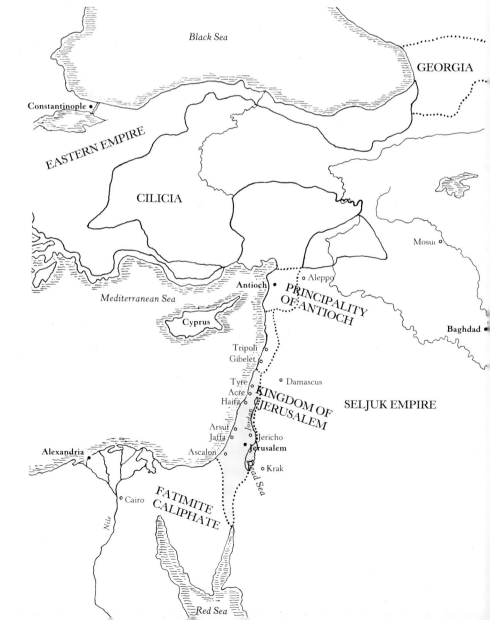

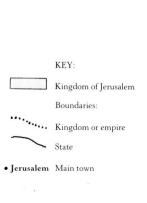

KEY:

Kingdom of Jerusalem

Boundaries:

Kingdom or empire

State

• **Jerusalem** Main town

Alarmed at such audacity, the king had his nobles forgather from all parts at Paris at Whitsun. Ethelulf the Dane, like a new Goliath, scornfully approached the city, demanding single combat with a French knight. When several of the bravest and noblest of the French had been defeated and killed in such combat, the king was overcome with grief and forbade anyone else to go out against Ethelulf.

When Count Geoffrey of Anjou heard the royal messenger who summoned him to the assembly at Whitsun, he prepared to leave his lands at Château-Landon. When he learned of the Dane's strength and cruelty, he set off in secret, with one knight and two squires.

He took just one horse and crossed the Seine, together with the knight and two millers. When he saw the Dane and heard his war cry, the count roared, swiftly armed himself and mounted his horse. Leaving his companions in the boat, he set out alone onto the plain to engage his foe. Spurring on his charger, each man closed on the other. The count pierced his enemy's chest and threw him to the ground with the steel emerging between the shoulder blades. As he looked back, Geoffrey could see the groaning Dane struggling to get up, with a threatening look in his fierce eyes; so he swiftly dismounted and drawing his sword, like a second David, he cut off his head. He immediately remounted and returned swiftly to the boat with the head and the horse of his enemy. After crossing the river, he gave the head to one of the millers to take to Paris, while he returned *incognito* to Château-Landon to rejoin his men.

The bearer of the head reached the city and, in the presence of the king, declared that although he did not know the identity of the knight he had no doubt that, if he saw him again, he would recognize him.

On the appointed day all those who had been summoned, the dukes and counts, the nobles of the whole of France, reached Paris: so all the chief men of outstanding skill and ability were gathered together in the royal palace. Geoffrey, count of Anjou, sat among the barons wearing a tunic of

A house of devils

'FROM the Devil they came and to the Devil they will return.' This saying about the counts of Anjou, reported by Gerald of Wales, refers to the legend that the Angevin counts and kings were descended from the daughter of Satan. In Gerald's story, an early count of Anjou returned from a journey with a woman, Melusine, famous for her beauty, whom he married. There were many strange things about her, the most shocking of which was that she was always absent from Mass at the consecration of the Host. Her true identity was discovered when her husband forced her to stay and see the body of Christ – a sight no evil spirit could contemplate. Melusine flew screaming out of the window and was never seen again. She left behind two sons, from whom the later counts were descended.

Other, more complimentary, legends were chronicled in the 12th century by the family's official historians, Thomas of Loches (*c*.1130) and John of Marmoutier (*c*.1164–73), and usually tell of soldierly prowess – for instance, how Count Geoffrey Greygown (*c*.960–987), single-handedly fought and killed a giant, Ethelulf.

The 12th century was a great period of legend-making, the time when the Arthurian tales first became widely known, and many noble houses invented pedigrees that gave them legendary ancestors, probably to explain obscure social origins. An earlier historian of the house of Anjou, Count Fulk Rechin (1068–1109), admitted that he knew nothing of the first three of his line, Ingelgar, who is said to have been granted the title of count of Anjou in the late 9th century, his son Fulk the Red, and Fulk the Good who ruled from 941 to *c*.960.

Sometimes the legends were blatant propaganda attempts. According to one, Fulk the Good, Geoffrey Greygown's father, was learned and saintly, dressed in cleric's robes and lived peaceably. Yet, when his simple ways were mocked by King Louis IV, he is said to have commented that, 'An illiterate king is a crowned ass.' As a holy man he would be expected to have the gift of prophecy and is credited with predicting that his descendants in the ninth generation would extend their power to the ends of the earth. By the time the prophecy was written down, it had come true.

Contemporaries enjoyed, and may have believed, the stories. Even Richard the Lionheart, one of the greatest of the descendants of the house of Anjou, laughed at his family's legendary origins: 'What wonder if we lack the natural affections of mankind – we come from the Devil, and must needs go back to the Devil.'

Right *Devils carry on their satanic work in hell.*

 unt enfant nomme guillau
me aatie de laatie de xv. ane
ou enuiron vid en dozmant

coarse grey cloth that the French call grising but which we Angevins call borrel.

The miller, who had been summoned by the king for this express purpose, looked at the count and recognized him immediately. With the king's permission, he approached him smiling. As he knelt, he caught hold of the count's tunic and said to the king and the rest of those assembled, 'This man, who wears a grey tunic, restored our honour when he slew the Dane and struck fear into their army.' The king decreed that henceforth Geoffrey should be called 'Greygown', and all present gave their assent.

Geoffrey Greygown was succeeded by his son Count Maurice who was 'wise, virtuous and peace-loving and who ruled in peace more as a result of wisdom than of fighting battles'. On his death in 987 his lands went to his son Fulk Nerra who, although only about 17 years old, had already proved himself a valiant soldier.

987

Fulk Nerra, ever a friend to God-fearing souls and a young man of no mean spirit, bravely set out to defend his land from its many enemies, for wars always break out quickly against a new ruler. On the advice of that scoundrel Landry lord of Châteaudun, Odo II, count of Blois and of Champagne and Gelduin lord of Saumur tried to expel Fulk from Touraine, imagining that the counts of Amboise and Loches would help them. Landry pointed out to them that the time was ripe for Sulpice the treasurer of St Martin's abbey at Tours had lost his brother recently, and was ruling Amboise for the count single-handedly. Our stout-hearted hero did not delay in preparing the enemy's defeat nor flinch from exposing himself to danger. He gathered together the largest army he could and boldly invaded the land of his enemies, marching past Blois to reach Châteaudun.

The inhabitants of that place girded their city well with rings of soldiers and, protected by their arms, they made ready for battle in the manner of defenders of a camp. Quickly crowding together, they attacked the count and his men. The

Angevins held off their repeated attacks until evening but, when they attempted to retreat, were unable to avoid the throng of attackers because the men of Châteaudun were pressing on them from behind, even as they yielded. When the count's army could toil no longer, neither to withdraw nor to check their opponents, the encircled men ventured to return step by step and fight them. With the men of Amboise forcing their way ahead, the Angevins attacked on every side and enclosed and overcame the enemy. The men of Châteaudun were seized by fear and, falling out of formation, took to their heels. But the battle continued, and the count pursued them into their own camp, capturing many of the populace and putting others to the sword. That night, the Angevins were able to rest there, guarding the two hundred knights who had been taken prisoner and bound with other captives. They pillaged the lands round about on the next day and brought ruin upon those who tilled the earth. Drunk with the joy of victory, they returned to Amboise three days later.

At Amboise, the count besieged the stronghold of Landry. So ferociously did his men gather to storm that man's house that they struck desperation into the hearts of those resisting. Knowing that they could not hold out and that if captured they would be unable to avoid the punishment of death they deserved, the besieged began to negotiate through envoys to surrender the stronghold to the count in return for their lives. When this was considered, it seemed good to everyone that such a great peril should be removed without danger to the attackers. And so the besieged were spared, the stronghold utterly destroyed and Landry and his men expelled from their encampment.

After this, the count crossed the Loire and stayed at a dwelling he had reinforced, known as Caramantum in years gone by, though now called Moraud; then to Semblançay, where he had also strengthened the defences, and through the land of his vassal and friend, Hugh of Alluyes, who was lord of Château-la-Vallière and of Saint-Christophe. He entered Vallée and descended freely to Angers, despite the wishes of the people of Tours. Indeed, he took control of Mirebeau,

The devout tyrant

FULK Nerra, by turns brutal monster and pious pilgrim, was one of the most dramatic figures of the 11th century. The extreme product of an age when appetite and emotion controlled men's behaviour, and religion was a materialistic tit-for-tat with God, his acts of atonement succeeded appalling acts of violence.

In 992, he won a major pitched battle against the count of Brittany at Conquereuil, a victory which was achieved only when he rallied his retreating army with the 'force of a gale sweeping corn'. Slaughter, pillage and devastation followed in the wake of this and his other triumphs and passion compounded violence: he had his first wife burnt at the stake for infidelity.

Yet Fulk Nerra undertook the pilgrimage to Jerusalem an astonishing three times in an age when few made this difficult journey even once. He also visited Rome, and founded two abbeys: Beaulieu-lès-Loches near Tours and St. Nicholas at Angers.

Behind these extremes was a man of policy and purpose, revealed in the effectiveness of his campaigns and the strategic siting of his castles. Fascinating yet repellent, he was a leader of undoubted if crude ability.

Below *The abbey-church of Beaulieu-lès-Loches, burial place of Fulk Nerra. Bones, probably his, were found there in 1870.*

Loudun, Chinon (which had been held by Odo), Saumur and Montsoreau, from which he frequently fought the men of l'Ile-Bouchard, before he returned to Loches through the territory of Guennon, lord of Nouâtre.

To complete his designs, Count Fulk selected a warlike man, the most accomplished of soldiers, Lisois of Bazougers, nephew of the viscount of Sainte-Suzanne, put him in charge of Loches and Amboise and instructed him to enforce obedience on the knights there, both great and small.

Fulk's wife gave birth to Geoffrey Martel and a daughter, Adela. Being a God-fearing man, Fulk made a pilgrimage to Rome to give thanks and, after receiving letters from the Roman pope with his blessing, started out on the road to Jerusalem, which at that time was held by the infidel. When he arrived at Constantinople, he met Duke Robert of Normandy, who had embarked on the same journey. (Richard, duke of Normandy, had had two sons, Richard and Robert, by Judith, daughter of Count Conan of Brittany. Richard, the elder, had been poisoned by his brother Robert. To offer atonement to God for having perpetrated this crime, Robert undertook the journey barefoot, seven years after becoming duke. That same Robert had a son, William, an upright man who conquered England.) When Fulk had found Robert and made his acquaintance, he showed the pope's letters to the emperor and at his command, they were both led through the land of the Saracens by the men of Antioch, who happened to be in the city. Robert died on the way, in Bithynia.

Fulk Nerra was led under escort to Jerusalem. At first, however, he was not allowed to go through the city gate where pilgrims were being forced to pay an entrance fee. But by paying for himself and for the other Christians delayed at the forbidden gate, he was able to go in with all of them. But then doors barred them from the Lord's tomb.

Once it was known that he was a high-born man, the guards said he could have access to the tomb but only, they added deceitfully, by urinating

East against West

THE medieval Church was utterly committed to the ideal of Christian unity, but was never able to achieve it. At no time in the Middle Ages was this regrettable failure more obvious than in 1054, when Pope Leo IX sent a diplomatic mission to Constantinople to denounce the patriarch there as 'a disobedient, insolent and corrupt daughter, sitting at home in peace and lasciviousness, and refusing to take part in the Christian fight waged by her Holy Mother, the Church of Rome'. Not surprisingly, the 'daughter' renounced her loyalty altogether; 1054 was the year in which a permanent schism between the Latin Catholic West and the Greek Orthodox East occurred.

The breach had been long in the making, ever since the first Christian emperor of Rome, Constantine the Great,

decided to inaugurate the Greek city of Byzantium as his Christian capital of Constantinople – or 'New Rome' – in 330. Rome and Constantinople were originally allies; but as the papacy of Rome gradually became cut off from Greek influences, it increasingly associated itself with western attitudes. After 752 there were no more Greek or Greek-speaking popes at Rome, while in the still powerful and highly sophisticated Byzantine Empire the patriarchs identified themselves and their Church absolutely with the interests of their all-mighty emperor. Doctrinal differences between the two Churches could have been resolved even in the 11th century. The western papacy's emphasis on discipline, obedience and rigid uniformity, however, did not easily allow it to accommodate alternative religious structures and, inevitably, Latin West and Greek East broke away from each other.

Until its capture by the Turks in 1453, Constantinople remained the centre of a highly learned Greek Church,

Above Hagia Sophia, Constantinople, dates back to the 6th century.

whose greatest achievement was the conversion of the Russian peoples to Orthodox Christianity. In Rome, the popes put themselves at the head of the great Church reform movement of the late 11th and 12th centuries. Under the aggressive Gregory VII (1073–85) and his successors the papacy began to enforce its will throughout western Christendom as never before.

For Count Fulk Nerra of Anjou, who died in 1040 while returning from his last visit to Jerusalem, the pope of Rome was a shadowy and insignificant figure. However, for his descendant, Count Fulk V of Anjou, who ruled as monarch of the Latin kingdom of Jerusalem exactly a century later, the Roman popes were the undisputed leaders of Christendom and the spiritual sponsors of the crusading movement.

upon it and upon the holy cross. Fulk being a wise man, assented, albeit unwillingly. He obtained a ram's bladder, cleansed it of impurities, filled it with the best white wine and placed it in a convincing place between his thighs. Then, after removing his shoes, he approached the Lord's tomb, poured the wine over it and was thus allowed to enter freely with all his companions. In the tomb he prayed, shedding many tears, and soon felt divine power when the hard stone became soft. After this, he tore himself away from the tomb, which he had smothered with kisses, and departed enraged because mocking and ignorant infidels had accompanied him. But giving generous alms to the needy, he earned a piece of the holy cross from the Syrians guarding the tomb.

When Count Fulk had returned to Loches, beyond the River Indre, he built a church in honour of the Holy Sepulchre, at Beaulieu to be precise, and installed some monks and an abbot there. In the church of St Mary the Virgin at Amboise, he placed a piece of the Saviour's cross and a fragment of the thongs by which the hands of Christ had been bound. To this church, the body of St Florentine was transferred in Fulk's time from Poitou and there, too, he and Sulpice, the treasurer of St Martin, established canons.

Odo, count of Champagne, in alliance with Gedouin of Saumur, was threatening Fulk's power in the east of Anjou. Fulk and his ally Count Herbert of Maine did battle against him and carried the day, slaying or capturing about 6,000 of their enemies. The next year Fulk founded the castle of Montboyau to threaten Tours which he hoped to capture from Odo. But Odo laid siege to Montboyau.

Fulk united as many as he could at Vallée and followed a shrewd plan, because he could not and dared not fight. He crossed the Loire and, riding fast all night, entered defenceless Saumur at daybreak where he immediately seized the whole town up to the citadel.

There was no hope of safety for the men in the citadel, no place of refuge, only the shame of surrender. They knew that the Angevins were a ferocious and warlike race and that they would not forsake their undertaking until their prayers were answered; they knew their attackers would be devoid of all mercy. So they came to terms with the count, according to the law of surrender. 'Lucky one,' they said, 'you order that we should cede the citadel and hand it over to you; protect us from those murderers and allow us to live to serve you.' The count listened and permitted them freedom with dignity, honouring them with great riches. He is said to have done this in order to bind the freed men to himself and to entice others to surrender. When the citadel had been handed over to his followers he ordered them to guard it diligently.

After taking control of Saumur as he had desired, Fulk crossed the Vienne near Chinon, between Nouâtre and Ile-Bouchard, on a bridge made of ships and besieged Montbazon. Odo abandoned the siege at Montboyau and directed his infantry against Fulk. The ingenious Fulk put an end to his siege and retreated to Loches, where he erected his tents on the meadows.

Both leaders were therefore quiet, their armies disbanded. While Odo was at Blois, a messenger informed him that the Germans, under the duke of Lorraine, had besieged Bar-sur-Aube. Hurriedly returning there, Odo pursued the Germans who had already departed into Lorraine. Although seriously wounded whilst fighting them, he returned victorious. He died shortly after, however, from his injuries and his son Theobald III inherited his territory. Meanwhile, Fulk besieged Montbazon again, this time capturing it and entrusting it to William of Mirebeau to be guarded. Airaud Brustulii and other traitors handed over their lord Geoffrey, ruler of Saint-Aignan, to Fulk. Later, in Fulk's absence, this man was strangled in his prison at Loches by the same traitors.

The count gave to Lisois, his steward, the niece of the treasurer Sulpice as a wife, and provided him with the citadel of Amboise, together with all its possessions, Verneuil-sur-Indre, Moré and vine-bearing Champagne. Establishing the man thus, the count commended him to his son Martel. And so the land was quiet and peaceful until Fulk died, not long afterwards.

The black monks of St Benedict

IN the great age of European monasticism – the 11th and 12th centuries – Benedictine monks were the most influential of all practitioners of the Christian religious life. Amidst the bewildering variety of monastic communities in Europe, the Benedictines or black monks – so called because they customarily wore black habits – owed their cohesion and success to the monastic rule originally compiled by St Benedict some years before he died at his famous foundation of Monte Cassino in Italy, during the first half of the 6th century. Simply but elegantly written, and described by its author as 'a little rule for beginners', it regulated the practice as well as the theory of the religious life. Supreme power was entrusted to the abbot, who was expected to 'do all things with the counsel of his brethren' but to be in complete control of the spiritual and material welfare of his community. The rule laid particular stress on the vows of obedience and stability; and at the centre of the monastic life lay the *opus dei*, the regular performance of communal acts of worship in the choir of the abbey's church. Benedictine monks were also committed to a regular routine which normally comprised four hours of private prayer, four hours of religious reading and four hours of manual labour every day. As far as possible, a Benedictine monastery was to be economically self-supporting.

The rule of St Benedict began to exercise its fullest influence in the two centuries after the abbey of Cluny was founded in Burgundy in 909. During the 11th century at least 70 important – and often new – communities of black monks came to accept the guidance of the abbey's monks, establishing the first large if informal federation or 'order' of Christian monks in western Europe. It would be hard to exaggerate the popularity of these Benedictine monasteries among the great men of Christendom. Just as Count Fulk Nerra's abbey of Beaulieu-lès-Loches (1004) later served as his burial place, so William the Conqueror was buried two generations afterwards in his own favourite Benedictine foundation of the Abbaye-aux-Hommes at Caen in Normandy.

This Benedictine expansion was especially important in Norman and Plantagenet England in creating magnificent new abbeys and cathedral churches like St Albans and Durham, and in ensuring that monasteries like Westminster, Glastonbury and Peterborough remained the wealthiest religious bodies in the country until the Reformation.

Such outstanding wealth was not without danger to men who were supposed to be living ascetically, withdrawn from the extravagances and cares of the world. By about 1100, new generations of monks were already beginning to argue that the religious life practised in most Benedictine monasteries was by no means as austere and zealous as St Benedict would have wished.

Below *A nun and monk are punished for immoral behaviour with a spell in the stocks.*

1040

After his father's death, Geoffrey Martel took possession of the count's fief. Martel, bolder than all the rest of his family, used to accomplish his designs with swift vigour. The people of Anjou incited the wrath of their lord Martel against both Theobald III, count of Blois and William, count of Poitou.

Martel frequently used force against many. When he was told, 'Men speak badly of you,' he would retort, 'They do what they are wont to do, not what I deserve; they do not know how to speak well.' So he stationed many troops at Amboise under the command of Lisois and they demolished whatever stood between Montbazon and Chinon.

Eventually, Martel besieged the town of Tours. He sent Lisois off to Amboise, however, with two hundred knights and fifteen hundred foot-soldiers who were to guard the roads lest the men of Blois descend on his army unhindered.

Having abandoned his siege, Martel came to meet the enemy at daybreak at Montlouis. On the morrow, the men of Blois rushed out of their camps in companies; the Angevins proceeded against them from Montlouis. And then, as they were checking one another's equipment over in turn, Martel, who had six swords, addressed his army with these words: 'Forward soldiers! You see and you have found that for which you came. In truth, you who are about to fight will be sustained in the Lord and in the power of his virtue, for the Almighty is strong to save. Let no one ever think of flight while Anjou is far away from us.'

Aroused by these and other such words from their count, every man proceeded to the fight and delayed the confrontation no longer. There was no hesitation; they assembled at a place popularly called Nouy, before the market town of Saint-Martin-le-Beau.

Trumpets resound together with shouts of 'Forward'. With all possible speed, they plunge themselves into the enemy ranks on every front and scatter those in their way, finding their

The castles of Anjou

THE remains of some of the castles in Anjou can still be seen: built in the early 11th century, they are amongst the earliest stone fortifications to survive from the Middle Ages, and seem powerful even today. At Montbazon, for example, a small, squat keep on top of a mound looks stark, forbidding and impregnable. At Langeais, parts of a rectangular stone keep still stand within the walls of the Renaissance château. At Loches the castle dominates its surroundings to this day.

Fulk Nerra was responsible for many of these castles, according to his grandson, Count Fulk Rechin, in his short *History of the Counts of Anjou* which names 13 and was written half a century after Fulk Nerra's death in 1040.

Some of Fulk's castles controlled lines of communication and important centres. Among them were Trèves on the River Loire, built in the 1020s to secure the Loire below Saumur, and Durtal (*c*.1040) on the Loire above Angers, capital of Anjou. Others were aggressive in purpose, such as the ring of castles which encircled Tours and enabled Count Geoffrey Martel, Fulk Nerra's son, to take the city and Touraine in 1044.

Certainly, Fulk Nerra was the first leader to grasp how strategically positioned castles could be the base from which to launch aggressive war. That realization has rightly earned him his reputation as an innovative strategist.

Left *Loches castle.*
Above *Château on the site of Langeais castle.*

Below *Carving of a lion, from Saint-Ours church, Loches.*

opponents not feeble but, on the contrary, resisting with all their strength. Martel's men are almost destroyed by the overpowering multitude and their foremost two ranks are quite devoured. Many men fall to the ground; many are wounded. The Angevins nevertheless check the onslaught of their foes and, attacking them in turn, bravely force them to give ground.

Martel, who had taken up position with his sword towards the back of his troops, hastened to where he perceived the enemy to be most hampered by its own numbers. Changing his appearance from that of a count to that of an ordinary knight, he prised some horsemen from their seats with his spear and clove others in their saddles with his sword. He rallied his men, encouraging those who were hard pressed. Having lifted their spirits, he rushed forward against the adversary.

Lisois, who was to bring help to his lord with his knights and a hundred banner-bearing foot-soldiers, came at full speed from Amboise. Catching sight of the battle, those in the right wing unloosed their whips and spurred on their steeds. With shields against their breasts, they scattered the mob that had gathered and cut down their opponents, each man stretching out one of the enemy on the ground.

The Angevins renewed the assault. Theobald's collaborators were no longer able to resist their prowess and turned their backs in flight, each suddenly engulfed by fear; many were pierced through by their pursuers' arrows. On horseback and on foot the Angevins pressed on them and forced them back, killing those horses which were alive and sparing few. Those with Martel put all to the sword and, rallying under their leader, who was bravest of all, pursued the runaways and strewed them upon the ground.

The men of Amboise followed, treading on the fugitives, overcoming their prey and beating them down, until they caught up with Count Theobald in a wood called Braye, near the hall of Hastuin and captured him and five hundred knights. For it was not possible to ride in Braye Wood. Having dragged the count out of the wood they returned to Martel. It was thus, with God's help, that the enemy was repulsed and fled ignominiously to scattered parts, while the Angevins returned and spent the year peacefully, untroubled by the turbulence of war.

1042

Since the wretch Theobald III was in chains and Geoffrey Martel would accept neither gold nor silver as a ransom for him, the prisoner, who feared for his life and cared more for his person than he did for his possessions, ceded Touraine to Martel, to be held in perpetuity in return for his deliverance. The year was 1042.

As Seneca affirms, 'Men lead the quietest lives if they obey this principle from natural order: thine and mine.' Now William of Poitou wanted the county of Saintonge and, occupying it, he held it down by force on the grounds that it had belonged to his father's brother. Martel claimed the same county because it had belonged to his great-uncle, whose direct heirs had died without children, and he asserted that for that reason it ought to revert to the heirs of his great-uncle's sister.

William of Poitou was truly warlike, second to none in daring and endowed with foresight and abundant wealth. With crowds of soldiers, he was, however, eager for praise and pompous in his boastful arrogance. His great reputation had earned him an enormous number of followers: men of Poitou, Limousin, Angoulême, Périgueux and Clermont-Ferrand, and Gascons, Basques, Toulousains and yet countless others whom he united to form a huge army.

Poitevins from all over the country were slowly gathering, as countless as the stars, and spreading out their innumerable forces in ranks from side to side, carrying chains with which they thought they would bind their opponents. Their companies were occupying agreed positions some distance away from Chef-Boutonne, as they had been instructed. They imagined that the Angevins would immedialty take flight, never considering that they might do the same because they thought they had already won. They derived confidence from their countless masses, from the spirit of animosity in the breast of their horde and from their leader's command never to flee.

Both sides were now ready for battle. Having drawn up at a little place where they could inspect each other more closely, the ranks clashed with equal force. The Poitevins were urged on by anger and fear, the Angevins by the hope of winning the county of Saintonge. Every man cries aloud and the heavens themselves resound with the confused clamour. The unbearable din resounds, be it of clashing arms, splitting helmets or breaking swords. The sobs and howls of the dying and wounded are heard on all sides.

Martel and the Angevins bravely assaulted the adversary, yelling and daringly thrusting swords into their midst. The throng of knights from Touraine, following their lord, scattered many and cut down the banner of William himself. The foot-soldiers, manfully following the horsemen, seized the banner and kept it because it had struck so great a fear in their hearts. All the men of Gascony and Limousin promptly took to their heels and the rest of the crowd went with them.

Lingering on, the bewildered Poitevins maintained their stand a little longer. Martel and his men turned on them there with their swords, scything them down like corn with horizontal strokes and cleaving the decapitated bodies in half; the fields were not moist but rather flooded with blood. The quaking Poitevins had nowhere to take respite and nor did they seek any. They pursued the runaways; or at least such men escaped as could somehow take flight. While the men of Touraine took many prisoners, the Angevins offered no truce to those whom they caught running away. They stabbed some through with spears and cut the throats of others, sparing the lives of none at all. Since Chef-Boutonne was situated a little way off, the exhausted few who remained were either captured or put to a swift death. That day was too terrible for the Poitevins; it was a day of distress and dispersion, a day of confusion and despair. They were bound with the very chains they had brought to bind their own enemies. The massacre complete, Martel and his men spent the night peacefully in their tents on the plain. Against the bitter north wind which was blowing, they piled up the dead bodies.

After this, Martel bore down on Saintonge as quickly as he could. Those in the city came to meet him and handed over the place with open gates. There, his men rested joyfully and took control of the surrounding county which Martel was to hold for the rest of his life, once he had made his peace with the count of Poitou. Having recovered from the wounds inflicted in battle, the latter had received homage from Martel upon the advice of his monks and bishops and conceded the county, which was now quiet. There was indescribable delight in Anjou and Touraine on account of this, and the victors reposed long in peaceful pleasure everywhere, thanking God with all their hearts.

In those days, Duke William of Normandy was greatly harassing Herbert, count of Le Mans. Since Martel was Herbert's ally and protector, Duke William, who later became king of the English, suffered much at Martel's hands.

Because he had no sons, Geoffrey Martel, son of Fulk, left his county, Anjou, and Touraine which he had conquered as I have described, to his nephews, Geoffrey the Bearded and Fulk Rechin. He gave Anjou and Saintonge to Geoffrey and Touraine and Château-Landon to Fulk. Martel was seized by an unexpected illness, an incurable sickness which grew worse from day to day, and he suffered right up to his death, dying in great pain amidst his family.

1060

As far as the number and nature of evils which occurred in the county while Geoffrey the Bearded and Fulk Rechin possessed the honour of Martel are concerned, their disclosure is ordered by true history but forbidden by the horror and scale of the destruction. Indeed, I do not know whether it is better for those malefactors if details of their evil accomplishments are omitted or rather whether it does them a disservice to suppress examples of their wickedness.

1066

Geoffrey the Bearded, a vigorous soldier, allied himself with the men of Maine. With his help Elias of La Flèche recovered Le Mans which William, king of the English, had appropriated for himself. Cunning Fulk began to fight against his brother Geoffrey, throwing the whole county into turmoil. The barons then started to fight each other all over the region, siding now with Geoffrey and now with Fulk. Treachery was rife.

In the year of our Lord 1066, there was betrayal at Angers. When Anjou and Touraine had almost been destroyed, Fulk Rechin cunningly captured his brother, put him in chains and took control of the county as though it were his own.

The count of Poitou, who was called William after his father, was the most skilful soldier, scheming and industrious. While the brothers were quarrelling as described, he assaulted, captured and occupied the county of Saintonge. Elias, ruler of Maine, and his fellow barons fiercely attacked Fulk on Geoffrey's behalf and demanded that he be freed, striving to release him from prison by force with the help of Philip I, king of the French and Stephen, count of Blois. But Fulk made a pact with Stephen and did homage to him. Then he went to the French king and, having made a treaty with him, he ceded him Château-Landon.

The king of France, Philip I, was effective ruler of only the Ile-de-France, although Paris, his capital city, was already established as an important centre of learning, and Abelard one of the university's most famous teachers. The chronicler sometimes uses the word 'France' to refer to this area.

Returning from France, Count Fulk went to Amboise where he was the guest of Ernoul of Meung-sur-Loire who had custody of the count's castle in the city from him in fee.

Fulk took away both his fief and the castle from him and, setting the guards where he would, kept it for himself. It was thus that Ernoul and his son Léon were expelled from Amboise.

Abelard and Heloise

ABELARD was famous as a teacher in Paris and as an original and provocative theologian, whose abilities placed him at the very heart of western European intellectual life in the 12th century.

He was born in Brittany in 1079 and for a number of years lived as a wandering scholar, typical of an age when there were as yet no established universities, and masters at various centres competed ferociously for pupils. Abelard's account of his life, *Historia calamitatum* (The History of his Calamities), shows how he destroyed the ideas and reputations of several of his teachers with an arrogance that made him enemies. By his late 30s he was himself a master in Paris, where his brilliance brought him crowds of pupils and established the basis for the city's great university.

In Paris, at the height of his fame he met and fell in love with Heloise, some 20 years his junior. She was the beautiful and learned niece of Fulbert, a canon of Notre-Dame Cathedral. In a Church where celibacy was expected, if not yet absolutely required, the liaison would have been harmful to his career, but not disastrous. But Heloise gave birth to a son and although a secret marriage was held to appease Fulbert, the canon continued to ill-treat her so that Abelard eventually took her to the convent at Argenteuil. Believing that Abelard intended to abandon his niece to the life of a nun, Fulbert wreaked a terrible revenge – his servants were sent to break into Abelard's room at night and castrate him. Abelard, filled with horror and humiliation, became a monk at the great royal abbey of Saint-Denis and, on his instructions, Heloise, even then only 19, despairingly entered the convent to which Abelard had taken her.

Abelard's contemporaries regarded him as a dangerous influence: in the 1130s he left Saint-Denis to resume teaching and attracted the opposition of conservatives in the Church, led by the formidable Cistercian abbot Bernard of Clairvaux. Abelard's mistake was to pronounce publicly and persuasively that the Christian faith should be subjected to rational enquiry. As a devoutly religious man, his aim was to deepen understanding, not to undermine faith. But he also adopted the radical position that intention was what mattered in determining whether a sin had been committed. All this was too much for the Church establishment, and he was condemned as a heretic in 1140, two years before his death.

Today Abelard is remembered as a passionate lover, and the *Historia* and an exchange of letters with Heloise, written when the two former lovers had retired to monasteries, reveal a desperate passion from which neither could release themselves.

Imbued with the conventions of their time, they agonized over their enjoyment of sexual pleasure. They appear less concerned with society's reactions to the relationship than with the parallels with Adam and Eve, and with the destructive consequences of a sinful relationship on the capacity of Abelard to interpret the scriptures.

Abelard tries to give spiritual counsel to Heloise, advising her to transform her love for him into love for God, advice which in the end she was able to take. In 1129, Heloise, already prioress of Argenteuil, became abbess of the Paraclete, a convent set up with Abelard's help on the site of an oratory which he had founded. Her learning, dignity, compassion and administrative abilities made her an admired and respected figure.

Eight centuries after their deaths, in the 19th century, the lovers' tombs were placed together in the cemetery of Père-Lachaise in Paris, where flowers are still brought to their ornate memorial.

More than just lovers forced apart by unsympathetic circumstances, Abelard and Heloise have inspired writers and artists over the centuries. Their portraits, carved in stone, decorate capitals in La Conciergerie, the first royal palace built in Paris.

Often, when acting in such a way, Fulk would make accusations of treachery against his own offspring, unjust though these were. 'For evil customs have this particular power to defile the innocence of the many with the crimes of a few, whereas a small band of good men is not able to mitigate the crimes of the masses by sharing its virtues. But who is not angered when he sees the sincerity of goodness impugned by the accusations of a few evil men?'

For many have been 'Slow to do good and swift to speak against evil, busy with plotting, weak in love, strong in faction and steadfast in preserving their enmities.' I mention these men because theirs is the story I tell.

Fulk took several wives: there was the daughter of Lancelin of Beaugency, whose own daughter became that countess of Brittany who led the life of a nun after her husband died at Jerusalem. After Lancelin's daughter died, Fulk took Ermengardine, daughter of Archenbaud the Strong of Bourbon, who bore Geoffrey Martel II, an admirable man, notable for his justice, who cultivated everything that is good and was the terror of all his enemies.

The lecherous Fulk then fell passionately in love with the sister of Amaury of Montfont, 'whom no good man ever praised save for her beauty'. For her sake, he divorced the mother of Geoffrey Martel II, declaring her to be his kinswoman, after which William of Jaligny married her.

Geoffrey Martel II, once of age, a wise and courageous young man, saw that the land was disturbed and that barons of the whole county were rebelling against his father. He resisted them bravely and wondered ceaselessly how he could avenge his father and his father's men. More farsighted than all, he summoned men back from their evil designs. He conducted his affairs sensibly and fought in neither too mild nor too foolish a manner.

When Geoffrey the Bearded heard of the upright qualities of his nephew Martel, he was pleased and calling him to him, said: 'I am

delighted that you have not departed from the worthiness of your ancestors. I bestow upon you that land which your father unjustly took from me; I want you to succeed to it.' Releasing his uncle from his chains, Martel II allowed him to travel freely through his towns and cities, although always under guard. But Geoffrey's mind had become confused in prison and his powers of reasoning were somewhat diminished. He did not live long after this.

In 1095 the Council of Clermont was called by Pope Urban II and the preaching of the First Crusade began.

Martel II gave his sister Elisabeth, born of the union of his mother and William of Jaligny, in marriage to Hugh of Chaumont. With her hand, he granted the whole of Amboise. To Martel himself, Elias count of Maine betrothed his only daughter, although she was not yet of age for marriage, and he surrendered Le Mans with all that belonged to it.

Martel was frequently in conflict with King William Rufus and ravaged and set fire to many towns in Normandy. Meanwhile the king tarried in England and Count Robert, the king's brother, remained in the army at Jerusalem with many pilgrims; for King Rufus held Normandy in pledge.

1106

In the year of our Lord 1106, there was a period of forty days when an ever-growing comet appeared every evening and filled the world with amazement. Casting its ray of shining splendour against the misty sunset, it seemed more fiery initially and then became less clear, gradually burning out until after forty days it disappeared altogether, or so they say.

On St. Michael's day, 29 September, Robert was captured by his brother King Henry I. William Clito espoused the daughter of Count Fulk of Anjou, but later separated from her because they were related and married the sister of the French queen, King Louis VI's wife; he thereby acquired Flanders. But his hand pierced by a spear, William did not live for long thereafter.

1107

The following year, Martel was killed in an ambush at Candé castle, supposedly with the connivance of his father and step-mother. It seems unbelievable to me that the father of such a son should have consented to his death, both when he was an old man and when his son, had he been granted longevity, would have recovered whatever he had lost. For Martel was challenging both the French king for Château-Landon and William of Poitou for Saintonge. Out of fear of Martel, the latter had built two towers at Poitiers, one at the entrance to the town and the other near the hall.

The lecherous King Philip came to Tours and, having conversed with Fulk's wife, decided to make her his queen. That evil woman abandoned the count the next night and followed the king, who had stationed his knights at Mindray near the bridge over the Beuvron, and he led her to Orléans. Thus the voluptuous king filled his house with marital crimes committed under ban of excommunication and begat two sons by the woman, Philip and Florus.

Although I found these things written in hidden volumes, I have not been at pains to conceal them. For the honour of our lords the counts of Anjou, I collected in writing what I perceived to be their deeds and those things which are designed for the instruction of their successors, praying that our work will be of assistance to the present generation when imitating their greatest ancestors.

1109

It is true that 'the father will not bear the iniquity of the son nor the son of the father'. Thus it is that after the death of Fulk Rechin, his son Fulk V, count of Anjou, abandoned the ways of his mother and father and led an honourable life, ruling his territory wisely. He negotiated with Elias count of Maine in order to marry the latter's only daughter, the girl whom Martel had been going to wed, and with her hand to acquire the county of Maine. It was in this way that the counties of Maine and Anjou were recognized as united.

Fulk V was an upright and vigorous man of orthodox faith who was benevolent towards the men of God. Having received both counties, he raised his friends up, put down the wicked and, in short, achieved a glorious and excellent reputation that was second to none. To Hugh of Chaumont, who did him homage, he granted the whole of Amboise as had done his brother Martel II, and he returned Montrichard which had been unjustly seized by his ancestors.

Fulk besieged Preuilly but did not take it, though he did gain control of Eschivard, a castle under the same lord with whom he then made peace. He bought Montbazon from John, the lord of that town. But when John forced his way back into the place after accepting part of the money, Fulk laid siege to it very courageously and made him return it. By handing over the money still promised, Fulk also obtained control of the castle. He blockaded Montreuil-Bellay, but once he had captured it and installed his own guards in the citadel, he was moved by pity to return the rest to the lord of the castle.

Henry I, king of the English, attacked Fulk many times because he hated the man. By giving money to the barons of Anjou and Maine, he frequently created great discord among them and did serious harm to Fulk.

King William, who had conquered England, divided his land between his three sons: he gave England to William Rufus, Normandy to Robert and the maternal inheritance to Henry. When Rufus died, Henry seized the crown of England while his brother Robert was tarrying in Jerusalem. Returning from Jerusalem, Robert had a son called William Clito by his wife.

Henry I, king of England, had a son William who married the daughter of Count Fulk V and received the county of Maine with her. After he had done homage to Fulk, William also received Normandy from Louis VI, king of France. In the summer of his seventeenth year, he was returning to England when he was drowned at sea and with him many nobles whose bodies were never recovered.

The loss of William, King Henry's son, in 1120, was to have momentous consequences as his only surviving legitimate child was his daughter Matilda.

1110

In the year of our Lord 1110, Fulk V had a son Geoffrey by his wife the daughter of Count Elias. The boy grew into an outstanding soldier and espoused Matilda, daughter of Henry I, king of the English and widow of the German emperor Henry V. By the same wife, Fulk had another son called Elias.

1128

While Fulk was ruling Anjou, Touraine and the county of Maine in prosperity, King Baldwin II of Jerusalem sent envoys who were to consult prudent men and then to persuade a suitable man to wed his daughter and accept the kingdom of Jerusalem. On the advice of King Louis VI of France, the bishops and many distinguished men, they chose Fulk V of Anjou, who had lost his wife.

1129

Crossing the sea with a large force, Fulk consummated his marriage with the king's daughter and became king of Jerusalem in 1129.

1131

After King Baldwin died, Fulk V ruled the kingdom manfully. He made the inhabitants of Damascus and Ascalon pay tribute and long before Raymond, brother of the count of Poitou, married the daughter of Bohemond of Antioch, Fulk sustained the principality of Antioch against the Turks with great effort, losing nothing. By his wife, he had two sons, Baldwin and Amaury. He himself lived to a great age and died still combative. The men of Jerusalem made Baldwin king after him.

While Geoffrey, son of Fulk V king of Jerusalem, was quietly governing his Angevin territories, his brother Elias, at the prompting of wicked men, frequently attacked him, demanding the county of Maine. Geoffrey captured him and held him prisoner at Tours for a long time, but

Fulk V, king of Jerusalem

IN 1128 a delegation from Baldwin II, king of Jerusalem, arrived in France. The king had no son to succeed him as defender of the Holy Sepulchre, only four daughters. His messenger requested Louis VII to select from the French nobility a man suitable to marry Baldwin's eldest daughter Melisande, and in due course to succeed as king of Jerusalem.

Louis's choice was Fulk, count of Anjou, Maine and Touraine, who accordingly travelled to the East to marry, in 1129.

Jerusalem was one of four Christian states that had been established in Syria some 30 years earlier, in the aftermath of the First Crusade, a giant armed pilgrimage which had resembled a vast raid, since few of the great concourse of princes, knights and humbler folk who made the journey settled in the East.

In 1096 a multitude had answered Pope Urban's call to arms in defence of Christianity. Yet although he had preached in Angers itself the rulers of the Angevins had been unmoved. Why, then, was Fulk chosen to be king of Jerusalem, and why was he prepared to quit the native land he had laboured hard to expand and consolidate?

In 1128 the count of Anjou was about 40 and had already made a pilgrimage to Jerusalem. An eye-witness, Archbishop William of Tyre, described him as '. . . a ruddy man, like David . . . faithful and gentle, affable and kind . . . a powerful prince . . . and very successful in ruling his own people . . . an experienced warrior full of patience and wisdom in military affairs.' His main fault was an appallingly bad memory for names and faces.

The offer of a crown was too good an opportunity to be missed by a mere count, and as Archbishop William

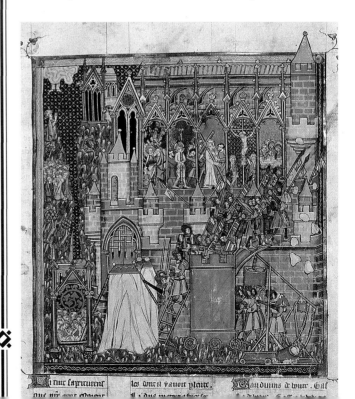

indicated, Fulk possessed all the qualifications required for the job. In addition, as a widower he was free to marry again, and could resign his lands confident that they were in reliable hands: his youthful but able son Geoffrey Plantagenet was knighted and betrothed to Matilda, the daughter and heiress of Henry I of England – in time he too stood to inherit a kingdom.

All in all 1128 was a good year for the house of Anjou and its spectacular advance had been achieved by astute marriages rather than by war.

Above Urban II's call to Christendom to go to war to recapture the Holy Land from the Muslims was the start of the Crusades. Urban preaching the First Crusade, in 1095, from a 15th-century French manuscript.

Far left Jerusalem was taken by the crusaders in 1099 and Baldwin I was the city's first king, in 1100; Fulk V was its third royal ruler. The fall of Jerusalem, from a 14th-century French manuscript.

after the young man was freed, he died from a serious illness which he had caught in prison.

Powerful brothers have always fallen, disunited through too much greed, refusing to hold their possessions in common when they quarrel between themselves and then, when their forces clash, they perish. But Geoffrey was a man of admirable worth, outstandingly just, dedicated to military deeds, exceedingly well educated, most eloquent amidst the clergy and the laity and, although he suffered much at the hands of his own men, was popular with all for accomplishing the acquisition of Normandy.

I think that enough has now been said about the deeds and acts of the counts of Anjou. If it seems to you that there are more besides (and I believe there are many), then ask someone who knows them better.

Feudal society

FEUDALISM, a word coined in the 17th century, is generally used to describe a social structure in which an aristocratic warrior class dominates a large peasantry and is sustained by its labour. More precisely, it refers to the social organization of the Middle Ages in which relationships between members of the aristocracy – and especially between the king and the dukes or counts – were based on lordship and vassalage.

The vassal, the inferior partner, received his fief – usually a parcel of land – and protection from the lord. In return he did service, either by taking a contingent of knights and other troops to fight in his lord's army, or by paying his lord money for the hire of mercenary soldiers. The fief was conferred by the ceremony of homage: the vassal, kneeling before his lord, solemnly vowed to give him service and obedience.

Medieval feudal societies took many different forms. From 1066 to 1135 England was strongly hierarchical, with the king firmly and unmistakably at the summit. In 11th-century France, however, kings had great powers in theory but were often overshadowed by powerful dukes and counts like the Angevins. Certain regions were dominated by these influential vassals but others – Berry and Picardy, for example – were split into much smaller units such as viscounties and castellanies (a castle and the land it controlled). Nobles might do homage to their king, but more as a mark of alliance than as an admission of their obligations to him. Such pacts could be, and often were, easily broken when necessary. In the same way, major local potentates made formal deals with their neighbours but regarded these as provisional.

To prosper in a world where local territorial advantages were all-important, it was necessary to proceed by methodical means, using castles and steady military pressure. It was essential to know how to make and break agreements, and when to retreat in the face of stronger rivals.

Fulk Nerra and his son, Geoffrey Martel were masterful exponents of this political game.

Above left *A king gives the sword of knighthood to a young man.*

Above *A later French chronicle shows the young Richard the Lionheart paying homage to Philip II for his French dominions. Public ceremonies like these created a bond of responsibility between lord and vassal.*

Part II

Geoffrey Plantagenet 1128–1154

In 1128 Geoffrey the Fair, nicknamed Plantagenet because of the sprig of broom he wore in his cap (Fr. genêt – broom), and soon to be count of Anjou, married the haughty Empress Matilda, daughter and designated heiress of Henry I, king of England and duke of Normandy. When Henry died in 1135, his nephew Stephen of Blois seized the English kingdom. Over the next 19 years, the houses of Anjou and Blois fought for control of England and Normandy. Matilda concentrated on the kingdom and Count Geoffrey on the duchy, where he became duke in 1144. In 1153. King Stephen was persuaded to acknowledge Geoffrey and Matilda's son, Henry, as his heir to England. Part II begins with a highly laudatory and at times florid biography of Geoffrey Plantagenet, written in about 1170 by John of Marmoutier. Full of chivalrous images and daring deeds, it was intended to please Henry II, Geoffrey's son. In contrast, Henry, archdeacon of Huntingdon, shows a relative lack of political prejudice in his History of the English. *It was completed by 1154, and in it he graphically describes Stephen's good as well as his bad qualities, bringing his reign to life.*

(Opposite: Geoffrey Plantagenet's enamel funerary effigy at Le Mans Cathedral)

IT is well known to everyone that the Angevin race has flourished under high-spirited and warlike rulers and that they have dominated the people surrounding them with terror. No one questions the fact that they wrought all the destruction within their power upon their neighbours and subjugated the lands around. For those for whom the dominion of Anjou was quite insufficient, bellicose labour acquired the territory of Tours when Odo of Champagne was defeated by the successful Fulk, nicknamed Nerra, in the battle of Braye and Odo's son, Count Theobald, was vanquished, bound by the law of war and taken prisoner. From the splendid stock of such princes came Geoffrey, the outstanding son of Fulk, king of Jerusalem.

Truly, Geoffrey had any number of outstanding, praiseworthy qualities. As a soldier, he attained the greatest glory and, benefiting equally from good fortune and his own hard work, dedicated himself to the defence of the community and to the liberal arts; he strove to be rightly loved and was honourable to his friends. Not only was he great in the eyes of the world at large, he was more trustworthy than the rest. His words were always good-humoured and his principles were admirable and likeable. He excelled at arguing his

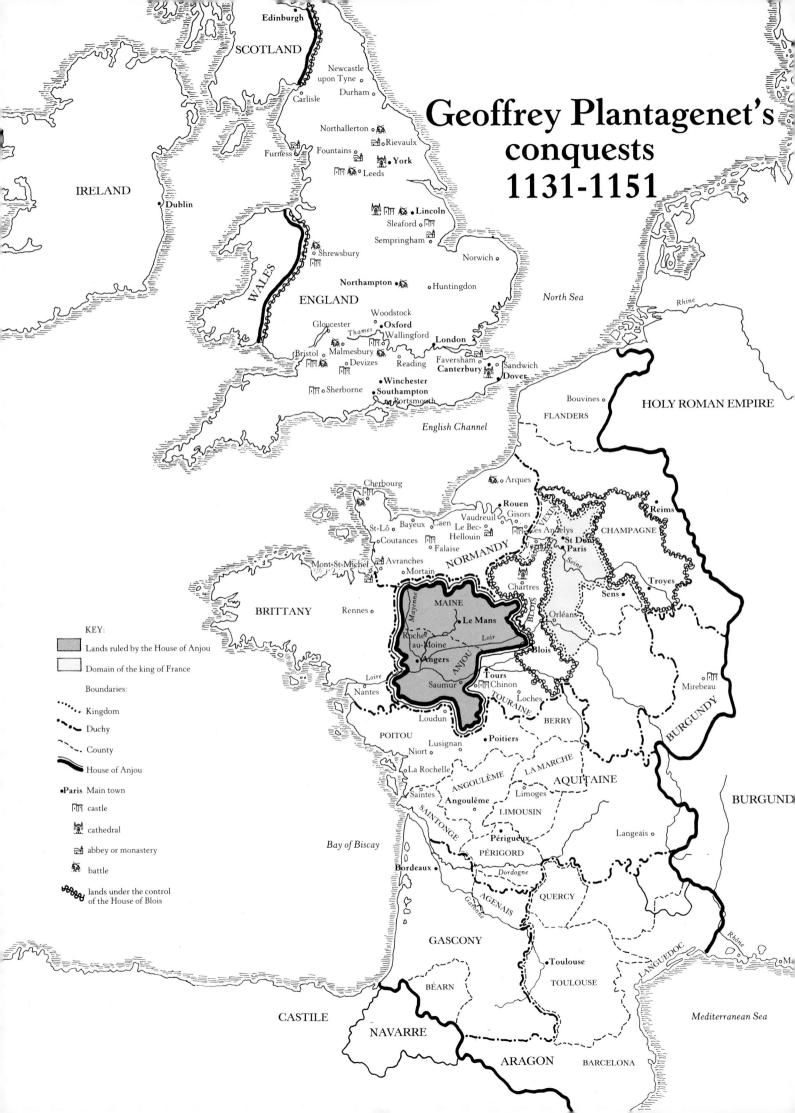

Geoffrey Plantagenet's conquests 1131-1151

SCOTLAND

Edinburgh

IRELAND

Dublin

Newcastle upon Tyne
Durham
Carlisle
Northallerton
Rievaulx
Furness
Fountains
York
Leeds

Lincoln
Sleaford
Sempringham
Norwich

Shrewsbury

WALES

Northampton
Huntingdon

ENGLAND

Woodstock
Gloucester
Oxford
Wallingford
Thames
London
Bristol
Malmesbury
Devizes
Reading
Faversham
Sandwich
Canterbury
Dover

Winchester
Sherborne
Southampton
Portsmouth

English Channel

North Sea

Rhine

Bouvines
HOLY ROMAN EMPIRE
FLANDERS

Cherbourg
Arques
St-Lô
Bayeux
Caen
Rouen
Gisors
Vaudreuil
Le Bec-Helloiun
Les Andelys
Reims
CHAMPAGNE
Coutances
Falaise
St Denis
Paris
Avranches
NORMANDY
Mont-St-Michel
Mortain
Chartres
Seine
Troyes
Sens
BRITTANY
Rennes
MAINE
Le Mans
Loir
Orléans
Roche-au-Moine
Mayenne
Loire
Angers
ANJOU
Blois
Tours
Chinon
Mirebeau
Saumur
Nantes
Loches
TOURAINE
BURGUNDY
Loudun
BERRY
POITOU
Lusignan
Poitiers
Niort
LA MARCHE
La Rochelle
AQUITAINE
BURGUND
Saintes
ANGOULÊME
Limoges
Angoulême
Langeais
SAINTONGE
LIMOUSIN
Bay of Biscay
Périgueux
PÉRIGORD
Bordeaux
Dordogne
AGENAIS
QUERCY
Garonne
Rhône
GASCONY
LANGUEDOC
M
CASTILE
Toulouse
BÉARN
TOULOUSE
Mediterranean Sea
NAVARRE
ARAGON
BARCELONA

KEY:

Lands ruled by the House of Anjou

Domain of the king of France

Boundaries:

············· Kingdom

─·─·─ Duchy

── · ── County

━━━━ House of Anjou

•Paris Main town

castle

cathedral

abbey or monastery

battle

lands under the control of the House of Blois

In 1128 Fulk's son Geoffrey Plantagenet married Matilda, dowager Empress and Henry I of England's daughter. To her Henry had promised the succession of England and Normandy. But on Henry I's death in 1135 Stephen of Blois, Henry's nephew and favourite, seized the kingdom and the duchy.

The counts of Blois had long been rivals of the Angevins whose lands abutted theirs; their possessions almost encircled the French royal domain. The two halves, Blois and Champagne, were several times divided between heirs. When Hugh, count of Champagne, became a Templar in 1125, his county went to his nephew Theobald II of Blois, the grandson of William the Conqueror, king of England and duke of Normandy.

Theobald's brothers, Stephen count of Mortain and Henry bishop of Winchester, had earned the trust and patronage of their uncle Henry I of England. In 1135 they together made sure that Stephen rather than Theobald took Henry I's lands.

In 1136, 1137 and 1138 Geoffrey and Matilda mounted campaigns in Normandy. With the help of Robert earl of Gloucester, a leading Anglo-Norman noble, Matilda invaded the kingdom of England in 1139, leaving Geoffrey to conquer the duchy. By April 1141 Geoffrey had taken control of much of Western Normandy. In 1144 he took Rouen and was invested as duke. In 1145 Arques, the last of Stephen's strongholds, fell to him. Insurrections in Maine and Anjou occupied the next few years, during which time his son Henry emerged as Matilda, his mother's champion, and ultimately as heir to her claims.

The duchy of Aquitaine

Aquitaine in the early tenth century was a large and diverse collection of counties and lordships, stretching inland to the heart of the Massif Central and South to the Pyrenees. Duke William the Great, who died in 1030, exercised effective authority in Poitou, Périgord and La Marche and had the overlordship of Limoges, Berry, Saintonge and Auvergne. In 1063 William VIII took Gascony; his son, William IX (1086-1126) married Philippa of Toulouse and was a noted troubadour with very much a southern outlook.

Eleanor of Aquitaine, daughter and heiress of William X (1126-37) thus grew up in the cultured and sophisticated ways of the Languedoc.

own case and possessed a thorough knowledge of antiquity; and because he was educated, he would remember precisely not only what was happening at home but also the wars and deeds of all abroad.

Not merely was he unusually skilled at warfare: it was with outstanding competence that he returned the principality to peace and his people to a quiet life. This man was an energetic soldier and, as I have said, was most shrewd in his upright dealings, exceptionally well educated, generous to all, tall in stature, handsome and red-headed, the father of his country and the scourge of pride.

He was enthusiastic about military feats, meticulous in his justice and graced with almost all good habits. He differed in no respect from the most excellent princes of his time and was loved by all, although he endured much trouble from his own men. Being intelligent and of strong character, he did not allow himself to be corrupted by excess or sloth in early adulthood, but spent his time riding around the country and performing illustrious feats, but saying little about himself as he did so. By such acts, he endeared himself to all and smote fear into the hearts of his enemies. Gentle and gracious, he had the kindest soul; clement to his citizens, he bore offences and injuries with equanimity. When he heard himself insulted in many quarters, he patiently hid what he felt; he was unusually affable and jovial to all but especially to soldiers. Such was his goodness and generosity that those whom he had subdued by force, he overcame rather by his mercy as I will relate in the following narrative.

1128

When he turned fifteen, Geoffrey was ending his boyhood, blooming in the first flower of youth. Rumour, whose truth was attested by ample evidence, proclaimed the talented youth far and wide until his celebrated name reached the ears of that most glorious king, Henry I of England. The king was well aware that the young man's forefathers were distinguished and sprung from ancient stock, upright in their customs and skilled in the arts of war. Hearing that the youth was no exception to this, as far as age allowed one to tell,

the king decided to join his only daughter Matilda, widow of the Emperor Henry V, to the young man in lawful matrimony.

Heralds were therefore despatched to make petitions to young Geoffrey's father, Fulk V, count of Anjou, and to inform him of the royal will. This man, wise and diligent in all matters, treated the royal legates with due honour and willingly promised to ensure that the royal request was granted. Pledges were given and a pact, supported by oaths, removed all trace of doubt. On the king's instruction, the count agreed to send his son, not yet a knight, in style to Rouen the following Whitsun, in order that he should be knighted with others of the same age amid regal festivities. There was no difficulty in arranging this: a just request warrants easy assent.

So, on his father's command, the future son-in-law of the king of England set out for Rouen with five barons: Jacquelin of Maillé, Robert of Semblançay, Hardouin of Saint-Mars, Robert of Blou, Paien of Clairevalle and fifteen of his contemporaries, accompanied by many knights. Rumour, ahead as ever, announced the arrival of the count's son to the king. Henry I rejoiced at what was being said about Geoffrey's arrival and sent some of his more distinguished nobles as his representatives to lead the young man into the royal presence with due honour and attention. Geoffrey entered the hall of the royal palace surrounded by his own men and the king's with a crowd of the common people standing around. The king, who was accustomed to stand for nobody, rose and went to meet him and, clasping him in an affectionate embrace, gave him a little kiss, as though he were his son. Then he took Geoffrey by the hand and bade him sit down with him. The king spoke of all manner of subjects to the young man, putting a great variety of problems to him to discover how wise his responses were during their private conversation. Geoffrey replied succinctly but, as is the wont of the wise, he embellished his words with rhetoric known to few. The king, whose profound admiration grew at every moment, was delighted by the youth's sense and his replies and so the whole day was spent in rejoicing and exultation.

Geoffrey and Matilda

GEOFFREY the Fair, count of Anjou, was the first of his line to bear the surname Plantagenet, an epithet he gained from the sprig of broom (*genêt*) he wore in his hat. He became count of Anjou in 1129 after his father, Fulk V, had gone to Jerusalem.

Geoffrey was a clever man, thought handsome by contemporaries. He was tall, graceful and strong, with a fair and ruddy countenance and sharp eyes. Well educated, he gloried in recalling the deeds of his ancestors and played up to the chivalric ideal. Yet he was also cold and cruel. His career as count was in large measure dominated by the pursuit of his wife Matilda's inheritance of Normandy and England, although he imposed limits on his participation: he was single-minded in his determination to conquer Normandy, Anjou's great enemy, but gave no help in England.

Geoffrey and Matilda had been married in 1128 when he was 15 and she was 26. Like so many marriages of the time, it was an arranged match, planned by Henry I, Matilda's father, to detach Anjou from a hostile coalition of northern French opponents and to assist Matilda's chances of succeeding him in Normandy and England. Her first marriage had been to the German emperor, Henry V, who had died in 1125. She had been despatched to Germany at the age of 12 and brought back to her father's court 12 years later, in 1126, as his sole surviving legitimate child.

From the start she despised her adolescent second husband as her social inferior and she seems never to have warmed to him.

Geoffrey equally disliked Matilda, yet both were tough and calculating, able to exploit their loveless marriage for mutual political gain. They produced the children necessary for the continuation of their lines, then went their separate ways, never deviating from personal political ambitions.

Matilda alienated all whom she ought to have wooed when she ruled England for a short period in 1141–42. During that brief episode of victory she refused to stand to greet her two chief supporters, her uncle, King David of Scotland, and her half-brother, Earl Robert of Gloucester, and greatly angered them. She also insisted on levying an unreasonably heavy tax from the citizens of London, and turned their loyalty and co-operation into hatred and resistance; she was forced to flee from the city. Driven by an iron will to gain what she regarded as her inheritance, her personality was one of the chief obstacles to the success of her cause.

Haughty, hard and inflexible, she was criticized by contemporaries for her lack of feminine qualities. The enduring image of her is of a daughter who was at war with her father, Henry I, when he died and who made no effort at reconciliation in his last hours. But she was handsome and brave, a powerful woman in an age dominated by men, and could inspire great loyalty in others – if not in her husband.

Below *A magnificent gemstone and gold filigree cross, given by Matilda to the abbey of Le Valasse in Normandy. The central cross is of paler gold and finer workmanship, probably 10th or 11th century; the empress had it set in a larger cross before giving it the abbey.*

As the next day was dawning, Geoffrey was prepared for his solemn bath, as custom demands of a young man about to become a knight. When the king learned from his chamberlains that the Angevin and those who had come with him had arisen from the ewer, he summoned them to his presence. After cleansing his body, the noble offspring of the count of Anjou was wrapped in crisp linen, dressed in a ceremonial robe interwoven with gold and covered with a cloak, dyed purple in the blood of oyster and murex. He was shod in silken shoes which had soles that were decorated with lion cubs. His comrades, who were expecting to receive the gift of knighthood with him, were likewise clothed in linen and purple. Decked out in such finery as I have described, the king of England's future son-in-law proceeded from a secret chamber into public view, accompanied by the assembled nobility of his country, bright like the flower of the lily and covered in red like a rose.

The horses were drawn up, the arms brought and distributed to each as was appropriate. To the Angevin, a Spanish horse was led, marvellously bedecked and reputed to outstrip many birds as it ran. Then the young man was fitted with a cuirass second to none, whose double layer of mail could be pierced by the blow of no lance or javelin, and with iron boots which were also reinforced with two thicknesses of compact mail; his feet were bound with gold spurs and a shield covered in gold motifs of lions was hung from his neck. On his head was placed a helmet, resplendent with many precious stones, which was of such a quality that it could be cut or destroyed by the blade of no sword; a spear of ash lengthened with Poitevin iron was brought; very last of all, a sword from the royal treasury was carried out to him. It had been preserved from long before, when it had been carefully crafted by that master, Weyland.

Armed thus, our young soldier, who was to be the new flower of knighthood, set forth on his horse, wonderfully fleet and poised, and graceful in his speed. What more? That day, dedicated to the honour and glory of the first campaign, was completely devoted to the practice of military games and to attending to the glory of the body.

For no less than seven days, the magnificent celebration of the first campaign of knighthood continued at court.

Once more, messengers were sent to Fulk V of Anjou, this time to announce that he should go to Le Mans eight days after Whitsun to celebrate his son's marriage in due pomp. Fulk did not delay, but assenting gladly, arrived as he had been commanded, in great splendour at the day and place assigned.

King Henry I of England set out from Rouen with Fulk's son and his daughter, the empress (for she had been the emperor's wife), and likewise arrived at Le Mans on the appointed day. From different quarters, they assembled for the service of the nuptial sacrament, which was to be performed by archbishops, bishops, abbots and priests of all ranks.

And so the king's daughter was given in wedlock to the son of the count of Anjou and the bishops investigated the mutual consent of the couple to the match. For all the strength and efficacy of marriage lies in consent; indeed, consent makes marriage. Both consented and each promised their faith to the other whom they were about to serve, and solemn Masses blessing their marriage were celebrated.

There was rejoicing amidst the clergy, dancing by the people and the shouting of praise by all and sundry, whether native or foreigner, rich, middling or poor, noble or commoner, soldier or husbandman drawn in by the general rejoicing. He who was unconcerned by the wedding festivities was doubtless deemed a traitor. Men and women spent the wedding feast taking their fill of the different dishes. For three weeks, the marriage was celebrated without a break and, when it was over, no one left without a gift.

Then Henry I left his son-in-law and daughter with the kiss of peace and turned his attention to other matters. Count Fulk of Anjou returned with the couple to Angers. While they were still some way off, the whole city hurried to prepare for them; instructions were given out and walls of the

Life in Anjou

KNOWN as the garden of France, Anjou lies in the fertile valley of the Loire. Its climate is gentle and tempered by cool ocean breezes.

The inhabitants of Anjou are the Angevins, and Angers is its capital. This is how it looked to the chronicler Ralph of Diceto, who wrote in *c.* 1200:

"The industry of the Angevins of early times caused their city to be sited in a commanding position. Indeed its ancient walls are a glorious testament to its founders, while its squared stones are a reproach to the penny-pinching of its present inhabitants. You would think from comparing its ancient with its recent buildings that the art of building on gravel with strong cement had quite disappeared. The southern part of the city has man-made defences, while the western part is protected by its natural position. The south-eastern quarter is dominated by a great house which is indeed quite worthy to be called a palace. For, not long ago, vast chambers were constructed, laid out and adorned in a luxurious manner entirely worthy of a king. Such is the extent of this great house that on one side it looks out over the river flowing past and on the other towards the vine-clad hills. Then, so that the town might be better able to provide shelter for the thousands of men who lived there, it was enlarged to include the neighbouring hill within its bounds. Indeed, it is my opinion that those who dwell in the new part are still more fortunate than those who live in the old city. It would be difficult to find another place so abounding in religious houses – pious communities, endowed by the generosity of princes and subject to rigorous discipline.

Moreover, although it is somewhat distant from the Loire, that noble river the Maine flows between the two hills on which the town is built. Thus it is as fortunate in relation to the river as it is in every other respect. In winter, the Maine swells into a flood, while in summer it shrinks down into a narrow trickle between sandy banks. However, that they might traverse it with ease in winter as well as in summer, the citizens were permitted to gather wood, earth and stones and erect structures on the opposite banks which met over the river to make a level platform. The middle part of the bridge is mostly made of wood and forms a kind of solid street which is accessible to those who wish to cross but protected from the rays of the sun. Indeed, the convenience and beauty of the bridge satisfy both those who merely wish to cross the river and those who also desire to see their city adorned."

Top *A farmer wielding an early form of sickle depicts July in 13th-century seasonal illustrations in the church at Pritz near Laval.*

Above *October: sowing the winter wheat. although Anjou was under threat of war during most of the 11th and 12th centuries, the land continued to be cultivated. Today, the area is still known for its rich variety of fruit and flowers, including eucalyptus and vines, palm trees and camellias, oaks, cedars, broom, chestnuts and fig trees.*

Above *Angers St Louis replaced the Plantagenet castle between 1228 and 1238, symbolising firm French rule in the former heartlands of the Plantagenet dominions.*

Right *The Loire river flows gently from the Ile de France to Anjou. This is the way the Plantagenets would have taken to Paris and to the court of Louis VI, nicknamed 'the fat', and his son Louis VII. This view of the Loire, near Château-du-Loir, is said to be the spot where Geoffrey went to swim on a hot summer's evening, caught a chill and died, leaving his eldest son, Henry, as duke of Anjou and Normandy.*

churches were decorated with hangings and covers; all the clergy went in loyal procession to meet them, in copes and albs, with candles, books and crosses, singing hymns and praises. The new lord and lady were received by priest and people with solemn dances. Thereafter, they lived comfortably and ennobled the island of Great Britain and the transmaritime parts with the issue of a magnificent heir [the future Henry II].

Once his father had been elevated to the kingdom of Jerusalem as I have described, Count Geoffrey devoted his time to feats of arms and strove for honour. Before long, a day was named for a tournament to be held between the Normans and Bretons on a sandy hill pasture. To the aid of the Norman side, came William Clito, count of Flanders, Theobald, count of Blois, and his brother Stephen, lord of Mortain, the future king of England. These three were nephews of Henry I. The count met them and increased their number. By way of an adversary, there stood the Breton line, agile in arms and mind but few in number.

When Geoffrey saw that the Breton troops which had assembled were few, he broke away from the multitude and offered his services to them. The company assembled and the lines joined battle. There was much clashing of arms, the clarions rang out and the voice of the horn resounded with many notes while their steeds let out dissonant neighs.

Mont-Saint-Michel itself glittered with the sunbeams reflected by their gold shields. The men were as one in the competition; the shafts of their spears were broken and their swords were destroyed. Now foot was bruised by foot and shoulder pushed back by shoulder. Saddles were emptied and horsemen flung to the ground. Horses which had thrown their riders and broken their reins wandered whinnying. A notable terror to the adversary, Geoffrey sought out and attacked his enemies and, running to and fro, hurling lances and brandishing his sword, he deprived many of their lives. The Bretons pursued their hope of victory, with the count leading the way, and inflicted many kinds of death on their foe. The Angevin pressed on more ferocious than the lion;

the Breton phalanx pushed forward, confident of victory, and the Normans, exhausted by the great struggle, showed their backs and took flight – the majority defeated by the few – forced to repair to their camp. Indeed, the Normans, disheartened by the unexpected confusion, proposed single combat to the Bretons.

When talk of the tournament spread beyond the sea, a Saxon soldier of enormous stature arrived, whose strength and daring gave the Normans confidence to assume victory. He set forth from the Norman camp, taller than any other human by far and, taking up position in a prominent place, he taunted the Breton line and dared them to name a man who would meet him in individual combat. The faces of his listeners grew pale and the strength drained from brave men. They feared for the person who went into single combat with such a huge monster.

Geoffrey watched these courageous men reduced to weakness and wailing when summoned individually. Then he yelled ferociously and refusing to suffer such taunts as were being thrown out, rode forward on his horse. Taking up his weapons and, in front of the crowd watching on all sides, he went into battle with the giant soldier. The fight was hard: that man, whose force was superhuman, had a lance like a beam and when he attacked the Angevin, he pierced the count's shield and cuirass, not without spilling much blood. But our hero remained immovable, as though rooted to his horse, and he transfixed his assailant by hurling his javelin. Then, standing over his impaled adversary, he beheaded him with his sword. Leading the horse of the defeated man by his victorious hand, as though in possession of a trophy, the shame of the Normans and the glory of his own men, the famous victor went away. Wicked noblemen are always jealous of the upright, and they say that Geoffrey, though the king's son-in-law, existed more safely among his own people where he was disturbed by no fear of capture. For this reason, this exceptional mirror of knighthood, who sought sweet fodder for his fame and was eager for sport, began to seek out tournaments in Flanders, striving there for opportunities to perform great deeds, desirous of praise as he was.

Geoffrey enjoyed hunting when he could afford the time; this diversion, pleasing and available to some, has often driven away dark cares and led men back, after their fill of recreation, all the more ready for duty. For this reason, the count hunted quite often. The hunters would enter the woods and unleash their cunning hounds as is customary, and the dogs, following the beast by the traces of its scent, would find it with a speed that was difficult to believe, leading the count by their barking.

On this particular occasion, the count hurries to anticipate the winding, circling paths of his almost runaway dogs. He climbs the quickest ways but has no luck, for while the beast he had hoped for is drawn down by his dogs, he is forced to flee elsewhere, and although he believes himself to be nearer to his companions than to his dogs, he is in fact further away. It was thus that he wandered all day, discovering neither his friends nor hounds nor anyone who had seen them. At last, as the sun was hastening to close the day, he caught sight of a peasant amid the undergrowth of a coppice. The man was covered in soot and the blackest of garments clothed his body down to his loins. His occupation was plain from what he wore: he sweated in making charcoal for workmen and it was for this reason that his face and clothing had acquired that colour.

When Geoffrey saw him, he did not despise him as a rich man a pauper but, as man acknowledges man in the suffering of an individual, he lamented the common misfortune of mankind, remembering that utterance of the first man: 'By the sweat of your brow will you eat your bread.'

Geoffrey greeted the man kindly and asked him, 'Can you tell me, my good man, if you know a road which leads to the castle at Loches?'

The other replied, 'If I did not know, I would not take my charcoal there so often to sell.'

The count said, 'So take me, dear fellow, along your path to the public highway, before I become completely lost in the lonely places of these woods.'

'Master,' said the peasant, 'you who ride a horse have no trouble in feeding your spirit and clothing your body. But if I stop work, I perish and my family with me.'

'Do not delay but come, I beg you, where I ask,' was the response, 'for I will pay the price of your journey.'

Then the fellow, looking at him and suspecting I know not what divine occurrence, bowed and answered, 'I am not afraid of what will befall me. I will go with you wherever you order.'

The count gratefully embraced him and bade him sit behind on his horse. The peasant gladly placed Geoffrey on the road he was seeking after a while, all the time taking note of the nobleman's humility and marvelling at his gentleness.

But more is to follow.

Now the count strikes up friendly conversation with the peasant. And among other things, he asks him, 'What do men say of our count? Tell me, good fellow. And what do they think of the nobility? What are the opinions of the populace?'

The other answered, 'As far as the count is concerned, and the things which happen in his presence, we neither say nor feel anything bad of him. But as for us, lord, we suffer many enemies of whom he is unaware, and the worse they are, the more secretive they are. For no enemy is so difficult to guard against or so ready to wound as the enemy at home, and it is these that we cannot and dare not resist.'

'And is it possible', said the count, 'for our lord to sway their opinion or to discharge them?'

The other replied, 'He could do both, my lord, if these wicked deeds were not done under guise of obedience to him.'

'Then', said the count, 'tell me carefully more about these enemies and explain their evil deeds to me. For perhaps when the time is ripe, I will not be silent before the count.'

'Lord, our oppressors are the reeves, bailiffs and other servants of our lord the count. Whenever he comes to one of his castles, his servants seize goods on credit, wherever they are available, without prayer or price. Those who have bought are silent, the count leaves and the creditors seek repayment. Then, lord, pitiful to relate, they either totally deny owing anything or they defer payment until their creditors are glad to accept half of what is owed.'

Then our wise hero, concealing the anger which he could not but feel at hearing himself so cruelly fed, said smiling to the peasant, 'But they have fertile land for nothing, these men who both usurp what is due to the count and make him live unawares on rapine.' And then he added, 'Peace, peace. But it is not peace where the land is so badly devastated by domestic enemies.'

The peasant told him, 'But you haven't heard all yet, master.'

'I will gladly hear everything,' said Geoffrey. 'Explain it all carefully and fairly, for I love the count and, presuming on my friendship, I will be sure to tell him what they do.'

'Perhaps', continued the peasant, 'it has happened by the will of God that I should tell to your ears today what I could not tell the count myself and that it will not be hidden from the count by you. Listen therefore, lord, and not for the worse. After the harvest has been gathered in, the count's reeves go out to the villages, and coercing one of the farmers by a new law, they place an exaction on his crop with much violence. Then, dreadful to relate, these men demand one-sixteenth of the crop, these two-sixteenths and those more if it can be hoped to obtain it. And if, perchance, there should be someone to contradict this levy, he is dragged into a law-suit and prosecuted by the reeves' followers. He is accused of false crimes, and thus no one escapes the greedy hands of the wicked judges until, purse exhausted, he regrets that his thrift contravened these perverse laws.'

The count thought, 'Evil be to him who founds such laws.' Aloud he said, 'Vengeance is mine and I will bring retribution on them before long. Tell me more and keep nothing back. What else is there to hear of those illustrious men? Would that the count (and here he spoke of himself) knew of their misdeeds.'

'It is a wonder, my lord,' the peasant said, 'to see how they conceal from our lord the count what is executed in the presence of all, unless it is usual for masters to be the last to know what happens in their own houses. I will add one more incident to what I have told and then I will put a stop to my tale lest, stammering in a country fashion, I cause offence to your fine ears.'

Geoffrey replied: 'Speak and fear not. No one speaks more elegantly than when he is speaking the truth.'

The other continued, 'When some warning of war begins to be heard, whether true or invented by them, then these reeves send out their hangers-on who put great effort into spreading the rumour and by means of a public edict announced by heralds, they gather husbandmen from all parts and fill the castles with them, under the pretext of guard duty, leaving the countryside deserted. Then their accomplices, secretly despatched, secretly summon individuals and console them for their loss as though they have always been their comforters. They encourage the husbandmen to buy permission to return from the reeves by offering secret gifts, as though this is good advice. And for every man allowed to return, there are others, wretched farmers, who are weighed down by debt and owe their few coppers to another and who are forced to stay in the castles. Such, my lord, are the men by whom the countryside is sorely afflicted. He who toils in peace is almost as unfortunate as he who perishes in war.' The peasant had said all and now they were entering the town.

I should not pass over the repeated, wretched murmuring that was growing at the count's absence. In his court, each man asked the others of Geoffrey's whereabouts and no one replied with good news; at dusk their distress greatly increased. One and all hung motionless with terrified eyes upon the road by which he was accustomed to

Aquitaine

THE mid-12th century *Pilgrims' Book of Compostella* describes the various people who lived in the duchy of Aquitaine. The Poitevins dressed elegantly, were good horsemen, and were witty, hospitable and handsome; in contrast the peoples of the Saintonge and Bordeaux regions spoke uncouthly, while the Gascons were frivolous, talkative, sardonic and debauched but, although far from prosperous themselves, gave generously to the poor. These characterizations should probably not be taken too seriously. But they do at least illustrate a medieval view of the diversity of Aquitaine, the largest duchy in France.

Stretching from Poitiers in the north to Périgueux in the south and close to the Rhône valley in the east, the region was extremely wealthy from the export of wine and salt. An astonishingly rich cultural life is typified on the one hand by such great Romanesque churches as Notre-Dame-la-Grande in Poitiers, the cathedral at Angoulême, the rich carvings on many country churches, and on the other by the Old Provençal love-poetry of William IX, duke of Aquitaine (1086–1126).

Duke William was the first of the troubadours, a breed in which Aquitaine was to be remarkably prolific. His writings encapsulate a new spirit of chivalry and individualism which was blasphemous, erotic, amoral and sensitive. His poems are an exuberant celebration of love and sensuality that was quite unknown before his time. They contain something of the spirit of renewal that is characteristic of the 12th century, as well as much self-indulgence: 'To refresh my heart in her/To renew my flesh in her/So that I shall never grow old.'

William's life-style was considered outrageous by many contemporaries. A great crusader, he is said to have had his mistress painted on his shield, saying that 'it was his will to bear her in battle, as she had borne him in bed'. As duke, his political legacy was unhappy. His many wars had allowed the Aquitanian aristocracy to attain an independence which neither he nor his son, also called William, could curb.

William X ruled from 1126 to 1137. As he had no male heir, it was decided to marry his young daughter Eleanor to the future king of France, Louis VII, so that the monarchy could protect the duchy. Louis first tried to play an active role in the government of Aquitaine, but subsequently spent little time there. In the long run, the result of the increasingly unhappy marriage was to plunge Aquitaine into the rivalry between the Capetians and the house of Anjou.

Above *Eleanor of Aquitaine gave this vase to Louis VII as a wedding gift; he subsequently gave it to the abbey of St-Denis. The rock crystal body is decorated with gold filigree and jewels.*

Below *Life in Aquitaine was rich in song and poetry, arts that Louis found difficult to appreciate.*

return from the forest when suddenly the longed-for figure arrives, cheerfully addressing the first man he meets, as was his habit. Recognizing the count's voice, that person could not answer for joy but ran on ahead shouting with what voice he had that the count had returned, and pointing to him.

Then the peasant realized whose guide he had been and with whom he had conversed. Convinced he could no longer cling to the count's back, he suddenly tried to jump to the ground. The count felt this and, holding him back as he lurched, said with a smile, 'So, ought I to dispense with my guide through whose assistance I have been brought back to my people? That will not do.' And with the crowd flocking round on all sides, the peasant was borne on high on the count's horse, whether he liked it or not.

They came to the time for a banquet. Changed into clothes generously provided by the count, he, a peasant, reclined amid the leading men of the court. A peasant was honoured with the most sumptuous dishes of food; a peasant dined off gold and most of the adventure was related to the court either by the count or by the peasant.

When the count had returned from Mass the next day, he ordered that his guide be summoned and said, 'I free you and your heirs from all exactions and services and I ordain that you be freemen, free in every respect. Return therefore to your family and lead a somewhat easier life.' Having said this, the count ordered that the man be escorted back to his own parts.

The count was outstanding above all because he made it his duty to spare the weak. Now, however, I shall lay before you an example of the way in which he knew how to subdue the mighty.

Count Theobald II of Blois and Champagne was an illustrious man, one of the richest of his day in France, utterly faithful and quite blameless. Within his dominion, William, count of Nevers and Hugh, lord of Cosne, nicknamed the 'Manceau', were constantly squabbling with each other, although Theobald would often invite them to bring their case before his court. At length, that

scoundrel of Nevers, who preferred to defeat his enemy by force rather than to have recourse to law, fled from Count Theobald's court.

King Louis VI of France was meanwhile quietly consolidating his power guided by Abbot Suger of Saint-Denis.

During the protracted and continuous struggle which ensued, the count of Nevers enlisted the help of the king of France, Louis VI, and of the bishop of Autun, both of whom brought large armies to his side, because he wanted to vanquish his opponent completely. So the king, the prelate and the count mustered their three armies and besieged Hugh in the castle which is known as Cosne. There was not the slightest hope of escape: with the forces entrenched on every side, none could enter and none could leave. In desperation, 'Manceau' sent envoys to Count Theobald to explain their plight and to beseech help. Without waiting, for there was danger in delay, that worthy man ordered his men to go there and asked his neighbours and allies for assistance too. Of these men he particularly implored Geoffrey of Anjou, but with confidence for he trusted totally in that count's help. Our hero did not delay; he was ever swift to assist his friends, would promise forces and be faithful to his pledge.

Geoffrey summoned a band of one hundred and forty knights, chosen and sturdy comrades, and with three hundred auxiliaries he hastened forward. He combined forces with Theobald and together the two hurried to rescue the besieged 'Manceau'. But rumour of their arrival flew ahead and reached the ears of the king of France, who wisely broke camp and left the siege.

Hatred for his enemy caused the count of Nevers to delay his flight a little, however. So Count Geoffrey set about pursuing him while Count Theobald dealt with those who remained. Then you should have seen the noble Geoffrey, with his companions of honour, holding up the lions emblazoned on his shield although, truly, he was inferior to no lion in ferocity. He chased fiercely those fleeing, as though he were a military thunderbolt, or went to the aid of his friends.

An unofficial minister

FOR nearly a quarter of a century, from 1127 to his death in 1151, Abbot Suger was chief adviser to Louis VI (1108–37) and Louis VII (1137–80).

A man of humble birth, who rose in the service of church and crown by his own abilities, Suger had no official position in royal government, but the value of the advice he gave to Louis VI and Louis VII was matched by his emphasis on the sacred and ceremonial side of kingship. He gave it a significance that far outstripped reality.

He rebuilt his abbey church of Saint-Denis, the burial-place of earlier kings, as a royal mausoleum in the new Gothic style – highly decorated, ornate and colourful. The beauty of this building was intended to transport the worshipper closer to God, and at the same time to glorify the French kings. Suger also involved his monarchs in ceremonies that demonstrated their links with a great past. In 1124, for example, Louis VI took the *oriflamme*, supposedly Charlemagne's standard, from the altar in Saint-Denis and made fervent and patriotic speeches before leading a formidable army of his nobles, great and small, to fight a war against the emperor, Henry V. The ceremonial and the number of vassals who answered the king's call made this the most impressive campaign in France for at least two centuries, and faced with this show of strength, the emperor retreated.

Although both kings might seem to have been mediocrities who made many mistakes, their reigns were crucial to the development of the image and status of monarchy in France; and Suger educated both of them in the subject, gave practical guidance and helped them to administer their lands.

Louis VI was a soldier king who subdued robber barons who pillaged and looted in the royal lands. Described by Suger as a man whose spirit was as large as his body, he gave way to lechery, avarice and gluttony and in his later years could no longer mount a horse – hence his nickname Louis the Fat. His son Louis VII, like him, improved the quality and efficiency of his administration and did his best to uphold royal rights. He was Eleanor of Aquitaine's first husband. The satirical writer Walter Map recorded how, as an old man, Louis could sleep alone in a wood almost unattended, so high was the esteem in which his people held him; and Map asked what other king could do likewise. Louis's temperament was indeed more suited to old age, when he could hide a lack of solid achievement and many disappointments behind a façade of gentleness and wisdom.

Above *Two details of the exterior of Saint-Denis. Although Abbot Suger started the great reconstruction of the abbey church, much of it was again rebuilt by Pierre de Montreuil in the 13th century.*

Above *Chalice, c.1140, given by Abbot
Suger to his abbey of St-Denis.*

Right *The abbot's choir in St-Denis.*

Below *One of the abbey's celebrated windows showing
the abbot kneeling before the Virgin.*

Some runaways he cut down with his sword, others he stretched out on the ground when he attacked. No one fled him unwounded.

What more? When many had died and more had fled, Geoffrey took the count of Nevers himself prisoner and handed him over, bound, to Count Theobald.

Our count, Geoffrey, was distinguished then by those outstanding virtues and by great integrity. He was at once human and mercifully gentle and upright, strong and courageously spirited. This is how it was true of him that he 'spared the weak and subdued the mighty'.

Meanwhile in the Holy Land Fulk of Anjou, king of Jerusalem, was struggling against the growing power of the Islamic champion Zengi, who ruled in Mosul from 1127 onwards. Such was Zengi's success that Jerusalem might well have fallen in the 1130s had not the emir of Damascus and the emperor of Constantinople come to Fulk's aid. In 1136 Fulk summoned Raymond of Poitiers, the handsome and able younger son of Duke William IX of Aquitaine, to Palestine. He was to be the bridegroom of the nine-year-old Constance, princess of Antioch. This was a strategically important dependent state of the kingdom of Jerusalem, and Raymond was needed to help Fulk in his defence of the Holy Land.

After several years had passed, while Count Geoffrey was flourishing in prosperity, Robert of Sablé with his allies made war against Geoffrey.

John of Marmoutier now describes in considerable detail the numerous campaigns of Count Geoffrey against his unruly castellans, among them the lords of Sablé.

Robert of Sablé made the barons of the entire territory by oaths his despicable comrades. Even Elias, then count of Maine, brother of the count of Anjou, by the advice of wicked men, attacked his brother. When Geoffrey had captured Elias, he kept him for many days at Tours; but after he had been released from there, the youth died, having caught a serious illness in prison.

Meanwhile, having conferred with his own men, Count Geoffrey seized the opportunity to enter his enemy's land, judging it more prudent to attack them in their own lands, rather than leaving it to them to attack him. Consequently, with hand-picked knights and many foot-soldiers, the count himself went after that rebellious and hostile people who were immediately forced to flee, even the foot-soldiers. Then Robert's men came out against the count. He held back from a headlong attack, for the men of Sablé, having been alerted to his approach, had set up ambushes. Geoffrey, seeing that it had become necessary for him to prepare his force for a battle, drove Robert of Sablé back within the castle, having both killed and wounded many of his men and captured others. The count, the victor, then retired to his own place.

1132

Then in the fourth year since the aforesaid marriage [of Geoffrey and Matilda], his first son, Henry, was born to Count Geoffrey. He was the future King Henry II of England. In the fifth year, Geoffrey was born, and in the sixth year William.

1135

In 1135, after precisely thirty-five years and four months of his own reign, in exactly the seventy-seventh year of his own age, on 1 December, King Henry I of England died at Rouen, in the place known as Lyons-la-Forêt. The Normans kept his intestines, and the rest of his body the English carried away to a tomb [in the abbey at Reading].

King Henry having died as we have said, Stephen, the count of Mortain, the brother of Theobald II, count of Blois and Champagne, a nephew of the dead king, was improperly elevated into the kingship and crowned king in England.

In that year Count Geoffrey of Anjou, with appointed men, entered Normandy, intending to conquer it as an inheritance for his son.

Meanwhile the Empress Matilda, the count's wife, having crossed the sea with a full band of

Princes of Antioch

IN 1133 Fulk V, king of Jerusalem and count of Anjou, selected the son of his former neighbour, Duke William IX of Aquitaine, to succeed as prince of Antioch. Raymond of Poitiers was 34 years old and his new capital was a flourishing centre, once the third city of the Roman Empire. Massively fortified with immense walls and 400 towers, Antioch had been captured by the crusaders in 1098, only after a siege of eight months.

The strategic key to north Syria, Christian Antioch was increasingly threatened as the 12th century progressed. The danger from Moslem Aleppo intensified with the capture of Edessa, and in 1149 Raymond was killed in a battle against its ruler. The Byzantine emperors had a claim to the city – it had been promised to them by the leaders of the First Crusade – and occasionally led armies to Syria to demand recognition of their overlordship.

Antioch was the second state founded by the First Crusade, and under its earliest rulers, Bohemond and Tancred, it had had a strong Norman flavour. This influence had faded by the time of Raymond of Poitiers, as the settlers had taken over many of the manners and customs of the East.

Raymond found that he, like the other emigrants from Europe, had quickly adapted to life in the East: 'We who were Occidentals have become Orientals . . . we have already forgotten the places where we were born . . . he who was once a stranger here is now a native,' wrote one of them in 1127. Some had married native women, 'a Syrian or an Armenian or even a Saracen who has received the grace of baptism'. An Arab emir told of meeting a knight who had adopted the Muslim way of life, to the extent of employing cooks from Egypt and eschewing pork.

The Western settlers, however, remained an alien minority who lived largely in the towns, and to those newly arrived from the West, full of crusading zeal, the Eastern manners of the settlers and their alliances with native princes represented a betrayal. Adaptations to the climate and political circumstances were only good sense; but for most Europeans, they were in reality only skin deep.

Left *Crusaders at the siege of Antioch.*

Below *From the same manuscript, within the initial, the patriarch of Antioch receives the emperor of Constantinople and, below, he is depicted with the count of Foix.*

knights, though by sex a woman yet with manly strength did she attack the English, maintaining that the inheritance which was hers by right she would obtain by arms. The news flew, and having come to the ears of King Stephen, it was declared that the kingdom was in danger, for the empress had overcome many of the English by force and many of them had at once surrendered to her; so that unless he hastened back to England quickly he would lose the crown of the kingdom. The king, compelled by the bad news, sailed with as many men as he could allow from his host of warriors.

John of Marmoutier next gives an idealized account of Geoffrey's conquest of Normandy (1142–4), which suggests — inaccurately — that the count's progress was met with more enthusiasm than hostility in the duchy.

Then the energetic Count Geoffrey, who was struggling in his fight against the collected army of Stephen, having ascertained that God would fight for him against the castles of the impious king, and having learned of his retreat, did not waste the advantage of the hour, but advanced. He entered the land, besieged Mortain, took hostages and sureties, received the inhabitants in peace, governed them humanely, protecting their possessions unharmed from the army.

The count then moving his army, came to Carentan. Having received that place in surrender without a fight, he hastened to the city of Bayeux. Both the citizens and the bishop, hearing of his approach, came in peace and with rejoicing, and accepted him in his authority, doing homage and swearing to aid him against all his adversaries.

Moving on from Bayeux, the count made for St Lô, which the bishop of Coutances, who controlled the place, had fortified against him. The soldiers within numbered about two hundred. And going out to battle against the count, they were forced to flee back to the town at his first attack. Holding up for the first and second day, on the third day they surrendered. The defenders opened the gates, sought peace, made over hostages, swearing homage and oaths to the count.

The first Plantagenet conquest

THE conquest of Normandy by Geoffrey Plantagenet, count of Anjou, was almost completed in 1144. It was a culmination of nine years of conflict, in which he and his wife the Empress Matilda tried to make good her claim to rule England and Normandy. In 1135, after Henry I's death, Stephen of Blois had taken both, but the Angevins now had a secure base from which to snipe at his power in England.

Initially, four expeditions into Normandy between 1135 and 1138 had achieved little. In 1137 the Angevin army had been smitten with dysentery and, in a contemporary's words, ran out of the duchy leaving behind a trail of filth.

Normandy was tied to England mainly because so many of the nobles held lands on both sides of the

Channel. Stephen made little effort to gain Norman loyalties – indeed he only visited the duchy once. But the Normans so hated their traditional enemies, the Angevins, that they put up stiff resistance to Geoffrey's troops. However, the news of Stephen's capture at Lincoln in 1141 by Matilda's followers undermined morale in Normandy. Castle after castle surrendered in rapid succession. In 1141 Geoffrey held most of the lands between Bayeux and the Seine, in 1142 he took the Avranchin and Mortain, in 1143 he overran the Cotentin and moved east of the Seine. Rouen fell in 1144 and Geoffrey was then invested as duke, leaving only a mopping-up operation in 1145 when Arques, the last castle, fell.

As a result of the conquest, the Angevins controlled half of the Anglo-Norman dominions. In addition, they could not be dislodged from western England. Their cause, therefore, became the better long-term bet. Contemporaries appreciated this: after 1144 no major baron with extensive Norman lands defected permanently to Stephen's side.

Above Falaise Castle, a powerful Norman stronghold that dates from the 12th century.

Below Tomb effigy of Robert Curthose, duke of Normandy. Deposed and imprisoned by Henry I in 1106, he was a captive until his death in 1134. Ten years later, Geoffrey of Anjou was duke of Normandy.

Then he came to the city of Coutances, in the province of Cotentin. This place the count entered, captured without opposition (for the bishop was away) and filled with a garrison and provisions. He then summoned the barons of the province of Cotentin, requesting homage from them. They came and performed the requested service, all except Ralph and his brother, Richard de la Haye. The former, fortifying his castles against the count, was known to be in rebellion; while the other, with a great force of two hundred or more soldiers, occupied Cherbourg, where he reckoned he would be able to withstand the count. But the great-hearted count first ravaged Ralph's land, besieged his castles, and then with martial strength captured Ralph himself. Too late to repent because he had already attacked others, Ralph accepted his captivity peacefully in submission.

Count Geoffrey now advanced to Cherbourg. Having organized his companies of soldiers, and with engines carefully and skilfully constructed, he made ready with warlike preparations. At Cherbourg Julius Caesar had erected a fortress in preparation for his invasion of Great Britain. It was surrounded by the most stout walls, frequent towers having been set into the circuit of the wall so that scarcely a soldier's spear would fit between them. Inside the fortification, he set a tower higher than the others and a royal hall. Into this fortress he fled at the first attack of the Britons. Not undeservedly tradition has named this fortress 'Caesar's Stronghold'.

After occupying this place, Richard de la Haye filled it with knights, squires, armed men and large supplies of provisions. Then he admonished them stoutly to resist Geoffrey. [Richard decided to cross the sea to King Stephen, from whom he would return leading forces of soldiers to break up the siege and drive Count Geoffrey to flight.] Meanwhile, those who were in the fortress continued to resist the count, trusting not only in their own valour and in the great hoard of provisions which the tyrant Richard de la Haye had stored up there, but also in the impregnable defence of the towers. They hurled darts of weaponry and verbal abuse. The attackers returned missile for missile, but not word for word, not wishing to respond to their

inanities. The Lord, however, in Whose hand are all the powers and kingdoms of every land, fought on the count's behalf, holding back his enemies and exalting him. For behold, when Richard de la Haye sailed, he was captured by pirates, and taken away to foreign lands.

The unhappy news was taken to those who were resisting the count. The defenders' faces fell from grief, their shaken hope collapsed, they could only think of flight, and no way out was seen. So they handed back the strong fortress, crammed with supplies, willingly surrendering themselves to the count's authority. They promised binding allegiance under the guarantee of fealty by oath. These things having been carried out, the count judged the onset of winter to be close at hand. And with what he had taken from the castles, he disbanded the expedition.

A long strife had been waged between Stephen, the false king, and Geoffrey, the count of Anjou: Geoffrey excelling and always more active in himself, Stephen weakening daily.

At the time when kings and princes are accustomed to advance to war, just after the bitterness of stormy Winter, when the gentle kindliness of Spring warms the scented airs and thickets blossom into flower, when rose-gardens, which but a little while ago were bare, are now garlanded with fresh roses, and when on wondering eyes the whiteness of flowering lilies plays. . . .

Henry of Huntingdon paints a quite different picture of the struggle between the houses of Blois and Anjou for domination of Normandy and England. Not only does the chronicler show some sympathy – albeit qualified – for Stephen, but he sees the events of his reign almost entirely in an English – and a Scottish – context. This is immediately apparent in his description of Henry I's death and Stephen's accession in 1135.

On the death of the great King Henry I (1135), his character was freely discussed by the people, as is usual after men are dead. Some contended that he was eminently distinguished for three brilliant gifts. These were: great wisdom, for his counsels were profound, his foresight keen and his eloquence commanding; success in war, for, besides other splendid achievements, he was victorious over the king of France [Louis VII]; and wealth, in which he far surpassed all his predecessors. Others, however, taking a different view, attributed to him three vices: avarice, as, though his wealth was great, in imitation of his progenitors he impoverished the people by taxes and exactions, entangling them in the toils of informers; cruelty, in that he gouged out the eyes of his kinsman the count of Mortain whom he held captive, though the horrid deed was unknown until his death revealed the king's secrets, and they mentioned other instances of which I will say nothing; and lasciviousness, for, like King Solomon, he was perpetually enslaved by female seductions. Such remarks were freely spread about. But whatever King Henry did, whether tyrannically or justly as king, seemed wonderful in comparison with the times that followed, which were set ablaze by the atrocities of the Normans.

For in all haste came Stephen, the younger brother of Theobald count of Blois, a resolute and audacious man who, disregarding his oath of fealty to King Henry's daughter Matilda, tempted God by seizing the crown of England with boldness and effrontery. William archbishop of Canterbury, who had been the first to swear allegiance to Matilda, consecrated the new king, alas; wherefore the Lord visited him with the same judgement which he had inflicted on the man who struck Jeremiah, the great priest: he died within the year. Roger, the powerful bishop of Salisbury, who had taken a similar oath and persuaded others to do the same, contributed all in his power to raise Stephen to the throne. He too, by the just judgement of God, was afterwards thrown into prison and met a pitiful end, afflicted by the very king he had helped to make.

In short all the earls and barons who had thus sworn fealty transferred their allegiance to Stephen and did him homage. It was a bad sign, that the whole of England should so quickly, without hesitation or struggle, as if in the twinkling of an eye, submit to Stephen. After his coronation he held his court at London.

1136

Stephen, coming in the first year of his reign to Oxford, was told that David king of the Scots, pretending to pay him a friendly visit, had marched to Carlisle and Newcastle and captured both by stratagem. The king replied to the messenger, 'What he has gained by stratagem I will compel him to yield.' King Stephen therefore immediately assembled one of the greatest armies levied in England within the memory of man, and led it against King David. They met at Durham, where the king of the Scots came to terms, surrendering Newcastle but retaining Carlisle by Stephen's permission; and King David did not do homage to King Stephen, because he had been the first of all the laymen to swear fealty to the late king's daughter, who was his own niece, acknowledging her queen of England after her father's death. But Henry, King David's son, did homage to Stephen, and Stephen gave him in addition the town of Huntingdon.

King Stephen, returning from the north, held his court during Easter at London, in a more splendid manner than had ever been known before, both for the number of attendants and the magnificent display of gold, silver, jewels, costly robes and everything that was sumptuous.

1137

In the second year of his reign, King Stephen spent Christmas at Dunstable, and in Lent he sailed over to Normandy. Alexander bishop of Lincoln and many nobles crossed with him. There, from his experience in war, the king succeeded in all he undertook, defeated the schemes of his enemies, reduced their castles and obtained the highest glory. He made peace with the French king, to whom his son Eustace did homage for Normandy, which is a fief of the French crown.

Geoffrey count of Anjou was King Stephen's mortal enemy, for he had married King Henry's daughter Matilda, who had been empress of Germany and who had received oaths of fealty for the kingdom of England; so that the husband and wife laid claims to the crown. But, seeing that at

present he could not make headway against King Stephen on account of his numerous forces and of the abundance of money found in the treasury of the late king, the count of Anjou came to terms with King Stephen. Thus successful, the king returned to England in triumph on the very eve of Christmas.

These first two years of King Stephen's reign were very fortunate; for the next year, of which I have now to speak, his fortunes were moderate and fitful; for the last two they were ruined and desperate.

1138

King Stephen, in the third year of his reign, with his usual energy went quickly to Bedford, and besieging it on Christmas Eve, pressed the siege during the whole festival, which was displeasing to God inasmuch as it made that holy season of little or no account.

After the surrender of Bedford King Stephen led his army into Scotland, for King David, in consequence of the oath which he had taken to King Henry's daughter, and under colour of religion, caused his followers to deal most barbarously with the English. They ripped open pregnant women and pulled out the unborn babies; they tossed children on the points of their spears, butchered priests at the altars and, cutting the heads off the images on crucifixes, placed them on the bodies of the slain while in exchange they fixed on the crucifixes the heads of their victims. Wherever the Scots came there was the same scene of horror and cruelty: women shrieking, old men lamenting amid the groans of the dying and the despair of the living. King Stephen therefore, invading Scotland, carried fire and sword through the southern part of the dominions of King David, who did not dare to oppose him.

The anonymous but contemporary author of The Deeds of Stephen, *takes a somewhat less critical view of the Scots.*

The king of Scotland, which country borders on England, only a river dividing the two, was a prince of great humanity who was born of religious parents and had not degenerated from them in goodness and piety. Along with the other great men, indeed the first of them all, he had taken the oath of allegiance to King Henry's daughter Matilda in that king's presence, and he was therefore deeply grieved that Stephen had usurped the crown of England; but as that was settled by the barons without his concurrence, he prudently awaited the result, watching the course of events.

At length he received letters from Matilda, complaining that she had been excluded from her father's will, robbed of the crown which had been secured to her and her husband by solemn oaths; that the laws were set aside and justice trodden underfoot; and the sworn fealty of the English barons was broken and disregarded. She therefore earnestly and sorrowfully implored him as her kinsman to succour her in her need, and as her liege vassal to aid her in her distress.

The king of Scotland was deeply grieved; and inflamed with zeal for a just cause, the ties of blood and regard for his oath induced him to foment insurrections in England, that by so doing, by God's help, Stephen might be compelled to resign to its rightful owner the crown which it appeared to him, had been unjustly acquired. The king of the Scots entertained at his court the English exiles who continually urged him to these measures. King David therefore, for that was his name, published an edict throughout Scotland calling his people to arms and, changing his line of conduct, let loose without mercy a most fierce and destructive storm on the English people.

Scotland, also called Albany, is a country covered by extensive moors, but containing flourishing woods and pastures which feed large herds of cows and oxen. It has safe harbours, and is surrounded by fertile islands. The natives are savage and their habits uncleanly, but they are neither stunted by extreme cold nor debilitated by severe want. Swift of foot and lightly armed, they make bold and active soldiers. Among themselves they are so fearless as to think nothing of death; among strangers their cruelty is brutal and they sell their lives dearly.

A brave and foolish king

STEPHEN (?1097–1154) was the third son of Stephen, count of Blois and Chartres, who had acquired European notoriety by running away from Antioch during the First Crusade, and of Adela, the tough-minded daughter of William the Conqueror who sent her husband back to Outremer.

Young Stephen was dispatched to the court of his uncle Henry I, probably in 1113, and given extensive lands in Normandy and England which made him one of the wealthiest of the Anglo-Norman landholders.

In 1126, along with many others, Stephen took an oath to accept the succession of Henry's daughter Matilda. However, on hearing of Henry's death on 1 December, 1135, he set in motion what seems to have been a premeditated and well-organized plan. He crossed to England, was accepted as king in London, gained possession of the treasury at Winchester, and was crowned on 22 December. A messenger then hurried to Normandy where the Norman barons, after hesitation, accepted him as duke. In this way, Stephen re-created Henry I's cross-Channel dominion. Early in 1136 his position seemed secure. His Easter court was attended by many of the major landholders, and even Matilda's half-brother, Earl Robert of Gloucester, had done homage. Matilda and her supporters had been able to occupy only parts of southern Normandy and there were isolated acts of defiance in the West Country by Baldwin of Redvers, and in the North by the king of Scots.

In the words of the chronicler Walter Map, Stephen was 'a good knight, but in all other respects a fool' – a stinging verdict that was perhaps over-harsh. No one doubted Stephen's personal bravery. At the battle of Lincoln on 2 February, 1141, he fought on foot long after much of his army had fled, wearing out a battle-axe and a sword before being captured.

He was a chivalrous figure – courteous, affable, kind-hearted and generous, if somewhat ineffectual when it came to carrying through the schemes he had conceived with such enthusiasm. He could also be sly and shifty, and on many occasions showed a considerable lack of judgement. He made many political blunders during his reign – arresting barons at court was one – and alienated vital supporters. On occasions his sense of chivalry led him to make mistakes that astonished and dismayed his followers, as in 1139 when he had Matilda at his mercy but gave her safe-conduct to her brother's castle at Bristol. Because Matilda, as wife of Geoffrey Plantagenet, had a secure base in Anjou and later in Normandy, Stephen had to deal with a combination of external and internal opposition the like of which none of his predecessors had faced. Many people concealed treacherous intent in their apparent loyalty to him. In the end, however, he simply lacked the dominant personality essential to successful 12th-century kingship.

Top left *Stephen with his pet falcon.*

Above *Stephen's seal.*

Pages 66 and 67 *Durham; the cathedral and the castle rise above the river.*

We now return to the narration of Henry of Huntingdon.

After Easter 1138, the treason of the English nobles burst forth with great fury. Talbot, one of the rebels, held Hereford castle in Wales against King Stephen, which, however, the king besieged and took. Earl Robert of Gloucester, bastard son of King Henry I, maintained himself in the strongly fortified castle of Bristol and in that of Leeds. William FitzAlan held Shrewsbury castle, which last the king stormed, and hanged some of the prisoners.

While the king was thus engaged in the south, David of Scotland again led an immense army into the north of England, against which the northern nobles, under the command of Thurstan, archbishop of York, made a resolute stand. The royal standard was planted at Northallerton and, as he was prevented by illness from being present at the battle, the archbishop commissioned Ralph bishop of Orkney to fill his place. Standing on a hillock in the centre of the army, Ralph roused the English nobles' courage with a speech.

Then all the English replied with a shout, and the mountains and hills re-echoed, 'Amen, Amen!' At the same moment the Scots raised their country's war cry, 'Alban, Alban', till it reached the clouds. The sounds were drowned amid the clash of arms.

In the first onslaught the men of Lothian, without asking the king of the Scots, had assumed the honour of striking the first blow and bore down on the mailed English knights with a cloud of darts and their long spears. But they found the English ranks as impenetrable as a wall of steel; while archers, mingling with the knights, pierced the unarmoured Scots with a cloud of arrows. The whole army of English and Normans stood fast round the standard in one solid body.

Then the chief of the men of Lothian fell, pierced by an arrow, and all his followers were put to flight, for the Almighty was offended at them and their strength was rent like a cobweb. Seeing this, the main body of Scots, which was fighting bravely in another quarter, lost courage and also retreated. When King David's chosen body of soldiers, which he had selected from various tribes, saw this they also began to flee, first singly and then in troops, until the king stood almost alone, whereupon his friends compelled him to mount a horse and escape. But his brave son Henry, heedless of what his countrymen were doing and inspired only by his ardour for the fight and for glory, left those who were fleeing and made a fierce attack on the enemy's ranks. The body under his own command, composed of English and Normans attached to his father's household, had retained their horses. But this body of cavalry could make no impression at all against men sheathed in armour and fighting on foot in close formation; so they were compelled to retire with wounded horses and shattered lances after a brilliant but unsuccessful attack.

It is reported that eleven thousand of the Scots fell on the field of battle, besides those who were found in the woods and corn fields and there slain. Our army gained this victory with very little effusion of blood. Its leaders were William count of Aumâle, William Peverel of Nottingham, Walter Espec, and Gilbert de Lacy, whose brother was the only knight slain. When the issue of the battle was reported to King Stephen, he and all who were with him offered thanks to the almighty God. It was fought in the month of August.

During Advent, Alberic, the papal legate and bishop of Ostia, held a synod at London in which Theobald, abbot of Bec, was made archbishop of Canterbury with the concurrence of King Stephen.

1139

In the fourth year of his reign, when Christmas was past, King Stephen besieged and took Leeds castle, after which he went into Scotland, and by fire and sword compelled the king of Scots to come to terms, and brought away to England King David's son Henry. Stephen then besieged Ludlow, where this Henry was dragged from his horse by an iron hook and nearly taken prisoner, but was gallantly rescued from the enemy by King Stephen.

Wild Scots

DAVID I, king of Scotland from 1124 to 1153, was a combination of administrator, church patron and freebooter. He invaded the north of England in 1138 to further his family's interests as English landowners, as well as his own as king of Scots, especially in the country between Forth and Tyne which was then almost as Scottish as it was English.

This provoked the nearest thing to spontaneous, popular resistance since the Viking invasions some 250 years earlier. He swept south from Northumberland, to which he had legitimate claims, into Yorkshire with such needless, gleeful violence that he forfeited any complicity he might have expected from the English barons, all of whom joined forces with the local militia to rout the Scots near Northallerton.

The English fought under the banners of their patron saints, waging a holy war against a barbarian, even heathen race. The half-naked wild men of Galloway were singled out as being especially depraved. They were considered so foreign that they were often picturesquely (but inaccurately) described as 'Picts' rather than 'Scots'. David and his eldest son gained considerably from their campaign. By 1149 they had extended their lordship, if temporarily, over lands stretching to the Ribble and Tyne and beyond.

Above *Men from the north had threatened England since the time when the Romans had built Hadrian's Wall to keep out the barbarians. A great many sections of the wall still survive.*

Below *Northallerton today, its peaceful green fields showing no sign of the violent battle which took place there in 1138 when the Scots were heavily – if temporarily – defeated by the English forces.*

Leaving Ludlow untaken he went to Oxford, where he perpetrated a deed of great infamy and beyond all precedent. For, after amicably receiving Roger bishop of Salisbury and his nephew Alexander bishop of Lincoln, the king violently arrested them in his own palace, though they refused nothing which justice demanded, and earnestly appealed to it. The king threw Bishop Alexander into prison, and took the bishop of Salisbury with him to the bishop's castle of Devizes, one of the most stately in all Europe. There he tormented Roger by starvation and tortured his son, the king's chancellor, who had a rope fastened round his neck and was led to the gallows. Thus he extorted from him the surrender of his castle, forgetting the services which the bishop, more than all others, had rendered him in the beginning of his reign. Such was the return for the bishop's devotion.

In a similar manner the king obtained possssion of Sherborne Castle, which was little inferior to Devizes. Having got hold of the bishop's treasures, he used them to obtain in marriage for his son Eustace the hand of Constance, Louis the French king's sister. King Stephen then took back with him to Newark, Alexander bishop of Lincoln whom he had previously thrown into prison at Oxford. The bishop had built at Newark a castle in a florid style of architecture, on a charming site among the meadows washed by the River Trent. Having inspected this castle the king imposed on the bishop a fast not authorized by the Church, swearing that he should be deprived of food until the castle should be surrendered to him. But the bishop had some difficulty in persuading his garrison with prayers and tears to deliver it into the custody of strangers. Another of his castles, called Sleaford, not inferior in beauty and site, was surrendered in a similar manner.

Not long afterwards, when Henry bishop of Winchester, the king's brother and the pope's legate, held a synod at Winchester, Theobald archbishop of Canterbury and all the bishops present joined him in imploring the king on their bended knees to restore their possessions to the above-named bishops, with the understanding that they would overlook the indignities to which they had been subjected. However, unmoved by the entreaties of such a distinguished assemblage, the king, following evil counsels, refused to grant their request.

This prepared the way for the eventual ruin of the house of Stephen. For the Empress Matilda, the late King Henry's daughter, who had received the fealty of the English, immediately came over to England and was received at Arundel castle. There she was besieged by the king who, listening to perfidious advice or finding the castle too strong to be taken, granted her safe-conduct to Bristol.

That same year there died Roger, the bishop of whom I have just spoken, worn out by trouble and weight of years. My readers may well marvel at his sudden change of fortune, for, from his youth on, her favours had so accumulated that we might say that for once she had forgotten to turn her wheel: not in his whole career did he meet with any adverse events until a cloud of miseries gathered about him and overwhelmed him at the last. Let no one, then, depend on the continuance of fortune's favours, nor presume on her stability, nor think that he can long maintain his seat on her revolving wheel.

1140

In the fifth year of his reign, King Stephen expelled from his see Nigel bishop of Ely, because he was the nephew of the late bishop of Salisbury, against whom the king was so incensed that his anger extended to all the kindred.

Where the king spent Christmas and Easter does not matter, for now all that made the court splendid, and the regalia handed down from the long line of his predecessors, had disappeared. The treasury, left full, was now empty; there was no peace in the kingdom, but slaughter, fire and rapine spread ruin throughout the land; cries of distress, horror and woe rose in every quarter.

1141

In the sixth year of his reign, over Christmas, King Stephen laid siege to Lincoln, the defences of which Rannulf, earl of Chester had siezed by a trick.

The king stayed there until 2 February. Then the earl, with Robert of Gloucester, his father-in-law and King Henry I's son, and other powerful nobles, assembled to raise the siege. The daring earl crossed an almost impassable marsh, drew up his forces and offered the king battle on the same day. He and his men formed the first line; those whom King Stephen had disinherited the second; and Robert and his men the third. A crowd of Welshmen, brave rather than well armed, was on the wings.

Meanwhile, King Stephen in great anxiety heard solemn mass. But as he was putting the wax candle, the usual royal offering, into the hands of Bishop Alexander, it broke. This was a bad omen for the king. The pyx, which contained the Lord's body, broke its chain while the bishop was present, and fell on to the altar – a sign of the king's ruin. Nevertheless, he set out bravely and cautiously drew up his forces. He himself was on foot, with all the men-at-arms dismounted and drawn up close around him; the earls and their men were ordered to form two mounted lines, but the cavalry force was extremely small. The false and factious earls had brought few forces with them, but the king's force was very large, some of them accompanying the king's standard. Then, as King Stephen lacked an agreeable voice, Baldwin FitzGilbert, a noble-man and a valiant knight, was told to address the army. Before he had finished his speech the sounds of the enemy were heard, trumpet blasts and the neighing of horses, making the earth shake.

The battle began. The disinherited, who were in the van, fell on the royal division in which were Earl Alan, the count of Meulan, Hugh, earl of East Anglia, Earl Simon, and the Earl Warenne with such impetus that the latter were scattered in the twinkling of an eye; some of them were killed, others captured, and some fled.

The division commanded by the count of Aumâle and William of Ypres attacked the Welsh on the wings, and put them to flight. But this group was then attacked by the earl of Chester's men, and scattered in a moment like the others. Thus, all the king's cavalry fled and also William of Ypres, from Flanders, a man of aristocratic blood and great worth. Since he was experienced in war and saw that it was impossible to help the king, he deferred his aid for better times. So King Stephen was left on foot in the midst of his enemies. They encircled the royal troops and attacked from all sides, like one attacks a castle. Then could be seen the horrible face of war all round the royal army, with sparks flying as swords crashed on helmets, and awful screams and shouts resounding from the hills and walls of the city. The cavalry charged the royal army; some were killed, others trampled, and many captured.

There was no respite or time to draw breath except where the king himself, who was very strong, was standing, his enemies being afraid of the incomparable force of his blows. When the earl of Chester saw this he envied the king's glory and charged him with the full weight of his armoured men. Then the king's power really shone as with a great battle axe he felled some and scattered others. A new shout went up: 'Everyone onto him! Him against everyone!' At length the king's axe was shattered by the repeated blows. Then Stephen drew his sword, worthy of the royal arm, and wrought wonders until it too was broken. Seeing this, William of Cahagnes, a valiant knight, charged the king and seizing him by the helmet shouted, 'Here everyone, here, I've got the king!' They all rushed in and the king was captured. Baldwin who had given the speech was also taken; he was severely wounded and his resistance won him eternal glory. Richard FitzUrse was captured as well; he had also gained glory in the fight.

The king's army continued the battle until he was captured; they were surrounded, so they could not flee, and were all either killed or captured. The city was given over to plunder, and the king led miserably into it.

And so God's judgement was passed on King Stephen; he was led before the Empress Matilda, and imprisoned in Bristol castle. The empress was regarded as their lady by all the English except in Kent, where the queen and William of Ypres fought against her with all their might. She was first recognized by the bishop of Winchester, the papal legate, and soon after by the Londoners. But she was puffed up with intolerable pride because her followers had been so successful in the uncertainties of war, and she alienated everyone from her. So, whether by conspiracy or by divine providence (for whatever men do is by the will of God) she was expelled from London. With a woman's bitterness she then had King Stephen, the Lord's anointed, put in fetters.

After a while, with her uncle the king of the Scots and her brother Robert of Gloucester, Matilda gathered her forces and besieged the bishop of Winchester's castle. The bishop sent for the queen and William of Ypres, and for almost all the barons of England. Both sides assembled large armies. There was fighting every day, not large battles but skirmishing. In these engagements valiant deeds were not lost, as they are in the blindness of war, but everyone's valour could be seen and glory be awarded for merit; so this interval was pleasing to everyone as their splendid deeds were more visible.

At length the Londoners' army arrived, and as it increased the number of the empress's enemies she had to flee. Many were captured in the flight, among them her brother Robert, in whose castle the king was imprisoned and whose capture alone let the king out: they were exchanged. And so the king, who had been captured by God's judgement, was set free by God's mercy, and the barons of England received him with great rejoicing.

1142

In the seventh year of his reign, the king besieged Empress Matilda at Oxford, from after Michaelmas till Advent. Not long before Christmas the empress escaped across the frozen Thames wrapped in white clothes, deceiving the besiegers by appearing so like the dazzling snow. She fled to the castle of Wallingford, and Oxford was surrendered to the king.

1143

In the eighth year of his reign, King Stephen was present at a synod in London in mid-Lent, which was held there by the legate, Bishop Henry of

Anarchy and War

CIVIL war and local disturbances were prominent features of Stephen's 19-year reign in England. The war of succession began soon after he had seized the crown in 1135, with Matilda's uncle, David, King of Scotland, invading northern England on her behalf in 1138. Conflict deepened when Matilda herself landed at Arundel in 1139, and continued up to and beyond her final departure from England in the early months of 1148. Her son Henry of Anjou, later Henry II, to whom she had transferred her claim, kept up the fight.

The war had its near-decisive moments. In 1141 Stephen was captured at the battle of Lincoln, only to be exchanged against Matilda's half-brother, Earl Robert of Gloucester, who was taken at Winchester in 1142. But it was mostly a struggle of attrition characterized by sieges and small military operations, with Matilda and her supporters entrenched in the West Country and Stephen unable to dislodge them. Matilda was normally on the defensive, occasionally desperately so, as when, in the depths of winter in 1142, with Stephen's army besieging her in Oxford Castle, she had to make a dramatic escape by walking in secret through enemy lines at the dead of night. From 1142 there was a stalemate which neither side came near to breaking.

Both Stephen and Matilda used mercenaries, usually unreliable Flemings. One of these, Robert FitzHubert, a man theoretically in the pay of the earl of Gloucester, captured the strategically crucial castle at Devizes for his patron in 1140 and then attempted to set up on his own. Another, Robert FitzHildebrand, took over the castle at Winchester from a fellow supporter of Matilda, seduced his wife, and then came to terms with Stephen. Both came to miserable ends: FitzHubert was hanged by the earl of Gloucester and FitzHildebrand devoured from within by a tape-worm.

England suffered the devastation typical of this kind of war. Contemporary chroniclers tell a grim story. In the West Country, for example, 'you could see villages with famous names standing solitary and almost empty'. They also tell of the construction of castles and of local tyranny.

Such conditions did not prevail everywhere; but the normally peaceful English countryside suffered the consequences of an unremitting struggle in which neither side could fully control its soldiers. Central government disintegrated, with taxes not collected in many regions and coins minted locally by barons. Power was assumed by local lords who were given earldoms by the contenders vying for their support

Local quarrels were interwoven within the struggle for the crown. Henry I's reign had left a legacy of claims to

Above *Wigmore Castle, one of the Bigod holdings. During the period of Stephen's struggle with Matilda and her son, many noble families had to decide who to support: the consecrated king or the woman who ruled as queen for two years, issuing writs and behaving as if the succession from her father were a simple matter of fact. In the early 1150s Hugh Bigod moved away from Stephen to the Angevin side.*

property and, soon after his death, violence broke out in, among other places, south Yorkshire and Warwickshire. As a result of rivalries which developed in Stephen's reign, Worcester was sacked twice, in 1139 and 1151. Barons paid off old scores and took property from both sides. Yet, from the late 1140s, they also organized local settlements which brought some measure of order. The treaty between the earls of Chester and Leicester which pacified the north Midlands is an example. Not all of them were greedy opportunists. Most were ordinary men. Ambitious, yet anxious to survive and keep local order, they were caught up in an apparently unending war of succession.

Above *A writ issued in 1141 by Matilda as empress and daughter of Henry I.*

75

Winchester, on account of the extremities to which the clergy were reduced. For no respect was paid to them or to God's holy Church by marauders, and the clergy were made prisoners and held to ransom just as if they were laymen. The synod, therefore, decreed that no one who laid violent hands on a cleric should be absolved except by the pope himself in person. This decree scarcely obtained any relief for them.

The same year the king arrested Earl Geoffrey de Mandeville, in the royal court at St Albans, an act more fitting the earl's deserts than public law, more expedient than just. But if he had not taken this step, the king would have been driven from the throne by the earl's treachery. To obtain his liberty Geoffrey surrendered the Tower of London, the castle of Walden and that of Pleshey. The earl, thus stripped of his possessions, seized the abbey of Ramsey and, expelling the monks, garrisoned it with robbers, turning the house of God into a den of thieves. He was indeed a man of great valour, but resolute in ungodliness; diligent in worldly affairs but negligent in spiritual.

1144

King Stephen, in the ninth year of his reign, laid siege to Lincoln. While he was preparing siege-works for the attack on the castle, which Rannulf earl of Chester had taken possession of by force, almost eighty of his workmen were suffocated in the trenches, whereupon the king broke up the siege in confusion.

The same year Earl Geoffrey de Mandeville gave the king much trouble, and distinguished himself more than others. In the month of August, providence displayed its justice in a remarkable manner; for two of the nobles who had converted monasteries into fortifications, expelling the monks, met with similar punishments, their sin being the same. Robert Marmion was one, who had committed this iniquity in the church of Coventry; Geoffrey de Mandeville had perpetrated the same, as I have said, in Ramsey Abbey. Robert Marmion, issuing forth against his enemy, was slain under the walls of the monastery, being the only one who fell though he was surrounded by his

troops. Dying excommunicated, he became subject to death everlasting. In like manner, Earl Geoffrey was singled out among his followers, and shot with an arrow by a common foot soldier. He made light of the wound but he died of it in a few days, under excommunication. This was the just judgement of God, memorable through all ages. While that abbey was converted into a fortress, blood exuded from the walls of the church and the adjacent cloister, witnessing the divine indignation and foretelling the destruction of the ungodly. This was seen by many, and I observed it with my own eyes.

1145

In the tenth year of King Stephen, Hugh Bigod was the first to make a movement, but in the summer, Earl Robert and the whole body of the king's enemies set to work to build a castle at Faringdon. The king lost no time in collecting troops and marching there at the head of a numerous and formidable body of Londoners. After daily assaults on the castle, while Earl Robert and his adherents were waiting for fresh forces not far from the king's army, the castle was taken with much slaughter.

1146

King Stephen, in the eleventh year of his reign, assembling a great army, built an impregnable siege-work against the castle at Wallingford, and Rannulf earl of Chester, who had now joined the royal side, was present with a large force. Afterwards, however, when the earl came peaceably to attend the king's court at Northampton, fearing nothing of the sort, he was arrested and kept prisoner until he gave up the strong castle of Lincoln which he had seized by a stratagem, as well as all the other castles which belonged to him. Then the earl was set free to go where he pleased.

1147

In the twelfth year of his reign, King Stephen wore his crown during Christmas at Lincoln, which no king, because of some superstition, had ever ventured to do before. This showed his great resolution and how little importance he attached to such superstitions. After the king's departure the

The Cistercian phenomenon

IN 1098 an obscure monk, Robert of Molesme, led a group of fellow brethren into the Burgundian forests south of Dijon and, at Cîteaux, established a small monastery in which to practise the primitive simplicity of the religious life advocated in the Rule of St Benedict. All the new orders of the 12th century (among them the Savigniacs, Carthusians and Grandmontines) had such simple beginnings, but at Cîteaux, within just a few decades, the most spectacularly successful of them all had developed. Under the influence of Stephen Harding, the Englishman who became abbot of Cîteaux in 1109, and then of the overwhelmingly powerful St Bernard, abbot of Clairvaux, people flocked to join the Order and to some observers it even seemed possible that 'the whole world might become a Cistercian monastery'.

It is difficult fully to explain the astonishing success of the Cistercian Order. Much of it was undoubtedly a result of its novel and highly centralized system of government. Even more important, however, were St. Bernard's personality and abilities. Not only did he fire his contemporaries with enthusiasm for the Cistercian ideals – infinitely preferable to what he called 'the vanities and insanities' of existing Benedictine and Cluniac religious houses – but he also became closely involved in many of the political and ecclesiastical controversies of his day. He upbraided Louis VI of France when he refused to allow French bishops to attend a church council in 1134, he comforted Queen Mélisande of Jerusalem on the death of her husband, Fulk V of Anjou, in 1143, and in 1146 preached the Crusade which was to come to her aid. Under his leadership, some 530 Cistercian abbeys had appeared in western Europe by the middle of the 12th century. Even today, scattered throughout the west European landscape, from Fontenay to Fountains and from Melrose to Maulbronn, the austere ruins of the 12th-century Cistercian houses still bear eloquent witness to the visionary idealism of St Bernard and his early followers.

Top right *St Bernard of Clairvaux, from a retable depicting his life and good works.*

Right *Fountains Abbey, one of the most majestic ruins in England. The tower, reflected in the water, dates from the 16th century, but the first and distinctive period of Cistercian building was over the the middle of the 13th century, when the abbey was first constructed.*

earl of Chester came to Lincoln with an armed force to assault the castle; but the chief commander of his troops, a man of great courage and fortune, was slain at the entrance of the north gate of the town, and the earl himself, having lost many of his followers, was compelled to retreat; upon which, rejoicing in their successful defence, the citizens offered special thanks to the Blessed Virgin, their patron and protectress.

At Whitsun, Louis king of France, Thierry count of Flanders and the count of St Gilles, with an immense multitude from every part of France and numbers of the English, took the cross and journeyed to Jerusalem intending to expel the infidels who had taken the city of Edessa.

1148

In this year the armies of the emperor of Germany and the king of France were annihilated, though they were led by illustrious commanders and had commenced their march in the proudest confidence. But God despised them, and their incontinence rose up to him, for they abandoned themselves to open fornication and to adulteries hateful to God, and to robbery and every sort of wickedness. First they were starved by famine, through the false conduct of the emperor of Constantinople; and afterwards they were destroyed by the enemy's sword. King Louis and the emperor took refuge at Antioch, and afterwards at Jerusalem with the remnant of their followers; and the king of France, wishing to do something to restore his reputation, laid siege to Damascus with the aid of the Knights Templar of Jerusalem and a force collected from all quarters. But lacking the favour of God, and therefore having no success, he returned to France.

1149

In the fourteenth year of King Stephen's reign David king of the Scots knighted his own nephew Henry. As a large force was assembled for this ceremony, David having a large retinue, and his nephew having in his own following the nobles of the west of England, King Stephen was alarmed lest they should proceed to attack York. He

The disastrous crusade

O N Christmas Eve 1144 the city of Edessa, capital of the first crusader state founded in 1098, was captured by Zengi, the Muslim ruler of the Islamic princedoms, Mosul and Aleppo, and the most dangerous enemy the Christians had yet faced. In response the pope proclaimed the Second Crusade, led by Louis VII and the German emperor, Conrad III. Louis had planned his own armed pilgrimage before he heard of the fall of Edessa – not least because he needed to restore his reputation following a series of setbacks in France.

The crusade was a *débâcle*: the crusaders skirmished with the Christian inhabitants of the Byzantine Empire as they travelled to the East; both armies were heavily defeated by the Turks as they crossed Asia Minor; and the attempt to capture the rich prize and strategically vital city of Damascus ended in fiasco.

For Louis there were deeper problems: the conduct of his headstrong wife Eleanor, who had accompanied him, was tainted with scandal. At Antioch she and Prince Raymond, her uncle, tried to persuade Louis to commit his army there, while he was eager to fulfil his oath by visiting Jerusalem. Worse, lewd rumours began to circulate that the affection between Raymond and Eleanor went beyond what was natural for uncle and niece. Louis believed them, and it was said that he had to drag his wife away by force. The affair dealt a disastrous blow to their marriage which was finally annulled in 1151, when Louis lost both his wife and her duchy of Aquitaine.

Right *A crude crusader figure painted on the wall of a small Romanesque church at Areines, where the 12th-century murals depict medieval religious images.*

Below *The siege of Damascus during the Second Crusade.*

therefore established himself in that city with a large army and remained there all the month of August. Meanwhile Stephen's son Eustace, who was also knighted the same year, invaded the territories of the barons who were in attendance upon Henry the empress's son, and, as there was no one to oppose him, he laid them waste with fire and sword. But the kings of England and Scotland, the one at York, the other at Carlisle, fearing to attack each other, avoided meeting, and thus separated peaceably, each to his home.

1150

King Stephen in the fifteenth year of his reign made an assault on the beautiful city of Worcester and, having taken it, committed it to flames; but he was unable to reduce the castle which was inside the city. It belonged to Waleran count of Meulan, to whom King Stephen had granted it, much to his own disadvantage. The royal army, having plundered the city, overran the territories of the hostile lords and, no one resisting them, carried off an immense booty.

1151

In this year, the count of Anjou, Geoffrey the Fair, who was King Henry I's son-in-law and the son of the king of Jerusalem and a man of great eminence, passed away.

Geoffrey's death is given far more lavish treatment by John of Marmoutier.

So, it was that in the forty-first year of his own age, on 7 September 1151, the victorious duke of the Normans, of the people of Anjou, Touraine and Maine, returning from a royal council, having been taken severely ill with a fever at Château-du-Loir, collapsed on his couch. Then, looking into the future of his land and his people with the spirit of prophecy, he forbade Henry his heir to introduce the customs of Normandy or England into his own county, nor the reverse, as it might be, according to the succession of changing fortune.

Then, having made bequests of grants, gifts and charities, the death of so great a prince having

been foretold by a comet, his body returned his spirit from earth to heaven. What wonder if death, which opposes and repels nature, should struggle for Geoffrey from his youth, since, according to Cicero: 'Young men often seem to die in the same way as with much water the strength of a flame is extinguished, and just as apples which are unripe have to be picked from the trees by force, yet fall if ripe and ready, so force bears away the life from young men and maturity takes it from the old.'

Geoffrey was buried in the most holy church of Saint-Julien at Le Mans, in a most noble tomb which the righteous bishop, William of pious fame, had built fittingly. Such a venerable likeness of the count was fashioned there, suitably ornamented with gold and precious stones, that it seemed to express their doom for the proud and grace to the humble. At the altar of the crucifix, at which the dead man lay, a chaplain was appointed by the bishop with a stipend in perpetuity, who each day offered the sacrifice to God for the count's sake, so that the holy and merciful Lord might deign to have mercy on the count's wretchedness, He who lives and reigns eternally.

Henry of Huntingdon, despite his not wholly unsympathetic approach to Stephen, prudently glorifies his successor to be, Henry of Anjou, duke of Normandy.

1152

Geoffrey left to his eldest son, Henry of Anjou and Normandy, the hereditary claim to England which he had never made good. Now it happened that Louis VII, king of the French, had been divorced from his wife, the daughter of the count of Poitou, on grounds of consanguinity. So the new Duke Henry married her, and through her held the county of Poitou, a great increase in his honours. This marriage was the cause and promoter of great hatred and discord between the king of France and the duke.

Eustace, King Stephen's son, with the king of France, now made considerable assaults on Normandy, and the duke valiantly resisted both of them and the French army. Then King Louis

An end and a beginning

THE marriage between Louis VII and Eleanor of Aquitaine was unsuccessful for a number of reasons. Kings required male heirs and Eleanor had produced only two daughters, born in 1145 and 1149. There were also serious differences that being married to Louis was like being married to a monk. Louis in turn was probably dominated sexually by his powerful and emotional wife and, as a result, lacked manliness in contemporary eyes.

Deep discord flared up in 1149 on the Second Crusade, when Eleanor was suspected of adultery with her uncle Raymond of Antioch. A remarkable reconciliation was, however, later achieved on the return journey by Pope Eugenius III which concluded with his arranging for the couple to sleep in a bed which he himself had decked out with valuable ornaments. But even this proved fruitless in the long term.

A divorce was granted to Eleanor and Louis by four French archbishops on 21 March 1152 on grounds of consanguinity. The two had ancestors in common within the degrees prohibited by the Church; a common excuse at this time for dissolving an obviously failed marriage. It is clear that Eleanor knew exactly what she wanted since she immediately sent messengers to Henry of Anjou. They were married on 18 May 1152.

The origin of the liaison must have been formed in August of the previous year in Paris, when the two had met. Like his father, Geoffrey Plantagenet, Henry took on a woman several years his senior. Like him, he also acquired great prospects through his wife: in this case, the duchy of Aquitaine which was Eleanor's inheritance. At a stroke Henry, who had become duke of Normandy in 1150 and count of Anjou after his father's death in 1151, became far more powerful than his lord, King Louis.

News of the marriage provoked Louis to make war. He was joined by Henry's younger brother Geoffrey, who must have realised that marriage with Eleanor meant that Henry would not relinquish Anjou to him, as he was supposed to do under their father's will. In England, King Stephen and his son Eustace also joined Louis.

But Henry's success in the war, easily achieved, established his dominance throughout all his French territories. A continuous block of land was now in his power, from Normandy in the north, through Anjou to Aquitaine in the south. A famous and turbulent marriage had been made, and the greatest period in Plantagenet history had begun.

Above *Eleanor and Henry were married in Poitiers Cathedral, and donated this stained-glass window in celebration of their alliance.*

collected all his foes and assaulted an immensely strong, almost impregnable castle called Neufmarché, captured it, and gave it to Eustace, son of the king of England, who had married his daughter.

In the seventeenth year of his reign, King Stephen proposed to have his son Eustace crowned. Asking the archbishop and other bishops whom he had assembled to anoint and bless Eustace, he met with refusal. For the pope, by his letters, had prohibited the archbishop from crowning the king's son because King Stephen was held to have seized the throne unlawfully. Both father and son were cut to the quick by this and, greatly enraged, they ordered the churchmen to be shut up in a certain house and tried to force them with threats to do what they asked. They were terrified for King Stephen never liked priests, and had once imprisoned two bishops but held firm though fearing for their heads. At length, they escaped unhurt, though despoiled of their goods which the king later gave back when he repented.

The same year, the king besieged Newbury castle, not far from Winchester, and captured it. From there he besieged Wallingford, building a siege castle at the entrance to the bridge which prevented free access and the delivery of supplies to the beseiged. Now hard pressed, they asked their lord, the duke of Normandy, either to send help or to give them permission to surrender the castle into the king's hands.

1153

In the eighteenth year of King Stephen's reign the duke of Normandy, Henry of Anjou, impelled by necessity, paid an unexpected visit to England. This miserable country, previously devastated, seemed to regain new life with his arrival.

When the glorious duke was blown by a tempest onto the shores of England the land rustled with rumours, like a reed-bed at a touch of wind. The news spread quickly, as usual, bringing joy and happiness to some, fear and sorrow to others. But those who were delighted at his arrival were a little alarmed that he had brought so few men with him,

Poitiers Cathedral

IN 1152, the marriage of Henry II and Eleanor of Aquitaine was celebrated in the 11th-century cathedral of Poitiers. Perhaps the building was too old-fashioned for Eleanor's taste: ten years later, according to local tradition, she began to fund the construction of the present building. Her involvement may be apocryphal, but work certainly started on the new choir in the 1160s, under the cosmopolitan Anglo-Norman bishop of Poitiers, John aux Belles-Mains, close friend of Thomas Becket and John of Salisbury.

Construction proceeded steadily during the rule of Eleanor and Henry – Poitiers was one of their most important cities, and money was plentiful – but came almost to a standstill as Poitiers lost its prestige in the 13th century. The west front was finally completed almost a century after work had begun.

The cathedral is a hall-church, with aisles as high as the central vessel – a common design in Romanesque Poitou – and dome-shaped vaults reminiscent of Fontevrault. These are ribbed, however, the piers slender, the scale spacious and the interior luminous. Poitiers is a genuinely Gothic building and it is tempting to see the influence of Eleanor, who, as queen of France, must have had many opportunities to admire the new architecture of Saint-Denis. Like Saint-Denis, Poitiers has large, richly coloured windows. The east window, which shows the crucifixions of both Christ and St Peter, was the gift of Eleanor and Henry, who appear kneeling at its base, presenting it between them.

Right *The interior of Poitiers Cathedral.*

Below *Modern Poitiers; its Palais de Justice was the ducal residence in the 12th century.*

while equally the worries of his enemies were lightened. Some thought that crossing the stormy sea in the middle of winter was brave, others found it rash. But the brave youth gathered together his supporters, both those he had brought and those he found, and hating delay above all, laid siege to Malmesbury castle.

Since the virtues of such a man are many and great I shall have to deal with them quickly or the story of his deeds will take too long. The castle was besieged (for he was never one to procrastinate), assaulted and soon taken. When the town had fallen, the great keep alone held out, held for the king by Jordan and conquerable only by famine. Jordan sallied out to tell King Stephen of these events. Disturbed by the evil tidings, the king's face changed from dignity to grief, and energetically he collected his forces and encamped not far from Malmesbury.

The day after his arrival he drew up his army containing a great number of excellent and distinguished knights. It was a huge army with many barons, their banners glittering with gold, beautiful and terrible indeed; but God, in whom alone is safety, was not with them. For the floodgates of heaven opened, and such bitter cold gusts of wind and pouring rain were driven into their faces that God himself seemed to be fighting for the duke. But the army marched in order, though as if fighting the power of God, and suffering greatly.

The young duke's army relied on valour rather than numbers, especially because the justice of the cause for which they were fighting ensured that they were strengthened by God's grace. It was drawn up not far from the walls of the town of Malmesbury, by the banks of a stream to which the inundations of rain and snow had lent such strength that to go in was terrifying and, once in, there would be no coming out.

The noble youth was at the head of his army, his physical beauty betokening that of the soul, and marked out by arms worthy of him, which suited him so well that we may say that his arms did not so much become him as he his arms. He

and his men had the gale at their backs, the king's army had it in their faces, so that they could barely hold their weapons or their dripping wet lances.

Since God intended that His child should be granted the land without shedding blood, and neither side would cross the river, the king, no longer able to withstand such floods of rain, retraced his steps to London, his discomfiture complete. So the besieged castle was surrendered to the duke, who hurried delightedly to do what he had come for, namely to relieve the castle of Wallingford by now on the verge of being starved out.

Collecting a large body of troops to take provisions to the beleaguered garrison, God so favoured his design that it was carried out without opposition. Although there were many castles in the area held by royal troops, through God's will they were not able to prevent his coming and going. After a little while the valiant duke assembled all the knights who were on his side and besieged the castle of Crowmarsh. He began this difficult and arduous task by digging a great ditch around both the king's castle and his own army, so that his own only way out was by Wallingford castle, while the besieged had no way out at all.

When the king heard this he mustered all the forces from the areas that obeyed him, and descended furiously on the duke, who, however, was not at all afraid even though his forces were less than the king's, and who promptly ordered the ditch he had had dug to protect his army to be filled in. Raising the siege Henry marched out splendidly to meet the king. When the royal army saw the unexpected sight of their enemies drawn up for battle in front of them, they were struck by sudden panic, but the king was not in the least afraid and ordered his men to march out from camp in battle array. But the barons, those betrayers of England, objected to this, trying for terms of peace. Although they loved nothing better than disunity, yet they were unwilling to fight a battle, as they did not wish either side to win. For if one side was defeated, they would be easily dominated by the other, but if each side had the other to fear, royal power could not be exercised over them.

The king and the duke did not wish to be compelled to make a truce, each realizing the treachery of his supporters. But as usual, God was on the duke's side. They agreed that the royal castle which the duke had besieged should be destroyed. The king and the duke had a conference alone together, across a small stream, about making a lasting peace between themselves, and each complained to the other about the treachery of his nobles. The peace treaty was begun here, but not completed until another occasion.

Their quarrel was still unsettled when the two went back to their quarters, but light had begun to dawn on the great duke's fortunes. For two of his most hostile and powerful enemies, namely the king's son Eustace and Simon, earl of Northampton, were snatched away by the providence of God at the same time, and in consequence all his opponents suddenly lost hope and courage.

They both died of the same illness in the same week. Earl Simon, who did everything that was unlawful and indecent, was buried at Northampton. The king's son was buried in an abbey founded by his mother at Faversham, an experienced knight but an ungodly man, very harsh with the leaders of the Church, being their determined persecutor. In removing the most formidable adversaries of his beloved Henry. God was most kindly preparing the way for his peaceful reign.

The third siege was of Stamford castle. The town fell at once, but the castle garrison sent to the king for help. The king was besieging Ipswich, held against him by Hugh Bigod and, as the king did not wish to raise his siege and so could not come to its aid, the castle was surrendered to Prince Henry; but the castle the king was besieging also surrendered. The Norman duke left Stamford and went to Nottingham, and immediately took the town, which was then burnt by the castle garrison. Moved by pity, the duke took his army elsewhere.

Meanwhile, archbishop Theobald was trying hard to arrange a peace agreement, having frequent discussions with the king and dealing with the duke by messenger. He was helped in this by Henry of Blois, bishop of Winchester, who had first stirred up the kingdom by giving his brother Stephen the crown; but now he repented, seeing everything destroyed by fire and slaughter, and tried to put an end to such evils by getting the princes to agree.

The providence of God, which creates both good and evil, put an end to the scourging of England, bringing a conclusion to what had been begun by having peace confirmed on both to shine in serenity.

What inestimable joy! O blessed day! when the king himself received the young prince at Winchester with a magnificent procession of bishops and nobles through the cheering crowds.

The king received him as his adopted son and recognized him as his heir. From there, the king took the duke to London, where he was received with no less joy by enormous crowds and splendid processions worthy of such a man. Thus, by God's mercy, peace dawned on the ruined realm of England, putting an end to its troubled night.

When this was over, King Stephen and his new son parted with joy and love soon to meet again, for the peace was confirmed before Christmas.

1154

On 13 January they again came together at Oxford, when the duke had just spent a year conquering, or rather resuscitating, England. There, all the great men of England, on the king's order, did homage and due fealty to their lord the duke, saving the honour and loyalty they owed to the king during his life-time. They all left this splendid assembly filled with joy and delight at the new peace.

It was not long before they had another meeting, at Dunstable, where, however, a small cloud appeared on the horizon. The duke was displeased that the castles built everywhere for nefarious purposes after King Henry I's death had not been destroyed as was provided for in the peace finally agreed between Stephen and himself.

Many of them already had been, but King Stephen, through mercy or guile, had spared some of his men's castles, which seemed to undermine the treaty. The duke complained to the king about this, but was rebuffed. Nonetheless, giving way to his new father, he reluctantly deferred the matter for fear that it would upset their agreement, and they parted amicably.

Not long afterwards, with the king's permission the duke returned triumphantly to Normandy. This was what Henry, the most illustrious of youths, did on his second visit to England.

Let me not be accused of telling his many glorious deeds too briefly; I have to tell the stories of so many kings and their acts over so many centuries, that to be exhaustive would have taken volumes. My idea was rather to summarize history in one book so that posterity will not be completely ignorant.

Now, back to business. When the duke returned to France he was duly received with joy and honour by his mother Matilda, his brothers and all the people of Normandy, Anjou, Maine and Poitou. King Stephen, now reigning in peace for the first time, was given the honour due to a king, thanks to his adopted son. But, how mad are mortals, and how endless their perversity! Certain men, 'whose teeth were spears and arrows, and their tongue a sharp sword', tried very hard to sow discord between the king and the absent duke. The king could hardly resist their persuasion and after a while, some thought he was no longer resisting them; but, pretending to disapprove, the king listened not unwillingly to evil counsel.

However men are one thing, God's judgement another, and He rightly finished what was started by bringing the wicked plotting of evil counsellors to nought. King Stephen besieged the castle of Drake near York, and having captured it, and destroyed many other castles, went to Dover to talk to the count of Flanders. During the conference he fell ill, and on 25 October, 1154, he died. He was buried in Faversham Abbey beside his wife and son, having reigned unhappily and with great labour for nineteen years.

Gifts to heaven

FURNESS Abbey stands in isolated medieval splendour on the outskirts of Barrow in Furness. Founded by Stephen of Blois in 1127, in what was then a wild and uninhabited area, it was first colonized by monks from Savigny in Normandy. This reformed order was similar to the Cistercians who absorbed it 20 years later, in 1147.

The austerity of the Savigniac order is reflected in its architecture: plain, practical, but not without a certain severe elegance. The original church at Furness was rebuilt in about 1160, and it is the remains of this second building that now dominate the site. The crossing and both transept arms are, miraculously, almost intact; only the wooden roof that would once have covered them is lacking.

Furness was not the most lavish of Stephen's dozen or so foundations. That was Faversham, a Cluniac abbey in Kent, founded in 1148 when he was king of England, and intended to be his burial place to rival Reading Abbey, Henry I's mausoleum. Tragically, both these monuments to royal wealth and dynastic pride have vanished almost without trace.

Stephen was quite outshone as a patron of the arts by his brother Henry of Blois, bishop of Winchester, abbot of Glastonbury, and papal legate, who played a key role in English politics and whose patronage was almost on the scale of a Renaissance prince. Henry bought antique sculptures in Rome to decorate his episcopal palace and commissioned numerous buildings, all sadly destroyed,

Top left *Henry of Blois.*

Above *Two gilded and enamelled* champlevé plaques from Henry's altar.

Right *Furness Abbey; the transepts, choir and west tower still stand but the roof is missing.*

manuscripts like the Winchester Bible, perhaps the finest book produced in England in the Middle Ages, and gilded and bejewelled altars and crosses.

Attached to one small portable altar were two gilded and enamelled plaques which show Henry himself presenting his altar to heaven, surrounded by inscriptions which make no pretence to false modesty:

'May the Angel take the giver to heaven for his gifts, but not just yet, lest England groan for it, since on him it depends for peace or war, agitation or rest.

'Art comes before gold and gems, the author before everything. Henry, alive in bronze, gives gifts to God. Henry, whose fame commends him to men, whose character commends him to the heavens, a man equal in mind to the Muses, and in eloquence higher than Marcus.'

Archbishop Theobald and many of the English nobles quickly sent messengers to tell their lord the duke of Normandy to come soon and take over the kingdom. Delayed by wind and sea, and other causes, he landed a few days before Christmas in the New Forest, with his wife, his brothers, many nobles and a large force. England was without a king for about six weeks, but by God's grace the peace was not disturbed, either from love or fear of the future king. When Henry landed he went to London, where, suitably for such a distinguished and favoured man, he was blessed as king with great joy, many crying for happiness, and splendidly enthroned.

Henry's succession

HENRY won his final victory in England because the great barons were increasingly reluctant to fight a decisive battle – whichever side won, a massive confiscation of property would undoubtedly follow: When Stephen and Henry finally faced each other across the Thames at Wallingford in 1153, there was general pressure on Stephen to acknowledge Henry as king of England.

Stephen had quarrelled with the archbishop of Canterbury in 1147, and the Church ever since had refused to confirm his son, Eustace, as his heir. Meanwhile, as a result of Henry's successes in France, and the steady support he enjoyed in England, allegiances had slowly drifted his way; by 1153, great barons like Earl Robert of Leicester were ostensibly on Stephen's side, but in practice had done secret deals with Henry.

Stephen had no choice but to come to an agreement with Henry, who was able to leave England confident that he was everywhere accepted as its next king.

Right *Wallingford, originally built by Alfred where the Ridgeway crosses the River Thames, was one of the most important towns in England. Stephen and Henry met here in 1153 when Eustace, Stephen's son, was already dead. Stephen remained king, acknowledging Henry as his successor; a year later he was dead. Henry was to give the town considerable privileges for the help it provided for his forces in 1153.*

Below *In 1152 Henry and Eleanor, pictured here in a window in Poitiers Cathedral, were married. A year later, Henry met Stephen at Wallingford.*

Part III

Henry II
1154–1189

In 1124 Fulk V, count of Anjou, ruled just one of the great French fiefs; 30 years later his grandson, Henry Plantagenet, had become king of England and duke of Normandy and Aquitaine as well as count of Anjou. Henry was a remarkably successful ruler, but the sheer size of his dominions created immense problems. He and the fiery Eleanor, duchess of Aquitaine, produced four sons who were as thirsty for power as their father. Louis VII and Philip II of France, overlords of the continental Angevin lands, were useful allies to them, as was Eleanor who became Henry's dangerous adversary and later his helpless captive. Thomas Becket, first the king's loyal chancellor and then his hostile archbishop of Canterbury, was another key figure. The History of English Affairs *by William, canon of Newburgh, sets the scene at the beginning of the reign, but the main chronicle in Part III is* Images of History *by Ralph of Diceto, dean of St Paul's Cathedral from c. 1180 until his death in about 1201.*

(Opposite: Henry II)

In the year of Our Lord 1154, after the death of King Stephen, Henry, grandson of King Henry I by his daughter the late empress, came over from Normandy and took possession of his hereditary kingdom to the acclaim of all, and was consecrated and anointed king, while throughout England the people shouted 'Long live the king'. Indeed, so many evils had sprung up in the previous reign that after their unhappy experiences the people hoped for better things from the new monarch, especially when they saw he possessed remarkable prudence, constancy and zeal for justice, and at the very outset already manifested the likeness of a great prince. First he issued an edict against the mercenaries who

under King Stephen had streamed into England from foreign parts, as much for the sake of booty as for the profession of arms, especially the Flemings, of whom a great host then infested the land. These he ordered to return to their own country and appointed a day after which to prolong their stay in England would be attended with certain danger. Terror-stricken by this edict, they slipped away in so short a time that they seemed to have vanished in a moment like phantoms, while many marvelled at the haste of their departure. Next he ordered the newly erected castles, which had not been standing in the days of his grandfather, to be razed to the ground, with the exception of a few sited in advantageous

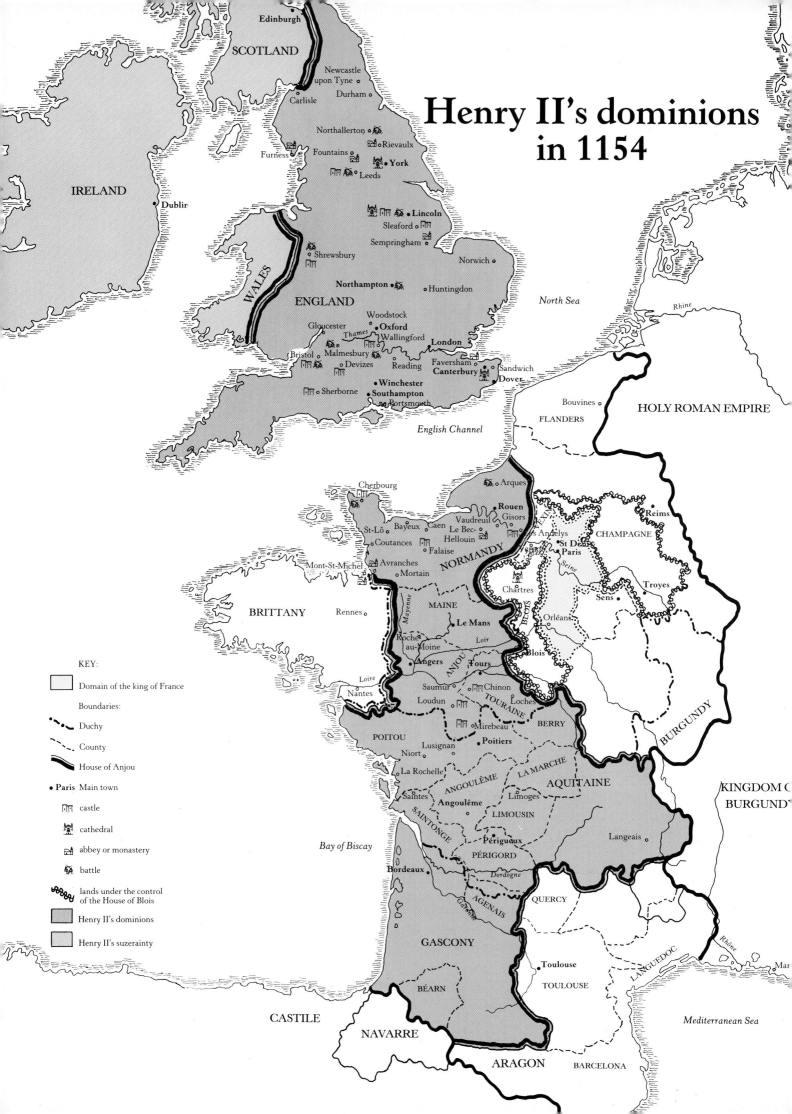

Henry II's dominions in 1154

KEY:

Domain of the king of France

Boundaries:

·–··–·· Duchy

–·–·–· County

House of Anjou

• Paris Main town

castle

cathedral

abbey or monastery

battle

lands under the control
of the House of Blois

Henry II's dominions

Henry II's suzerainty

SCOTLAND

Edinburgh

Newcastle
upon Tyne

Carlisle

Durham

Northallerton

IRELAND

Furness Fountains Rievaulx

York

Leeds

Dublin

Lincoln

Sleaford

Sempringham

WALES Shrewsbury

Norwich

Northampton Huntingdon

ENGLAND

Woodstock

Gloucester Oxford

Thames Wallingford **London**

Bristol Malmesbury

Devizes Reading Faversham

Canterbury Sandwich

Winchester **Dover**

Sherborne **Southampton**

Portsmouth

North Sea

English Channel

Cherbourg

Arques

Rouen Gisors

Vaudreuil Les Andelys

Reims

St-Lô Bayeux Caen Le Bec-
Hellouin

CHAMPAGNE

Coutances Falaise **St Denis**
Paris

NORMANDY

Mont-St-Michel Avranches Mortain

Seine

Chartres Troyes

Sens

BRITTANY Rennes MAINE

Orléans

BLOIS

Mayenne **Le Mans**

Roche-
au-Moine Loir

Angers **Tours**

ANJOU

Loire Saumur Chinon

Nantes Loudun Loches

Blois

TOURAINE

BERRY

Mirebeau

POITOU **Poitiers**

Lusignan

Niort

La Rochelle LA MARCHE

Saintes ANGOULÊME **AQUITAINE**

Limoges

Angoulême LIMOUSIN Langeais

SAINTONGE

Bay of Biscay **Périgueux**

PÉRIGORD

Dordogne

Bordeaux QUERCY

AGENAIS

GASCONY

BÉARN Toulouse

TOULOUSE LANGUEDOC

CASTILE

NAVARRE

ARAGON BARCELONA

Mediterranean Sea

HOLY ROMAN EMPIRE

Bouvines

FLANDERS

Rhine

BURGUNDY

**KINGDOM OF
BURGUNDY**

Rhône

Mar

In 1150 Geoffrey Plantagenet transferred the duchy of Normandy to his elder son Henry. He intended to grant Anjou to his second son Geoffrey, but in 1151 he fell seriously ill and on his deathbed decided that for financial reasons Henry should keep Anjou until he had secured his claim to England.

In 1152 Henry's marriage to Eleanor of Aquitaine brought him his third great acquisition – her wealthy duchy which gave him a commanding position in France. Henry then sailed for England to press his claims to the throne. Eustace, King Stephen's son, died in 1153. This proved a major blow to Stephen. He recognised Henry as his heir, and when in 1154 he died, Henry was warmly welcomed by the war-weary English nobility as king of England.

During his reign Henry made further gains on the peripheries of his lands. In 1157 he compelled the Scottish king to pay him homage, Henry retaining the disputed Northumbrian lands. In the 1150s and 1160s he turned the Welsh into valued allies. In 1171 he invaded Ireland and by 1175 he had compelled all the native kings to do homage to him. He made his youngest son, John, lord of Ireland. Finally in 1160 he took the Vexin, the crucial strip of land between the duchy of Normandy and the French royal lands. This was as the dowry of Margaret, Louis VII's daughter, who was married to the Young King, Henry's heir. With her too came the hope of the Crown of France, but this final prize was to elude the male Plantagenet line.

Henry's plans for his sons

In 1169, Henry II was under considerable pressure from his sons and had potentially dangerous rebellions in Brittany and Aquitaine to contend with. He worked out a scheme for the future division of his lands which was confirmed in the will he made in 1170.

Henry, the young king who was crowned in that year, was to inherit England, Normandy and Anjou; Richard was to have Poitou, and Geoffrey, Brittany, but as a vassal of the young king. At this stage John got nothing, but in 1173, Henry decided that Chinon, Loudun and Mirebeau should be made over to him as part of a proposed marriage settlement. That plan angered the young king and was a factor in the outbreak of war between Henry II and his sons.

KEY:

The young king's lands (1169-1170)

Geoffrey's lands (1160-1170)

Richard's lands (1169-1170)

John's castles (1173)

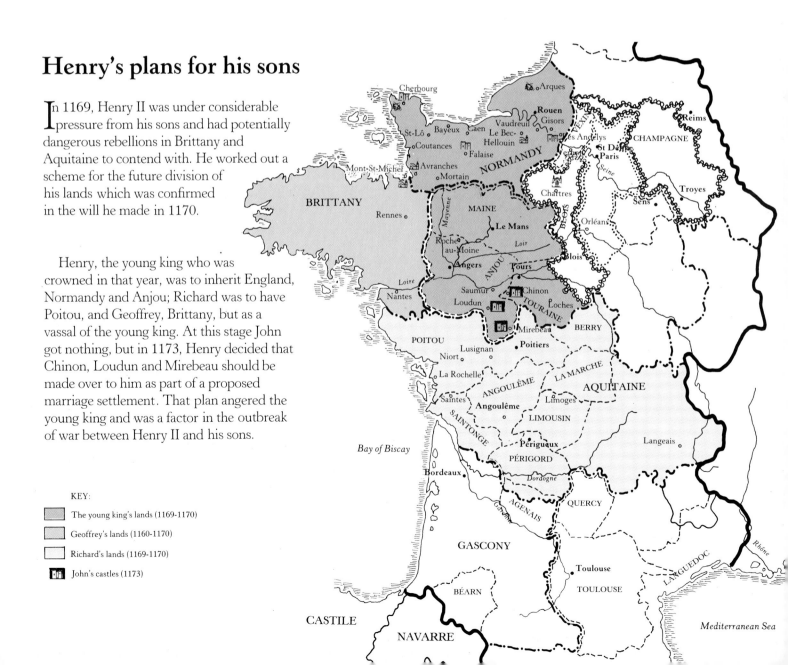

places, which he desired either to retain for himself or to be maintained in the hands of peaceful men for the defence of the realm.

In these early days, also, Henry II paid due regard to public order and was at great pains to revive the vigour of the laws in England, which had seemed under King Stephen to be dead and buried. Throughout the realm he appointed judges and legal officials to curb the audacity of wicked men and dispense justice to litigants according to the merits of their case; he himself, whether engaged in pleasure or in affairs of State, jealously watched over the royal interests. For as often as any of his judges acted either too leniently or too harshly and he was alarmed at the complaints of the men of the shire, he applied the remedy of a royal ordinance to amend effectively their negligence or excess.

Such were the first acts of the new monarch, which earned the praise and thanksgiving of peace-loving men but induced the murmuring and pertur-bation of the wicked. The ravening wolves were put to flight or turned into sheep, or, even if they were not really changed, they were made through fear of the law to dwell harmlessly with the sheep. Swords were beaten into ploughshares and spears into pruning-hooks, and none now girded himself to battle, but all with God's favour tasted the joys of peace which they had previously longed for, whether they pursued their pleasures or were intent upon their business.

As Henry II's reign began, so Thomas Becket was rising in the service of Theobald, archbishop of Canterbury. William FitzStephen gives a hagio-graphical but lively account of Becket's childhood and early career.

The Lord knew and predestined the blessed Thomas [to His service] before ever he issued from the womb and revealed to his mother what manner of man he would be. For during preg-nancy she saw in a dream that she carried in her womb the whole church of Canterbury. As soon as the child saw the light of day, the midwife lifted him up in her arms saying, 'I have raised from the ground a future archbishop.' While he was yet a babe lying in his cradle, his mother dreamed one

A remarkable king

HENRY II, one of the most powerful rulers in the western Europe of his time, made a vivid and lasting impression on his contemporaries. Lively pen portraits by Gerald of Wales, Walter Map and Peter of Blois among others give a sense of the contradictions in his character, contradictions which left many people baffled and many afraid. His most striking characteristic was his boundless, incessant energy. It kept him constantly on the move around his vast dominions, his household always one step behind, striving desperately to catch up. Herbert of Bosham compared him with a human chariot which drew all behind him. In his youth he showed a rash and impulsive valour and although this diminished with the years, he never lost his love of active outdoor pursuits such as hunting. He was an able military leader, but seems not to have relished war for its own sake in the way that Richard the Lionheart, his son, was to do.

Henry was tall, with broad shoulders and the strength and endurance to match. His dress was usually informal – like that of a huntsman – and his manner courteous and charming, although he was quick to take offence if he felt his authority as king was being threatened. His sense of humour was strong and his wit mordant, but his temper was unpredictable and he could be bitterly vindictive towards anyone who roused his anger. His violent Angevin rages were legendary. Nevertheless, he bore, and enjoyed, the self-inflicted hardships of his constant travels, and was unfailingly patient with the crowds of suitors and litigants who at times thronged around him seeking justice. Generous to the poor, he gave alms frequently, and often in secret. In 1176 he bought large amounts of grain to relieve a famine in Maine and Anjou.

Henry was well known for his love of holy men, such as Hugh of Lincoln and Gilbert of Sempringham, and founded and endowed a considerable number of religious houses. He was less respectful towards the secular clergy, many of whom he treated harshly during the Becket dispute. William of Newburgh reports that, when criticized for holding bishoprics vacant so that the Crown could enjoy the revenues, the king replied that it was far better to spend the money for the benefit of the realm than for the pleasures of bishops; a remark that Newburgh found shocking rather than humorous. Another contemporary, Ralph Niger, castigated Henry for spending too little time in church and for constantly muttering and doodling during Mass.

Despite his frenetic energy and love of hunting, Henry had a serious and scholarly side. 'With the king of England', wrote Peter of Blois, 'it is school every day, constant conversation with the best scholars and

discussion of intellectual problems.' The king read books regularly, had an excellent memory, and according to the chronicler Walter Map, understood all the languages from the coast of France to the River Jordan, although he normally spoke in French or Latin. His serious side also emerges in the many legal, administrative and financial developments of his reign, developments for which he has been much praised by posterity.

Above *The king's seal. Traditionally it showed the man of judgement and the man of action; in Henry's case both images were appropriate.*

Below *The keep of Orford Castle was built with unusual projecting corners, against the unruly behaviour of Hugh Bigod, one of Henry's most difficult East Anglian barons. Orford proved effective, and was symbolic of the king's secure hold on the throne.*

night that she rebuked the nurse for not putting a coverlet over him. 'Nay, my lady,' replied the nurse, 'he has the best of coverlets.' 'Show it me,' said her mistress. The nurse brought it and showed it her, but when she tried to unfold it, she could not do so and said to the mother, 'It is too large for me to spread over the bed.' Whereupon the mother answered, 'Come into the hall and unfold it there.' The nurse tried hard to do so, but failed and said, 'I simply cannot unfold the whole of it here.' The astonished mother then said, 'Go out into the street of the market-place, which is now empty; no doubt you will succeed in unfolding it there.' But neither could the nurse do so there, whereupon she exclaimed, 'The coverlet is so large that I cannot find the end of it; methinks all England would be too small for it to cover.'

Thomas, then, was born in lawful wedlock and of honourable parents, his father being Gilbert, sometime sheriff of London, and his mother Matilda. Both were citizens of London, of the middle class, neither making money by usury nor engaged in business, but living respectably on their income.

That his father received some divine intimation concerning his future we may learn from this. While still a child his father commended him to Robert, prior of Merton, to be educated for a time in that religious house. One day the father came to see his son. When the boy was brought into the presence of the prior and his father, the latter fell prone before him worshipping him. Indignantly the prior exclaimed, 'You foolish old man, what are you doing? Would you fall at your son's feet? The honour you do to him, he ought rather to do to you.' To whom the father replied in an undertone, 'My lord, I know what I am doing: this boy will be great in the sight of the Lord.'

So Thomas spent his years of infancy, boyhood and adolescence in simplicity in his father's house and the schools of the city. As a young man he studied in Paris, and on his return took part in the affairs of the city of London, being made clerk and accountant to the sheriffs. In this employment he conducted himself in a manner worthy of all praise, and acquired such a knowledge of the

world that in afterlife he had no difficulty in managing with caution and prudence the common interests of the Church in England and the public affairs of the kingdom, which he dispatched efficiently and with due magnificence.

Becket showed such great promise in his work for archbishop Theobald that in 1155 the king made him Chancellor of England. That gave him responsibility for supervising Henry's Chancery (writing office) as well as a role in the royal administration.

1155

After Henry II had been crowned king of England at the hands of Archbishop Theobald, by the latter's recommendation and through his good offices, and also at the instigation of Henry of Blois, bishop of Winchester, King Stephen's brother, Thomas was made the king's chancellor in preference to all others. Being a man of diligence and industry, revolving great matters in his mind and experienced in many and great affairs, he discharged the onerous duties and obligations of his office to the praise of God and the well-being of the whole realm: so much so that it may be doubted whether he served the king with greater distinction and efficiency or to greater advantage in peace or in war.

Through the energy and counsel of the chancellor and the wholehearted co-operation of the clergy, earls and barons, this noble realm of England enjoyed, as it were, a second springtime. Holy Church was respected; vacant bishoprics and abbacies were bestowed on honest clerks without simony; the king, by favour of the King of Kings, prospered in all his undertakings; the realm of England increased in riches, and a shower of blessings flowed from the horn of plenty. The hills were cultivated, the valleys teemed with corn, the fields with cattle and the folds with sheep.

Becket's birthplace, London, was the largest and most prosperous city in the land. By the 1170s, when FitzStephen wrote his life of Becket, it had become the capital of England. FitzStephen brings its buildings and people vividly to life.

A very political queen

ELEANOR of Aquitaine was one of the most vivid and remarkable figures in 12th-century Europe. As a patron of the arts, as a politician and as a mother, her influence was pervasive for more than six decades. Her forcefulness, ability, beauty and charm were such that once she had turned against her second husband, Henry II, he felt compelled to imprison her for 16 years to prevent her from tearing his dominions apart.

Born in 1122, Eleanor was the eldest child and heiress of William X, duke of Aquitaine. In 1137 she was married to the young Louis VII of France, over whom she soon exercised a profound personal and political influence. The union was barren for some years until, in 1144, Eleanor met St Bernard of Clairvaux. He regarded her as an evil influence upon the king, and promised that she would conceive only if she strove for peace. Her first child, a daughter, was born in 1145, and was named Mary, after the queen of heaven and the patron saint of Fontevrault Abbey, for which Eleanor had a particular affection. In 1147 she and Louis went on Crusade, but were almost estranged as a result of her flirtation (and perhaps worse) with her uncle, Raymond of Antioch.

After Eleanor and Louis had been reconciled by the pope in the course of their return to France, she bore a second daughter, Alice. Shortly afterwards she met Henry of Anjou, 11 years her junior, and seems immediately to have set her sights on him. When she and Louis were divorced in 1152, she returned to Poitiers and immediately sent messengers to Henry to announce that she wished to marry him. He, desiring her duchy quite as much as her person, hastened to her. To the fury of Louis VII the nuptials took place and in 1153 Henry declared himself duke of Aquitaine. In the same year Eleanor bore him a son, William, who did not survive; Henry (the young king) followed in 1156. Subsequently Eleanor produced three more sons and three daughters.

Her influence on the artistic, literary and cultural life of the 12th century was as great as her impact on its politics. Brought up in her father's court in the sophisticated ways of the Languedoc, she felt an exile among the uncouth Parisians, and surrounded herself with troubadours and ladies from the south. Her marriage to Henry allowed her to found her own literary court which, as she travelled around Henry's dominions, became a melting-pot for various cultural traditions. Under her patronage the ideals and codes of courtly love began to emerge. Her son, Richard the Lionheart, inherited her love of music, and another daughter, Eleanor, took with her to Castile the distinctive Angevin style of building.

Eleanor's legacy to the 13th century was an important one. In her old age she chose the best of her Castillian grand-daughters, Blanche, to be the bride of Louis VIII of France. Blanche shared many of her grandmother's characteristics. As queen of France she was a major patron of art and of building, and an effective politician.

Below *Celebrations of courtly music, painted on the side of a 12th-century marriage casket.*

In the church of St Paul's there is the episcopal seat. Once it was an archbishopric, and some think it will again become so, unless perhaps the archiepiscopal title of the blessed martyr, Thomas, and the presence of his body preserves that dignity for ever at Canterbury where it is at present. But as St Thomas has made both cities illustrious, London by his rising and Canterbury by his setting, each can claim advantage of the other with justice in respect of that saint. As regards the practice of Christian worship, there are in London and its suburbs thirteen greater conventual churches and, besides these, one hundred and twenty-six lesser parish churches.

It has on the east the Palatine castle [the Tower of London], very great and strong: the keep and walls rise from very deep foundations and are fixed with a mortar tempered by the blood of animals. On the west there are two castles very strongly fortified, and from these there runs a high and massive wall with seven double gates and with towers along the north at regular intervals. London was once also walled and turreted on the south, but the mighty Thames, so full of fish, has with the sea's ebb and flow washed against, loosened, and thrown down those walls in the course of time. Upstream to the west there is the royal palace [of Westminster], which is conspicuous above the river, a building incomparable in its ramparts and bulwarks. It is about two miles from the city and joined thereto by a populous suburb.

Everywhere outside the houses of those living in the suburbs, and adjacent to them, are the spacious and beautiful gardens of the citizens, and these are planted with trees. Also there are on the north side pastures and pleasant meadow lands through which flow streams wherein the turning of mill-wheels makes a cheerful sound. Very near lies a great forest with woodland pastures in which there are the lairs of wild animals: stags, fallow deer, wild boars and bulls. The tilled lands of the city are not of barren gravel, but fat Asian plains that yield luxuriant crops and fill the tillers' barns with the sheaves of Ceres.

There are also outside London on the north side excellent suburban wells with sweet, whole-some and clear water that flows rippling over the bright stones. Among these are Holywell, Clerkenwell and St Clement's Well, which are all famous. These are frequented by great numbers and much visited by the students from the schools and by the young men of the city, when they go out for fresh air on summer evenings. Good indeed is this city when it has a good lord!

Those engaged in business of various kinds, sellers of merchandise, hirers of labour, are distributed every morning into their several localities according to their trade. Besides, there is in London on the river bank among the wines for sale in ships and in the cellars of the vintners a public cook-shop. There daily you may find food according to the season, dishes of meat, roast, fried and boiled, large and small fish, coarser meats for the poor and more delicate for the rich, such as venison and big and small birds. If any of the citizens should unexpectedly receive visitors, weary from their journey, who would fain not wait until fresh food is bought and cooked, or until the servants have brought bread or water for washing, they hasten to the river bank and there find all they need. However great the multitude of soldiers and travellers entering the city, or preparing to go out of it, at any hour of the day or night — that these may not fast too long, and those may not go out supperless — they turn aside thither, if they please, where every man can refresh himself in his own way. Those who would cater for themselves fastidiously need not search to find sturgeon or the bird of Africa or the Ionian godwit. For this is a public kitchen, very convenient to the city, and part of its amenities. Hence the dictum in the Gorgias of Plato that the art of cookery is an imitation of medicine and flatters a quarter of civic life.

Immediately outside one of the gates there is a field which is smooth [Smithfield] both in fact and in name. On every sixth day of the week, unless it be a major feast-day, there takes place there a famous exhibition of fine horses for sale. Earls, barons and knights, who are in the town, and many citizens come out to see or to buy. It is pleasant to see the high-stepping palfreys with their gleaming coats, as they go through their paces, putting down their feet alternately on one

Peace and prosperity

HENRY II succeeded peacefully to the English kingdom after Stephen's death on 25 October, 1154. After the long civil war the aristocracy was tired of fighting and ready to accept Henry, who, from the first, set out to restore the powers of monarchy. His policy was to rule as if Stephen's reign had not existed. He regarded the kingdom as his legitimate inheritance through his mother Matilda from his grandfather Henry I and, therefore, set out to reclaim royal rights as they had been before 1135. Stephen's land grants were not respected, and royal lands and castles that had been taken over by barons were taken back by the king. Although this led at times to conflicts, all rebellions had been defeated by 1158.

The king took control over the Church immediately after his succession and supervised appointments to bishoprics as his grandfather had done. The kingdom's chief ecclesiastic, Archbishop Theobald of Canterbury, was, fortunately, a long-standing Angevin supporter and there were no difficulties with the Church before his death in 1162. Henry also made use of those of Stephen's followers who were willing to serve him. The capable Richard de Lucy, for example, shared control of the royal finances administered at the Exchequer.

All this was part of a general recovery and resumption

Above *'The Sower', in Canterbury Cathedral, represents peaceful agriculture.*

Below *The mayor of London was one of the witnesses to this deed of sale.*

of order. Financial records from the first part of the reign show large areas of the kingdom unable to pay tax. Later records show returning prosperity helping to increase the government's revenue. The early years of Henry II's rule laid the foundations of the peace, widespread prosperity and well-organized government that is associated with the first of the Plantagenet kings.

side together. Next, one can see the horses suitable for squires, moving faster though less smoothly, lifting and setting down, as it were, the opposite fore and hind feet: here are colts of fine breed, but not yet accustomed to the bit, stepping high with jaunty tread; there are the sumpter-horses, powerful and spirited; and after them there are the war-horses, costly, elegant of form, noble of stature, with ears quickly tremulous, necks raised and large haunches. As these show their paces, the buyers first try those of gentler gait, then those of quicker pace whereby the fore and hind feet move in pairs together. When a race is about to begin among such chargers that are so powerful to carry and so swift to run, a shout is raised, and orders are given that the inferior animals should be led apart. Three jockeys who mount these flying steeds (or at times two, as may be agreed) prepare themselves for the contest; skilled in managing them, they curb their untamed mouths with bitted bridles. To get a good start in the race is their chief concern. Their mounts also enter into the spirit of the contest as they are able; their limbs tremble, and so impatient are they of delay that they cannot keep still. When the signal is given, they stretch their limbs to the uttermost, and dash down the course with courageous speed. The riders, covetous of applause and ardent for victory, plunge their spurs into the loose-reined horses, and urge them forward with their shouts and their whips. You would agree with Heraclitus that all things are in motion! You would know Zeno to be completely wrong when he said that there was no motion and no goal to be reached!

By themselves in another part of the field stand the goods of the country folk: implements of husbandry, swine with long flanks, cows with full udders, oxen of immense size, and woolly sheep. There also stand the mares fit for plough, some big with foal, and others with brisk young colts closely following them.

To this city from every nation under heaven merchants delight to bring their trade by sea. The Arabian sends gold; the Sabaean spice and incense. The Scythian brings arms, and from the rich, fat lands of Babylon comes oil of palms. The Nile sends precious stones; the men of Norway and Russia, furs and sables; nor is China absent with purple silk. The Gauls come with their wines.

London, as historians have shown, is a much older city than Rome, for though it derives from the same Trojan ancestors, it was founded by Brutus before Rome was founded by Romulus and Remus. Wherefore they still have the same laws from their common origin. This city is like Rome divided into wards; it has annual sheriffs instead of consuls; it has its senatorial order and lower magistrates; it has drains and aqueducts in its streets; it has its appointed places for the hearing of cases deliberative, demonstrative and judicial; it has its several courts, and its separate assemblies on appointed days.

I do not think there is a city with a better record for church-going, doing honour to God's ordinances, keeping feast days, giving alms and hospitality to strangers, confirming betrothals, contracting marriages, celebrating weddings, providing feasts, entertaining guests, and also, it may be added, in care for funerals and for the burial of the dead. The only plagues of London are the immoderate drinking of fools and the frequency of fires.

To this it may be added that almost all the bishops, abbots and barons of England are in a sense citizens and freemen of London, having their own splendid town-houses. In them they live, and spend largely, when they are summoned to great councils by the king or by their metropolitan, or drawn thither by their private affairs.

On feast days throughout the summer the young men indulge in the sports of archery, running, jumping, wrestling, slinging the stone, hurling the javelin beyond a mark and fighting with sword and buckler. Cytherea leads the dance of maidens, and until the moon rises, the earth is shaken with flying feet.

In winter on almost every feast day before dinner either foaming boars, armed with lightning tusks, fight for their lives 'to save their bacon', or stout bulls with butting horns, or huge bears do battle with the hounds let loose upon them. When the great marsh that washes the north wall of the city is frozen over, swarms of young men issue forth to play games on the ice. Some, gaining speed in their run, with feet set well apart, slide sideways over a vast expanse of ice. Others make seats out of a large lump of ice, and whilst one sits thereon, others with linked hands run before and drag him along behind them. So swift is their sliding motion that sometimes their feet slip, and they all fall on their faces. Others, more skilled at winter sports, put on their feet the shin-bones of animals, binding them firmly round their ankles, and, holding poles shod with iron in their hands, which they strike from time to time against the ice, they are propelled swift as a bird in flight or a bolt shot from an engine of war. Sometimes, by mutual consent, two of them run against each other in this way from a great distance, and, lifting their poles, each tilts against the other. Either one or both fall, not without some bodily injury, for, as they fall, they are carried along a great way beyond each other by the impetus of their run, and wherever the ice comes in contact with their heads, it scrapes off the skin utterly. Often a leg or an arm is broken, if the victim falls with it underneath him; but theirs is an age greedy of glory, youth yearns for victory, and exercises itself in mock combats in order to carry itself more bravely in real battles.

Many of the citizens take pleasure in sporting with birds of the air, with hawks, falcons and suchlike, and with hounds that hunt their prey in the woods. The citizens have the rights of the chase in Middlesex, Hertfordshire, all the Chiltern country, and in Kent as far as the River Cray.

In Christian times this city produced that noble emperor Constantine, son of the Empress Helena, who bestowed the city of Rome and all the imperial insignia on God and St Peter and on Sylvester, the Roman pope [the Donation of Constantine] to whom he dispensed the office of a groom, no longer rejoicing to be called emperor but rather the defender of the Holy Roman Church; and, lest the peace of the lord pope should be disturbed by the uproar of secular strife occasioned by his presence, he himself altogether abandoned the city which he had bestowed upon the lord pope, and built for himself the city of Byzantium. And in modern times also London has given birth to illustrious and noble monarchs, the Empress Matilda, the young King Henry, son of Henry II, and the blessed Archbishop Thomas, that glorious martyr of Christ, than whom she bore no purer saint nor one more dear to all good men throughout the Latin world.

There are considerable contrasts between FitzStephen's hagiography and the witty, gossipy writings of Gerald of Wales. Looking ahead to events later in the reign, this short account of Henry II and Eleanor of Aquitaine shows him at his most malicious.

When the two-year war was over (1174) and the fighting and persecution had stopped, the king, attributing his success like another Pharaoh not to divine mercy but to his own strength, hardened his heart and returned incorrigibly to his usual abyss of vice, or rather, to an even worse one, since, going downhill things can only deteriorate. And to mention only one thing, omitting the rest, he imprisoned Queen Eleanor his wife as punishment for the destruction of their marriage; his adultery, previously hidden, now became open and blatant, not with a 'pure rose' (Latin *rosa munda*), falsely and frivolously named, but rather with an impure one. And since the world copies a king, he offended not only by his behaviour but even more by his bad example.

How Eleanor, queen of France, behaved when she was across the sea in Palestine, and how she conducted herself on her return, towards her first husband and her second; and how her children aroused such hopes when young, but withered away; all these things are well enough known.

Of two of her daughters, the Sicilian and the Saxon, the first died without children and the second without happiness, one without fruit, the other not without misery. As far as the others are concerned, the Spanish branch, the German one and the Breton, subsequent ages will be in a position to tell their fate; let us not go through them all, as some may find it offensive. It is to be hoped that, God willing, some good may come from the fortunate Spanish marriage.

It is very well known how, of her two daughters by Louis king of the French, one married to Henry count of Champagne, the other to his brother Theobald count of Blois, both failed of their fruit in Palestine and in the land of the Greeks.

To demonstrate how King Henry's stock was blighted, we only have to remember that the Emperor Henry V, to whom King Henry I's daughter and King Henry II's mother Matilda was married, for the sake of worldly ambition captured and held in chains first his natural father and afterwards his spiritual father, namely Pope Paschal; resigning the empire he went into a hermitage in western Britain, near Chester, and lived a holy life of repentance until his death. When the Empress Matilda came home her father gave her in marriage to Geoffrey count of Anjou, though her husband was still alive, and Geoffrey had sons by her of whom two quickly vanished, nipped in the bud despite the great hopes held of them — and the third, began better than he ended.

Then again, Count Geoffrey of Anjou when he was seneschal of France took advantage of Queen Eleanor; for which reason he often warned his son Henry, telling him above all not to touch her, they say, both because she was his lord's wife, and because he had known her himself. As the final culmination of these outrages it is related that King Henry presumed to sleep adulterously with the said queen of France, taking her from his own lord and marrying her himself. How could anything fortunate, I ask, emerge from these copulations?

Unlike Gerald of Wales, the chronicler Ralph of Diceto set out to write about historical events in an objective way. He takes up the story of Henry II's reign with the events of 1155.

A son, Henry, was born in London to Henry king of England and Queen Eleanor on 28 February, and was baptized by Richard bishop of London.

Robert dean of Salisbury was elected bishop of Exeter and was consecrated by Theobald archbishop of Canterbury.

The English borough

TWELFTH-CENTURY England was predominantly rural, and with the exception of London, the few existing towns tended to be small by continental standards. However, Lincoln, Norwich, York and Winchester all had populations approaching ten thousand, and there were many other smaller urban settlements throughout the country, although these retained very close links with rural life – their inhabitants cultivated the fields on their outskirts. In 1086 about one person in every ten had lived in one of these settlements. This proportion grew in the 12th century and a number of new towns developed which were often 'planned', sometimes on a grid system like Leeds and Liverpool.

Places described as boroughs in the 12th century usually had a fairly sizeable population, and always contained people known as burgesses. Living on messuages (plots of land each with a house and garden), these were people who made their living wholly or partly from the profits of trade. A 12th-century borough would therefore contain a market; it might also have walls for protection. The burgesses had their own courts and customs, a considerable say in the running of their town and might have been granted a charter of protection or privileges by the Crown.

The social composition of borough communities varied, but in larger towns usually included merchant and commercial groups who also participated in town government; Jewish communities involved in money-lending; and a diverse 'industrial' population which could be significant and influential. As early as 1130 the weavers of Huntingdon, Oxford, Lincoln and Winchester bought the protection of their interests from the king. The growing importance and wealth of these groups in the 12th century made the towns increasingly a force to be reckoned with in the political and economic life of England.

*Right **This map of Britain was drawn around 1250 by Matthew Paris to illustrate his** History of England. **A fascinating and relatively accurate example of medieval cartography, it depicts many of the larger towns and boroughs which would have been well known to the more seasoned traveller of the day. The county names are also clearly visible.***

Frederick king of Germany was crowned emperor by Pope Adrian in the church of St Peter's [Rome]. Henry of Blois bishop of Winchester left England without the permission of the king. In consequence the king ordered the destruction of six of his castles. William Peverel of Nottingham was disinherited because he had given poison to Ranulf earl of Chester. The king took over the tower of Gloucester and the castles of Bridgnorth and Wigmore, which Hugh of Mortimer had fortified against him.

1156

King Henry crossed the Channel from Dover and anchored off Wissant, where he was met by Thierry count of Flanders and Countess Sibyl, who was his aunt.

1157

Queen Eleanor bore a son at Oxford who was christened Richard. King Henry crossed back to England, and Malcolm king of Scotland returned to him the city of Carlisle, the town of Bamburgh, Newcastle-upon-Tyne and the county of Lothian.

Thierry count of Flanders and Countess Sibyl arrived at Jerusalem.

1158

Henry king of England went to a crown-wearing at Worcester, but after the divine service he placed the crown on the altar, not wishing to be crowned again [because he had little taste for ceremonial].

Queen Eleanor bore a son Geoffrey.

A new coinage was issued in England.

Thomas, the king's chancellor, came to Paris with great ceremony to receive Margaret, daughter of the king of France, to be the wife of Henry, son of the king of England.

Immediately after the death of his brother Geoffrey, Henry king of England crossed the Channel and seized Nantes.

Royal mistress, social outcast

HENRY II first openly acknowledged 'Fair Rosamund' as his mistress when he was 40 and she in her early 30s. The daughter of a nobleman, Walter Clifford, and possibly the one love of Henry's life, she lived in the royal palace of Woodstock, Oxfordshire, which the king refurbished specially for her, during the two or three years before she died in 1176. Chroniclers regarded her death as the just deserts for her adultery.

The sorrowing Henry had her buried in an unusually magnificent tomb before the high altar at Godstow nunnery. Later, both he and her father made generous gifts to the house in her memory. But in 1191, after Henry's death, St Hugh, bishop of Lincoln, was horrified to find an adulteress's tomb inside the church and to see its lavish decoration. To put a stop to such profanity he ordered the removal of the shrine, and Rosamund was reinterred outside the church.

Within a century of her death, chroniclers had begun to fabricate legends about her. According to one, she had been hidden away at Woodstock in a secret chamber within a maze, to protect her from Eleanor of Aquitaine's jealousy, but the queen had found her and bled her to death in a hot bath. In later centuries Eleanor was said to have used a dagger and poison cup, and to have found her way into the maze by following a silken thread.

Legends aside, the story of Rosamund and Henry II illustrates the difficulties women encountered when they set themselves outside society – a society orientated towards, and dominated by, men. Although royal bastards like Geoffrey Plantagenet and William Longsword, Henry II's sons by earlier liaisons, were given recognition and honours, their mothers, who had broken the laws of the Church and the rules of society were treated with contempt and revulsion. Even fortunate and respectable women who were heiresses in their own right – Mélisande of Jerusalem, the Empress Matilda or Eleanor of Aquitaine – were normally used as political pawns by their fathers, and only the most determined of them could make any real personal impact on the high politics of the 12th century.

Above *Woodstock Palace, from a Victorian representation.*

Below *An anonymous ballad about Rosamund.*

The Flower of the World

When as king Henry rulde this land,
The second of that name,
Besides the queene, he dearly loved
A faire and comely dame.

Most peerlesse was her beautye founde,
Her favour, and her face;
A sweeter creature in this worlde
Could never prince embrace.

Her crisped lockes like threads of golde
Appeard to each mans sight;
Her sparkling eyes, like Orient pearles,
Did cast a heavenlye light.

The blood within her crystal cheekes
Did such a colour drive,
As though the lillye and the rose
For mastership did strive.

Yea Rosamonde, fair Rosamonde,
Her name was called so,
To whom our queene, dame Ellinor,
Was known a deadlye foe.

The king therefore, for her defence
Against the furious queene,
At Woodstocke builded such a bower,
The like was never seene.

Most curiously that bower was built
Of stone and timber strong,
An hundered and fifty doors
Did to this bower belong.

And they so cunninglye contriv'd,
With turnings round about,
That none but with a clue of thread
Could enter in or out.

The Ballad of Fair Rosamund

Louis VII, king of France progressed through Normandy intending to fulfil a vow at Mont-Saint-Michel. He was received in the cathedral churches with solemn ritual. One by one men came to pay him honour, presenting him with many gifts.

The king of England came to Paris on the invitation of King Louis VII of France and was received in his palace and was offered lodging in the cloister of the canons of Notre-Dame.

1159

Henry II king of England led an army against Toulouse and took some well defended castles in that region. However, they say that the king of England did not attack Toulouse itself, out of respect for the king of France, who was staying there. For the king of France, out of good will towards the count of St Gilles, who had married his sister and had children by her, refused to retire from Toulouse. Thus the two kings became enemies.

1160

On the death of Pope Adrian there was a schism and two popes were elected, though it was Alexander who was the true pope. The king of England and the king of France accepted Alexander as pope, but the emperor of Germany and all the German clergy supported Octavian. The emperor sent messages to the kings of France and England requesting that they too might lend their support to the same pope, but in vain.

The queen of France, daughter of Alfonso emperor of Spain, died in giving birth to a daughter who fortunately survived. King Louis, however, did not observe the proper time of mourning but within two weeks had married Adela, daughter of Count Theobald of Blois. Samson archbishop of Reims refused to anoint her as queen, for the marriage of the said Adela's sister with the king's brother, Philip, had been dissolved because they were too closely related.

Henry king of England betrothed Margaret, daughter of the king of France, who was under his

The Gilbertine nun

IN about 1131 Gilbert, the parish priest and school master of Sempringham, Lincolnshire, built a convent on his lands for a group of fervent young women from among his pupils. Local people flocked to join; and lay sisters and lay brothers soon became an integral part of the order. Within the next 60 years 12 houses had been founded, some for canons only, in Lincolnshire and beyond.

The Gilbertines' reputation for sanctity was high, but the order experienced problems from the beginning. The Cistercian abbot, Ailred of Rievaulx, tells the story of a nun of Watton, Yorkshire, who was admitted to the Gilbertine order at the age of only four. As she grew to maturity she became 'frivolous and lascivious', rejecting the discipline of the cloister. Attracted to a young lay brother, she met him in secret: 'She went out a virgin of Christ, and she soon returned an adulteress.' Discovering this, and feeling she had disgraced them by her conduct, the younger nuns beat her and imprisoned her in fetters. Only the orders of older and wiser sisters prevented them from flaying and branding her. Frustrated, they persuaded some of the lay brothers to seek out her lover and bring him to them. The young man was pinioned to the ground and his mistress forced to cut off his offending parts and place them in her mouth. She was sent back to prison, and later gave birth to a child; but the very next day she was miraculously healed and restored to her state of virginity as a reward for the repentance she had shown. Later, her fetters fell away. Gilbert, informed of these wonders, decided it would be impious to return her to captivity.

A few years later, in the 1160s, the lay brothers at Sempringham revolted against Gilbert, complaining that they were underfed and overworked, and alleging that the proximity of the nuns and canons produced moral lapses. The order was cleared of the charges of immorality by five bishops, all of whom wrote to Pope Alexander III on Gilbert's behalf, and by Henry II, who took a particular interest in the Gilbertines.

Gilbert himself remained in charge until his death in 1189 at the age of more than 100; he died, according to his biographer, without ever having touched a woman. Within little more than a decade he had been canonized.

Top right *Sempringham parish church. Part of the present building dates from the 12th century, when it became the temporary home of the first Gilbertines.*

Right *The door at Sempringham is remarkable for its original wood and iron work. There were 24 Gilbertine houses at the time of the Dissolution in the 16th century.*

protection, to his son Henry, and thus gained possession of the castle of Gisors. He had long had designs on this fortification, which had been entrusted to the Knights Templar, according to an agreement between the two kings, until such time as the day of the wedding between their children should be fixed. However, the king of France and the queen's brothers now claimed that the day had been fixed far earlier than they had anticipated and were greatly aggrieved. And so, feeling enmity toward the king of England, the king of France and Count Theobald, with their allies, set about strengthening the defences of Chaumont, hoping to bring disgrace upon their enemy. However, the king of England came swiftly with his men and besieged the castle, when the French king and Count Theobald had fled. After a few days, he compelled its surrender and held fifty-five of Theobald's knights prisoner within. The marriage of the king of England's son and the king of France's daughter was celebrated with the alleged authority of Henry of Pisa and William of Pavia, cardinal priests and legates of the Holy See, even though the boy was only seven years old and the girl, three. This came to pass at Neufbourg on 5 November.

1161

Richard archdeacon of Coventry, whose father was Richard bishop of Chester, was consecrated bishop of that same see by Archbishop Theobald. For the sons of priests, if their mode of life shows them worthy, are neither to be excluded from holy orders, nor from cathedral churches nor yet from the papacy itself. Nicholas, for example, an Englishman by birth, whose father was a priest, became Pope Adrian IV.

1162

Louis king of France and Henry king of England assembled their troops from all quarters and armed conflict between them seemed inevitable. However, they were reconciled with one another near Fréteval.

The queen of England gave birth to a daughter at Rouen and gave her her own name, Eleanor.

Richard bishop of London died on 5 May. The bishops and abbots of all England, on the orders of the king, swore fealty to Henry his eldest son. Thomas, the king's chancellor, was the first among them to pay homage, saving his faith to the king for as long as he lived and wished to rule.

Frederick, the Holy Roman emperor, and Louis king of France met near Besançon to decide which pope, Octavian or Alexander, was to be preferred, and thus heal the schism which afflicted the Church.

The death of Theobald, archbishop of Canterbury, in 1161 necessitated the choice of a successor.

The clergy of all the province of Canterbury were summoned to London and, in the presence of Henry, the king's son and the judges, Thomas archdeacon of Canterbury was solemnly and unanimously elected archbishop. Henry bishop of Winchester carried the news that Thomas had been elected unopposed to the refectory of the monks at Westminster on the Wednesday before Whitsun.

On the following Sunday, he was consecrated by Henry bishop of Winchester, who was at that time vicar of the vacant see of London.

Messengers were sent to pope Alexander that the suffragans of Canterbury had chosen their pastor, who, on the unanimous vote of all, had been consecrated by their own synod. On hearing this, the pope gave his approval. And so, when the letters of the bishops, the prior and convent of Trinity [i.e. Canterbury Cathedral priory] and the king had been read out, the request for ratification was put to the cardinals assembled in the consistory. They all agreed without doubt or hesitation. The archbishop's pallium was then handed over to the messengers with all due pomp and ceremony. Archbishop Thomas, bound by the customary conditions and under the terms of the sacrament, took up the pallium from the high altar of Canterbury Cathedral.

However, as he put on those robes reserved, at God's command, to the highest of his clergy, he changed not only his apparel but his cast of mind. For he wished no longer to be bothered with the concerns of the chancery but rather that he might be allowed to retire from it and thus have more time to devote to addressing his flock and watching over the affairs of the Church. Therefore, Thomas sent a message to the king of England, then in Normandy, resigning his chancellorship and surrendering the seal. Such a sudden resignation had its sole cause in his own conception of the duties of his new office.

William FitzStephen's panegyric about Becket's conversion contrasts with Diceto's measured analysis.

In his consecration Thomas Becket was anointed with the visible unction of God's mercy; putting off the secular man, he now put on Jesus Christ. He vacated the secular duties of the chancellorship and was at pains to fulfil the functions of a good archbishop. To this end he kept a strict watch over his mind. His speech was grave and to the edification of his hearers; his works were those of mercy and piety; his decisions in conformity with justice and equity.

Clad in a hair shirt of the roughest kind, which reached to his knees and swarmed with vermin, he mortified his flesh with the sparest diet, and his accustomed drink was water used for the cooking of hay. He was always, however, the first to taste the wine before giving it to those who sat at table with him. He would eat some of the meat placed before him, but fed chiefly on bread. Yet all things are pure to the pure, and it is the appetite, not the food, which is to blame. Frequently he exposed his naked back to the lash of discipline. Immediately over his hair shirt he wore the habit of a monk, as abbot of the monks of Canterbury. Above this he wore the garb of a canon, in order to conform to the custom of clerks. But the stole, the emblem of the sweet yoke of Christ, was every day and night around his neck. His outward visage was like that of ordinary men, but within all was different. In this he took for his pattern St. Sebastian and St Cecilia, the former of whom under cover of a warrior's cloak conducted himself as a soldier of Christ, whilst the latter mortifying her flesh with sackcloth, appeared outwardly adorned with vesture of gold.

In his private cell every day he washed the feet of thirteen beggars, kneeling on his knees, in memory of Christ, and after replenishing them with victuals he gave four shillings to each of them. If he was on any occasion, though rarely, prevented from performing this act in person, he took great care to have the duty discharged by proxy. When he was alone, it was marvellous how often he dissolved into tears, and when he celebrated at the altar it was as if he discerned the Lord's Passion present in the flesh before him. He handled the holy sacraments with the utmost reverence, so that his very manner of doing so strengthened the faith and conduct of those who observed it.

Furthermore he entertained in his house the outcast and the needy, and clothed many against the severity of winter. At Canterbury he received many of them in person, sitting in the cloisters like one of his monks, studying some large volume. Afterwards he would go and visit the monks who were sick, in order to learn their wants and fulfil their desires. He was the consoler of the oppressed, the husband of the widow, the friend of orphans. He was besides humble and amiable to the gentle, but stern to the proud.

The glorious Archbishop Thomas, contrary to the expectation of the king and everyone else, so utterly abandoned the world and so suddenly experienced that conversion, which is God's handiwork, that all men marvelled thereat.

We next return to Diceto's discussion of the growing rift between king and archbishop.

1163

King Henry of England, when he had arranged his lands in Normandy, Brittany, Maine, Anjou, Touraine and Aquitaine as he thought fit, returned to England, anchoring at Southampton on 25 January. Thomas archbishop of Canterbury came to meet the king and embraced him but without true goodwill, turning his face away as all those present could see. Thomas, who had risen from archdeacon of Canterbury to archbishop, had put off resigning the archdeaconry for some time despite the most urgent request of the king. Eventually, he did resign it as the king had asked. However, although he was thus restored to the king's favour from which he had been excluded as a consequence of his delay, he never properly acknowledged this.

Roger de Clare earl of Hertford was summoned to Westminster on 22 July by Thomas archbishop of Canterbury to pay him homage in respect of Tonbridge castle and its domain. But the earl firmly resisted the archbishop's request, asserting that the fief in question was held of the king not the archbishop and it was to the former that its military service and public payments were due.

Malcolm king of Scotland, Rhys prince of the southern Welsh, Owen prince of the northern Welsh and all the noblemen of Wales paid homage to the king of England, and to Henry his son, at Wood-stock on 1 July.

A general inquiry was made throughout England to find out who ought to be by right holding in secular services of whom. While making inquiries in Kent, the justiciars decided that William of Ros owed allegiance to the king not the archbishop in whatever business he did. Thus personal hatreds caused harm to the Church as a whole.

When Archbishop Thomas transferred the vacant living of Eynesford to one Lawrence, William lord of Eynesford claimed that he himself had the right of appointment to that living and expelled Lawrence. In response to this the archbishop excommunicated him. Because this had been done without informing the king, the latter was most indignant. He asserted, indeed, that the king's dignity was inseparable from that of his kingdom and that no captain, or soldier of the king, none of his ministers, no one, of his tenants-in-chief (as they are commonly styled), whether they hold castle, town or woodland, was to be excommunicated by any one without the king's knowledge. For otherwise, the king might in ignorance be defiled by the excommunicate, embracing a captain who came to visit him or receiving him into his council.

King Henry sent Arnulf bishop of Lisieux and Richard archdeacon of Poitiers on an embassy to Pope Alexander, who was then travelling in the area of the schismatics in France. Over the space of three

Archbishop against king

ALTHOUGH more was written about Archbishop Thomas Becket of Canterbury than almost any other personality in Plantagenet England, his character sharply divided opinion among his contemporaries and has remained controversial ever since. Born at London in 1118 of a Norman merchant family, he was educated at Merton Priory and then joined the household of Archbishop Theobald of Canterbury, where his administrative talents marked him out for rapid promotion. In 1154 he was appointed archdeacon of Canterbury and later that year, on Archbishop Theobald's recommendation, Henry II made him Chancellor of England. For the next eight years Becket was totally absorbed in affairs of state and completely in the king's confidence, not least because he invariably tended to support the latter in his conflicts with the Church. This loyalty made Becket Henry II's ideal candidate for the archbishopric of Canterbury on the death of Theobald in 1161. The king was therefore surprised and angered when Becket, his most trusted servant, resigned the chancellorship immediately after being elected archbishop and became his most formidable opponent.

The best explanation for Becket's remarkable change of front – and for the bitter dispute which followed – was that on being consecrated at Canterbury the new archbishop transferred his allegiance from Henry II to an even greater lord: God. As Becket put it, in a heated interview with the king in 1163, 'in the dread Judgement Day we shall both be judged as servants of one Lord; for temporal lords should be obeyed, but not against God.' The only answer Henry II could find to this argument was the threat of physical force – an unwise weapon to use against the most senior prelate in his country.

The struggle between king and archbishop was fought out over judicial responsibility and, in particular, over Henry II's determination to limit the powers of the Church courts: he believed that their activities were beginning to undermine the legal powers he had inherited from earlier English kings. At Westminster in October 1163 Henry proposed that clerks (i.e. people in holy orders, and therefore connected with the Church) found guilty of criminal offences should be handed over to the secular authorities for punishment. Even under considerable pressure from the king and after several changes of mind, Becket refused to consent to this demand – or to others which Henry presented in writing at a council meeting at Clarendon in January 1164.

The king was by now increasingly intent on his archbishop's submission. After a final stormy confrontation at another council of barons and bishops

held at Northampton in the autumn, Becket escaped to France, where he appealed for protection to Pope Alexander III, who was then himself living in exile at the cathedral town of Sens. For the next six years the archbishop stayed at the Cistercian abbey of Pontigny while he waged a war of words against his monarch and the latter's new advisers.

Most educated churchmen in western Europe would have conceded that Becket had justice on his side in his conflict with the king. However, the functions of Church and State were inseparably intertwined in Plantagenet England: the English bishops were a powerful group who owed their appointments to royal favour and were heavily involved in administrative and judicial work on the Crown's behalf. They therefore had a vested interest in maintaining their crucial role as the leading intermediaries between Church and king and were reluctant to see this prejudiced by Becket's intransigence towards Henry.

There was little sympathy for an archbishop who took his opposition to the king to extremes and Becket was gradually forced to realize that his long years of self-imposed exile made remarkably little difference to the running of the English kingdom. According to Bishop Gilbert Foliot of London, who knew Becket well, 'he always was a fool, and always will remain one'. This judgement on the exiled archbishop is less than fair. However, it is an accurate comment on how Thomas Becket courageously exposed the tensions between the lay and spiritual powers without being able to resolve them — except by his own death.

Illustrations from the only known medieval illustrated life of Becket, c.1235:
Above *Becket leaves Henry and Louis.*
Below *He leaves for England after his long exile.*
Bottom *Becket arrives at Sandwich.*

months, they suffered exposure to the dangers of the fierce seas and stormy waves six times; but although they laboured long to find support for the laws of the kingdom in the authority of the pope, they were able to achieve nothing. Thus when they finally returned they could do nothing to mitigate the king's anger which now raged against many persons.

1164

The king of England wished, so he said, to inflict severe punishment on individual members of the clergy who were guilty of crimes, considering that for such men to receive less punishment than they deserved derogated from the dignity of the order as a whole. Therefore he decreed that members of the clergy who were considered by his own judges to be flagrant criminals should be turned over to their bishop. Those whom that bishop found guilty he should deprive of their authority in the presence of one of the king's judges and should, after the trial, hand over for punishment.

The archbishop of Canterbury was then put on trial for his actions as chancellor, appearing at Northampton on 12 October. The bishops, earls and barons of the whole kingdom gathered there at the king's urgent command. Roger archbishop of York was summoned and appeared. It was by order of Thomas's chancery that overseers had been appointed to the possessions of bishoprics. Since Thomas had as chancellor exceeded the limits of his authority in the king's household (for many years he had held the castles of Berkhamsted and Eye, doing what he liked with them), it seemed to most people to be consistent with the law that he should be made to account for the sum of the profits, even though, before his consecration, the archbishop had been granted by Henry, the king's son and heir, freedom and exemption from the obligation to render accounts. However, since it was impossible for Thomas to prove that this immunity had been granted him, the leaders of the church did bring judgement against him though he had neither confessed to the charge, nor been convicted, but was laying claim to benefit of clergy.

Thus the archbishop was in dire straits, accused of many wrongs, wounded by many insults and bereft

of the support of the bishops. He raised up the cross which he carried and left the court room. The following night, he left the town in secret. Concealing himself from the view of men by day and travelling by night, after some days he came to the port of Sandwich and crossed over to Flanders in a small boat. After the disappearance of the archbishop, the king sent messengers to Pope Alexander III at Sens.

Among their instructions from the king, the messengers carried a request that the pope might send two judges to England who, in the presence of the king and the archbishop, might resolve the non-ecclesiastical quarrel between the king and the archbishop which had been first discussed at Northampton, and any other matter which might emerge during the course of the discussion, after the appeal had been withdrawn. However, when the king's messengers arrived at the palace of the archbishop of Sens, as the archbishop was not present, the court could give no decisive response to their request, for what was being asked seemed neither to accord with the law nor with reason.

1165

Adela, the queen of France gave birth to a son who was called Philip. The queen of England, Eleanor, gave birth to a daughter who was called Joanna. Pope Alexander returned to Italy and was welcomed at Rome.

While the king was staying at Westminster [the royal palace near London], Reginald archbishop of Cologne came to England to receive Matilda, the king's eldest daughter, as a wife for Henry, duke of Saxony. However, when the nobles of the kingdom came, with great ceremony, to meet him, Robert earl of Leicester, the king's justiciar, refused to embrace him on the grounds that he was a schismatic. And all the altars upon which the schismatic had celebrated Mass were overturned.

Becket had fled to the pope at Sens, and from there went to the Cistercian abbey of Pontigny. Here he adopted an austere and scholarly way of life. At Whitsun 1166, while on pilgrimage, he visited Vézelay, where he excommunicated several English bishops who were supporting the king.

A daughter's alliance

NEGOTIATIONS for the marriage of Matilda, Henry II's eldest daughter, to Henry the Lion, duke of Bavaria and Saxony, started in 1165 when Archbishop Reginald of Cologne, close adviser of the Emperor Frederick Barbarossa, led a delegation to Henry II at Rouen. The proposal was that one of the king's daughters should marry Frederick's young son while another (Matilda) should marry the duke, the emperor's most powerful subject and – at this stage – his close ally. Frederick, whose rule theoretically extended throughout Germany and northern Italy, needed support in conflicts with the papacy – he had just established an antipope as a rival to the hostile Alexander III – and the cities of northern Italy. Henry II, for his part, was embarrassed by the dispute with Thomas Becket, who had gone into exile at the end of 1164 and had appealed for the pope's assistance. Henry saw friendship with the empire as a means of putting pressure on Pope Alexander in order to influence him against Becket.

Since Henry II annoyed Barbarossa when he finally refused to transfer his allegiance to his antipope Victor IV, the marriage between Duke Henry and Matilda was the only one to take place. The ceremony took place in February 1168 at Brunswick. Henry, in his late 30s, had been married before, but the marriage had produced no male heir and was dissolved on the usual grounds of consanguinity. Matilda, who had been born in 1156, was either 11 or 12 when she married. She bore her husband two sons, and until her death in 1189, administered her husband's vast lands during absences such as his pilgrimage to the Holy Land in 1172–3.

The political consequences of the marriage were totally unexpected, eventually involving Henry II and his sons deeply in German politics. Duke Henry and the Emperor Frederick quarrelled in the late 1170s and in the autumn of 1182 Henry and his family arrived at the court of Henry II, his father-in-law, as exiles. The king gave them his protection and tried to secure their return to Saxony through diplomatic pressure against Frederick. The children, notably Otto, the second son, became protégés of the Plantagenets and stayed at their court when Henry and Matilda returned to Germany in 1185.

Above *The tomb and effigies of Henry the Lion, duke of Saxony, and his second wife Matilda, daughter of Henry II of England. There had been long links between the English and German royal families: Henry II's mother, the Empress Matilda, had lived for more than 20 years in Germany before she married Geoffrey of Anjou, and she kept her imperial title until she died. Matilda, her grandchild, had a son, Otto, by Henry the Lion. He was brought up at Richard the Lionheart's court and eventually became German emperor from 1209 to 1218, as Otto IV. His coat of arms was derived appropriately from the Plantagenet emblem of three lions. Duke Henry used a naturalistic picture of a lion as a seal, and there was a monumental bronze lion outside his castle in Bavaria.*

Although the tomb shows a young and peaceful couple, Henry was an able, if not always successful, military leader.

1166

"Thomas archbishop of Canterbury to the king of the English.

I greatly desire to see your face and talk with you; much for my sake, but even more for yours, that seeing my face you would be brought back to the memory of the services I did for you when I was in your obedience, devotedly according to my conscience, as God may help me at the last judgement when all shall stand before his tribunal to receive good or ill according to how they acted when alive; and that you would be moved by pity for me, who must live as a beggar among foreigners even though, thank the Lord, we have plenty of sustenance."

Queen Eleanor bore a son whom she called John.

Cardinals William of Pavia and John of Naples, the pope's legates, called the king of England and the archbishop of Canterbury together at Montmirail; and although the archbishop felt them to lean more to the king's side, he allowed the case to be dealt with, the legates sitting in public, so that full restitution to himself and his followers would have to be made according to ecclesiastical law. But the despoiled archbishop did not want to undergo judgement and could not be compelled to in any way; as the legates could not and did not want to do so, they returned to the papal court in failure.

Louis VII king of France came to Pontigny, where the monks had shown Archbishop Thomas every kindness for two years, and in case any harm should be done to the Cistercian Order in England took him with him to Sens and paid his expenses at Ste Colombe for four years.

1167

King Henry II's daughter Matilda married Henry duke of Saxony. The earls of Arundel and Pembroke, and many others, escorted her to him.

The kings of France and England fell out: the Normans burnt Chaumont near Gisors, capturing many knights and civilians, and in revenge the French king burnt Andelys, a country house of the archbishop of Rouen, and returned to France the same day losing more than a thousand men on the journey. Afterwards a great number of French knights were captured by the Normans in Perche; but the two kings made peace, as Richard duke of Aquitaine, the English king's son, was betrothed to Alice of France, the king's daughter.

1169

Eleanor, daughter of the king of England, married Alfonso VIII king of Castile.

On 18 November a conference was held between King Louis VII of France and King Henry II of England near Paris, which was where the archbishop of Canterbury was, but Thomas did not present himself to the king of England. There was lengthy discussion about making peace between the king and archbishop, so the archbishop, on the advice of the king of France and the bishops and nobles, provided the king of England with his petition in a letter, which ran thus:

"We seek from the lord our king, on the advice and mandate of the pope, that for the love of God and the pope and honour of the holy Church, and his own and his heirs' salvation, he receives us into his grace and concedes to us, and all who with us and on our behalf left his kingdom, his peace and full security from him and his men, without bad feeling, and that he returns the church of Canterbury to us as freely and fully as we held it after we were made archbishop, and all possessions which we had, to have and hold as freely, honourably and peaceably, as the church and ourselves had and held when we were promoted to the archbishopric; and similarly for our followers. He should likewise permit us to have all those churches belonging to the archbishop, which fell vacant after we left the country, so that we may do with them what we please."

The king of England did not provide his full assent to two details. Since he had not expelled the archbishop, he was not obliged, in accordance with the dignity of the kingdom, to discharge anything in the name of restitution. Nor was he obliged to

Las Huelgas in Castile

THE royal abbey of Las Huelgas in Spain was founded in 1187, at the request of Eleanor of England, wife of Alfonso VIII, king of Castile, and daughter of Eleanor of Aquitaine and Henry II. Although richly endowed – Alfonso, a pious man, was always generous to the Church – its nuns belonged to the strict and ascetic Cistercian order, and were almost totally cut off from the world.

They were drawn only from the highest ranks of the Spanish aristocracy. The first abbess was a princess of Aragon; the second, from 1205 to 1218, was Princess Constance, one of Eleanor and Alfonso's daughters. The king and queen and their immediate entourage were allowed to visit the whole of the abbey on only one day in every year. On all other occasions, they were restricted to the choir and transepts, which they used as a royal chapel, looking through a small glass window into the nave where the nuns, their daughter among them, were at prayer.

Las Huelgas was not just a haven for noble ladies with strong religious convictions. It was also to be the royal mausoleum or burial place for Eleanor and Alfonso, in the tradition of Henry I's Reading Abbey and Stephen's Faversham. A beautiful building, with the elegance befitting a royal nunnery, Las Huelgas mainly reflects the influence of the Ile de France. But one feature is purely Plantagenet in style: the vaulting – domed, with small additional compartments and ribs – of the transept

chapels. These are identical to a group of vaults, known as Angevin vaults, that were built in and around Angers in the early 13th century. It seems certain that Eleanor of England or her daughter, Abbess Constance, brought an architect from Angers to leave a Plantagenet imprint on the abbey that was so much their own in a foreign land.

Below *The cloisters of Las Huelgas.*

Bottom *The tomb of Alfonso VIII and Eleanor.*

declare invalid the possession of vacant property which he had already given to certain persons. But so that he could profess himself to be a ruler bound by laws, he was prepared, before the king of France, to satisfy the archbishop in all respects, or if he had decided to dispute the matter, to submit to judgement in the palace at Paris, with the nobles of France there, or with the French Church using its influence, or with scholars from the different provinces examining the business fairly.

Thus the king of England, who previously had excited the hatred of many against himself, with these words turned many in his favour. In this way the king of England and the archbishop would have come to some sort of agreement, if the king had not absolutely refused to give the archbishop the kiss of peace.

1170

On Christmas Day the king held court at the town of Nantes, with the attendance of the bishops and barons of the whole of Brittany, who swore allegiance to him and his son Geoffrey all together. In Lent he returned to England, and when many of his retinue were endangered by a sudden storm at sea, he himself escaped unharmed by virtue of his great gift of piety to God.

In Becket's absence from England, Henry II decided to use the archbishop of York to crown his son the Young King, thereby reopening the longstanding rift between the two English archbishops over precedence.

On 14 June, Henry, the first-born son of Henry king of England, was consecrated as king at Westminster by Roger archbishop of York.

After the coronation of his son the king crossed the Channel. A conference was held at Montmirail between him and Archbishop Thomas, where the king of France was present. But after much else, when it came to the embrace, because the archbishop said, 'I kiss you in honour of God,' the king refused the kiss as made only conditionally. For just as our ancestors used to pay very close attention to formulae in law, so the king kept taking issue with

certain phrases in the archbishop's words, though uttered with the purest conscience, that is to say sometimes 'saving my order', sometimes, 'saving the honour of God', sometimes, 'saving God's faith'.

The king of France, William archbishop of Sens, and the bishop of Nevers met again at Fréteval. When, however, the king of England and the archbishop parted twice, and twice dismounted and mounted their horses, the king twice held the stirrup for the archbishop. And again at Amboise, to put it briefly for easier understanding, the king and the archbishop entered an agreement, this time peace being procured by Rotrou archbishop of Rouen.

"Henry king of England, to his son Henry king of England, greeting.
May you know that Thomas archbishop of Canterbury has made peace with me in accordance with my wishes. Therefore I order that he and his followers may have peace and that you see to it that he and his followers, who on his behalf left England, should have their possessions in peace and with honour, as they did three months before they left England. Summon before you some of the best and oldest knights of the honour of Saltwood and on their oath you should make an inquiry as to what of the fief of the archbishopric of Canterbury is there, and make sure that the archbishop gets what has been recognized as part of his fief. Witness Archbishop Rotrou of Rouen, at Chinon."

On this security the archbishop therefore returned to England, and landed at the port of Sandwich on 1 December.

Thomas archbishop of Canterbury, after he entered England, wrote a letter to the pope, running partly as follows:

" . . . After we reached our church, and were received with great devotion by the clergy and the people, several angry officials of the king approached us, demanding on his behalf that we should absolve those bishops who had been excommunicated or suspended, because what had been done against them amounted to injustice against the king and overturning of the customs of the kingdom. . . . We

Politician, prisoner and queen

DURING the early years of her marriage to Henry II, Eleanor was actively involved in the political life of his domains. She travelled a great deal, exercising considerable administrative responsibility and, until about 1161, was regent of England in Henry's absences. After 1163, however, she was less in the public eye, and it may have been at this time that her resentment against Henry began to grow. Although Henry gave her full control of the duchy of Aquitaine in 1168, perhaps to allow him to pursue his own political and amatory adventures unhindered and elsewhere, Eleanor's rancour against him did not diminish. A year later, when Richard was named as heir to the duchy, he became her constant companion and fellow conspirator against his father. The coronation of the young Henry as king of England in 1170 gave Eleanor another useful focus for her schemes against her husband. In 1173 her plotting reached fruition and the Young King, Richard and Geoffrey all rebelled against their father and fled to Louis VII. Eleanor was captured when she tried to follow them disguised as a man, and was imprisoned by her angry husband.

Henry knew it would be a grave political error to divorce Eleanor and also that he could never compel her to become a nun at Fontevrault. But he recognized the danger she posed to the precarious stability of his lands, and kept her in close confinement in England, supervised by his most trusted men, treatment which she bore with fortitude. With her spiritual advisers she was allowed to travel only the short distances between Winchester, Salisbury, Ludgershall and other royal residences in the south of England.

In 1183, after the Young King's death, she was released for a time to tour Aquitaine in order to counter a French claim to the duchy, and in the following year was allowed to come to court to see her daughter Matilda, in exile from Saxony with her husband Henry the Lion. Then, in 1185, she was escorted to Normandy to receive Aquitaine from Richard, who had been persuaded to give up his beloved duchy by his father's threat that Eleanor would lay waste the region with an army.

In the last three years of Henry's reign, Eleanor began once more to plot against him. His death, in 1189, liberated her and allowed her to assume powers far greater than she had enjoyed before.

Above *In the first years of their marriage, Henry and Eleanor were to cross the Channel many times, travelling frequently between the towns and palaces of their English and French dominions.*

Below *Ruins of the Great Hall at Chinon Castle, one of the main centres of Plantagenet power in the Loire region.*

replied to them that if the bishops of London and Salisbury would⁴ swear in our presence that they would obey our order, we would absolve them, for the peace of the Church and from reverence to the king. When this was passed on to the bishops they replied that an oath of this kind ought not to be made except in accordance with the king's wishes.**"**

While Thomas archbishop of Canterbury was on the way to visit the young King Henry, who was at that time staying at Woodstock, he was received with all honour by the inhabitants of London, and on 18 December, when he was a guest at Southwark, messengers came from the Young King to him, prohibiting him on the king's behalf from going to see him; he was instead to return to his church. So returning to Canterbury, he arranged to celebrate Christmas there, with many clerks from different places meeting there on various matters of business.

On Christmas Day, Thomas archbishop of Canterbury mounted the pulpit to give a sermon to the people. When that was done, and he had made the customary prayers to the Lord for the pope, the king and the salvation of the populace, with candles lit he solemnly excommunicated Nigel de Sackville, a violent oppressor of the church of Hardres, and the vicar of the same church, and also Robert de Broc, who had himself mutilated a certain horse of the archbishop himself which was carrying victuals, to his disgrace and ignominy.

On the fifth day of Christmas around dusk, while the archbishop was residing in his chamber with his clerks, as if carried by a fury, William de Traci, Reginald FitzUrse, Hugh de Moreville and Richard Brito, four knights who had come from Normandy, burst into the chamber, and threatened on behalf of the king, who was staying in Normandy, that the archbishop should restore the suspended bishops of England to their offices and absolve those excommunicated. He replied to them that it was not for a lesser judge to dissolve the sentence of a superior, and that it was not for any man to undermine what had been decreed by the apostolic see; however, if the bishops of London and Salisbury would swear that they would obey his command, he would absolve them for the peace of the Church and through reverence to the king. They, white with

anger hurrying to bring the wicked crime which they had conceived, to its execution, rapidly withdrew.

The archbishop, despite the warnings of his clerks, entered the main church, since it was nearly time to sing vespers. And so the aforementioned accomplices to the crime, who had in the meantime armed themselves, followed in the archbishop's footsteps. When they came to the church they found its doors open, just as the archbishop had instructed. 'We shall not', he said, 'change the church of God into a castle; it should be a universal refuge at times when order is thrown into chaos.' With commotion converging from all sides, the four irreverently entered the church and began to shout, 'Where is the betrayer of the king? Where is the archbishop?' When the archbishop heard the mention of his name, he descended to meet them from the third or fourth step of the presbytery, which he had already started to mount, saying, 'If you seek the archbishop, I am here.' To their very harsh response, his words were, 'I am prepared to die: I prefer an assertion of justice and the Church's liberty to my life. I ask however that my followers are not liable to punishment, just as they were not instigators of the situation.' While the accomplices of the crime rushed forward with drawn swords he said, 'I commend myself and the cause of the Church to the blessed Mary, the patron saints of this church and the blessed Dionysius.'

In his life of Becket, William FitzStephen gives a highly coloured description of the archbishop's murder by the four knights.

One of the knights struck him with the flat of his sword between the shoulders, saying, 'Fly, you are a dead man.' But the archbishop stood unmoved, and offering his neck [for a blow] commended himself to God, while his lips repeated the names of the holy archbishops who had been martyrs before him. Some of the enemy cried, 'You are our prisoner, come with us,' and laying hands upon him, they would have dragged him out of the church, but for fear that the people might rescue him from their clutches. The archbishop made answer, 'I will not go hence. Here shall you work your will and obey your orders.' He struggled

A question of murder

THE final act in the six-year conflict of wills between Henry II and Thomas Becket was as abruptly decisive as the conflict itself had been long and inconclusive. In 1170 a compromise was reached between king and archbishop: Becket could return to England, the confiscated property of the archbishopric would be returned, and Becket could re-crown the young king who had only weeks earlier been crowned by the archbishop of York. Nothing was said about the council meeting at Clarendon. On 1 December 1170, therefore, the archbishop returned to England after his years of exile – in a mood that was aggressive rather than conciliatory – and excommunicated the archbishop of York and the two bishops who had assisted at the young King Henry's coronation. When the news reached Henry in Normandy, he flew into a violent rage, and four of his knights travelled to Canterbury to take a revenge so terrible that it is hard to believe the king would ever have contemplated it.

In the late afternoon of 29 December, the archbishop was assassinated in his own cathedral, provoking a tide of indignation across the whole of Europe.

Becket dead was immeasurably more powerful than Becket alive. Within a few months many miracles were reported at his tomb; and less than three years after his death he was canonized by Pope Alexander III in February 1173.

During the following year Henry II did public penance at his old enemy's shrine – a shrine which rapidly became, and remained, one of medieval Christendom's principal pilgrimage centres. Not by nature a saint, Thomas Becket had become the most influential martyr in the history of the English Church.

Below *This casket, which contained relics of St Thomas, was made in Limoges in about 1190; the copper plaques are engraved and gilded, and laid over wood.*

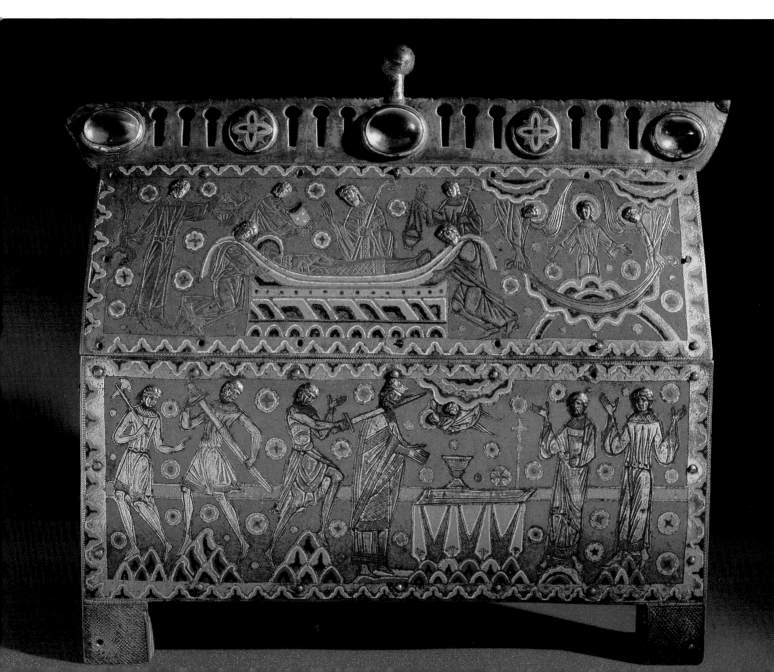

with might and main against them, while the monks too held him back. With them also was Master Edward Grim, and he, putting up his arm [to ward off the blow] received the first stroke of the sword aimed by William de Traci at the archbishop's head. By this same stroke the archbishop was wounded in the head as he bent forward, and Grim in the arm severely.

Wiping off with his arm the blood that streamed from his head, the archbishop gave thanks to God, saying, 'Into thy hands, O Lord, I commend my spirit.' As he knelt down, clasping and stretching out his hands to God, a second stroke was dealt him on the head, at which he fell flat on his face hard by an altar there dedicated to St Benedict. He took care, however, and was granted grace, to fall in honourable fashion, covered down to the ankles with his pallium, as though in the act of prayer and adoration. On the right hand he fell, as one proceeding to the right hand of God. While he lay there stricken, Richard Brito smote him with such force that the sword was broken against his head and the pavement of the church: 'Take that,' said he, 'for love of my lord William, the king's brother [whose marriage with the countess of Warenne Thomas had prohibited].'

Four wounds in all did the saintly archbishop receive, and all of them in the head: the whole crown of his head was lopped off. Then it was seen how his limbs obeyed the motions of his spirit. For, as in mind, so too in body, it was manifest that neither by parrying blows nor in evading them did he struggle against death. For he accepted it of his own free will and from a desire to be with God rather than as a violent death from the knights' swords. A certain Hugh of Horsea, nicknamed Mauclerk, put his foot on the neck of the fallen martyr and extracted the blood and brains from the hollow of the severed crown with the point of his sword. A sorry spectacle, an unheard-of cruelty on the part of so-called Christian men! A terrible storm cloud overhung the firmament, sudden and swift fell the rain and the thunder rolled round the heavens. After this the sky turned a deep red in token of the blood which had been shed and in horror of the outrage.

Diceto, unfolding the events which followed Becket's death, writes in a less dramatic way than FitzStephen, but his outrage at the archbishop's murder is still evident.

Robert de Broc and his accomplices plundered the property of the archbishop, the clothes of the clergy and servants, and even the utensils from the workshop. They swiftly made off with all the horses which they found in his stables, as spoils.

The body of the archbishop, which had sunk onto the pavement to the right-hand side of the altar of St Benedict, was carried and placed in front of the main altar at twilight. There, what had been known only to his chamberlain, became evident to bystanders. For although the archbishop had quite secretly concealed a monastic habit, which he had worn for a long time, by covering it with his canonical garb, he had also taken care to tame his flesh with undergarments of haircloth. The following day, Wednesday, early in the morning, a wicked rumour became prevalent: that the wicked executioners had conspired to drag away the body of the archbishop from the holy place, and to cast it outside the walls of the city to be torn by dogs or birds. So the abbot of Boxley and the prior and convent of the church of Canterbury wisely decided that they should give the body a somewhat late burial; it seemed not to need washing with water, especially since it had been purged by the long abstinence of the archbishop, and wiped by the haircloth, and purified by his own blood.

1171

King Henry of England was at this time staying in Normandy, at Argentan, when certain people conveyed the unhappy rumour to his notice. At once, in the very first stages of the evil story, he turned to all sorts of lamentation and misery, and completely exchanged, as it were, his royal majesty for sackcloth and ashes, calling almighty God to witness for the sake of his soul that the evil deed had not been committed by his will, nor with his knowledge, nor was it brought about by his plan, unless perhaps he had sinned by being believed to bear little love for the archbishop up to then. On top of this he directly submitted himself to the judgement of the Church, and with humility, promised to undertake whatever it should decide.

Envoys were sent from the king to the pope, to defend the king, and to plead his innocence; the pope did not wish to see them, nor embrace them, nor have them kneel at his feet. The envoys tried a second time, and were received by some cardinals but only to speak to. Therefore, they were thrown into confusion for a long time by the sorrow of their own spirits, but they supplicated those who were consistently more favourable, so that by their intervention, the pope should at least indulge some of them with an audience, but they made no progress at all. The Wednesday before Easter approached, on which, in accordance with the custom of the Roman Church, the pope usually either made a public excommunication or absolution. By way of several of the pope's secretaries, it reached the ears of the envoys that on the said day the pope had decided immutably to impose the sentence of interdict against the king of England by name, and against the whole of his land on both sides of the Channel.

On the same day, the pope generally excommunicated the most evil murderers of the archbishop of Canterbury, and all those who provided assistance or assent, and all those who might help or shelter them. The murderers nonetheless stayed at Knaresborough in the province of Northumbria for a year.

Around Easter, Lord Jesus Christ, who is always present in his saints and everywhere, miraculously began to shine on the praiseworthy life of his most glorious martyr, Thomas archbishop of Canterbury, and his insuperable constancy in death, by means of frequent miracles, so that he who put up with the proscription of himself and his followers for so many years to protect the endangered liberty of the Church should be recognized by all to have won a worthy victory.

On 6 August the elder king arrived in England, and on his journey he visited Henry of Blois, bishop of Winchester, who was on his deathbed; the king was reproached for the death of the glorious martyr by the bishop, who predicted that he would suffer

much because of that death. So the bishop, an old man and full of days, died on 8 August.

1172

On Christmas night, thunder was heard in Ireland and England and in all of France generally, sudden and dire, portending something great, new, and unusual.

From the king's arrival in Ireland, where he had landed with an army in October 1171, for almost twenty weeks on end no report reached him from his kingdom, or any part of his domain, so extensive and broad, nor could it reach him, as there was a contrary wind blowing.

While the king delayed in Ireland, Hugh of Saint-Maur and Ralph de Fayes, uncle of Queen Eleanor, on her advice, so it is said, began to turn away from his father the mind of the Young King, suggesting that it seemed incongruous to be a king and not exercise the rule of a kingdom.

Many men in King Henry II's army in Ireland were afflicted with a flux of the stomach, through eating fresh meat and drinking water, which was unprecedented; they suffered from lack of bread.

When, however, the inhabitants of Ireland had understood how completely the intentions of the king of England were completely concerned with establishing and maintaining peace, and that he did not encourage crimes by his indulgence, nor hurriedly sentence anyone to death, when summoned by an edict they met him to discuss peace. Because there was no publicly constituted power among them which would give them safety, through fear of punishment and since they very often had grieved that their fathers killed each other in civil wars, they transferred their jurisdiction and power to him and in him, so that because of the king, they should have peace.

Since various matters of business called him, Henry boarded ship at twilight and the next day arrived in Wales near Saint Davids. From there he went directly, turning neither to the left nor right as if post-haste, to Portchester, where, boarding a vessel, he said goodbye to England and after a fair crossing arrived in Normandy. When this came to the notice of the king of France, he sharply remarked, 'At one moment the king of England is in Ireland, the next in England, the next in Normandy – he must fly rather than travel by horse or ship.'

When Henry arrived in Normandy he at once hurried to visit Albert and Theodin, the cardinals and papal legates. Finally, after protracted dealings, firstly at Savigny, then at Avranches, the king swore in the presence of the legates that the death of the most glorious martyr Thomas was not perpetrated in accordance with his wishes, nor with his knowledge, nor brought about by his planning; but since the villains had taken the opportunity of killing a holy man because of words which he had very carelessly brought forth when inflamed by the heat of anger, he with all humility sought absolution from them, and was granted it. Therefore in the eyes of the Church he was solemnly absolved, and he promised in accordance with the wishes and orders of the cardinals that as from Whitsun he would give each year an amount of money which in the judgement of the Knights Templar would pay for two hundred soldiers for the defence of the land of Jerusalem for one year.

He promised that appeals could freely be made, and that practices which had in his reign been introduced against the liberty of the Church would be revoked, and that the possessions of the church of Canterbury, having been removed after the departure of the archbishop of hallowed memory, would be restored complete; also that it would freely be allowed for the clergy and laity of both sexes, who had left the kingdom on Thomas's behalf, to return in the king's peace and receive their belongings. For promising and carrying this out, the pope granted the king the remission of his sins. The young King Henry, son of Henry II, swore and promised as his father had done.

In the following August, the Young King and his wife Margaret, daughter of King Louis of France, arrived in England. The archbishop crowned Margaret queen of England on 21 August at Winchester and placed the royal diadem on the

England and Aquitaine

THE Romanesque sculpture of western France, deeply undercut and exuberant with small monsters and grotesque figures, seems to have had an extraordinary appeal for the English. The elegant and distinctive arches of Aquitanean portals, with one beast or figure to each constituent stone (or *voussoir*), radiating out like flower petals from the archhead of the door, inspired the west portals at Rochester cathedral, and the doors of innumerable small parish churches in Yorkshire.

Although much of this was a result of the marriage between Eleanor and Henry and the cultural interchange that followed between Aquitaine and England, it is clear that the rich sculpture of Aquitaine had already struck an answering chord in the English imagination. In the 1130s, Oliver of Merlimond, a Herefordshire baron, had gone on pilgrimage to Santiago de Compostella in northwest Spain, travelling through Aquitaine. He must have had a sculptor in his retinue, who drew anything which impressed him on the way, to adapt for his own work on his return to Herefordshire. These new ideas were used at Merlimond's small Augustinian foundation of Shobdon, now decayed, and at the well-preserved and enchanting rural church at the Benedictine cell of Kilpeck. The finesse of the Aquitanean models, carved in the kind of fine limestone that must be a sculptor's dream, is lost in the more lumpen Herefordshire sandstone, but the copies have their own rustic and earthy charm.

Right *The doorway to Kilpeck church.*

Top *Examples of corbels: the innocent animal faces (far right) seem out of place near this female fertility symbol (near right).*

Below *Grotesque figure playing a viol.*

Young King's head with the bishop of Evreux ministering to him as well as several of the suffragans of the church of Canterbury.

In accordance with the petition and wishes of the king of France, the archbishop of York and the bishops of London and Salisbury [because they had performed the Young King's coronation in Becket's absence in 1170] were forbidden to be present at the coronation, or to presume to impede it in any way.

1173

Henry II, king of England betrothed his son John, called 'Lackland' [because he had received nothing when Henry II divided his estates in 1169], then barely seven, to the eldest daughter of Humbert count of Maurienne whom the widow of Duke Henry of Saxony had borne him. And since the count had no hope of male children, four of his castles reputed to be the best fortified by man or nature were, as the king wished, handed over into his custody.

King Henry the king's son, following wicked advice, turned away from his father; and leaving Argentan by night, the servants of his father who looked after his needs knowing nothing about it, he went on 23 March via Mortagne, a castle of Theobald count of Perche, to his father-in-law, King Louis of France. That same night his father, sleeping at Alençon, was woken and told of his son's flight. With only a few companions he mounted his horse and, riding along the borders putting his castles in a state of defence, with many changes of mount came at dawn to Gisors, which King Louis had given to the Young King as the dowry of his daughter Margaret. Richard duke of Aquitaine and Geoffrey duke of Brittany, the king's younger sons, chose to follow their brother rather than their father – in this, so they say, following the advice of their mother Eleanor. Everywhere there was plotting, plundering and burning. And to take an omen from the seasons, the son took up arms against his father at just the time when everywhere Christians were laying down their arms in reverence for Easter. Dissensions of this sort cannot end happily.

One hundred and forty Flemings, coming in near Passy, invaded Normandy by means of a bridge, and immediately the place was full of blaring trumpets, shouting people and armed men running about. The Normans' courageous resistance made the Flemings think about retreating as soon as possible. But the bridge by which they had crossed was broken down by a certain little woman; deep waters were in the way of their retreat, and rushing into them all the Flemings were drowned. When he heard this King Louis VII said: 'The elements are on the side of the Normans! When I invaded Normandy last time a large part of my army died of thirst, and now we can complain of too much water.'

Letters from the elder king and the cardinals were sent to England on 6 July urging action about the church of Canterbury. When the bishops had conferred on this. Odo prior of Canterbury Cathedral and the better part of the convent constantly started asserting the unheard-of view that the archbishop should be elected by their chapter and publicly nominated by them. And since it greatly concerned Henry II at that time to have an untroubled election, two were selected from the large number of monks, namely Odo the prior of Canterbury and Richard prior of Dover; when the monks presented them to the bishops, all hoping for the election of their prior, Gilbert bishop of London rising before them all heaped praise on prior Odo but with the agreement of the bishops came down on the other side, saying, 'We elect Prior Richard.' All this happened in St Catherine's chapel, in the presence and with the agreement of the king's justiciar. On the same day that the council about the election to Canterbury was held, the following letter from the pope was read out in public:

"Pope Alexander to his venerable brothers the archbishops and bishops, his dear sons the prelates of other churches and all the clergy and people of England, greeting and apostolic blessing.
England emits the fragrance and virtue of those miracles which almighty God works through the merits of the holy and reverend Thomas, formerly archbishop of Canterbury. His praiseworthy life shone with much meritorious glory, and at length was closed in the glorious battle of martyrdom. No one who hears of his admirable life, and considers

The castle at Mirebeau, said to have been left by Count Geoffrey Plantagenet of Anjou to his second son and namesake.

Mirebeau lies between Le Touet and La Vienne rivers, and played an important part in the lives of the Plantagenet family. After the old count's death, young Geoffrey tried to keep his older brother Henry from retaining Anjou as well as Normandy. In the summer of 1156, Henry, now the new king of England came back to Anjou, put down the rebellion fostered by Geoffrey and took over Mirebeau for himself.

Eventually the castle was to arouse another dispute between brothers; Henry II proposed that it, with two others, should be part of his son John's inheritance, while the Young King fought bitterly to retain all three castles for himself.

Mirebeau became a symbol of the problems Henry continued to have with his children, and it was mentioned by name in a song written by the troubadour, Bertrand de Born ... 'between Poitiers and L'Ile-Bouchard and Mirebeau and Loudun and Chinon ...'

After John became king, he fought Philip Augustus at Mirebeau in 1202. It was their first real contest and John won a clear victory, rescuing his mother Eleanor, who had been trapped in the castle by the enemy, and capturing most of Philip's allies and barons. It was a shining light in what was to be a story of lost inheritance and defeat.

his glorious passion can have any doubt of his sanctity. Being told constantly by all the faithful of the great and innumerable miracles worked through his merits, and according due credence to the testimony of many, we do hereby solemnly, before a great Lenten gathering of clergy and laity, canonize the said archbishop and decree him to be inscribed in the catalogue of saints. We therefore advise, and by our authority order, all of you to celebrate solemnly the feat of the said glorious martyr every year on the day of his passion. Given at Segni, 13 March."

Hardly had the letter been read than all those there raised their voices on high to the praise of the martyr and the triumph of his glorious struggle, intoning, 'Praise be to the Lord.'

On the instigation of Louis king of France, the Young King attracted to his side Philip count of Flanders and Matthew his brother, count of Boulogne, winning them over with generous promises. They summoned a large number of armed men by proclamation as soon as possible, in the face of resistance from the Flemish nobles, and invaded Normandy in great splendour. The castle of Aumâle was swiftly taken, to the discredit of several men. They then besieged Drincourt, a castle which was very well fortified and in the hands of a select company of knights. It too was stormed and put under guard. They proceeded from there towards the castle of Arques; the count of Boulogne was mortally wounded by a mercenary on St James's Day, 25 July. Count Philip, who was anxious for a swift return, would then have gone home rejoicing in his victory, had it not been that treachery blackened his success, and his brother's death, which was shortly to take place, renewed uncertainty as to the outcome of the war. So he returned through the county of Eu, which the Young King had entirely in his control.

When King Henry heard that Philip count of Flanders had left Normandy, he immediately collected together as large an army as he could, so that if he met the king of France within the borders of Normandy he could engage him in battle.

On hearing this the king of France, knowing that the king of England was very powerful and

had bitter feelings towards him, like a bear whose cubs have been stolen and who is raging in the forest, decided that the best course of action for his men, and for himself, was flight. Mounting a swift horse, he retreated with all speed into France. The baggage which belonged to the French was left to be plundered by the besieged, and other Normans who had arrived. All the supplies of food which had been brought in for the French army by wagons, carts, or packhorses, were pillaged by the Brabançon mercenaries, on 9 August.

William king of Scotland demanded that Henry II should restore to him the estates in Northumberland which had been a gift to his grandfather King David, confirmed to him in a formal charter, and which King David had in fact occupied for years; but his claim was rejected. So he gathered an army from the large number of Galwegians at his disposal, light-armed, agile men, easily recognized by their bald heads, who carried a knife at their left sides, enough to frighten any soldiers, and who were skilled at hurling spears long distances; they lifted a long lance as a signal as they marched into battle. King William had a safe passage through the estates of Hugh bishop of Durham and began to devastate England, setting fire to towns, seizing vast amounts of plunder, taking women prisoner and tearing children half-alive from their mothers' wombs. To prevent these atrocities, the English nobles took up arms as swiftly as they could and at once forced the king of the Scots to take flight and retreat into Scotland. Following on his trail they destroyed the whole of Lothian by fire; anything found outside city walls fell to the English as plunder. At the request of the king of Scots a truce was made until 13 January [1174] and the English nobles returned in victory.

1174

The Young King, accompanied by Theobald count of Perche, the count of Alençon, and with them about fifty knights, attacked the city of Sées, but even though the citizens had no prince or leader they resisted valiantly, and nothing was achieved.

Henry II, fearing that either the Young King or some other neighbour on the borders would invade his territory and devastate Normandy, entrusted

Normandy to the protection of his closest friends and those who had previously given him loyal support. He himself took only two companions, Alured de Vavaci and Geoffrey Esturmi, as a test of their loyalty to him, and on 30 April entered Maine. The inhabitants flocked to him from all directions and offered him their allegiance in every way, whether against the threat of war, or any other crisis, even at the risk of death.

So he travelled through the country, surrounded by large numbers of soldiers, strengthening their confidence in him and exhorting the local nobles to defend and protect their country. When he reached the border with Anjou, he dismissed everyone, except for the two men named above. The Angevins welcomed the king sooner and in greater numbers than the inhabitants of Maine, for they submitted to all his wishes with more devotion and readiness.

Now that everything had worked out according to plan, Henry II celebrated Whitsun at Poitiers. When he heard that the army of his son Richard was occupying the city of Saintes, he took the inhabitants of Poitiers with him and went quickly to relieve it. His soldiers, showing no reverence for God or the Holy Church, entered the great church with torches and lanterns and immediately turned it into a fortress, filling it with weapons and supplies of food. The king approached the city sooner than the soldiers expected, and was told that it was defended by three fortifications; he concentrated on attacking the city. To begin with he captured the first fortress, which had been built long ago at the entrance to the city. Proceeding from there he attacked the citadel with similar success; it was a larger fortress, but much older than the first one. Finally he reached the great church, which was crammed with armed soldiers, full to bursting with archers and trampled by brothel-keepers. Realizing as he approached that, if a crime was committed against holy religion, everyone would suffer, he approached it nonetheless, not wanting to impugn or violate or contaminate the church, but rather to cleanse it of filth. He dragged from the church those who had violated it, dragged them out because anyone who violates a law invokes it in vain. About sixty knights and about four hundred archers were captured in that stronghold and in the two others.

Aware of what was happening in Flanders, Henry king of England debated returning. He entrusted Aquitaine to six noblemen. On the border between Nantes and Angers he built, at great expense, a fortress called Ancenis, which displays all the knowledge and skill of the carpenter. Anjou, Maine and in particular this castle of Ancenis he entrusted to the protection of Maurice of Craon. On arriving in Normandy he issued an edict at Bonneville, naming all those he had put in charge of the borders and those he had made wardens of his castles.

In front of King Louis and the nobles of the realm, Philip count of Flanders swore, by placing his hands on some sacred relics, that within fifteen days after the coming feast of St John on 24 June, he would invade England with a strong force and make her subject to the control of the Young King. Impressed by this display of loyalty, the Young King went to Wissant on 14 July to send Ralph of La Haie off to England with a large army. The count of Flanders sent three hundred and eighteen men on ahead for the crossing, not, it should be stressed, local men who happened to be available, but experienced soldiers selected from a large number of Flemings. After landing in England in Orwell on 15 May, at a time when their allies were for the most part in danger, they attacked Norwich from there, accompanied by Earl Hugh, and captured it on 18 June, pillaged it, carried off vast sums of money, took away large numbers of prisoners and forced them to pay a steep ransom.

King Henry II's justices, seeing how grave the state of affairs was in England, sent large numbers of messengers across the Channel, but received no certain news that Henry planned to return to England; as a last resort they sent Richard bishop-elect of Winchester to talk with the king, a man they knew for certain was a much closer friend than the others, much keener and more enthusiastic, and who could be relied on to point out to the king all the losses, difficulties and risks his people had endured, and to give an accurate picture of the squabbles of the nobles, the unstable situation in the cities, the clamouring of the people, which would steadily grow worse as they longed for change and would produce movements which would be difficult to repress. So the elect crossed the Channel in haste and found the king at Bonneville, holding a general conference with the Normans on 24 June.

The Normans, learning that the elect of Winchester had arrived and of his reason for coming, said: 'Since the English have sent so many messengers, and now this one, it seems that nothing less than an attack on the Tower of London would call the king back to England.'

The king received this special messenger with due respect, and events showed how much he trusted his words. That very day he discussed the defence of the country's borders and the protection of the castles with his friends, and prepared to return within a few days with his entire household, taking with him Queen Eleanor, Queen Margaret, his son and daughter John and Joanna, and his sons' wives.

He sent the earl of Chester, the countess of Leicester and several others he had taken prisoner on ahead to Barfleur, where there were plenty of ships moored and a huge crowd awaiting the king's arrival. A vast army of Brabançon mercenaries with their weapons and baggage crossed the Channel at Ouistreham. The king sped to the harbour on 8 July, the ships were unmoored and at midday he embarked. As they put out to sea, the waves started to look rough. The wind rose and fell hourly and made the sailors hesitant about the crossing. They put on subdued expressions in front of the king, their faces betraying signs of doubt.

When the king learned that the wind was blowing directly against them, while the ship was taking a direct route to England, and that the strong gusts were steadily growing worse, he lifted his eyes to the sky and said in front of everyone: 'If peace among the clergy and the people is my mission, if the Lord of the heavens has ordained that peace will be restored when I arrive, then in his mercy may he grant me a safe landing. But if He is hostile to me, if He has decided to visit the kingdom with the rod, may it never be my fortune to reach the shores of my country.'

It could be assumed that his prayer was heard, since on the same day as he embarked he was blown

at dusk to Southampton, with everything intact. There he ate a simple meal of bread and water, put off the business of restoring order and avoided meeting the citizens until he had fulfilled the promises made in his prayers by praying at the shrine of the glorious martyr Thomas.

After a short interval he made a hasty journey across England. When he reached Canterbury he leaped off his horse and, putting aside his royal dignity, he assumed the appearance of a pilgrim, a penitent, a suppliant, and on Friday 12 July, went to the cathedral. There, with streaming tears, groans and sighs, he made his way to the glorious martyr's tomb. Prostrating himself with his arms outstretched, he remained there a long time in prayer. During this time, in front of the bishop of London, who was preaching to the people, he protested publicly, calling on God as his witness, that he had neither ordered, nor willed, nor plotted the death of the archbishop. But since the murderers had been incited by his own words, which were not carefully enough considered when he had uttered them, he asked for absolution from the bishops then present, and subjected his flesh to harsh discipline from cuts with rods, receiving three or even five strokes from each of the monks in turn, of whom a large number had gathered.

Rising from his prayers and putting on the clothes he had removed before, he honoured the most esteemed martyr with precious gifts, allotting an annual rent of £40 to provide for lamps to be lit perpetually around the martyr's tomb to venerate it.

He spent the rest of the day and also the whole of the following night in bitterness of soul, given over to prayer and sleeplessness, and continuing his fast for three days. And because a repentant spirit and a contrite and humble heart are the kind of sacrifice most pleasing to God, every time that, in imitation of King David, he called out repeatedly, 'I have sinned against the Lord, I have sinned against the Lord,' he deserved to hear from the prophet the words: 'The Lord also hath put away thy sin.'

There is no doubt that he had by now placated the martyr, and we can safely say that his sin was put away from him. That very sabbath day, when he

The price of repentance

THOMAS Becket was canonized by Pope Alexander III on 1 March, 1172, and two months later the papal legates absolved Henry II of any part he might have played in the archbishop's murder. In return for his absolution Henry made some vague concessions to the Church, and also promised to do public penance and to lead a Crusade to the Holy Land. However, although the king submitted himself to a public flogging before Becket's tomb in 1174 (an astute move politically as he was thereby seen to enlist the saint's help against his rebellious sons) he showed no intention of departing for Palestine. Instead, according to Gerald of Wales, in 1177 he founded three monasteries at minimal cost to himself: Waltham (Augustinian), Amesbury (Fontevraldine) and Witham (Carthusian). However, Gerald continued, the Almighty would not be deceived by such a paltry, shamming effort.

Henry certainly showed good business sense in founding monasteries to supply prayers for his soul: at Waltham and Amesbury he took existing priories, introduced new orders, added to their estates, and took full credit. But this approach to 'founding' was not unusual and contemporaries other than Gerald admired the king for removing nuns known to be scandalously corrupt from Amesbury and replacing them with the austere and cloistered sisters of Fontevrault. (Many people thought that the stricter the order, the more efficacious its prayers.) Gerald also ignored the numerous other monasteries Henry founded. Among these were a second priory for the Carthusians at Le Liget near Loches; several cells for the austere order of Grandmont, two Augustinian priories, one in Dublin dedicated to Becket, and another in Nottinghamshire; and several hospitals, including two for lepers at Angers and Le Mans.

Such largesse was expected of kings and had been taught to Henry by his mother, the Empress Matilda. In the early 1150s she had associated him with several Cistercian foundations which she established, after which he continued making foundations and donations, stepping them up to a far higher level after Becket's death. Despite his methods, Henry II was therefore far more open-handed to the monastic orders than his predecessors or his contemporaries; his generosity to monks makes him one of the most munificent of all the Plantagenet kings.

Above *Small chapel at Le Liget, the Carthusian monastery built by Henry.*

Below *Henry prays for forgiveness at Becket's tomb.*

prayed that Thomas should show mercy to him, God delivered William [the Lion] king of Scots into his hands, surrendered into his custody at Richmond, so that [Merlin's] prophecy was fulfilled which said: 'Between his jaws there will be found a bit which was forged in the bay of Armorica'; meaning by 'the bay of Armorica' the castle of Richmond, for it had been occupied by Breton princes by the law of inheritance now as from ancient times.

In his metrical chronicle, written before 1183 and in French, Jordan Fantosme describes the joyful re-action of Henry II to William the Lion's capture.

Thus they accompanied the king as far as
Westminster.
The Londoners make rejoicings at the coming
of their lord.
They give him presents, they pay him great respect.
But he was pensive and somewhat distracted
On account of the king of Scotland who had
acted madly,
And Roger de Mowbray, a noble warrior,
Who were laying waste his land by night and by day.
But before the right hour came for going to bed,
There came a piece of news from which he gained
great honour.
The king had entered his own chamber
When the messenger came; he had gone through
much fatigue:
He had neither drunk nor eaten for three days
of the week,
Nor slept a wink on account of the certain news,
But by day and night fatigues himself with
journeying.
He has acted very wisely, he will have a good gift.
The king was leaning on his elbow and slept a little,
A servant at his feet was gently rubbing them;
There was neither noise nor cry, nor any who were
speaking there,
Neither harp nor viols nor anything was sounding
at that hour,
When the messenger came to the door and gently
called.
And says the chamberlain: 'Who are you there?'
'I am a messenger, friend; now come more this way.
'Lord Ranulf Glanville sent me here
'In order to speak with the king, for great need
he has of it.'

And says the chamberlain: 'Let the business be
till the morning.'
'By my faith!' said the messenger, 'but I will
speak to him forthwith.
'My lord has in his heart sorrow and vexation:
'So let me enter, good chamberlain.'
And says the chamberlain: 'I should not dare
to do it.
'The king is asleep: you must withdraw.'
Whilst they are speaking the king has awaked,
And he hears a crying at that door: 'Open! open!'
'Who is that,' said the king, 'can you tell me?'
'Sire,' said the chamberlain, 'you shall know
directly.
'It is a messenger from the north, very well
you know him.
'A man of Ranulf Glanville's: his name
is Brien.'
'By my faith!' said the king, 'now am I very uneasy:
'He is in need of aid, let him come in here.'
The messenger, who was very well bred, entered,
And saluted the king, as you may shortly hear:
'Sire king, may God who dwells in
Trinity save you,
'Your person first and then all your
intimate friends!'
'Brien,' said the king, 'what news do you bring?
'Has the king of Scotland entered Richmond?
'Has Newcastle-upon-Tyne been seized, and the
fortifications?
'Odinel of Umfravile been taken or driven away,
'And all my barons ousted from their estates?
'Messenger, by thy faith! tell me the truth.
'Badly have they served me, so now may they be
punished for it.'
'Sire,' so said the messenger, 'hear me a little.
'Your barons of the north are right good people.
'On behalf of my lord kindly listen to me,
'He sends to you by me salutation and friendship,
'And my lady much more, with whom you are
well acquainted,
'He sends you word by me, that you would do
wrong to torment yourself.
'The king of Scotland is taken and all his barons.'
And says King Henry: 'Do you speak the truth?'
'Yes, sire, truly, in the morning you will know it:
'The archbishop of York a wise, learned man,
'Will send you two private messengers;
'But I started first, who know the truth.

'I have hardly slept during the last four days,
'Neither eaten nor drunk, so I am very hungry:
'But, in your kindness, give me a reward for it.'
And the king replied: 'You would be wrong to
doubt it.
'If you have told me the truth, you are
rich enough.
'Is the king of Scotland taken? Tell me the truth.'
'Yes, sire, by my faith! On a cross may
I be crucified,
'Or hanged by a rope, or burnt on a great pile,
'If tomorrow, before noon, all be not confirmed.'
'Then,' says King Henry, 'God be thanked for it,
'And Saint Thomas the Martyr and all the
saints of God!'
Thereupon the messenger went to his hostel,
He has abundance to eat and to drink,
And the king is so merry and joyful that night
That he went up to the knights and
awoke them all:
'Barons, wake up. It has been a good night for you.
'Such a thing I have heard as will make you glad:
'The king of Scotland is taken, so it has been
told me for truth.
'Just now the news came to me, when I ought to
have been in bed.'
And the knights say: 'Now thank the Lord God;
'Now is the war ended, and your kingdom
in peace.'
This night seemed very fine to King Henry.
Next day, before noon, the news again
reached him
From the archbishop of York, whom they
call Roger,
Who salutes his lord and who cares for the loyal.
When the king saw the messengers, never was
he more delighted,
And perceives that they say the same thing, so he
answered them:
'Last night I heard the news when I was
very irritable;
'To him who brought it to me a reward
shall be given.'
He took a little stick, to Brien he gave it.
Ten librates of his land for the trouble which
he has had.

*We now return to Diceto's account of Henry II's
campaigns against his enemies.*

Now that the promises made in his prayers had
been fulfilled with such devotion, the old king
returned and stayed a short time in London,
discovering that the English nobles had come to
meet him there. He set off in force and arrived at
Huntingdon capturing the castle, which had been
under siege since 8 May, on the following day.

The Northumbrian nobles, with the king's son,
the bishop-elect of Lincoln, as their leader, took
Kirkby Malzeard, the castle of Roger Mowbray, by
force. When the king had gathered a large army at
Bury St. Edmund's, with a host of soldiers flocking
from all directions, he ordered them, on general
advice, to besiege the two castles of Hugh Bigod earl
of Norfolk, Framlingham and Bungay. The earl,
who had fifty knights and a sizeable army, but was
nevertheless greatly inferior in strength and despaired
of anyone coming to his aid, was compelled out of
necessity to offer hostages and pay thousands of
marks to win peace from the king; on 26 July he did
homage to the king, swore loyalty, and renewed his
allegiance to him.

The army of Flemings which Count Philip had
arranged to send on ahead of him before he came to
England, giving his solemn promise to the French
king by putting his hands on some holy relics, swore
an oath never again to invade England with hostile
force, and went back to their own country with
Henry's permission. The Young King's army, under
the leadership of Ralph of La Haie, departed freely
with their weapons and equipment. Thus, at a
critical moment, through the intercession of St.
Thomas the Martyr, the old king, who now had
control throughout his kingdom, was able to embark
on 7 August at Porchester, with the king of Scots in
tow. On 11 August, after a prosperous voyage, he
arrived at Rouen, which he found under siege.

King Louis of France, the Young King and Philip
count of Flanders collected forces from every region
and amassed a huge army. Leaving the Seine on
their left they besieged Rouen on 22 July, hoping
that, if they took Rouen, this would remove the stain
of ignominy which the breaking of an oath at the
French siege of Verneuil and the act of treachery
which was known to have played a part at the siege
of Drincourt by the Flemings had caused. The

Normans, of whom there were now few compared with the host which had arrived, resisted valiantly. Relying on the defences of the walls and using square stones, sharp stakes or long pieces of wood, they forced the enemy, who were attacking the outer walls in formation using siege engines, into head-long flight. But so that those who were under siege should have no respite, and so that they could put their own strength to the test with more energy and precision, the Flemings and the French alternated in the attack; as the French grew weary, the Flemings would stir themselves into action, using all their strength to undermine the walls. The Normans remained unperturbed by the enemy's threats or by any incursion, confidently expecting to win; they survived frequent attacks and bitter encounters resolutely. Their number rose daily, and their food supplies were plentiful. On the other side, there were many people who deserted the army every day because they were in danger of starvation.

This critical situation persisted for many days until the French king received reliable reports that the king of England had approached Rouen in force and was reduced to a state of utter bewilderment, for he was afraid that, as spreading rumours suggested, the king would invade France and lay siege to Paris. He discussed with his councillors the best method of stopping the siege without harm to themselves. After a general resolution had been taken, both the French and the Flemings burned their engines, tore down their tents, set fire to their huts and other makeshift buildings, and, on 14 August, despite the fact that the rumours had died down, retreated from the city, putting off for the time being all their threats, boasts and vows to destroy Rouen, which they had made so often and so rashly. People from the border country attacked the furthest part of the fortification and hastily plundered large numbers of weapons as well as equipment.

The French, worried at the expense, and the Flemish, fearing for their lives, got together to discuss the damage inflicted on them. And as they both saw that they were wasting their efforts they decided to stop attacking the Normans and withdraw from the frontiers. Looking out for their

Allies in heaven

THE intense devotion given to the legion of Christian saints in the Middle Ages can only be explained in terms of a society which preferred to put its trust not in forms of government, nor even in princes, but in a select band of holy men and women who could intervene on its behalf with God himself.

Christ's own immediate disciples, and increasingly his mother, the Virgin Mary, were regarded by the 12th-century Church as the most powerful of all saintly intercessors. However, the increasing popularity of shrines and statues of Our Lady did nothing to lessen popular enthusiasm for a host of local saints, whose spiritual influence was often thought to be all the greater if he or she was closely associated with one particular place or region. The body, or *corsaint*, of St Cuthbert at Durham Cathedral priory continued to be the most popular relic the north of England, even when its miracle-working powers had been eclipsed by those of St Thomas Becket after his martyrdom at Canterbury in 1170.

It was important to Becket's unparalleled position as England's leading saint that not only did he gain a large popular following immediately after his death, but that Pope Alexander III canonized him so soon, and at a time when most people in western Europe finally accepted the papal claim that no one should be venerated as a saint without the authority of the Roman Church. From then on, it was harder to become a duly canonized saint, although popular respect for saints already in being did not diminish.

Right *Reliquaries were vitally important assets of a house of worship. Abbeys and churches vied with each other to acquire bones, fragments of cloth, parts of a saint's body or any personal possessions that might be a focus for prayer, and even work miracles. Well-known saints were given jewelled and marble reliquaries while lesser saints were often honoured with simpler reliquaries, carved, like this one in Cunault church, out of local stone and wood.*

own peace and quiet, they did all they could to heal the breach between the king of England and his sons. You may say the sons have incurred their father's curse, the hatred of the clergy and the imprecations of the people, but still they should be forgiven because of their youth.

The archbishop-elect of Canterbury set out for Rome, intending to avoid the ambushes of the schismatics. At this time the whole world was terrified by an infection deriving from a cloudy corruption of the air, causing a general coughing, a catarrh of the stomach, which was dangerous to all and led to many deaths. He arrived in Rome, and crossing beyond its boundaries, went to find Pope Alexander, who was then living at Anagni. There at the court he found agents of the Young King opposing him, doing all they could to black the characters of the bishops-elect. Finally the question of whose assent to the elections and subsequent proceedings was to be preferred, the elder or the younger king's, was raised at length and discussed in consistory and, as it appeared, fairly settled. Then, since a long tract had been put out concerning his birth, a number of wise men, of whom there were many on the archbishop's side, swore on the gospels that neither before nor during the election had they heard other than that he was conceived and born in legitimate wedlock. After this, on 2 April his election was confirmed.

The archbishop returned to London and was honourably received by a crowd of the barons of England who had gathered there on 3 September. But because unhappiness is often mixed with joy, just as he happily completed his journey, the cathedral at Canterbury, alas, was destroyed by fire on 5 September.

The principal dignitaries of vacant churches were called together to elect bishops for themselves. And since the Young King's agents had told the pope a lot of things about the bishop-elect of Ely whereby his reputation might be damaged among good men, in a ceremony in St Catherine's chapel at Westminster he swore his innocence of the death of Archbishop Thomas, that neither by word nor deed had he knowingly procured it, and also that after his ordination he had not slept with any woman.

The elder King Henry always rejected tyranny with his heart and soul, and considered it a duty of his royal majesty to call his subjects away from running about the country plundering the poor, harming widows and orphans, raping virgins and especially from shedding blood. Furthermore, he knew that the unusual humility of the French and Flemings and their desire to make peace between himself and his sons proceeded from their inability to resist him. He would have avoided the French even when bearing gifts, had he not thus been inveigled into any sort of humiliation and alliance with enemies of this kind, through foreseeing the possibility of recalling his sons, whom almost everyone thought had gone seriously astray, to the fruits of a better life — his sons whom he loved so much, whom he had made lords of so many nations, whom he had unceasingly tried to raise to the heights of honour, so as to curb the peoples and rule them wisely to the terror of tyrants and the extermination of his foes.

Since his enemies were speaking words of peace, and wanting to confer with him, he went to meet them on 11 October between Tours and Amboise. What emerged is revealed in the following document:

"The king of the English to all his faithful subjects, greeting.
Know that by the grace of God I have made peace with the French king, my sons and my men, for God's honour and mine. It is agreed that I shall give my eldest son Henry fifteen thousand pounds Angevin money per annum, and two castles in Normandy at my pleasure. To Richard I shall give half the revenues of Poitou, and two castles from which he cannot harm me. To Geoffrey, half the revenues of Brittany. All my men who left me have returned to my homage and allegiance, in my sons' presence and by their command, and have sworn fealty against all men. They shall have the lands they had when they left me. The king of Scotland and the earls of Leicester and Chester and others who have made agreements with me or who have given hostages before this peace are at my mercy and outside this agreement with my sons. Those men I have captured, who neither gave hostages nor made any agreement, shall be freed against good security

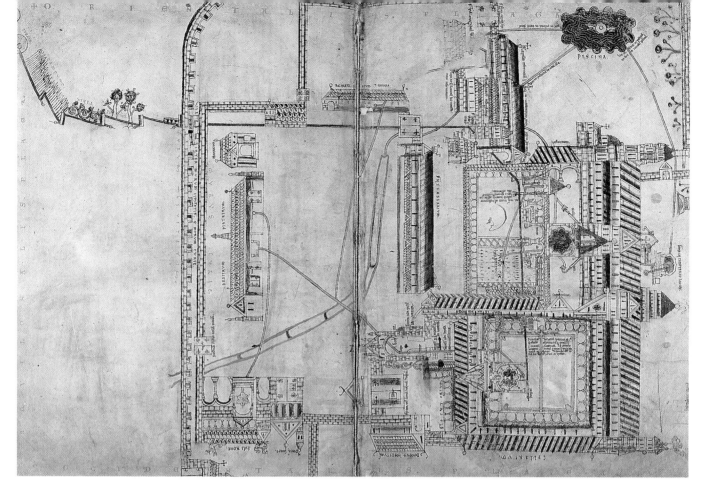

Becket's shrine

THERE was more than a hint of arson when the choir of Canterbury Cathedral burnt down in September 1174. Bitter arguments had been raging over whether a new one should be built to house the shrine containing the precious relics of St. Thomas Becket and these were decisively settled by the fire. Rebuilding took ten years, and Gervase, a monk at the cathedral priory, wrote a full account of how it was done, describing the way in which a great Gothic cathedral was built.

Normally the first step was to raise funds, usually from other ecclesiastical establishments. Canterbury was lucky in that this was not immediately necessary. It was a wealthy see, and the pilgrimage to Becket's tomb had already brought in enormous riches. Even so, work had to be suspended during 1183 while the treasury was refilled.

The next step was to appoint an architect. Several candidates, from both England and France, were invited to Canterbury to discuss their ideas with the monks. A Frenchman, William of Sens, rapidly emerged as the clear victor.

William retained the aisle walls of the previous choir, but otherwise built anew. In 1178, he was directing the vaulting of the eastern crossing when he plunged some 50 feet from the primitive medieval scaffolding. Miraculously, he survived. Although he tried to carry on directing the work from his sickbed, ill-health soon forced him to return to France, leaving the choir in the capable hands of

Above This remarkable plan for Canterbury Cathedral in c.1160 shows the vineyard and orchard which were considered necessary for the maintenance of the monastery.

Overleaf The cathedral and cloisters today, and inside the cathedral, looking from the choir towards the west end.

another William, an Englishman, who finished the eastern transepts, extended the crypt, and built the Trinity Chapel and corona.

The floor of Canterbury's Trinity Chapel was unusually high to allow the entire congregation to see the shrine, and a broad ambulatory surrounded the chapel's marble piers so that pilgrims could be conducted round the shrine and past the corona, where the scalp of the sainted archbishop was displayed. These arrangements were important: the easier the pilgrims' access to the shrine, the greater their numbers and the greater the gifts of gold and jewels they brought with them.

The shrine was not finished and placed in the Trinity Chapel until 1220 – mainly because of bitter quarrels between King John and Stephen Langton, archbishop of Canterbury – and the saint's body lay in the old Romanesque crypt, where it had been hastily buried, beneath a provisional shrine. It had already attracted magnificent gifts, including the famous Regale of France, an enormous ruby, given by Louis VII on his visit to Canterbury in 1179.

137

at my sons' request. All the castles I or my men had in all my lands at the start of the war have been returned to me, and those that have been fortified against me shall be returned to the state they were in when the war began."

In defeating his enemies the Lord had put into the elder king's hands nine hundred and sixty-nine knights whom he did not compel to ransom themselves for money; in fact he released the conquered from their chains if they gave hostages, or just their word. There were a few kept in close custody whose enormous outrages and hateful perfidy would have driven the most merciful prince to anger and thoughts of punishment.

The younger king on the other hand released only those whom he or his allies had captured, or intercepted by the law of war or other means, for money. They numbered a little over a hundred.

On 4 November, at about midnight, for the space of an hour and more the whole of the northern sky was observed to be a bloody red colour.

William king of Scots, held in chains in Normandy, had the consolation of being visited by a large crowd of his subjects; the bishops, abbots, earls and barons of his kingdom made peace with the English king at Valognes on 8 December.

The king of Scots did homage to Henry II and bound his heirs to do the same. He also promised that the Scottish Church would be subject to the English Church, and that the Scots would not harbour fugitives hostile to England. As a final sign of submission he handed over Roxburgh and Berwick castles to Henry II's men.

Geoffrey Plantagenet, Henry II's father, count of Anjou, as a result of a not altogether legitimate affair with a certain lady from Le Mans, had a daughter called Emma; David prince of North Wales, understanding her to be King Henry's sister, asked for her as his wife and only just obtained her by urgent pleading. He wanted to give the pride of descent from a royal house to his descendants, if he should have sons, and to strike terror into the other Welsh because of his new relations.

1175

William king of Scotland, having left hostages in Normandy, came back to England on 11 December [1174] and was kept in fairly free custody until the castles mentioned in the agreement should be handed over to the king of England's safekeeping as had been agreed.

Everywhere in England and Normandy the castles of those whom the king thought had oppressed the poor during the long conflict with his son were demolished.

So that the king of England's sons, whom the counsel of wicked men had turned away from their father, might return to favour and their old familiarity they decided to remove all suspicion by doing homage and allegiance to their father. The younger sons, Richard and Geoffrey, did so first at Le Mans, and later the younger king at Bur on 1 April.

The two kings of England, whom the previous year the kingdom had not been big enough to contain, came together and crossed to England in a single boat on 9 May. They ate together at the normal meal times on the same table, and rested their limbs in the same bedroom. The egregious martyr Thomas entertained them both equally on their pilgrimage to Canterbury, on 28 May. He entertained them in the same way, except that the elder king stayed up on all-night vigils, with prayer, fasting and scourging lasting into the third day.

Philip count of Flanders, it is said, caught Walter of Fontaines in adultery with his wife Countess Isabel; he had him clubbed to death, on 2 August, and hastened to have his body hung upside down on a lavatory seat, with its feet tied together, from hurriedly prepared gallows; and so that no cruelty should be missing and his rage against the dead man be complete, he ordered him to be publicly exposed to the gaze of all.

John dean of Salisbury was called to the episcopate at Eynsham on 26 November, receiving the rule of the church of East Anglia with the agreement of the people from Norwich, the king's assent, the archbishop's connivance and with the cardinal's

Wales on Wales

An able and highly educated man with an inquiring mind and a talent for lively observation, Gerald of Wales was at his best when writing about his beloved native land.

Born c.1145 at Manorbier near Pembroke, his father was a Norman knight and his mother the grand-daughter of a Welsh prince. He was appointed archdeacon of Brecon at the age of 28, but the bishopric of St. David's, which he long coveted, never became his. In these extracts from his Description of Wales, *written in about 1191, he brings his countrymen to life with his acute and affectionate descriptions.*

Welsh characteristics

The Welsh people are light and agile. They are fierce rather than strong, and totally dedicated to the practice of arms. Not only the leaders but the entire nation are trained in war. Sound the trumpet for battle and the peasant will rush from his plough to pick up his weapons as quickly as the courtier from the court.

They plough the soil once in March and April for oats, a second time in summer, and then they turn it a third time while the grain is being threshed. In this way the whole population lives almost entirely on oats and the produce of their herds: milk, cheese and butter. They eat plenty of meat, but little bread. They pay no attention to commerce, shipping or industry, and their only preoccupation is military training. They are passionately devoted to their freedom and to the defence of their country: for these they fight, for these they suffer hardships, for these they will take up their weapons and willingly sacrifice their lives . . .

The Welsh are given neither to gluttony nor to drunkenness. They spend little on food or clothes. Their sole interest in life consists of caring for their horses and keeping their weapons in good order, their sole preoccupation the defence of their country and the seizing of booty. From morning to evening they eat nothing. In the evening they eat a modest meal. If food is short or if they have none at all, they wait patiently for the next evening. They spend the dark and stormy nights in observing the movements of their enemies.

Hospitality – a way of life

In Wales no one begs. Everyone's home is open to all, for the Welsh generosity and hospitality are the greatest of all virtues. They very much enjoy welcoming others to their homes. When you travel there is no question of your asking for accommodation or of their offering it: you just march into a house and hand over your weapons to the person in charge. They give you water so that you may wash your feet and that means that you are a guest. With these people the offering of water in which to wash one's feet is an invitation to stay.

Guests who arrive early in the day are entertained until nightfall by girls who play to them on the harp . . .

When night falls and no more guests are expected, the evening meal is prepared, varying according to what the house has to offer, and to the number and importance of the men who have come. You must not expect a variety of dishes from a Welsh kitchen, and there are no highly seasoned titbits to whet your appetite. In a Welsh house there are no tables, no tablecloths and no napkins. Everyone behaves quite naturally, with no attempt whatsoever at etiquette. You sit down in threes, not in pairs as elsewhere, and they put the food in front of you, all together, on a single large trencher containing enough for three, resting on rushes and green grass.

Alongside one of the walls is placed a communal bed, stuffed with rushes, and not all that many of them. For sole covering there is a stiff harsh sheet, made locally and called in Welsh a *brychan*. They all go to bed together. They keep on the same clothes which they have worn all day, a thin cloak and a tunic, which is all they have to keep the cold out. A fire is kept burning all night at their feet, just as it has done all day, and they get some warmth from the people sleeping next to them. When their underneath side begins to ache through the hardness of the bed and their uppermost side is frozen stiff with cold, they get up and sit by the fire, which soon warms them up and soothes away their aches and pains. Then they go back to bed again, turning over on their other side if they feel like it, so that a different part is frozen and another side bruised by the hard bed.

Music and singing

The Welsh are very sharp and intelligent. When they apply their minds to anything, they are quick to make progress, for they have great natural ability. They are quicker-witted and more shrewd than any other Western people.

When they play their instruments they charm and delight the ear with the sweetness of their music. They play quickly and in subtle harmony. Their fingering is so rapid that they produce this harmony out of discord. The Welsh play three instruments, the harp, the pipe and the crwth [a stringed instrument] . . .

When they come together to make music, the Welsh sing their traditional songs, not in unison, as is done elsewhere, but in parts, in many modes and modulations. When a choir gathers to sing, which happens often in this country, you will hear as many different parts and voices as there are performers, all joining together in the end to produce a single organic harmony and melody in the soft sweetness of B flat.

authority; he was consecrated by the archbishop of Canterbury at Lambeth on 14 December.

The king, turning his fatherly gaze to the needs of his sons, paid the younger king's onerous debts. Whatever the elder king's ministers had taken for the younger king's use in the way of food and drink throughout Normandy, Maine and Anjou during the previous three years was reckoned up. When the king's treasurers had paid in full for everything, the creditors were sent away.

1176

The king, with the advice of his son and the consent of his bishops, earls, barons, knights and other men who were present, appointed justices, three for each of six areas of the kingdom, who swore to give justice to everyone. This was done on 26 January at Northampton.

On the orders of Cardinal Hugh Pierleoni the clergy of all England were assembled at London on 14 March. The archbishop of York rose up against the archibishop of Canterbury, claiming that Pope Gregory the Great's words 'Let there be between the bishops of London and York distinction of honour according to seniority of ordination' should be applied to Canterbury and York. He kept on saying that, because he had been ordained first, he should sit on the cardinal's right hand. The archbishop of Canterbury on the other hand said that his church was of such dignity and seniority that in line with the statutes of the fathers, royal charters and papal privileges it had always rightly claimed for itself the primacy of all England.

With the two archbishops at loggerheads in this way, the following Thursday the cardinal set up his chair in St. Catherine's chapel at Westminster. The archbishop of Canterbury arrived, assisted by the bishop of Ely. Hardly had he sat down on the cardinal's right hand when, with fights breaking out all around, the tumult growing worse, the clamour rising and threats worsening, some people were beaten and the cardinal left very quickly. The archbishop of York in person was assaulted, he said, and in the presence of the king and the cardinal blamed his injuries and torn clothing on the bishop of Ely.

The struggle for primacy

ONE of the unusual features of the Church in England is that it has always had only two archbishops, ever since St. Augustine, the first archbishop of Canterbury from 601, began the work of converting England to Christianity.

After the Norman Conquest, when the Church was more centrally governed than before, it became positively embarrassing that neither the archbishop of Canterbury nor the archbishop of York would give precedence to each other. As early as 1071 the vigorous Lanfranc of Canterbury had tried to establish his ascendancy by obtaining a papal judgement that he and his successors should consecrate the archbishops of York and receive oaths of obedience from them. However, in 1118, Archbishop Thurstan of York refused to submit, inaugurating a long and bitter battle between the two cathedral churches. Some of the documents the Canterbury clergy produced in favour of their case were such blatant forgeries they made papal officials 'smile, turn up their noses and laugh aloud'.

In the reign of Henry II the controversy became more acute, above all when the king's savage conflict with Thomas Becket led him to favour the latter's counterpart at York, Roger of Pont l'Evêque. Archbishop Roger actually crowned the heir to the English throne, the young Henry, at Westminster Abbey on 14 June 1170, 'against the desire and opinion of almost everyone in the kingdom'. This direct challenge to a traditional prerogative of the archbishops of Canterbury did more than anything else to force Becket out of his self-imposed exile in France and bring him home to martyrdom in Canterbury cathedral at the end of the year.

However, this was one dispute which even Becket's murder could not resolve; six years later (in 1176) there was a violent brawl when the partisans of Archbishop Roger tried to eject the archbishop of Canterbury by force from his seat at the right hand of a visiting papal legate. Only in the 14th century was this long-running and at times hilarious controversy brought to a compromise solution, whereby the archbishop of Canterbury gained precedence as 'Primate of all England' and the archbishop of York had to be satisfied with the title of 'Primate of England'.

Top right *Canterbury Cathedral, still a place of pilgrimage for many admirers of Thomas Becket, and the setting for T. S. Eliot's* Murder in the Cathedral.

Right *York Cathedral, one of the great attractions of northern England.*

On this account there were appeals from both sides. The council was abandoned. The cardinal made a speech to the clergy and people in the cloister court at Westminster and he requested leave to withdraw. But afterwards, soothed by the pleas of the king, he acquiesced in the wishes of the bishops.

"Pope Alexander.
Desiring to preserve entire the dignity of the church of York, and following in the footsteps of our predecessors of happy memory the pontiffs Calixtus, Honorius, Innocent and Eugenius, by apostolic authority we prohibit the archbishop of Canterbury from exacting any profession from York, and the archbishop of York from making any; neither should York be in any way subject to Canterbury, as was prohibited by St Gregory, but instead that distinction of honour should be preserved between them which was constituted by that father, so that what takes place should be what was ordered earlier."

The country on the borders of Anjou and Maine was suffering from lack of bread, and Henry II found sufficient food for ten thousand people every day from 1 April until there was enough of the new grain. Whatever had been reserved in England for the king's use, whether in barns, wine cellars or storehouses, was all given out on the royal command to our pious colleagues and to the poor.

Vulgrin count of Angoulême gathered together a gang of wicked Brabançons and dared to invade Poitou. John bishop of Poitiers on the other hand summoned troops from all sides and collecting many mercenaries joined together with Theobald Chabot, the leader of the knights of Richard duke of Aquitaine – who was then in England with the king his father – to rescue the people entrusted to his care from the clutches of their enemies. Ordered in three divisions, they met these evil destroyers of castles, depopulators of fields, burners of churches and oppressors of nuns in the vicinity of Barbezieux. A lot of them were killed in the fields, and not a few shut up in a fortress were burnt. The rest deciding on flight they left their equipment as booty. So the Poitevins, protected not so much by swords and helmets as by divine favour, penetrated the squadrons of their

Sexual politics

ANECDOTES told by 12th-century chroniclers and moralists illustrate the reality, then as now, of eroticism, sexual jealousy and romantic love, and show there was a ready audience for a spicy story. We know, too, that in their daily lives people were bounded by the conventional ideas of Christian marriage; and we must suppose that ordinary human passions played their part. But despite these clues, the relationship between the sexes in the 12th century remains shadowy and elusive, with little indication of how men and women thought about each other.

The subjection of women – ideally, subordinate in society and submissive in the home – was fundamental to the medieval interpretation of Christian ethics, and was largely reflected in law and custom. On marriage, at or before 14, women gave up their rights to their husbands who, at least in theory, had almost absolute power over their wives and their properties. Their betrothal often required them to go to strange courts, far from home, perhaps to be returned to their fathers when a better match presented itself. Depending on a woman's social status, her marriage was in the gift of her father, or of her lord or the king; in a society acutely conscious of family position and ambitions, the marriage of a daughter or ward was too important to be left to chance or personal choice.

Characteristically, these restrictions were accompanied by the habit of blaming women for departures from the sexual code. Female virginity was highly prized, and its loss outside marriage brought disgrace – but only on the woman. If virtue was the virtue of the Mother of God, the responsibility for sin rested with the daughters of Eve, and the Church identified women as the source of human lechery. In the king's courts a sexually experienced woman was not allowed to bring an accusation of rape. In the manor courts, even when both partners were known, only the woman was fined for fornication or the pregnancy which would devalue her as a marriageable asset.

Yet many women were far from being meek and submissive chattels. Henry II's mother, Matilda, and his wife, Eleanor, were formidable and ambitious, with evident capacity and opportunity for political power; Nicola de la Haye became constable of Lincoln castle and sheriff of Lincolnshire. Such examples were not confined to the nobility and royalty. Throughout the social spectrum, capable women did the jobs of capable men while those men were away in the fields or on Crusade, and must have received a measure of trust and respect for doing so.

With marriage a matter of dynastic economics, female sexuality both exploited and closely circumscribed and

childbirth a very real hazard, the apparent room for tenderness between the sexes was limited. Yet paradoxically it was in this society that the romantic notions of courtly love and devotion flourished; the Arthurian myths, fostered at the court of Eleanor of Aquitaine, are an example. In the circles of the élite, therefore, fantasy often conflicted with reality.

Top Pope Gregory IX celebrating a marriage. The ring was a sign of the bride's unavailability to all other men.

Above Adulterers made to walk naked through a town. In spite of punishments such as this, many men openly supported and acknowledged mistresses and illegitimate children.

145

enemies unharmed, losing only four of their number. Thus safety came from the hands of priests, which showed them to be lacking not in spirit but in arms.

At the king's summons the Young King, who was busy abroad, and the prelates of the Church and barons of the kingdom came together at London. Ambassadors sent with a great train by William king of Sicily to ask for the hand of Joanna the king's daughter in marriage were answered, after deliberation, on 20 May. The mention and promise of a future marriage were turned, with oaths on each king's soul, into a definite wedding. In order to bring about the alliance with the king of Sicily effectively and enter more closely and solemnly into it, the king of England sent ambassadors to Sicily who, after settling what gifts were to be made on account of the marriage, hurried back. This was done in the presence of the cardinal, with the assent of the archbishops and bishops, and strengthened by the consent of the nobles.

Joanna, Henry II's youngest daughter, sailed on 27 August to marry the king of Sicily; the bishop of Winchester provided the expenses and provisions needed for the journey, together with a large number of servants. On the king's orders, honourable men were assigned as escort, some to go as far as St Gilles, some to climb the mountains of Sicily and go up to the palace of Palermo; they were not to contemplate returning until they had witnessed the marriage ceremony and had seen the king of Sicily and Joanna crowned in wedlock.

Once the king of Sicily's ambassadors had braved the rough seas, the king of England's daughter was assigned to the king before a company of nobles at the church of St Gilles on 9 November by John bishop of Norwich, as he had promised at Palermo on 23 August.

John bishop of Norwich set sail for Sicily on the king's orders in dangerous weather conditions, and endured many different discomforts. While he should have headed straight for Rome had the Lombards not still been involved in the schism, the southern region, through which it was still possible for him to pass, was gravely affected by famine. They could scarcely afford fodder for beasts. On his

Working the land

THE threat of famine was always present in the Middle Ages. Farming was done almost entirely by hand – the only major labour-saving device was the water- (and later the wind-) mill to grind corn – and the slow harvesting of crops could be disastrously interrupted by bad weather.

Crops included cereals like wheat, barley and oats and vegetables such as peas, beans, leeks and onions. But yields were abysmally low compared to today: a figure of three to four bushels of wheat harvested to one sown was normal. Agricultural technology was basic. Ploughshares were tipped with iron to turn heavy soil and ploughs were guided by hand. A large plough was often attached to a wheeled carriage and pulled by as many as eight oxen or horses, although small ones could be pulled by just one animal – a donkey perhaps. Scattering seed by hand was wasteful, and reaping, which relied on scythes and sickles, was exceptionally labour-intensive. Manure, the main fertilizer, was generally in short supply. Pasturing animals on land left fallow for a season could help to increase the soil's productivity, but peasants' flocks were usually too small to supply enough dung.

Throughout the 12th century, therefore, poorer and poorer land was brought into cultivation to feed western Europe's growing population. Inevitably, the margin of risk narrowed and agriculture teetered constantly on the brink of catastrophe.

Above *Two men, one with a hoe and the other using a spade.*

Left *A farmworker carries his rake and fork.*

Below, left to right *Cultivating the ground; harvesting grain; picking fruit. There were few farm implements during the 12th century and yields were low compared to the 20th century; unsurprisingly, the threat of famine was always present.*

journey through Auvergne the bishop was tortured by the cries of people lying in the streets, swollen with hunger. He was still in good health when he entered the city of Valence, but questioned the honesty of his hosts. Their beds were infested with fleas, which caused sleepless nights. The bishop passed by the territory of Embrun, avoided the region of Mont Genèvre and reached the Italian border; then he set sail on the Tyrrhenian Sea.

From then on, because of the diversity of the terrain, he invested in a variety of ships, fast and light, relying on rowing-boats rather than sailing-ships. He passed the duchy of Apulia, the principate of Capua and the promontories of Calabria after some delay, observing the cities of Reggio and Messina at close quarters on either side of the straits. I shall not omit to mention those hazards known also to the men who sailed to Italy after the fall of Troy: the bishop avoided the cape of Palinurus, the rocks of Scylla and the whirlpool of Charybdis with some trepidation. For it was not only momentarily that he meditated on the fact that the depths of the sea can be churned up in an instant. So the voyage was doomed by lack of rest and persistent anxiety. The threat of pirate attacks would have frightened even the most resolute sailor. Seasickness was brought on by the squalid conditions in which the rowers lived; their vital organs were affected by the unhealthy air. One can imagine the sort of dangers that beset people abroad (among all their other troubles) when in Sicily the leaves on the trees, the shoots on the vine and the reeds in the marshes were all withered by drought, as it was then the middle of August. When they put in to land at dusk, their skiffs, scarcely large enough to hold eight people, were washed up by the waves. Desperate as they were to restore their strength, they slept reluctantly under the open sky for many weeks. At night they made do with hard stones instead of soft bedstraw, or sometimes the tide gave them the use of the sand, and mistress necessity taught them to strew their beds on the gravel.

After many days spent in this sort of comfort, the bishop entered Palermo, was united with three of his fellow ambassadors, and within a few days received a favourable response from the Sicilian king. Had he had time he should have asked whether Sicily was

called Trinacria because of its three mountain peaks, or because of its triangular shape, but he was spending a somewhat irregular autumn. Two of the companions mentioned above lost their lives in an accident. The third was struck down by a serious fever and confined to a sickbed. So it was alone that the bishop returned to England, after a successful mission, concluding with the marriage of the princess to the Sicilian king; he found the king at Nottingham on Christmas Eve.

1177

The city of Palermo was resplendent with the marriage celebrations of the king of Sicily and the king of England's daughter. Archbishops and bishops, counts and barons, clergy and people, flocked at once to solemnize the marriage and crowning of the new queen, and Walter archbishop of Palermo performing the marriage ceremony on 13 February.

After organizing his kingdom according to his will, King Henry went to France on 18 August.

"I, Louis king of France, and I, Henry king of England, wish everyone to know that we have solemnly promised, inspired by God, to take up the cross and go to Jerusalem. We wish also that everyone may know that we are, and from now on always wish to be friends, and that each of us is willing to save the life, limbs and worldly honour of the other against all men to the best of his power. If anyone tries to do harm to either of us, I Henry will swear to protect Louis king of France, my lord, against all men to the best of my power, and I Louis swear to protect Henry king of England against all men to the best of my power, as he is my man and my ally, saving the faith which we owe to our men as long as they are loyal to us. This was enacted at Nonancourt on 25 September."

Saladin, a brutal persecutor of the name of Christianity, subdued Egypt and Syria, and seized Babylon and Damascus by force. When the count of Flanders and Earl William de Mandeville had collected a large force from the inhabitants of Jerusalem to harass the 'Agarenes' on the border with Antioch, they laid siege to Hareng on 4

nozarii Greci   ʃ Noͭ ʃaraceni   ʃ neͭ latini   Bigamꝰ nocte ʃcribes tancred.

Language: a link and a barrier

Above *The Sicilian court in the 1190s,
with different scribes working a
manuscript in Greek, Latin and Arabic.*

NORMAN French became the language of the
English court and nobility after the Conquest in
1066, and remained so for several centuries. By the late
12th century, many town and city dwellers were bilingual,
as were the lesser knights, many of whom, although born
into French-speaking families, were cared for by English-
speaking wet nurses. Most of the peasants, however,
spoke only English.

The ruling classes were able to communicate across
frontiers with other French-dominated regions, including
Outremer – the Crusader states in Palestine – and Sicily.
When Joanna, daughter of Henry II and Eleanor, married
the king of Sicily, she was not so isolated as other noble
wives, who had to adapt to foreign environments while
unable to speak the language of their new country.

In the *Song of Roland*, the French converse with
impossible fluency with their Saracen enemies. In reality,
armies of local interpreters were employed in the Holy
Land, as they were in England in 1066. Duke William
reputedly tried to learn the English of his new subjects.
Henry II is flatteringly credited with an understanding of
all European tongues, while his Sicilian son-in-law
probably did, through necessity, possess more than a
smattering of all the languages spoken in his kingdom,
French, Italian, Greek and Arabic.

This babel was unified by the common heritage of the
Church. Latin was the *lingua franca* of educated people
everywhere, while the uneducated but powerful turned to
clerics, fluent in the language of learning, to help them in
international negotiations, as they did in law and
administration, and in mediating between the laity and
their God.

November, a feast day. Saladin, who had achieved eminence by reason of arms rather than nobility, thought that the holy city of Jerusalem was empty of warriors, so he gathered a huge army, and invaded the territory of Ascalon in force, pitching camp in a place called Ramlah. The king of Jerusalem, the patriarch and the small army of knights that remained to him, either in the Temple or in the Hospital, together with a number of warriors, prepared themselves hurriedly for war. Relying not on spears and swords, bows and arrows, but only on the aid of religion, armed and inspired at once by the sign of the Lord's cross, they made haste by night to meet the 'Agarenes', remembering that it is easy for a multitude to be pinned down by a few, and that in the eyes of God there is no difference between winning among many or among few.

When morning came and the sun gleamed on their golden shields, the Christians climbed to the top of a mountain while the 'Agarenes' were drawn up for battle on the plain below: it seemed to those who could see clearly that the infidels outnumbered the Christians one hundredfold. So the Christians learned from mistress necessity to find a new remedy. The four ranks which had been drawn up for battle they reduced to one wedge shape; thus they steadfastly received the harsh assaults of the people surrounding them on all sides. While the Christians were in this threatening situation, a matter of life or death, Odo, master of the Knights Templar, another Judas Maccabeus, took eighty-four knights of the order with him and joined their side with his knights, defended by the sign of the cross. The knights dug in their spurs and, like one man, attacked, not swerving from right or left and, after recognizing the battle line in which Saladin was in command of many soldiers, valiantly attacked, rode through them without hesitation, struck incessantly, scattered them, crushed them and wore them into the ground. Saladin was astonished by this feat, and, seeing his men scattered in all directions, driven to flight and put to the sword, he decided himself to resort to flight, and swiftly throwing down his cuirass, he climbed on his travelling camel and barely escaped, together with a few men, hardly caring that he left this old reminder to his descendants: 'One chased a thousand, and two put ten thousand to flight.' Thus on 25 November the Christians won the victory, and

'Soldiers of Christ'

THE Knights Templar were formed in 1118 when a small group of French crusaders solemnly vowed to defend the recently recaptured Jerusalem from the Moslems, and were given a house near Solomon's Temple as their first home. After ten years of living on alms, they adopted a form of the Cistercian Rule, and rapidly began to acquire and administer estates all over Christendom. The expansion of the Knights Hospitaller was almost as remarkable. First organized in the 11th century (c.1070) under the Rule of St. Augustine at the Hospital of St. John the Baptist in Jerusalem, their first obligation had been to provide pilgrims to the Holy Land with hospices and hospitals; but like the Templars, the Hospitallers became an international military order.

Both orders had emerged to meet the needs of the crusading movement, so it is hardly surprising that their wealth, influence and prestige were at their height in the years before the fall of Jerusalem to Saladin and the Saracens in 1187. But, well into the 13th century, the Templars were still building and extending their great castles – Safed, Karak of the Desert and Castle Pilgrim – to defend a beleaguered Holy Land.

There were comparatively few Templars and Hospitallers actually resident in the British Isles, and the final and highly controversial suppression of the Templars by Pope Clement V in 1312 – among other things the order was accused of sacrilege – caused relatively little opposition or disruption in England. Their only important memorial is the church south of the Strand in London. (This, and other churches of theirs in England such as Garway and the Round Church in Cambridge has a round nave like the church of the Holy Sepulchre at Jerusalem.) The English province of the Hospitallers, however, directed by its chief prior from the house of St John at Clerkenwell, London, survived as a religious order until the Reformation.

Right *Garway, in Herefordshire, was a small settlement at the time of the Domesday Book. The church of St Michael is one of six in England attributed to the Knights Templar; the land at Garway was given to the order around 1170, and confirmed later by King John in 1199. The massive square tower, 70ft high, was a fortification as well as a church, providing protection during the continual border wars. The original chancel and nave were probably built around 1170, the chapel a little later.*

by divine command the power of the Gentiles was destroyed.

Beacons were lit all over the kingdom on 29 November.

On 1 December a high wind came from the east, destroying woods and buildings.

1178

Heavy snow.

On the coast huge earthworks made of turf were destroyed by flooding from the sea, especially from the north. On 8 January inhabitants, herds and flocks were swept in all directions by the blasts of the north wind.

King Henry of England, after consolidating his control of the defences in all the provinces under his jurisdiction, which lay near the borders of France, the Pyrenees or the English Channel, and arranging everything as he wished, returned to England on 15 July, and on his return visited the tomb of the glorious martyr Thomas.

William archbishop of Reims, to fulfil his vows made in prayer to the glorious martyr Thomas, went to Canterbury with a huge escort on 27 July. The king of England, several bishops and many nobles came to meet him, and having been thus received with the greatest honour, he spent three days in the king's palace in London at royal expense. When the king sent him as gifts of hospitality a large number of precious vases, he refrained from touching any of them, contrary to French custom, but accepted certain things which were not offered as part of the gift, as tokens of the king's love.

King Henry of England gave his son Geoffrey the belt of knighthood at Woodstock on 6 August.

There was an eclipse of the sun on 13 September.

1179

Young King Henry, the king's son, left England and passed three years in tournaments, spending a lot of money. While he was rushing around all over France he put aside the royal majesty and was transformed from a king into a knight, carrying off victory in various meetings. His popularity made him famous; the old king was happier counting up and admiring his victories, and although the Young King was still under age, his father restored in full his possessions which had been taken away. Thus occupied with knightly matters until no glory was lacking to him, he sailed from Wissant and was received with due honour by the king his father on 26 February.

We have heard that at Easter at a great court, Agnes the daughter of Louis VII, king of France, was married to Alexius, son of Manuel, the emperor of Constantinople. God will it more fortunate than the marriage between the daughter of Charlemagne and the Emperor Constantine, who withdrew from a childless marriage. Constantine expelled his mother Irene from the empire and after Irene was restored to power she blinded him.

Duke Richard of Aquitaine, having suffered many attacks, at length decided to conquer the proud Geoffrey de Rançon. He collected a force and on 1 May besieged the castle of Taillebourg. It was a most desperate venture and something which none of his predecessors had dared to attempt. The said castle was in those days completely unfamiliar to enemy troops; it was enclosed by a triple ditch, with three walls to resist rebellion, well supplied with arms, bars and barriers, adorned with towers placed at regular intervals, fortified by stone battlements, abundant in supplies, filled with thousands of men trained to fight; it hardly feared the arrival of the duke. The duke himself violently invaded the region; he took much booty, cut down the vines, burnt villages and demolished and laid waste the rest.

He reached the castle and set up his tents and machines near the wall and thoroughly terrified the occupants of the castle. But as it seemed to them shameful to stay enclosed within the walls without making an attack, they agreed to rush out of the gates and suddenly attack the duke's army. When the duke realized this, he ordered his men to arms and forced the enemy back. There was fierce fighting at the gateway: no matter what horse, lance, sword,

mir treuge ad
to certamen. Quod
de popilatui
Andiur.
u kt fob . dyr ecin
ueti hug denunac
cefti

tio quinto scilicet & quarto nonas iulii infra
octauas aplop petri & pauli. Euasit etiam ab
hac clade theodoricus magister milicie templi.

Balaadin   Guido
rex
Cru
sca

Voyage to Jerusalem

Above *The legendary Saladin defeats the Christians and then seizes the Cross.*

THERE were two possible routes for westerners who wished to visit Jerusalem. The quickest and safest way was by sea, but the resources necessary to transport whole armies were available to only a few commanders. As a result, until the end of the 12th century most crusaders took the land route.

As far as Constantinople, they travelled through lands which were Christian and, at least nominally, friendly. Once in Asia Minor they were in hostile territory; this area, which had once been the powerhouse of the Byzantine Empire, had been overrun by the Turks in the 12th century. The crusaders had to fight their way through Anatolia against such powerful enemies as the Seldjuk Sultan of Iconium (modern Konya) before they reached the safe haven of the Christian principalities.

The First Crusade had been lucky, for the Turks did not take the Christian threat seriously at first, but those who followed in 1100 were cut to pieces and only a pitiful remnant struggled on to Syria. The Second Crusade also suffered grievous losses on the march through Asia Minor in the winter of 1147–8.

In 1174 Saladin became the new ruler of Syria. He came from a Kurdish military family, but received a political education at the court in Damascus and learned the value of Holy War in uniting the forces of Islam.

Widely respected by friend and foe, Saladin became a legend even in his own lifetime. Pious and honest, he could be cunning and utterly ruthless when necessary: after Hattin, he ordered the execution of the captured knights of the Hospital and Temple, the élite troops of Christendom. Although he was not a great warrior, he was a masterful politician, and an honourable man who was admired even by his Christian enemies.

Nevertheless, his success in forging alliances with Egypt and neighbouring rulers was watched with mounting horror in the kingdom of Jerusalem, which addressed increasingly frequent appeals for help to the West. These were answered only when the Third Crusade in 1189 brought Richard the Lionheart and Saladin face to face.

The Turks were not the only enemies of the Christian army. Drought and famine were constant problems, and much of the land was rugged and mountainous, laced with torrents that had to be forded. When Frederick Barbarossa drowned in one of these in 1190, the German contingent to the Third Crusade dispersed, and most of its members returned to Germany. Richard the Lionheart and Philip II of France had taken their forces by sea, and the success of this strategy set the pattern for future crusaders.

helmet, bow, crossbow, shield, hauberk, stake, or mace was used by those fighting, experience won. The occupants of the castle could not withstand the very fierce assault of the leading cohort which the duke commanded outside, and quickly withdrew within the walls. Unwearied, the duke entered the town. There was a rush hither and thither throughout the place and then the burning and pillage began. On 10 May the castle was surrendered and within a few days the walls were flattened. Other castles throughout the area submitted to defeat within one month. Therefore with everything completed as he wished, the duke Richard crossed to England and was received with great honour by his father Henry II.

Louis VII king of France, surpassing his ancestors in magnificence with his generosity, had relieved the exile of St Thomas, formerly archbishop of Canterbury, in France for many years with abundant kindness in accordance with his character. He hoped to show obedience to God by treating the archbishop with piety and respect. As stories of his miracles were circulating far and wide, Louis decided that he wished to venerate his body with all devotion, in order that by his prayers and intercession he might deserve to cross from this transitory kingdom to the eternal kingdom. Neither he, nor any of his ancestors, at any time either in peace or in war had visited England. Assuming the name and dress of a pilgrim, accompanied by a modest group of nobles, he very devotedly made his visit.

Henry II, king and father of the English, as soon as he heard of his imminent arrival, hurried to meet him at double speed and met the French king at Dover on 22 August. Whatever honour could be conceived of or bestowed was shown to the French. There was a solemn procession at the great church attended by the archbishop, bishops, earls and barons, the clergy and the people on 23 August. There were hymns, songs and great joy, celebrating the arrival of such a great prince. I do not know how much French silver and gold was given as an offering. The king of France granted a hundred Parisian measures of wine per annum on behalf of himself and his heirs in perpetuity out of reverence for the martyr. This was for the use of the monks of

The cult of chivalry

ALL kinds of men were knights, from individuals who served for pay and in expectation of being rewarded with a grant of land, to the rulers of society – kings, dukes and counts. They were part of a military élite who practised the art of fighting on horseback with lance grasped firmly under the arm (a technique known as 'jousting'), and shared a common code of values embodied in chivalry – the French word, *chevalerie*, means 'cavalry' – which was celebrated in the vernacular works of the minstrels, the *chansons de geste* ('songs of deeds') of which the epic *Song of Roland* is the most famous. The songs extolled loyalty and prowess in battle, strength and endurance, a sense of honour and *courtoisie*: manners fitting to the court. In return, it befitted a lord to be generous to his followers. Clerics had some success in grafting on other values, such as the protection of the Church, widows and the poor.

The ceremony of initiation into knighthood varied according to wealth and circumstances. A landless younger son was knighted by his father and invested with the arms of knighthood. More elaborate rites were developed for the powerful. An account of the magnificent ceremony in which Henry I knighted Geoffrey the Fair in 1128, on the eve of his marriage to Matilda, tells how, after a purifying bath, Geoffrey was dressed in a tunic of cloth of gold and a purple cloak. The king then bestowed on him symbols of knighthood: golden spurs, a renowned sword and an emblazoned shield. Thirty of Geoffrey's companions were knighted at the same time, and the feasting and tournaments that followed lasted for a week. His grandson, Henry the Young King, was given a 'tutor in chivalry', William Marshal, who knighted the youth in 1173 on the eve of his first campaign (against his father!).

There is a temptation to dismiss chivalry as a romantic ideal, and to some extent it was. Yet the deeds of fictional heroes were emulated in life and beneath tales of knight-errantry lay a sense of realism. The 'Story of William Marshal' – written in 1225–6 in Anglo-Norman verse by an unknown poet, John – shows great admiration for William, who seems to have been a genuinely honourable and chivalrous person, and tells how a career devoted to chivalrous deeds was not confined to the *chansons*.

Top right *A faded fresco showing two knights engaged in battle.*

Right *Marriage casket, illustrated with a knight mounting his horse and receiving his shield from the lady of the castle.*

Canterbury and we commend his memory. But lest the French should seem to anyone to have sought anything other than the martyr, they restrained their hands from the treasure of the martyr, something which perhaps they had in mind.

Thus the king of France spent three days at Canterbury in fasting, prayer and vigil and he accepted from Henry some small gifts as a mark of love. On 26 August Louis left again from Dover.

Leaving campaigns and politics for a while, we turn now to Adam of Eynsham's life of St Hugh of Lincoln. A much-admired and loved figure at the monastery of La Grande Chartreuse near Grenoble, Hugh was chosen by Henry II to be prior of his new monastery at Witham in Somerset. Founded in 1177, it was still struggling for existence some three years later when Hugh arrived there.

Hugh found his brethren in Dothan, which is a synonym for penury. They were living in a wood near the royal vill of Witham, a prophetic name. It means in Latin, house or home of the mind, which is exactly what the place became by the coming of Christ's true philosopher. Hugh found the brethren living there in cells made of stakes surrounded by a narrow ditch and a stockade. At the time of his arrival and until he could reform it, to put it briefly, they lacked everything or almost everything essential even for the modest requirements of their order. It was not yet decided where the greater church, with the cells and cloister for the monks, or the smaller one, with the quarters and houses for guests and lay brethren, could best be erected. The former inhabitants were still living on the site which was to be handed over to the monks, nor had provision been made to enable them to give up their ancestral homes to their successors without indignation and serious loss to themselves.

First of all Hugh held a meeting of those who had holdings or other possessions and would have to give them up because the noise and the frequent visitors would destroy or at least disturb the monks' privacy and perpetual silence. On the king's behalf he offered them the choice of two alternatives: either to be given fields and dwelling-sites of the same type as at Witham on any royal manor they

chose, or to be freed from villeinage and go and live wherever they wished. When some had chosen lands and others freedom, Hugh, who was determined to temper justice with generosity, said to Henry II king of England, 'Now, my lord, you must also see that they are given monetary compensation for their homes, and for whatever expense or labour they have bestowed on their holdings and buildings of every kind for otherwise I cannot accept this place.' Thus, the king was compelled to buy goods which he thought completely worthless, old hovels, decayed beams and half-destroyed walls, laying out a considerable sum of money to little advantage. The sellers when they were paid were absolutely delighted at this new type of sale which enriched them considerably. They blessed the new prior who had brought his bread from afar; the bread which strengthened everyone.

This good businessman was not, however, content with a deal which seemed to him to be just but not generous, and therefore once more spoke to the king with a smile. 'See, my lord king, how I, a poor stranger, have enriched you in your own land with many houses.' The king laughed at this and replied 'I had no wish to receive this sort of riches, which have made me almost destitute. I don't even know anyone to whom they could be of any use.' His answer gave Hugh the opportunity he had sought for. 'Very good,' he said, 'I see you don't think much of your bargain. It would be an action in keeping with your munificence to give these buildings to me who have nowhere to lay my head.' The king was dumbfounded at the request and stared in amazement at the petitioner. 'You are', he replied, 'an extraordinary prior. Do you really believe that I cannot erect new buildings for you? At least tell me what you are going to do with these.' Hugh answered 'It is unworthy of your royal generosity to ask about such trifles. This is my first request to you, and, as it is so trivial, why shouldn't it be granted at once?'

The king, who had a sense of humour, thoroughly enjoyed his ready wit, and intentionally prolonged the verbal duel. 'Can a man on foreign soil be so bold? What would happen if he were to use his fists, when his tongue is so violent! Lest worse should befall us, let him have what he asks.' Hugh then gave back the buildings he had received to their former owners, although they had already been paid for. The owners either sold them once more, or took them away to live in them elsewhere. Thus he, being endowed with the foresight and devotion of Nehemiah, the favour of Solomon and the zeal of David, was enabled to build Jerusalem without blood, and immediately set about erecting the edifice which we now see.

When the buildings required by the customs of the order were almost finished and the number of brethren was complete, the good shepherd concentrated upon the training of the souls committed to his care in their holy profession. He devoted much labour to the making, purchase, and acquisition by every means of manuscripts of religious works, since these were a great assistance in this task.

Once in private converse with the king, the lack of books happened to be mentioned. When he was advised to do his best to get them copied by professional scribes, he replied that he had no parchment. The king then said, 'How much money do you think I should give you to make up this defect?' He answered that a silver mark would be enough for a long time. At this the king smiled. 'What heavy demands you make on us,' he said, and immediately ordered ten marks to be given to the monk who was his companion. He also promised that he would send him a Bible containing the whole of both testaments. The prior returned home, but the king did not forget his promise, and tried hard to find a really magnificent Bible for him. After an energetic search he was at last informed that the monks of St Swithun [Winchester] had recently made a fine and beautifully written Bible which was to be used for reading in the refectory. He was greatly delighted by this discovery, and immediately summoned their prior, and asked that the gift he desired to make should be handed over to him, promising a handsome reward. His request was speedily granted. When the prior of Witham and his monks received and examined the Bible given to them by the king they were not a little delighted with it. The correctness of the text pleased them especially, even more than the delicacy of the penmanship and the general beauty of the manuscript.

When a monk of Winchester visited Witham, he told Hugh that Henry II had taken the fine new Bible from his community. Hugh immediately returned this valuable manuscript to its rightful owners, despite the fears of the Winchester monks that the king would be angry. Hugh, however, was well able to cope with Henry's Angevin rages. The following story shows how, as bishop of Lincoln, he had aroused the King's ire by excommunicating his chief forester.

When the behaviour of the new bishop of Lincoln became public property at court, many people did their best to fan the already strong indignation of the king against Hugh by poisoned words. 'Sire,' they said, 'the black ingratitude of the man for your unusual favours is now obvious, the reward you have received for taking so much pains for his advancement is notorious.'

In spite of his great anger, the king behaved with restraint. He sent a summons to the bishop, and when he knew that he was about to arrive, mounted his horse, and withdrew with all his nobles, who were there in considerable numbers, to the neighbouring forest.

He sat down in a pleasant spot and the earls and other barons formed a circle round him. These he commanded not to rise or greet the bishop when he arrived. To make a long story short, the bishop came and greeted the king and the company, but no one returned his greeting. When he saw them sitting there silent and indifferent, he came up and put his hand lightly on the shoulder of the earl who was sitting next to the king, and made him give him his seat by the king. A heavy silence ensued, and all of them waited for a long time.

Finally, the king raised his head and ordered one of the attendants to give him a needle and thread. Having received it, he began himself to put stitches into a bandage wound round an injured finger on his left hand. There was silence, whilst he did this for some time to avoid the embarrassment of doing nothing. Angry people are accustomed to behave in this way, since their rage has rendered them speechless and they cannot give vent to it.

The bishop looked on and realized that this display of anger was for his benefit. He contemplated this conflict of human passions as though from some lofty watchtower of inward reason. At last he turned to the king and said, 'How you resemble your cousins at Falaise.' This shaft, said lightly and in a low tone, pierced the king to the heart. He pressed his fingers together, and, dissolved in helpless laughter, rolled on the ground. For a long time he could not restrain his merriment. The people present who understood the gibe were absolutely amazed that a man in Hugh's position had dared to make fun of so mighty a king at such a moment. They were not, however, able to refrain from smiling, and waited in suspense to hear the king's reply. Most of them, however, not understanding the meaning of what Hugh had said, were absolutely at a loss to account for the king's sudden change of attitude.

At last, the king became aware of their confusion and spoke thus 'You cannot understand the way this barbarian has insulted us, so I will explain. The mother of our great-grandfather William, the Conqueror of this land, is reputed to have been of humble birth, and to have come from the important Norman town of Falaise, which is celebrated for its leatherwork. This giber saw me sewing my finger, and so complimented me on my resemblance to my cousins at Falaise.'

'Now, tell me', he said to the bishop, 'my good friend, why without informing me have you thought fit to excommunicate my chief forester, and to treat my trifling request to you with such contempt, that you neither came yourself to explain why you had refused it, nor sent any excuse by our messengers?' The bishop at once answered these remonstrances in these words: 'I know that you worked hard to make me a bishop. I am therefore bound to save your soul from the perils which would befall it, if I was not careful to do my clear duty to the church entrusted to my charge. It is essential to excommunicate the oppressor of my church, and still more to refuse those who try to obtain prebends in that church illegally. I deemed it unnecessary to approach your highness since you are quite wise enough to recognize what is right, and would certainly wish

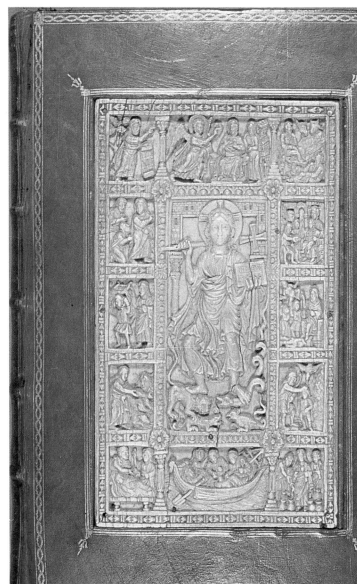

Words and images

ILLUMINATED manuscripts were the coffee-table books of the Middle Ages and, at a time when only a minority of writings were lavishly illustrated, were almost invariably for special use: a bible or psalter for the church or refectory lectern, or a diplomatic gift from a baron to his lord, a church to its patron, or from one monarch to another. Most books produced in the 12th century were religious, mainly bibles and psalters, with some biblical commentaries and lives of the saints. Of the secular books, bestiaries seem to have been fashionable towards the end of the 12th century and scientific books, derived from Latin or Greek sources via the Moslems, included herbals, and astronomical and medical treatises.

Although the Church had a virtual monopoly of book production, not all the illustrators were monks; many were versatile artists involved in other, quite different enterprises. Master Hugo of Bury St Edmunds, who painted the Bury Bible, also produced sculpture and metalwork.

One of the artists who illustrated the Winchester Bible was equally at home working on a large scale: he painted frescos in Winchester Cathedral and at Sigena in Spain. An artist of international stature, he had learnt his distinctive, Byzantine style in Sicily.

The scribe and the painter-illuminator were sometimes one and the same person. The monk Eadwine of Canterbury was both, and drew a magnificent picture of himself at his writing desk in what is now known as the Eadwine Psalter. Produced at Canterbury in c.1160, it is a copy of a famous Carolingian Psalter, the Utrecht Psalter, which was at Canterbury Cathedral in the 12th century and shows how closely and carefully medieval illustrators copied older models. It also has bound into it a plan of the waterworks installed at Canterbury in the 1160s by Prior Wybert, showing the 12th-century choir before it burnt down in 1174.

Top left *One of the many delightful illuminated letters in the Winchester Bible. This was probably commissioned by Henry of Blois in 1160, and at least five artists worked on it over a period of about 20 years; but, like many large projects which outlived their patrons, it was never finished.*

Left *An ivory and velour book cover of the 12th century. The covers of workaday manuscripts were usually made from leather-covered oak boards; but the most precious books, and especially those fully illuminated for religious houses or commissioned by wealthy patrons, or intended as personal psalters, could be magnificently ornate, with gold and metalwork filigree, jewelled inlays, and decorative panels of ivory.*

Right *Henry of Blois was a leading patron of the arts in England and France. This cover, from a psalter made for his use, is marvellously decorated with a painting of the horrors of damnation, and a view into Hell. The highly imaginative treatment, with its gaping mouth, and rather sad angel locking in the wicked, is one of the finest examples of the period. Even the devil's horns are decorated with dragon ears. It is perhaps a sign of piety or of political astuteness that two of the figures in Hell are a crowned king and queen.*

to show your approval of what you know to be so.'

The king found nothing to take exception to in this explanation, and the last traces of his hasty resentment being now dissipated, he embraced the bishop with a beaming face and commended himself urgently to his prayers. He left to his decision the question of the absolution of the excommunicated man, who, being thoroughly contrite and humbled, took the oath in the form prescribed by the Church and, after being publicly flogged with his accomplices, was absolved. The bishop gave him his blessing, and all the rest of his life he was devoted to him and became his especial friend and benefactor.

Henry II's harsh but fair cast of mind is also stressed by Diceto in his description of the king's judicial changes in England (1179).

The elder king, Henry II of the English, asked these days for much to be done that was scarcely possible. He found that the sheriffs were reluctant to perform public functions, careless of their duties and more concerned with their own affairs. He was more and more anxious about the common welfare and he granted jurisdiction in certain places to other faithful men, so that the arrival of public authority in the provinces should deter criminals and that those withholding money and damaging royal majesty would incur royal anger. Those who rashly hunted wild animals would be punished with a heavy fine or a long imprisonment; the punishment should deter the criminal and those caught would receive a heavy sentence. Murder was to be punished by hanging, traitors were condemned to exile, those caught for lesser crimes would have their limbs cut off; the justiciar should vigorously restrain trespassers and satisfaction should be made for the damage.

Once more after a lapse of time, the king was most intent on showing justice to everyone and, in order to provide more protection for his subjects, he wanted to test the loyalty of many men. He carefully looked for lovers of justice among various classes of men, and he sought among thousands of men he whom money could not corrupt, for an offer can change one's mind and among change-able people an unalterable sentence may be changed. How far the clergy had relieved the complaints of the poor, or the authority of the belted knight had resisted the more powerful and forced them to live by the common law, the disasters of the oppressed make obvious. For he appointed now abbots, now earls, now captains, now his household men or those closest to him to hear and determine cases.

The king, therefore, since he had appointed so many of his faithful men of all classes who were prejudicial to the public welfare and since none of them had retracted any sentences, not finding any way of helping private citizens, decided that he could separate some men from the generality; who, although they lived among men, were above them, and who had felt and experienced something more than men. Thus transcending everything that could be changeable the king turned to the Church and appointed the bishops of Winchester, Ely and Norwich as chief justices of the realm, but for certain areas only, thinking that if those whom he had appointed long ago were less respectful, these ones on the other hand, ardently and attentively fearing God, the king of kings, the creator of men, judge of consciences, avenger of deeds, turning neither to the left or the right, would not oppress the poor in court nor be biased by accepting bribes. And then if the prelates got involved in secular affairs contrary to the canon, and on account of this were dragged into a lawsuit, they could plead that it was at the instance of the king, and that it was the pious intention of the king to please God by his action and to be praised by men. Cases were to be heard by these bishops and their fellow justices, but some cases were reserved for the king and were heard at Westminster on 27 August.

This year was a good one: after a dry winter, after the northerly winds of spring, after lightning in the midlands from west to east, a light rain watered the fields on 13 June. It revived the spirits of the farmers who had given up their seeds for lost, and it helped the growth of fruit trees and young animals which had almost died. The weather was kind to the seeds, just touching the little roots, and successive rain and showers restored fertility. The

Sheriffs and shires

EXCEPT on the rare occasions when the king or his judges came to a shire, the sheriff and his officials were the only representatives of Henry's government. The sheriff was the 'shire-reeve', the person responsible for supervising the king's estates in the shire and collecting the income from them to pay into the Exchequer as a sum called the sheriff's 'farm'. The amount for each shire was fixed at the beginning of Henry's reign.

The sheriff also presided over the shire or county court where he dispensed justice and carried out administrative tasks, supervised the keeping of the peace through the lesser courts of the districts, called hundreds or wapentakes, and was responsible for delivering writs summoning litigants to appear in the royal courts. In times of war he was expected to maintain military control of the shire for the king. In many shires his activities centred on a royal castle in the county town.

Sheriffs must have struck awe into the hearts of local men, and many exploited the power their position gave them for their own financial gain. As a result, in 1170, Henry held inquiries into their conduct and dismissed most of them. From then on, sheriffs were usually professional administrators rather than local barons. However, although the Exchequer could control them financially, the problem of controlling their local political activities remained to trouble later kings.

Above *A Pipe Roll recording the sheriff's accounts which were presented twice every year at the Exchequer.*

Left *Detail from a letter sent in 1190 by William Longchamp, the Chancellor, to all the sheriffs, ordering them to collect dues for St Paul's Cathedral.*

more intense heat of the sun's rays helped the abundant fruit; and unexpectedly the land, previously dry, produced a great crop, so that in many places you could see seven ears of corn on one stalk. You ought to be reminded that something or other, suddenly, unhoped for and unusual, will perhaps happen to you in your time.

Again, in this year the grace of heaven bestowed its affection and earthly powers on its subjects, so that anyone who has a case in a civil or ecclesiastical court cannot doubt that the outcome will be favoured by divine consideration. For it was decreed that, in the counties, as we have said before, bishops should be appointed on the king's orders to hear disputes over service, but could not impose the death penalty. If you are honest you can come safely to the consistory court of the archbishop of Canterbury, with all peace of mind for the reason about to be reported. So that his assessors, whom he has for giving advice and conducting suits, should not stray from the path of truth, and be corrupted by money on behalf of the litigants, they introduced an oath on the Scriptures according to civil law. For all bearing a common responsibility, swore publicly on the Gospels that they would never dirty their hands with money, and no one was exempt. The archbishop promised this on his word at Pagham.

Cadwallon, who held a principality in South Wales, often crossed the ancient border between the English and the Britons and, entering the Marches, violently murdered many men and spent his life making raids and secret attacks. At length, accused by many, he was dragged before the king. While he was with the king he was under his protection, but because of the cruelty of his crimes he was always very frightened.

On his way home he was caught and killed in an ambush by his enemies on 22 September. This greatly injured royal authority and damaged the public law by which the state ought to be kept safe. For Cadwallon, although he ought to have been hanged many times for his crimes, should have been safe out of respect for the king from whose court he was returning, and because he had been granted a safe conduct for a fixed length of time.

Clerical justice

CHURCH and lay courts existed side by side in Plantagenet England and, to an extent unparalleled in modern times, a man's political power went hand in hand with his right to try offenders in his own court. It was, therefore, inevitable that the great power of the Church was expressed in a complicated hierarchy of ecclesiastical courts.

By the mid-12th century all Henry II's subjects must have been familiar with the way in which many offences could lead to a summons to the court of a bishop or his chief subordinate, the archdeacon, with the further possibility of appeals to the archbishop and even to the court of the pope himself. Although it was generally accepted that these courts should confine themselves to 'causes touching the rule of souls', such causes were notoriously hard to define.

Cases involving sexual immorality or irregularities in making wills and testaments were undoubtedly matters for the spiritual authorities; while the king's monopoly over serious crimes such as treason, murder, violent robbery, arson and false coining was undeniable. But there were many other offences over which clerical and royal lawyers competed incessantly for jurisdiction.

The influences of Church and State were so inextricably combined that neither side could hope to win the struggle outright. However, by the end of the 12th century – not least as a result of the confrontation between Henry II and Thomas Becket – England's Church and lay courts settled down to a comparatively peaceful coexistence for the rest of the Middle Ages.

Right A monk in the stocks, and his admonishing bishop. Clerical courts remained an important part of the system of judicial punishment, and the disputes between Thomas Becket and Henry II came to a head over who had the power to discipline the clergy. Although Henry seemed to have lost the battle when Becket was murdered and subsequently canonized, the power of the lay courts and especially the power of the English king to dominate those courts continued to increase.

quiere̅
i sup
cozz
ueiss
os xr
quod
rozcc
iat̅ xc
pret̅
pados
nchil
tius
etius
alti
entiaq
uizi
animoz
n aud
otc
lexit
q̅ si
statt
ncta
non

floz igitur q̅ pados mediatozes si-
lxx actum̅ e̅. auct. ap confirma̅s
C ompmissum n̅o exteat̅. Ioz
in compmittentis hexedes si de-
ip sis n̅o cauetur ibidem.
I napit libez. ij. de iuditijs. ꝝ

G x con. africiano ·   ꝓum nomen est   suple ta sta
                                          tute e
          E QVO LICET DŌ
          centurien epo que
          eam adversari ipi
          cum petiss. ad aliu:
          introduci. introgat
an cum eo uell. et expta. primo
io pmiserat et alt̅ die ꝝndit hec
sibi n̅o placere. atꝗ diceffit. pla
aut ut nullius eidem comu
nic; doce satisfactioeq; pmissa fi

If, however, anyone is frightened by this example, though nothing similar has happened in our day, the king did not let it go unpunished. He punished the offence severely and if summoned to the king's court you need have no fear. The Welsh could comfort each other in their turn, for the death of one of their men meant the sad and hateful funerals of many of the Normans and English of the Marches. The king took those who knew of the murder and those whom he suspected and proved their guilt in a public trial. He pronounced harsh sentences: some were hanged on the gallows, ruined by the forfeiture of their goods; others were forced to lead a wretched life in the woods as fugitives.

Fate was kinder to Louis VII of France in his last days as regards his third marriage. Three times he married legitimately and at the time most happily, as was written in the French annals. His third marriage was made to produce a male heir. From his first two marriages the king had had four daughters only; at length by his third wife, Adela, the daughter of the great Theobald, count of Blois, most happily he had a son, Philip, loved by the people and devotedly and readily sought by the clergy.

When Philip was fourteen, after meeting with the archbishops, bishops and princes of the kingdom, whose assent was needed according to the custom of the realm, he went to Reims. On 1 November by hereditary right, as the comfort, father and governor of all his subjects, in the solemnity of all the saints, so that he might deserve their protection against his enemies, he was consecrated king of France by William archbishop of Reims, the king's own uncle. At his coronation Philip king of France had Philip count of Flanders as his special official, who bore his sword and arranged the royal feasts. The count of Flanders had a twofold right to this office, through his father and his wife.

King Henry, son of Henry II, king of England, the husband of the French king's sister, attended the coronation because he was a close relation and because he was invited to observe. Although Britain almost deserves to be called another world and you will often hear that Britons are divided amongst themselves, it remains clear that no king of Britain or England ever acknowledged the king of France as a superior, rather they were more accustomed to be friends. In the letters passing between them they decided that they would call each other brothers, a custom which even Charlemagne had observed after he had been made emperor by the Romans. The young King Henry, realizing he had an interest in the solemnities, exercised his prerogative and talked with all the nobles in his presence, and thus from the mouths of the French people he learned of future events. King Henry II of England held the crown on the new king's head, lest, since he was still young, it injure him, the claims of those more suited to this duty being rejected. This implied that if ever the French needed help they could safely ask for it from one who had helped at their king's coronation.

1180

Knowing that under a new prince, especially when he is a child king, the designs of evil councillors often prevail, King Henry of England took precautions lest this should be to his own disadvantage. He feared that those who wished him ill would suggest to the king of France some plan injurious to the land of Normandy. For those who lived near its borders feared the power of the Normans and the might of their name, which was known throughout the world. Richard bishop of Winchester was charged by the king with the care of this matter. He crossed the Channel on 6 March, taking with him, as fellow ambassador, Master Walter of Coutances, keeper of the king's seal. When they arrived in Paris they found King Louis confined to his bed, bowed down with old age and sickness.

The clergy of Limoges, without the knowledge or consent of Henry II king of England or Richard duke of Aquitaine, elected Sebrand, dean of the church of Poitiers, to be their bishop. As punishment for this insolent conduct, their property was confiscated, their houses ruined, their vineyards uprooted. When Pope Alexander learnt of this, he sent instructions to Warin, archbishop of Bourges, to investigate the matter and negotiate a settlement. However, when the clergy of Limoges came to the archbishop, they found him dead. Then, so that they might not seem to have laboured in vain, the archpriest of Brive inserted the letters of the pope, which were still sealed, into the hands of the dead man, saying, 'What he could not accomplish in life, let him accomplish in death.' By his skilful mediation, they say that the bishop of Limoges achieved reconciliation with the king and the duke.

Young King Henry, son of the elder king, came to England on 1 April and was most honourably received by his father. He swore at Reading, in the presence of holy relics, that he would follow his father's instructions in all matters, particularly in the distribution of the towns, castles and benefices as mentioned in a charter which was there. After this, the elder king crossed the Channel from Portsmouth, the younger from Dover. On arriving in France, the elder king at once celebrated Easter at Le Mans. Philip king of France married Margaret, daughter of Baldwin count of Hainault, whose mother Margaret was sister of the count of Flanders, at Le Tronchet. The wedding was celebrated at Bapaume. We heard much about the splendid celebration of that memorable marriage. On Ascension Day, 29 May, at Saint-Denis, Guy, archbishop of Sens anointed Margaret, wife of King Philip, as queen of France.

Louis VII, having already given over his jurisdiction and power to King Philip, surrendered his seal also, so that no decisions concerning the kingdom could be made without his son's knowledge. A quarrel arose between King Philip and his mother Adela. Some castles which Queen Adela had received as a wedding gift were taken over and their guardians violently ejected by King Philip's ministers, on his instructions. However, the king and his mother were reconciled when they appealed to the king of England's judgement in a council of the kings which took place at Gisors on 28 June.

"I, Philip, king of France by the grace of God, and I, Henry, king of England by that same grace, wish to bring to the notice of all men, both now and in the future, that we renew by faith and oath, the treaty and friendship which my lord father the king of France and I, Henry II, king of England, confirmed at Ivry in the presence of Cardinal Peter and Richard bishop of Winchester. And that all cause for discord between us be removed, we each grant that neither shall seek from the other any of the territories or lands or other goods which he possesses. The only exceptions to this shall be the Auvergne, which is a cause for dissension between us, and the fief of Châteauroux and the small fees of the land of Berry, if our men occupy any part of it whether against each other or against one of us. However, if we are unable to reach an agreement through our own negotiations, concerning those territories which we have excepted from the general provisions, I, Philip king of France, have chosen three bishops and three barons and I, Henry king of England, have chosen three bishops and three barons to discuss the matter. We shall faithfully observe whatever they recommend. We promise by faith and oath that we shall abide by all the preceding conditions. This agreement was drawn up on 28 June between Gisors and Trie."

And now Louis VII king of France lay gravely ill in Paris. He ordered that all his gold, his silver, his jewels, his rings, his rich garments and his regal ornaments be brought before him. Then, on the advice of the bishop of Paris, the abbot of St-Germain and the abbot of Ste-Geneviève, he instructed that they be distributed among the poor. On 13 September he died and was buried in a monastery of the Cistercian order called Barbeaux, which he had built at his own expense.

Philip Aimery, a man from the region of Tours by birth, came to England summoned by the king and undertook the task of reforming the coinage. And so that winter, on 11 November, the old money was recalled and a new coin, round in shape, was issued throughout the kingdom for use in all business dealings. Philip himself was charged with the duty of watching over the interests of the Treasury. Thus it fell to him to contain the devious plans of forgers. When the minters were discovered to have tampered with the coins, he was much criticized. However, he did not incur the anger of the king who relieved him from fear of punishment. Nevertheless, he was dismissed and sent back to France without ceremony.

1181

Four kings, so they say, came together in one battle and – what is more remarkable – four kings came peacefully to a conference and left it on good terms. Philip, the king of France, Henry, the king of England, Henry, the son of the king of England, and William, the king of Scotland, came to take council together and parted peacefully. At the insistent suggestion of his palace advisers, Philip king of France decided to follow the example of Henry king of England, who managed to exercise government over his vast kingdom, beset though it was with the incursions of the barbarous Scots and Welsh. That he might learn more exactly the methods of his fellow prince, he decided, on the advice of his domestic councillors, to submit himself entirely to Henry's guidance.

The elder king of England surrendered all of Normandy to the control of his son, the younger king, charging all the ministers of that land with obedience to him, and left him to watch over and protect Philip king of France, should the need arise. Now that all the provinces were ordered according to his wishes and, respectful of his laws, were enjoying the benefits of peace brought by his rule, he returned to England on 28 July. He paid a visit to Canterbury where he offered prayers to St Thomas.

Philip count of Flanders, when he heard how Philip king of France and Henry king of England were so closely associated, raised up as many of the Flemings as he could to fight against his liege lord. He declared that matters had come to such a head that they must either destroy the enemies' fortifications or else capture them and so force the king to negotiate. He even tried now sending messengers, now going in person, to persuade Frederick emperor of the Germans to rise against the king of France and extend the borders of his kingdom to the English Channel. And so Count Philip, having no regard for the tender age of his lord the king and quite unmindful of the assurances he had given to King Louis that he would watch over, protect and guide his son according to what is right, attacked Noyon with as large a force as he could muster. They devastated the area around Senlis, demolishing houses and uprooting vineyards.

Young King Henry, son of the elder king, Richard duke of Aquitaine and Geoffrey duke of Brittany — three sons bearing witness to the fruitfulness of their mother — were eager to make up for the absence of the king their father by giving proof of their own valour. Planning to oppose with all their might the designs of those wicked men who desired to oppress the innocent young king of France, they gathered a great force from all the land and came as a united band to his aid.

They decided first to dispose of Count Stephen, the evil lord of the castle of Sancerre. Within a few days they had ravaged his property, his towns, his castles and his lands. They gave about five thousand yoke of oxen to the men of Brabant as booty. Since the count's forces were outnumbered and he was unable to resist, he fell at the feet of his nephew, King Philip, asking and receiving forgiveness for his offence. Moving on, the two kings (Philip and the young Henry) and their forces inflicted severe losses on the duke of Burgundy, the countess of Champagne, sister to both kings, and their accomplices, whose forces they again outnumbered. Moving back northwards, they compelled the count of Flanders to retreat. The count feared to meet King Henry, son of the king of England, face to face and shut himself up in the castle of Crépy. Indeed, they say that, had the deceitful advice of the king of England's councillors not thwarted his plans, the count, shut in the castle, would soon have been forced to surrender, as he only had food for a few days.

1182

Philip king of the French, the kings of the English, father and son, Philip count of Flanders and those from all over France who on his advice had broken faith with their lords, met together at Senlis after Easter. Henry bishop of Albano, the pope's legate, was there, and William archbishop of Reims with many bishops. What was agreed can be seen from the following document:

"The king of the English to Richard bishop of Winchester, greeting.
Philip count of Flanders has returned Pierrefonds to the king of the French, the king to the bishop of Soissons, and the bishop to Agatha widow of Hugh of Oisi who holds it by hereditary right from

Red Beard

FREDERICK I, Barbarossa, was one of the great medieval emperors. Like Charlemagne five centuries earlier, and Frederick II in the 13th century, he expended tremendous energy on war, travelling and ceremonial in order to maintain his authority throughout far-flung lands. But by 1178 the Holy Roman Empire was in crisis. Frederick I had then been its ruler for 26 years, during which he had first calmed the feuds which had torn his German kingdom apart in the reign of his predecessor Conrad III, then made five military expeditions into Italy in an attempt to enforce imperial authority over its populous, wealthy and independent northern cities which had largely escaped previous emperors' control. He also set up the first of several antipopes in 1159 as a rival to Alexander III.

The cracks in Frederick's grand schemes were opened wide on 29 May 1176 when he was defeated at Legnano by a league of the Italian cities. He was then forced into an apparently disadvantageous settlement with them and the papacy, in the peace of Venice of 1177. This gave cities like Milan and Verona effective self-government within their walls, even though the emperor's overall authority was confirmed. However, it left Frederick free to pursue his German interests more fully. In that kingdom, his

policy of allowing the aristocracy considerable independence in the hope that they would be loyal had crumbled. Henry the Lion, duke of Bavaria and Saxony, was in rebellion and had refused to send troops to Italy for the Legnano campaign. Frederick had relied on him to keep order in Germany, especially in the north where his power was greatest. Frederick was given a suitable pretext in 1178–9 – a dispute between Henry the Lion and the bishop of Halberstadt – for trying Henry in his absence in the imperial court and sentencing this great prince to be deprived of his lands. The emperor managed to enforce the sentence and, in 1181, to drive his enemy into exile at the court of Henry II. During the next nine years Frederick I consolidated his successes, married his son Henry to the heiress to Sicily, and went on Crusade, meeting his death in Asia Minor in 1190 soon becoming the focus of myths and legends.

Left *Frederick I's reliquary bust.*

Below *Portrait of Frederick from a 13th-century history of the Crusades.*

full justice to him in his own court or the king's. The count of Clermont and Ralph de Chuci remain completely in the king of France's hands, free of the count of Flanders. Philip count of Flanders releases my son Henry from all agreements made between them. He has also agreed that the Flemish barons should do me full service for the fees they hold of me, and that they should irrevocably lose those fees if they do not perform my service. Furthermore, we also agreed that none of his men should lose his land in Flanders on account of my service if he came to serve me in my lands. With all things reduced to peace, all those who renounced the fealty of the king of the French by counsel and action of the king of the English shall return to his allegiance. Damages on both sides have been amended by mutual compensation."

Roger archbishop of York, while still alive, requested from Pope Alexander the following privilege: that if a cleric under his jurisdiction made a will on his deathbed but did not distribute his goods with his own hands, the archbishop would have the power to lay hands on the dead man's goods. Since 'whoever decrees a law for someone else ought to observe it himself', it was God's just judgement that after the archbishop's death everything found in his treasury was confiscated. This amounted to eleven thousand pounds in silver of old money, three hundred gold pieces, a golden bowl and seven silver ones, nine silver cups, three bowls of maplewood, three silver salt-cellars, forty silver spoons, eight silver plates, a great silver dish and silver basins.

Henry duke of the Saxons, the husband of the king of England's eldest daughter Matilda, rose up against Philip archbishop of Cologne and did him enormous damage. The archbishop raised forces from all around and manfully resisted the duke, receiving aid and favour from the emperor. Things happened in such a way that when the sentence of all the princes of the empire was made public, the duke was forced to submit to exile. Coming to Normandy to his father-in-law with the duchess, two of his sons, Henry and Otto, and a marriageable daughter — the third son, called Lothar, stayed in Germany — he was honourably received

and for more than three years shown sumptuous hospitality and royal generosity.

1183

In 1143 John Porphyrogenitus emperor of Constantinople had died, poisoned, at Antioch, leaving two surviving sons. The elder brother disappeared, leaving a son called Andronicus. Manuel, the younger one, was made emperor, as he was more popular with the Greeks.

Now about this time Emperor Manuel died at Constantinople, after reigning for about forty years, leaving as his successor his young son Alexius, whom he had had by the daughter of Prince Raymond of Antioch, Eleanor of Aquitaine's uncle. Andronicus, feigning peace, came to Constantinople and swore fealty to Alexius in the church of St Sophia. He placed the royal crown on Alexius' head and rode through the city with Alexius on his shoulders.

But after a little while Andronicus changed his policy: he cruelly murdered the protovestiarus [a court official], killed the empress, Alexius's mother, and everyone whom he knew to have been faithful to the emperor Manuel, and usurped the throne for himself. It is said that he drowned Alexius and then married his widow, that is Agnes, daughter of King Louis VII of France.

While human fate answered to the elder king Henry's nod in almost everything, he was careful to exercise foresight for his posterity lest anything useful for peace was let slip. Anxious to make peace more firm between his sons and to avoid the arguments between brothers which are natural in many generations, he asked the Young King his son to receive the homage and allegiance of his brother Geoffrey for the duchy of Brittany, which the latter possessed as the dowry of his wife Constance, the only daughter and heiress of Count Conan. From ancient times the counts of Brittany had been bound by this chain of due subjection to the dukes of Normandy, through the liberality of the kings of France.

What the father requested took place at Angers. Afterwards, to complicate matters, the father asked his son Henry to concede to his brother Richard the

The 'New Rome'

Above **The ruins of Istanbul's walls, originally built in about AD 413, still show traces of the magnificence and strength described by medieval chroniclers.**

'CONSTANTINOPLE, the glory of the Greeks, rich in renown and richer still in possessions. . . .' So wrote a chaplain to Louis VII who accompanied his master on the Second Crusade. The city had been founded some 800 years earlier, in AD 330, by Constantine as a 'New Rome' – it too had a senate and was built on seven hills – and as a new capital was rapidly provided with the necessities of civilized life: palaces and public buildings, a hippodrome, monumental squares, markets and baths. As befitted the capital of the first Christian emperor, there were many splendid churches but no temples to the pagan gods.

For centuries Constantinople stood as a bulwark between Europe and Asia, holding at bay the advancing Arabs and then the Turks, and preserving much of western Europe's inheritance from the Graeco-Roman civilization. Yet in 1204 it was crusaders from the West who captured and sacked the city, establishing a short-lived Latin empire.

Constantinople occupied a peninsula between the Bosporus and the Golden Horn. The landward side was cut off by an impressive double line of walls erected in the 5th century, the first sight to greet a visitor from the West. At their northern end a great pleasure garden and game reserve had been built for the imperial palace of Blacharnae. Within the city walls there were several exquisitely wrought palaces and churches, but the most remarkable building was Justinian's Saint Sophia whose massive golden dome floated, according to the 6th-century Greek historian Procopius, as if 'suspended from heaven'.

Fresh water was piped into the city and stored in vast cisterns, of which nearly 60 survive. Like all great cities it had its dark side – the dank and lawless slums which the wealthy shunned.

The jealousy of westerners was excited each time they visited Constantinople on their way to the Holy Land: it was, wrote one of its attackers in 1204, 'a city richer than any other since the beginning of time . . . there were at that time as many people in Constantinople as in all the rest of the world'.

It contained immeasurable wealth in precious metals, stones and cloths, and its churches were packed with the holiest relics of the Christian Church – the holy lance, part of the true cross, the crown of thorns and the shroud in which Christ had been wrapped. In the West its inhabitants were widely thought to be treacherous and heretical, and to kill them was judged no crime. It was only a matter of time before an attempt was made to seize this jewel.

Left *Emperor Alexius Comnenus; a*
mosaic portrait in Hagia Sophia. The
Comnenus family were able rulers who
held back the flood of Islam.

Above *Interior of Hagia Sophia.*
Originally a Greek Orthodox church, it
was a mosque for many centuries after the fall
of Constantinople in 1453 and is now a museum.

duchy of Aquitaine to be held by Richard and his heirs in perpetuity. Then at last the younger king openly demonstrated to his father that he was allied with many Aquitainian barons against his brother Richard. He had been led to this at the time when Richard had, against his wishes and to his disadvantage, strongly fortified the castle of Clairvaux which of olden times had been subject to the counts of Anjou. But so as not to incur his father's displeasure he solemnly swore to do what his father asked at Mirebeau, as long as Richard, after doing homage and allegiance to him, would also swear fealty to him on sacred relics. At this Richard exploded in anger, apparently saying that since he came from the same father and the same mother as his brother it was not right for him to acknowledge his elder brother as superior by some sort of subjection; but by the good law of the first-born the paternal goods were due to his brother, and he claimed equal right to legitimate succession to the maternal goods.

Hearing this the elder king fell into a rage and threatened difficulties for Richard, vehemently saying that the younger king was going to rise up and tame Richard's pride. He told Geoffrey duke of Brittany to stand faithfully by his brother as his liege lord. So the young king took up arms not against his father, as he constantly said, but to come to the aid of the Poitevins whom Richard was oppressing with violence and harrying unjustly – the Poitevins who were fighting to be subject to him by the common law without any of his brothers standing over him.

They had many talks amongst themselves, but as no hope of peace emerged the Young King gathered a numerous army, and leaving his father, to whom he knew the rule of Aquitaine belonged during his lifetime, he ordered all his allies, whoever and however many they were, to join battle with Richard. Then his life was cut short, as if by a weaver, and with it the hopes of many fighting for him and hoping to rule with him after his father's death.

For on 11 June in the region called Turenne in Gascony, among quite barbarous people at the castle of Martel, Henry the Young King passed away having lived twenty-eight years, fourteen weeks and six days, leaving for the approval of the wise the

opinion that sons who rise up against fathers to whom they owe everything that they are and everything from which they live, and by whose goods they expect to be enriched, are worthy only of being disinherited.

The Young King's body, carefully anointed and wrapped in the linen garments which he wore at his coronation, was carried on the shoulders of his comrades through villages, castles and towns, with people running from everywhere to look until they reached Le Mans, where it was set down in the choir of the church of St Julien. The great men of the town suddenly rushed in, and with popular approval speedily buried the king's body there, as his paternal grandfather rested in the same place. But afterwards he was moved to Rouen on the request of Robert, the dean of Rouen, because while the Young King lived he had chosen that as his place of burial. He was interred with the honour due to a prince in the cathedral of Rouen, on the north side of the high altar.

1184

When he had arranged all the provinces under his jurisdiction according to his wishes, and all his subjects were enjoying the delights of peace, the king of the English crossed over to England on 11 June, going through Flanders with the permission and goodwill of the French king. About this time the duke of Saxony with his household and goods came to England, and within a few days, at Winchester, the duchess bore a son, called William.

Philip archbishop of Cologne, accompanied on his journey by Philip count of Flanders, came to England to offer prayers to St Thomas at Canterbury. The king came to meet the archbishop and the count and besought them to travel as far as London. When they arrived, they were met with an unparalleled reception. The city was decked with garlands and all the streets were filled with joyful crowds. The visitors were received with honour and great delight. The archbishop, accompanied by a stately procession, was welcomed in St Paul's Cathedral and was received at Westminster, too, on the same day. There he beheld another stately procession splendid with regal ornament. No expense was spared. The

The body royal

HENRY II was not a great lover of the ceremonial side of kingship, but he was interested in his own genealogy and in honouring the remains of his forbears. The canonization of Edward the Confessor in 1161, a triumph for the monks of Westminster where he was buried, was achieved with Henry's help. But the king had no ambition to build himself a great burial church. When he was seriously ill in 1170 he announced, to the horror of his courtiers, that he intended to be buried in the tiny church of Grandmont, the mother-house of the Grandmontine order which carried asceticism to its furthest extremes. His barons retorted that this would be against the dignity of the realm, and when Henry eventually died at Chinon nearly 20 years later, his entourage made sure he was given a suitably regal funeral. His body was placed on an open bier and, wearing his regalia and with his face exposed, he was carried the ten miles to Fontevrault Abbey, the favourite monastery of Eleanor of Aquitaine. This resting-place was almost certainly chosen for him by his courtiers.

Some 12th-century kings died far from the churches which they had selected as their burial places. Henry I, for example, had founded Reading Abbey as his mausoleum, but in 1135 died in Lyons-la-Forêt in Normandy. Contrary winds prevented the funeral party from crossing the channel, and decomposition set in while the body was still in the duchy – an attendant died after coming into contact with the putrid corpse before it could be buried. Henry had been disembowelled and his entrails presented to a nunnery he had founded in Rouen. The practice spread: in 1199 Richard I was split three ways – his body went to Fontevrault, his heart to Rouen Cathedral and his entrails to Charroux in Poitou.

Monks, canons and the communities they served were as anxious to obtain royal remains as were kings to gain intercession from suitably holy monks after death. Although the Young King had been violent and unruly, after his death the citizens of Le Mans considered that his body would bring them honour and prestige. They kidnapped his cortège on its way through their town and buried him in their cathedral. The citizens of Rouen, where he had promised to be interred, threatened to raze Le Mans to the ground; in the end, Henry II had to intervene. On his ruling, his son was moved to Rouen and buried in the cathedral he had originally chosen.

Below *Effigy of Richard I at Rouen, where his heart is buried.*

sumptuous banquets offered more food than the guests could eat. The archbishop stayed for five days as a guest in the king's palace at Westminster and, when he left, was presented with many gifts.

The order of Santiago was confirmed by the lord pope. These soldiers, who are distinguished from all others by the red sword that is their emblem, have their base in Spain. They seek to use their might in the struggle against the Saracens.

Arnauld, master of the Knights Templar, died at Verona.

1185

Heraclius, patriarch of Jerusalem, and Roger, master of the house of the Knights Hospitaller at Jerusalem, came on a journey to the West. They travelled through Italy to France, seeking assistance neither from the lord pope nor from the Roman emperor nor from the king of France. Instead, they sailed to England and came to the king at Reading. And as they explained their reasons for their great journey (such as was without parallel) and told in detail the devastation of the holy city, they moved the whole company, the king and all those who were present, to sighs and tears. And they gave into the king's hands memorials of the birth of Jesus Christ, of his passion and of his resurrection. For they gave the keys of David's tower, a piece of the holy cross and the keys of the holy sepulchre. All these things the king displayed with great reverence.

Richard, the new archbishop of Canterbury, was enthroned on 19 May; he was received in solemn procession at St Augustine's Abbey and celebrated mass there. The abbot, Roger, ministered to him, and wore a mitre in the procession on 26 May.

Herbert, an Englishman from Middlesex, when passing through Sicily, was made archbishop of Cosenza with the agreement of William king of Sicily. But then there was a great earthquake and the archbishop, his clergy and household, and a large part of the city were swallowed up, many castles destroyed and many people killed. A city was submerged by the Adriatic sea during the night,

Le Mans Cathedral

THE striking silhouette of Le Mans Cathedral still dominates the city, as it did in the 12th century. Although the choir, with its spectacular forked flying buttresses, is early 13th century, the nave was given its present form in the 1150s when the city belonged to the Plantagenets, and was solemnly dedicated in 1158 in the presence of Henry II and his court. The aisle walls, incorporated from the previous building, are almost entirely 11th century, their slightly uneven texture and striped light and dark stone details contrasting with the perfect surfaces and exquisitely carved capitals of the blond 12th-century limestone. Medieval patrons and architects always preserved as much as possible from previous buildings, partly because of their immense veneration for the past, but also because it was cheaper to re-use material: building a Gothic cathedral was an immensely expensive undertaking.

The nave of Le Mans is grandly spacious, very typical of the west of France. The striking domes of the big, square vaults, each covering a double bay, reflect the local Romanesque tradition. But Le Mans also contains elements of the new Gothic style; with the ribbing in its vaults, alternating arcades of simple columns and massive piers, and slightly tentative flying buttresses, the nave resembles the cathedral of Sens, one of France's oldest Gothic buildings, to the south of Paris.

The south porch was modelled on the Portail Royale at Chartres. Elegant figures of Old Testament kings and queens, dressed exactly as Eleanor or Henry would have been, flank the portal. Above, the figure of Christ in Majesty implacably pronounces the Last Judgement. The whole entrance was originally painted in bright red, blue and gold, like a wall painting, or a page of manuscript coming to vibrant, gaudy, three-dimensional life.

Top *The tympanum above the South Porch.*

Right *The great nave, with its Plantagenet vaulting.*

while all the people were asleep. In England too, in the north, there was an earthquake and in some places buildings were destroyed.

There was an eclipse of the sun on the afternoon of 1 May.

The king of France visited the king of England, who was ill, at Beauvoir on 9 November, and stayed for three days.

1186

On 27 January the archbishop of Vienne crowned Frederick as Holy Roman emperor at Milan, and on the same day the patriarch of Aquileia crowned Henry king of the Germans – and from that day he was called Caesar. A certain German bishop crowned Constance, William of Sicily's aunt. All this took place in the monastery of Sant'Ambrogio.

The French and English kings, the count of Flanders, the countess of Champagne and Margaret, the widow of Henry the Young King, met at Gisors on 10 March. The disagreement between the king of England and Margaret about her dowry and marriage-portion was brought to an amicable conclusion.

There was an eclipse of the moon on 16 April, just after sunset, and an eclipse of the sun on 21 April just after dawn.

King Henry took into his own hands the castles of Aquitaine which were most strongly fortified by nature or human skill and gave them to whatever custodians he wanted; although Richard count of Poitou was very offended he made no complaints to his father. And so, with Anjou, Touraine, Maine, Brittany and Normandy enjoying peace and tranquillity, the king came back to England, landing happily at Southampton on 27 April. The queen crossed with the king, in the same boat.

After disembarking the king visited the bishop of Winchester at Marwell, and spent the night at Winchester. The archbishop of Canterbury was coming to see the king, but the latter hurried out to meet him, showing all due respect, and in this his

The path to holiness

PILGRIMAGES – ranging from an individual's visit to the shrine of his local saint to the Crusades – are remarkable manifestations of the intense popular piety of medieval Christendom. Although the natural desire of men and women to visit holy places believed to be particularly cherished by their god is not confined to the Middle Ages or to Christianity, the widespread belief in the potency of the relics of Christian saints in medieval Europe was exceptional and gave pilgrimages their particular appeal.

With little direct encouragement from Church leaders, the overwhelming majority of clerks and laymen alike came to believe that a visit to a saint's shrine was the equivalent of visiting the person of the saint; the touch, or even the sight of the relics was a sure means of bringing health to the diseased and tranquillity to the troubled.

This pervasive belief in divine intervention led to a flourishing if often dubious traffic in relics, and also to saints' cults growing up in places which later became the

great pilgrimage centres of medieval Christendom. From the 11th century onwards, in addition to the prospect of a personal cure, pilgrims had the assurance that their *peregrinatio* might enable them to atone for past sins and earn some remission from the trials of purgatory. Although Jerusalem and Rome remained the most sacred places in the history of the Christian religion, the popularity of innumerable alternative centres waxed and waned according to how accessible they were and to changing fashions.

Pilgrims did not necessarily, or usually, confine their veneration to just one saint. Godric, a merchant from Norfolk (and later a saint) had visited Jerusalem, Rome and St. Andrews, before settling down to become a hermit at Finchale near Durham. He was also one of the first Englishmen known to have made the lengthy journey to Santiago (St. James) de Compostela. A tomb alleged to be that of St. James the Apostle had been discovered in the diocese of Ira Flavia in northern Spain in the 9th century. As a succession of ever more splendid churches on the site testified, it became the most successful pilgrimage centre of the age and increasing hordes of Christian pilgrims took the long *routes de Saint Jacques* – either by sea or land – to worship at his shrine.

Top left *Pilgrims from St Lazare cathedral, Autun.*

Above *The Door of Glory, Santiago Cathedral.*

Below *Pilgrims arrive late at a town's gates.*

humility exceeded that customary with his ancestors. The archbishop was received in solemn procession at Winchester on 1 May.

Geoffrey duke of Brittany, the king of England's son, passed away on 18 August, aged 28. He was buried in the choir of Notre-Dame at Paris. He left two daughters by his wife Constance, daughter of Count Conan of Brittany. Margaret, the sister of King Philip of France and widow of young King Henry, returned to Paris with a great train on 24 August. She was then married to Bela, king of Hungary, Dalmatia, Croatia and Ramma.

On the king's order, Richard dean of Lincoln and most of his chapter met at Eynsham on 24 May. After a long meeting about the affairs of their church, Hugh, a Burgundian from Grenoble, prior of the Carthusian order in England, was elected bishop of Lincoln in the presence of several bishops. Messengers were sent to Burgundy to tell the prior and convent of La Grande Chartreuse, who gave their assent. Thus Hugh, as most people wished, was consecrated bishop of Lincoln on 21 September in St Catherine's chapel, Westminster.

Adam of Eynsham also discusses Hugh's election to the bishopric of Lincoln, and follows it with a lively account of his sanctity.

This important see had been vacant for nearly eighteen years. The king realized his culpability for its neglected condition, since the deplorable vacancy was patently due to him. He therefore did his utmost to make amends for the havoc caused by the long neglect, through the energy of a carefully chosen husbandman.

As the clergy were hopelessly divided, since each of them, it is said, at heart desired the election of no one but himself, many persons urged and advised them to try to obtain as their bishop Hugh the prior of Witham, a man of exceptional goodness. Many commended his sanctity and wisdom, and lauded his charm and piety to the skies. All agreed that he was the only person who combined all the virtues with good breeding, and it was almost universally agreed that no more suitable bishop could be found.

The art of worship

TWELFTH-CENTURY mainland Italy falls into four artistically distinct regions: Rome, Tuscany, Venice and Lombardy.

Rome's art was conservative and its new churches, like S. Maria in Trastevere, with its slender columns and wooden roof, could have been built at any time during the previous ten centuries.

Tuscan architects, centred on the rich trading cities of Pisa and Lucca, were scarcely more enterprising. Pisa cathedral, however, begun in the 11th century and still under construction in the 13th, is a splendid, double-aisled building, encrusted inside and out with multicoloured marble. Its west front has a series of elegant, arcaded passages, one above the other, like a many-tiered wedding cake. Pisa, like many Italian cathedrals, follows the early Christian tradition of a cathedral complex with separate baptistery and bell tower.

In Venice, San Marco, originally the chapel of the ducal palace, was begun in 1063 and finished in the 1150s. It was built on the 'Greek cross' plan with its nave the same length as the transepts and eastern arm. Crowned by five domes, and with splendid mosaics, it might almost be in Constantinople and was undoubtedly built by Byzantine artists.

The most interesting artistic developments were in the politically active cities of northern Italy – Milan, Parma, Pavia, Modena and Verona – where architecture was valued for its own sake, and not swamped under sheets of marble or mosaic. Here, throughout the 12th century, a series of brilliant sculptors developed a new, lively, narrative style.

While French sculpture concentrated on religious themes, and drew its power from an intense spirituality, Italian sculptors remained closer to reality. They loved to produce jovial, secular scenes, like the Labours of the Months, carved in the capitals of Ferrara cathedral, and even their religious figures have a certain earthy corporeality.

Italy and its Roman heritage were of immense significance to the rest of Europe. In the 1140s, Bishop Alexander of Lincoln commissioned a frieze, to be modelled on one at Modena by Willigelmo, for the façade of his cathedral. Henry of Blois bought antique sculpture in Rome. Abbot Suger, in imitation of Italian churches, had a mosaic set into the west front of Saint-Denis. Needless to say, it did not stand the test of the inclement north European weather.

Left The bell tower at Pisa was begun in 1173, to match the earlier baptistery (begun in 1153) with its marble arcading. It began to tilt when it was only 35ft high.

Right A richly decorated mosaic at San Marco in Venice, showing the Creation.

Below St Ambrose in Milan is dedicated to the influential bishop of that city, who held office there from 374 to 397.

As this has already been described by Gerald, archdeacon of St David's, amongst certain other outstanding events connected with the saint, it seems best to quote his words. Here is his account:

"To return to the bishop of Lincoln, I do not think I should omit an incident which undoubtedly was intended to be a sign and portent of what his coming implied. On the very day of Hugh's enthronement, or thereabouts, as bishop of Lincoln, at his manor near Stow, which is about eight miles from the city of Lincoln, a delightful spot surrounded by woods and lakes, a swan suddenly arrived which had never been seen there before. In a few days, by reason of its weight and size, it had fought and killed all the other swans there, except for one female which it spared for company and not for breeding purposes. It was about as much larger than a swan as a swan is than a goose, but in everything else, especially in its colour and whiteness, it closely resembled a swan, except that in addition to its size it did not have the usual swelling and black streak on its beak. Instead, that part of its beak was flat and bright yellow in colour, as were also its head and the upper part of its neck.

This royal bird of unusual appearance and size, the first time the bishop came to the place, suddenly became completely tame. It let itself be captured without any difficulty and was brought to the bishop for him to admire. It immediately let him feed it, and remained with him as a pet, and for the time being apparently lost its wildness, and did not shun his attentions. It even seemed indifferent to the noise made by the crowds everywhere and the mob of spectators who constantly came and went. When the bishop fed it, the bird used to thrust its long neck up his wide and ample sleeve, so that its head lay on its inner fold, and for a little while would remain there, hissing gently, as if it were talking fondly and happily to its master, and seeking something from him.

The officials and bailiffs in charge of the manor, moreover, declared that whenever the bishop returned after one of his usual absences, for three or four days beforehand, the bird displayed more excitement than was customary with it. It flew over the surface of the river, beating the water with its wings, and giving vent to loud cries. From time to

time it left the pond, and hastily strode either to the hall or to the gate, as if going to meet its master on his arrival. It is quite conceivable that, as the fowls of the air are so sensitive because their natures contain so large an element of air and future events have frequently been predicted owing to their behaviour, that this bird may have known this instinctively from the preparations and bustle of the servants. Curiously enough, however, it was friendly and tame with no one but the bishop, and indeed, as I have sometimes seen myself, kept everyone else away from its master when it was with him, by hissing at them and threatening them with its wings and beak and emitting loud croaks as is the habit with swans. It seemed determined to make it completely clear that it belonged only to him, and was a symbol imparted to the saint alone.

When the bishop visited that place the last Easter before his departure from this earth, not only did it not come to meet him as usual, but it refused to be chased from the pond on which it was swimming in order to be brought to him. To the surprise of everyone, there it remained on the water looking depressed and ill, and its movements were languid. Finally, the bishop ordered that it should be brought to him, whether it wished it or not. For three days, a large number of people tried hard to do so, but their efforts were fruitless. It was at last captured amongst the rushes in a very remote part of the pond where it had taken refuge from its would-be captors. When it was brought to the bishop, with its hanging head and general air of wretchedness it seemed the very picture of grief, which strange occurrence amazed all who saw it.

The bishop's visit was exceedingly short, and just six months afterwards he had gone the way of all flesh, and so was never seen again by his friend the bird. Those who thought about the matter, then realized that its melancholy air meant that it was very sadly taking leave of its master for the last time. It survived him, however, for a long time."

Lincoln

IN 1185, when an earthquake struck the city of Lincoln, the cathedral's late 11th-century west front was undamaged. Built with positively military solidity, and even military technique – it contains slits through which boiling oil could be poured over attackers – it still stands today. The rest of the Romanesque cathedral was shattered; and in 1192 Bishop Hugh of Avalon began rebuilding it in the new elegant Gothic style. Only the choir and eastern transepts were built when he died eight years later, but the western transepts and nave soon followed in the early 13th century. In the 1250s Hugh's apse was destroyed, ironically to make way for the present angel choir, which was built to provide a more spacious setting for his relics. He had been canonized in 1220, and from the start his shrine had attracted a substantial pilgrimage.

The interior of Lincoln, with soft gold limestone offset by dark polished Purbeck 'marble' shafts, has a remarkable coherence, and is even richer than Canterbury. Rib and arch mouldings are more elaborate; capitals have lusher, windswept foliage and shafts spring from the heads of kings and queens instead of from leafy corbels or capitals, as at Canterbury. This lively, decorative approach to architectural form reached its peak in Lincoln's famous 'crazy vaults', where the vaulting is a continuous pattern of ribs, zigzagging along the full length of the choir, rather than a series of independent bays. The new opulence of Lincoln Cathedral, rather than Canterbury's severe, structural style, inspired English architectural development during the following centuries.

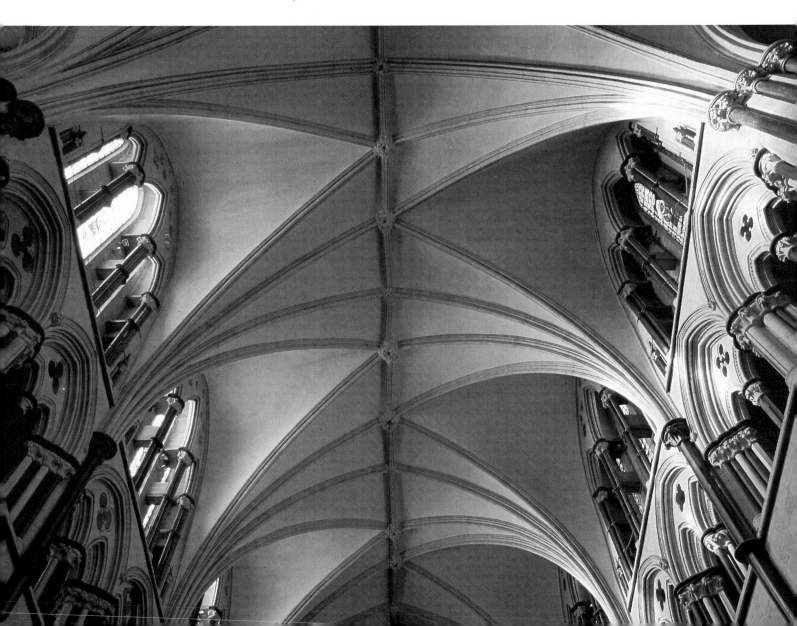

Below *Lincoln's unusual vaulting. Bishop Hugh of Avalon expended every effort to create a cathedral to reflect the greater glory of God, and Lincoln remains a remarkable testament to the inventiveness of medieval craftsmen.*

In spite of it being my great aim to avoid wearying my readers by long-windedness, I believe that I should mention that he was somewhat less abstemious in the matter of food after his assumption of the episcopal office than had been his wont before. He never touched flesh meat whether in sickness or health, but frequently ate fish. He did not abstain from wine altogether, but drank it in moderation, both on account of bodily weakness as the apostle advised and also as following his example to be all things to all men, and with the most exquisite courtesy to put those who ate with him at their ease. He was gay and lively at table, but at the same time dignified and restrained, always remembering, and sometimes even quoting to those who urged him to be merry, the text from the book of Esther 'The beauty of the saints has made us glad.' If, as occasionally happened at the grandest banquets, either in his own household or when he was a guest elsewhere, there was music or acting, he displayed the greatest detachment, hardly ever raising his eyes from the board. Every word and gesture made it apparent to those present how completely withdrawn he was, as if only his exterior senses were being charmed by these sweet delights.

Because of his unsullied innocence, which made him set great store by sincerity and simplicity, the saint had an unusual affection for children because of their complete naturalness. In this he resembled the Author of perfection, who said to his disciples 'Suffer the little children to come unto me and forbid them not, for of such is the kingdom of heaven.' Wherever he found them, he caressed them lovingly with angelic tenderness, and even when they could hardly talk, they made affectionate noises. He used to make the sign of the cross on their foreheads and their mouths and eyes, and bless them again and again, praying for their welfare. They in their turn made friends with him surprisingly quickly, and even those who generally were terrified of almost everybody, came to him more readily than to their parents.

I saw a child of about six months, who, when he made the sign of the cross on its forehead with the holy oil, expressed such great delight by the movement of its limbs, that it reminded one of the joy of the Baptist, leaping up in the womb. The

St Hugh and Witham

IN about 1163 Hugh of Avalon in Burgundy, a young man of noble birth, became a monk at La Grande Chartreuse monastery, high in the mountains near Grenoble. He had been admitted to the religious life as an Augustinian canon when still a child, but now sought the ascetic and largely solitary life of the Carthusian order. Such was his zeal, devotion to his ideals and desire for learning that his master early prophesied that he would one day be a bishop. But when Henry II, hearing about Hugh's qualities, asked him to go to England to head the new royal priory at Witham, Somerset, Hugh at first

refused. It took the strict orders of his prior to persuade him to depart.

Hugh found Witham priory only half planned and half endowed. Its monks lived huddled in a wood and lacked even basic essentials. Hugh immediately confronted the king, and persuaded him to grant adequate funds and to compensate the former peasant owners of the land where the monastery stood. Royal courtiers were taken aback by the directness with which Hugh approached the king, but Henry was captivated by his personality and delighted by his wit. They were strikingly similar in appearance and many people thought Hugh was Henry's natural son.

The king tried to heap favours on Hugh who, more often than not, refused. Henry presented Witham Priory with a fine bible which he had taken from Winchester

Above The site of the main church at Witham Priory; a few swans make their home on the lake, recalling St Hugh's friend, described on the previous page.

Cathedral, but Hugh, unafraid of the royal wrath, returned it to its rightful owners. Nor did Hugh wish to expand Witham once it had been properly established. Instead, he kept it a small, ascetic community, true to its Carthusian ideals.

In 1186 the king and the prior of La Grande Chartreuse persuaded Hugh to become bishop of Lincoln. However, according to his biographer, Adam of Eynsham, he retained his links with Witham and, in his old age, returned there for a month each year to live the solitary life of a Carthusian monk.

tiny mouth and face relaxed in continuous chuckles, and it seemed incredible that at an age when babies generally yell it could laugh in this way. It then bent and stretched out its little arms, as if it were trying to fly, and moved its head to and fro, as if to show that its joy was almost too great to bear. Next, it took his hand in both its tiny ones and, exerting all its strength, raised it to its face. It then proceeded to lick it instead of kissing it. This is did for a long time. Those present were amazed at the unusual spectacle of the bishop and the infant absolutely happy in each other's company. The bishop gave the boy an apple and several other things which children usually like, but he refused to be amused by any of them. He rejected them all and seemed completely absorbed and fascinated by the bishop. Disdainfully pushing away the hands of the nurse who was holding him, he gazed hard at the bishop, and clapped his hands smiling all the time.

When finally he was taken away, the company expressed surprise at such an unusual spectacle, and declared that they had never seen such a tiny being express such immense joy.

When Hugh was at the celebrated monastery of Fécamp, he extracted by biting two small fragments of the bone of the arm of the most blessed lover of Christ, Mary Magdalen. This bone had never been seen divested of its wrappings by the abbot or any of the monks who were present on that occasion, for it was sewn very tightly into three cloths, two of silk and one of ordinary linen.

They did not dare to accede even to the bishop's prayer to be allowed to see it. He, however, taking a small knife from one of his notaries, hurriedly cut the thread and undid the wrappings. After reverently examining and kissing the much venerated bone, he tried unsuccessfully to break it with his fingers, and then bit it first with his incisors and finally with his molars. By this means he broke off the two fragments, which he handed immediately to the writer, with the words, 'Take charge of this for me with especial care'.

When the abbot and monks saw what had happened, they were first overcome with horror,

and then became exceedingly enraged. They cried out, 'What terrible profanity! We thought that the bishop had asked to see this holy and venerable relic for reasons of devotion, and he has stuck his teeth into it and gnawed it as if he were a dog.' He mollified their anger with soothing words. Part of his speech is worth recording. 'If, a little while ago I handled the most sacred body of the Lord of all the saints with my fingers, in spite of my unworthiness, and when I partook of it, touched it with my lips and teeth, why should I not venture to treat in the same way the bones of the saints for my protection, and by this commemoration of them increase my reverence for them, and without profanity acquire them when I have the opportunity?'

1187

As Diceto shows, in 1187 the English and French kings prepared once more for war.

With his kingdom enjoying the delights of peace King Henry crossed the Channel from Dover on 17 February. Going through Flanders, he stayed at a castle called Hesdin and three days later entered Normandy, at Drincourt.

Constance countess of Brittany, who was pregnant at the death of her husband Geoffrey the son of the king of England, bore a son whom the Bretons called Arthur.

While the kings of France and England were gathering armies in the region of Bourges, drawing up their forces and arming them for war, they made a truce at Châteauroux on 23 June for two years, having paid each other compensation for damages, rather than submit matters to the doubtful judgement of Mars.

Margaret queen of France bore King Philip a son whom she called Louis.

The Knights Templar wrote the following letter to all Christians:

"Alas! no letters and no tearful voice could describe or enumerate the calamities that the anger of God, provoked by our sins, has visited upon us. The Turks gathered an immense army of their peoples and invaded the Christian kingdom. We brought together our own forces on 3 and 4 July, marched out and attacked them, moving towards Tiberias which they had taken by force, excepting only the castle. They drove us back to a most fearful cliff, where we were so badly overcome that the holy cross was captured, and the king of Jerusalem and our own master killed, and with them almost all our army and our own brothers, so that we truly believe two hundred and thirty men to have been beheaded that day, not counting the sixty who were killed on 1 May. The count of Tripoli, Lord Reinald of Sidon, and the Lord Balian (of Ibelin) and ourselves were barely able to escape from that miserable field. From there, wallowing in Christian blood, they quickly went with all their army to Acre. They took over almost the whole country, leaving only Jerusalem, Ascalon and Tyre in our hands. Almost all the townsmen of those places were killed in the battle, and unless divine assistance and the aid of noblemen come quickly we shall not be able to hold onto them. The city of Tyre is hard pressed at this moment, and they attack it continually day and night. They are in such numbers that the whole country from Tyre to Jerusalem and down to Gaza looks like an antheap.*"*

Richard count of Poitou, son of Henry II and first among the barons of France, took the cross, from the hand of the archbishop of Tours, without asking his father or waiting to hear his wishes.

1188

On 22 January the king of the French and the king of the English met for a conference. After long discussions the English king was the first to take the cross from the archbishops of Tyre and Rouen. Afterwards the French king took the cross from the archbishops of Tyre and Reims, and then Philip of Flanders took it and very many joined him. They agreed amongst themselves that the French should wear red crosses, the English white crosses and those from Flanders green crosses. After he had taken the cross, the English king sent his household clerk Richard Barre, archdeacon of Lisieux, to the emperors of Rome and Constantinople.

At about this time Geoffrey of Lusignan killed a friend of Richard count of Poitou in an ambush. Count Richard took up arms to punish this crime, but mindful that he had taken the cross, he permitted those of Geoffrey's men who were willing to take the cross to do so; many he put to the sword and he captured many castles. Geoffrey, maintained with forces and money by the English king, it is said, resisted the count but made little progress. Because of this Richard count of Poitou was alienated from his father. Count Richard crossed into Gascony and attacked the count of Toulouse and within a short time, reinforced by Brabançons, he had taken seventeen castles in the region of Toulouse. But the king of France was outraged that Richard count of Poitou had attacked his kingdom, for he had neither renounced his homage nor informed him; and he surprised the castle of Châteauroux in Berry on 16 June and forced all the inhabitants to do him fealty. This seemed to be greatly unworthy of a prince, especially since after taking the cross the king of England had crossed to England leaving all his lands in the keeping of the king of France, who undertook the custody in good faith.

Then the king of France won over to his side with threats or promises certain castellans who were subjects of the English king. When he heard this King Henry crossed to France around 25 July. He gathered a large army of English, Marchers, Welsh and Bretons. But he kept them restrained for many days living in tents in Normandy when they were eager to make an attack on France.

At length the kings held a conference on 16 August between Gisors and Trie which lasted for three days. When however the kings on both sides withdrew in discord, the king of France ordered a certain tree near Gisors, but rooted within the French kingdom, to be cut down. The English king, leaving Gisors the next day, crossed through Vernon and invaded France, laying waste as far as Mantes.

On 18 November a meeting was held between the French and English kings at Bonsmoulins, which Richard count of Poitou had arranged. When it came to the conference the French king proposed that he should restore to the English king everything he had gained since taking the cross and that afterwards everything should remain as it had been before he had taken the cross. The king of the English replied, on the advice of the clergy as much as the barons, that it was better to enter a firm peace than to drag out a damnable quarrel.

When he heard this Henry's son Richard count of Poitou spoke against it, for it seemed to him incongruous to return Quercy on this condition, and also to return the whole county and much else in his demesne worth one thousand marks or more per annum, for the fee of Châteauroux, the castle of Issoudun, and Graçay. The count of Poitou wanted something else, asking his father to give him the sister of the French king as his wife, and demanding that King Henry would confirm his land to him as the king's heir. This he had to ask through the French king. The English king replied that he would not do this, since it would look as if he had been coerced. After this the count of Poitou, in the sight of all, did homage to the French king for all his father's holdings which pertained to the French kingdom, saving his father's lands while he lived and the loyalty which he owed his father. Thus the conference ended and the truce was prolonged until 13 January.

1189

A newsletter from the East.

"Saladin's army was defeated at Antioch. The prince of Antioch rode out each day as far as Aleppo. Admiral Margarit took Jaffa, and killed all the Turks there, about five thousand of them, and he took eight emirs. He also took Jebail and killed everyone. The lord of Mulla, one of Saladin's chiefs, attacked Saladin, and so did the Lord Marendim. The caliph, lord of Baghdad, the chief of all the Turks, attacked Saladin as far as he was able. You know that the sultan of Iconium married his daughter to Saladin's son, and Saladin married his daughter to a son of the sultan, and it is well known how Kutepez, Saladin's son, killed his wife the daughter of the sultan. For it is certain and beyond doubt, as all say, that the prophecy of Daniel of Constantinople is true, that in the year when the Annunciation falls on Easter Day the French will restore the promised land, and they shall stable their

horses in the palm groves of Baghdad and set up their tents beyond the dry tree and the tares will be separated from the wheat. And you know most certainly that a causeway has been found in the Hellespont.

"It is openly acknowledged that the sultan hates the emperor of Constantinople, because he has not paid the four hundred pounds of gold he ought to have paid each year since he became emperor, nor the other three hundred pounds. Take note, brothers, of what the emperor once said to us, so that the eye may not be deceived. Otherwise I can tell you that so many Turks were captured at Tyre that two Turks could be bought for one bezant. Saladin said that he had in his custody a messenger of Eustace Patricius and Balian, who had the wife of the king of Jerusalem, when the count of Tripoli handed over to him the promised land. And you know that the emperor showed greater honour to the envoys of Saladin in his palace than to anyone else of high rank there. Saladin then handed over all the churches of the Holy Land to the emperor's envoys, so that they might be served according to the Greek custom. Nor is trust to be placed in anyone Greek, even if he gives his hand. You know that Saladin with the agreement of the emperor sent his idol to Constantinople to be publicly worshipped there; but by the grace of God it was captured at sea by the Genoese, and it together with the ship was taken to Tyre. And now there is news that Saladin's army is stopped at Antioch.

"The prophecy which an old Greek from Astralix told the Lord Walter of the Templars, which offended the rest of the Greeks, will now be fulfilled as they say, that the Latins will govern and be lords in the city of Constantinople, because it is written on the golden gates which have not been opened for the past two hundred years, that 'when a red-haired king comes from the west, I shall open by myself'. Asan, that worthy man, has been poisoned in his imperial vestments. The emperor promised Saladin one hundred galleys and Saladin gave him all the promised land if the emperor would prevent the arrival of the French. Truly I tell you that if anyone touches the cross of Constantinople he is immediately taken and put into prison. This, however, is the

Stars of fortune

THE great increase in the study of astrology during the 12th century can only be understood in the context of contemporary beliefs. For medieval man the supernatural world was ordered and meaningful, while human existence was disorderly and could be predicted only in terms of God's intentions. When Arab texts describing a direct relationship between the movements of the stars and events on earth poured into the West during the 12th century, they were readily received by Europeans. Genethliac astrology, interpreting the positions of heavenly bodies at the moment of an individual's birth, particularly interested people at this time. Astrologers were in permanent residence in royal palaces – in 1228 Michael Scot completed his great encyclopedia of astrology at the court of the Emperor Frederick II of Hohenstaufen.

Astrologers were tolerated by the Church, as were popular preacher-prophesiers, as long as neither stepped beyond the canons of orthodoxy. But there appeared some strange messianic figures in the popular religious movements of the 11th, 12th and 13th centuries – Fulk of Neuilly, for example, a fiery preacher who made a series of evangelistic missions in the 1190s and who was particularly concerned with converting prostitutes from their sinful ways. In 1198 he began to arouse popular fervour for what was to become the Fourth Crusade. He was an ascetic miracle worker with the alleged power to heal the blind and dumb, who wanted – and raised – an army only of the poor; he set hordes of people in motion and they perished on the coast of Spain. Joachim of Fiore,

a Cistercian abbot from Calabria living as a hermit (between 1190 and 1195), worked out a highly popular, complex, revolutionary theory of history that made present and future comprehensible: Man was moving through a succession of ages culminating in the Last Judgement. In 1190–1 Joachim met Richard the Lionheart *en route* for the Third Crusade, and prophesied that, since Saladin was the identifiable sixth of the seven persecutors of the Church, he and his armies would soon fall. Richard would be the instrument of this inevitable event.

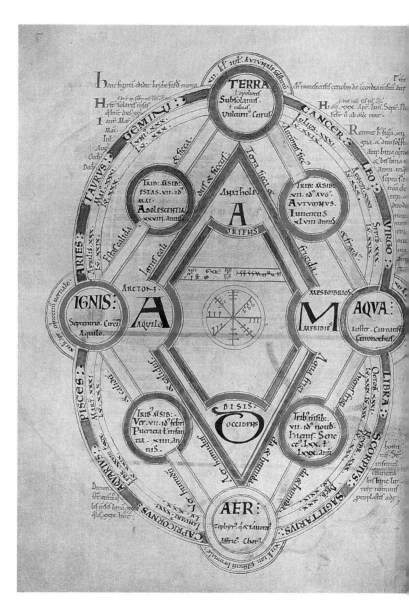

Top left *The signs of the zodiac, still used in casting horoscopes, are shown in an 11th-century manuscript.*

Above *The four elements of fire, water, earth and air were used to foretell health and fortune, and in prescribing medicine for illness or other disorders.*

187

prophecy of the Turkish astrologers, that within these three years, a third of the Turks will perish by the sword, another third will flee beyond the dry tree and the other third will be baptized. We know indeed that Saladin could not find any Turks who would build in the promised land or take their families there for fear of the arrival of the French. On the day that the bearer of this letter left Constantinople there came certain messengers saying that Saladin's army had been destroyed at Antioch and that Saladin's brother and his son had been captured. On the day that I left the emperor ordered the extermination of all the Latins in his empire. And you know that by the grace of God in the kingdom of Iconium there are five thousand good Armenians and twenty-five emirs ready to go with the French in the defence of Christianity and for the liberation of the land where our lord Jesus Christ was born and died."

After the following Easter, negotiations were held twice between the kings of France and England and Richard count of Poitou at La Ferté Bernard. But in the end, after lengthy talks, they withdrew on both sides as enemies.

The tragic final days of Henry II's reign, and the king's death, are well described in The Deeds of King Henry II.

Philip king of France departed and took La Ferté Bernard. On the Monday following, when the king of England and his men appeared to be at a safe distance from the farthest point of the French king's advance, the latter arranged his army in line of battle in preparation for an attack upon the city of Le Mans. Seeing which, Stephen of Tours, the seneschal of Anjou, set fire to the suburb. But the fire immediately grew to immense proportions and leaping across the city walls set the city itself aflame. Many of the English king's army were taken. The rest incontinently took to flight, desiring to retreat into the city. But the French forced an entry together with them; seeing which the king of England, despairing of his lot and breaking his promise, fled from the city with seventy knights. For he had promised the citizens that he would not leave them in the lurch, in the first place because his father's body rested there, in

the second because he himself was born there and loved the city above all others. The French king, however, pursued him for three miles, and had the River Sarthe by which the French crossed not been running enormously high, they would have pursued the other fugitives with such swiftness that, as is commonly asserted, they would all have been taken prisoner.

The English king, however, came with a small retinue to Chinon and withdrew into the fortress there. But the remnant of the king's household retired into the citadel of the castle at Le Mans. At once the king of France besieged the citadel and assaulted it both with his engineers and with missiles of war; at length within three days the citadel surrendered with thirty knights and sixty men-at-arms.

On the Sunday next following, Philip count of Flanders, William archbishop of Reims and Hugh duke of Burgundy came to the king of England, who was then at Saumur, rather of their own initiative than at the king's will, to make a settlement between them. But the king of France had warned them before they set out on their journey that he would, notwithstanding, prepare an attack upon the city from the fortress of St Martin, to which he had retired across the River Loire.

On the following Monday 3 July, about the third hour, the city of Tours was taken by storm by an assault from the bank of the Loire, in consequence of the lower level of the river – the volume of water being reduced beyond measure – and ladders being placed against the walls; within the city eighty knights and a hundred men-at-arms were taken prisoner. For shame! The king of England, placed in a difficult position, made peace with Philip king of France, in this wise.

"Henry, king of England, has put himself in all things at the advice and will of Philip, king of France, to the effect that, whatsoever the king of France has provided and decreed, the king of England will wholly perform without opposition. First, the king of England again paid homage to the king of France because, as related above, he had

Father of the common law

HENRY II was a man of wide abilities and considerable learning, and one of his greatest interests was in the workings of the law. Almost fortuitously, he was king of England during a century that saw a revived interest in Roman law and customs and produced flourishing schools of jurisprudence. To anyone well versed in this new learning, the English system of customary law, much of it rooted in the Anglo-Saxon period, must have seemed needlessly complex, cumbersome, unreasonable and slow.

There were a great many courts of law in England – royal, county, hundred and borough courts, courts of the feudal honour, manor and village courts, and Church courts held for or by archbishops or archdeacons – and many had overlapping jurisdictions. A man's status in society and how he held his lands was as important as his alleged offence or the nature of a dispute in determining which court he had to attend. Instead of trying to sweep this morass aside, Henry and his advisers, recognizing that there was some good in the system, took the best elements of what was there and made them work more efficiently.

Kings traditionally intervened to remedy complaints that justice had not been done, and Henry did so, in person, on many occasions.

The royal court, which sat in the king's absence under the control of his justiciar, met more frequently than before, heard more cases and sent groups of justices to hear more pleas in the shires. Legal changes were made as a result of cumulative case law and through assizes – judicial instructions issued by the king.

Traditionally, the truth or otherwise of evidence in a case was established by oath or through ordeal by fire, water or battle. During Henry's reign, the jury of 12 sworn men began to replace this method. One of the most difficult areas of the law involved the possession of land, and the crown standardized the wording and procedures of the writ of right, which ordered lords to do justice in such cases. People unjustly dispossessed of their lands were later given redress through new writs. The most important of these was the writ of *novel disseisin*, by which a royal justice summoned a jury to establish whether the man bringing the action had indeed had his lands seized and if so by whom. A heavy fine was imposed on the loser. Settlements of land disputes were recorded in the form of final concords or agreements. (The text, if not the use, of these documents continued virtually unchanged into the 19th century.) There is no doubt that Henry II was personally, and sustainedly, involved with these developments.

The changes and clarifications which the Plantagenet king and his justices made to the laws of England, and to the procedures through which they took effect, were crucially important to the development of the English legal system.

Below *Henry's writ ordering restoration of land to the canons of Lincoln, and telling the sheriff to have a jury ascertain the facts.*

Overleaf *The castle at Chinon.*

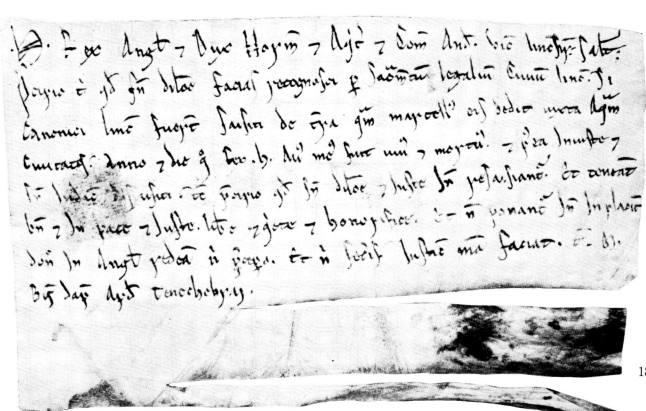

189

surrendered his dominions to the king of France, who had requited him at the beginning of this truce. Secondly, the king of France has appointed that his sister Alice, whom the king of England holds in wardship, shall be surrendered and handed over to the custody of one of five [barons] whom Count Richard of Poitou shall choose. Moreover, the king of France has provided that his sister shall be granted safe-conduct on the oath of the men of the land for her marriage to Count Richard on his return from Jerusalem, and that Count Richard shall have the fealty of the men of his father's lands both on this side of the channel and beyond. Also, none of the barons or knights, who have withdrawn their allegiance from the king of England in the recent war and have come over to Count Richard, shall in future return to the king of England, except within the last month before the king sets out for Jerusalem.

The time-limit for this journey shall be mid-Lent. So the said kings and Richard count of Poitou shall meet on that date at Vézelay.

Also, all the townsfolk of the demesne vills of the king of England in all lands of the French king shall be quit by their lawful customs and shall not be impleaded in any matter unless they have trespassed by a felony.

Also, the king of England shall pay twenty thousand marks in silver to the king of France; and all the barons of the king of England shall swear to stand by the king of France and Count Richard and to assist them to the utmost of their power against the king of England, if he does not fulfil these agreements. Also, the king of France and Count Richard shall take possession of the city of Le Mans and the castles of Château-du-Loir and Trou; or if the king of England shall prefer, the king of France and Count Richard shall hold the castles of Gisors, Paci and Nonancourt, until everything is carried out as the king of France has appointed above."

Henry, king of England died in the year of our Lord 1189, in the month of July, on the sixth day of the month, within the Octave of the Apostles Peter and Paul, in the nineteenth lunation, on the fifth day of the week, at Chinon.

He was buried at Fontevrault in the abbey of the nuns who served God there.

The day after his death, when he was borne to burial, he lay in state robed in royal splendour, wearing a gold crown on his head, gauntlets on his hands and a gold ring on his finger, holding the sceptre in his hand, with gold-braided shoes and spurs on his feet, girded with his sword, and his face uncovered. When this had been reported to Count Richard, his son, he came post-haste to meet the cortège. At his coming blood began to flow forthwith from the dead king's nostrils as if his spirit was moved with indignation. The said count, weeping and lamenting, followed his father's corpse in procession as far as Fontevrault, where it was given burial.

The old king at bay

HENRY II was denied the peaceful and honourable end to his reign which he so fully deserved. This was largely because of the dissensions within his own family. Although the death of the Young King in 1183 removed a dangerous threat – a hostile and cunning crowned heir in league with the old king's enemies – the remaining sons were anxious to know what was going to happen. Henry quickly forced Richard to return Aquitaine to his mother, and sent John to Ireland on what proved to be an abortive expedition, but otherwise kept his intentions secret. His sons steadily became more angry and restive.

Family relationships deteriorated from then on, and in 1188, two years after Geoffrey had died, Richard and Philip of France resolved their many differences and united against Henry II. In 1189 Philip and Richard together attacked Normandy. Henry at first put up a spirited defence but his phenomenal energy suddenly left him and he fell ill. Accompanied by only a few retainers, he left his army and retreated to Chinon, the heart of his Angevin lands, to die.

Below *Henry's tomb at Fontevrault.*

Philip and Richard overran Normandy and Maine and forced the sick king to travel to Ballan, where they compelled him to accept humiliating terms. Henry was to do homage to Philip for all his French lands, and place himself in his hands, while Richard was to inherit all the Plantagenet dominions, including England. Henry was carried back to Chinon in a litter where, the next day, he learnt that John, his favourite son, had deserted him. He became delirious and died the next day, 6 July.

One chronicler describes how, when Richard went to attend the corpse lying in state at Fontevrault Abbey, blood gushed from the dead king's nostrils as a sign of anger with his faithless son. Henry II's reign, which had begun in triumph, ended in defeat and tragedy.

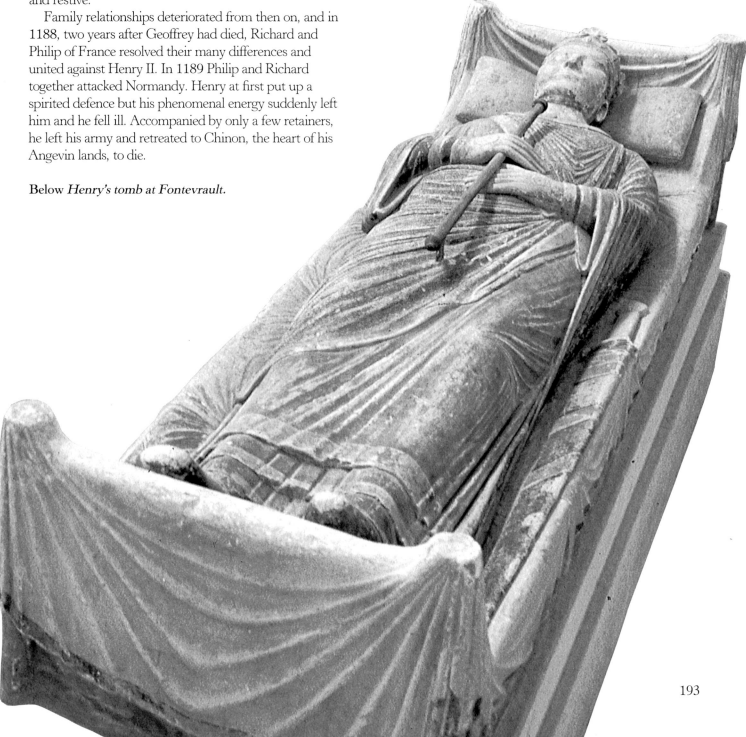

Part IV

Richard I
1189–1199

Richard the Lionheart shared some of his father's administrative capacity, but his raison d'être was the battlefield. He waged war ferociously, savagely and charismatically for most of his reign, sucking his vast dominions almost dry of funds in the process. His obsession took him to the Holy Land in 1191–2 on a crusade which, although in many ways successful, ended in disaster. He was captured while returning to England, and held to ransom in a German prison in 1193–4. On arriving home Richard returned to the battlefield, this time against his fellow-crusader Philip II of France. Richard met his premature death in 1199 during a minor skirmish with an Aquitanian ally of Philip.
The French king's hostility towards Richard stemmed partly from the Lionheart's rejection of his sister Alice, despite being betrothed to her since childhood, for Berengaria of Navarre. Berengaria did not produce an heir for Richard and this gave his brother John, count of Mortain, extra scope for his numerous conspiratorial schemes.
In Part IV, Ralph of Diceto's Images of History *is once again the main chronicle, this time describing the events of Richard's reign.*

(Opposite: Richard I)

Richard count of Poitou, after arranging matters the best to ensure peace and tranquillity in Aquitaine, Anjou, Touraine and Maine, arrived in Normandy three weeks after his father's death, on 6 July 1189, and met the archbishops of Canterbury and Rouen at Séez. He asked and received pardon from them for his offence in taking up arms against his own father after the launching of the crusade. He came thence to Rouen where he received the sword and standard of the duchy of Normandy from the hands of the archbishop of Rouen, before the high altar in the church of the Blessed Virgin, while a great crowd of nobles looked on.

He then went on to England and was received with stately ceremony at Winchester on 15 August. Queen Eleanor, who for many years had been under close guard, was entrusted with the power of acting as regent by her son. Indeed he issued instructions to the princes of the realm, almost in the style of a general edict, that the queen's word should be law in all matters.

Since Richard had resisted his father and had, as it seemed, done much to stir up the French factions that were hostile to the Normans, he had earned the disapproval of good and wise men. Now, however, he sought to make up for all his past excesses by

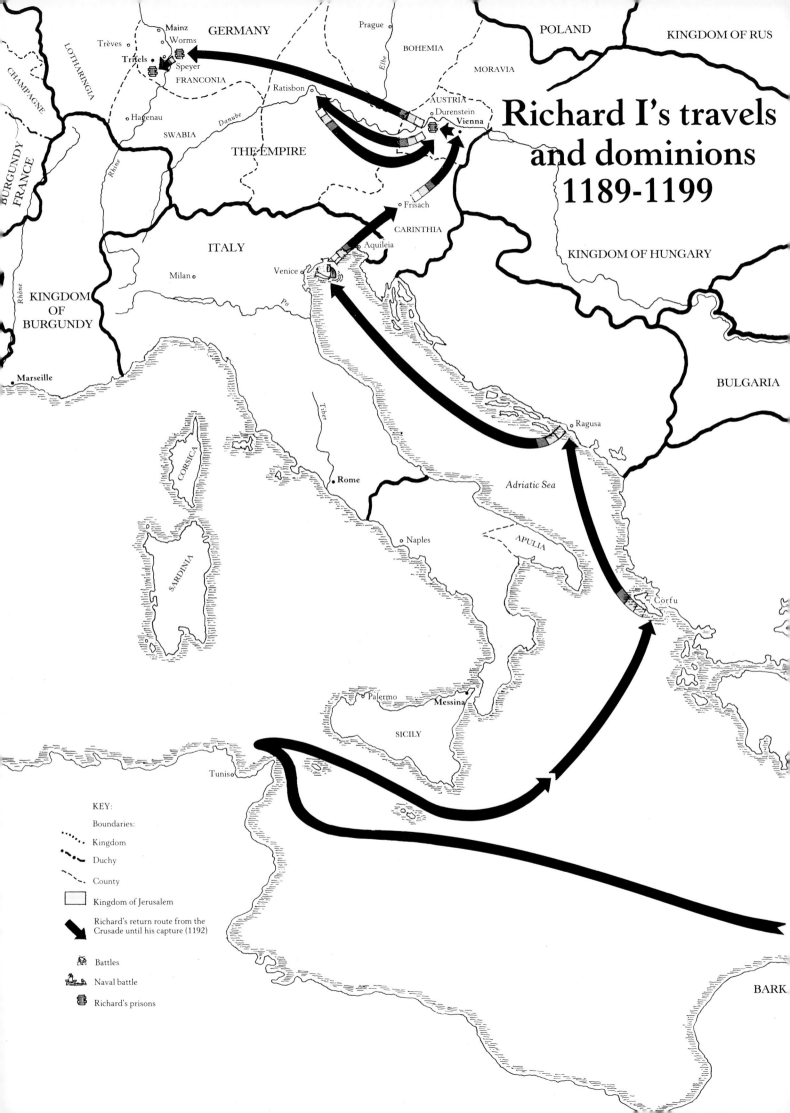

GERMANY

Mainz

Trèves
Worms

Triels
Speyer
FRANCONIA

LOTHARINGIA

Hagenau

SWABIA

Danube

CHAMPAGNE

BURGUNDY
FRANCE

Rhine

Rhône

KINGDOM
OF
BURGUNDY

Marseille

Prague

POLAND

KINGDOM OF RUS

BOHEMIA

Elbe

MORAVIA

Ratisbon

THE EMPIRE

AUSTRIA
Durenstein Vienna

Frisach

CARINTHIA

Aquileia

Richard I's travels and dominions 1189-1199

KINGDOM OF HUNGARY

ITALY

Milan

Venice

Po

Tiber

CORSICA

Rome

SARDINIA

Naples

APULIA

Adriatic Sea

Ragusa

BULGARIA

Corfu

Palermo

Messina

SICILY

Tunis

KEY:

Boundaries:

.... Kingdom

––·––·–– Duchy

– – – – County

Kingdom of Jerusalem

Richard's return route from the
Crusade until his capture (1192)

Battles

Naval battle

Richard's prisons

BARK

The first year of his reign Richard spent in preparing and financing his great Crusade, and he was then away from his dominions for more than four years.

His expedition to the Holy Land was undertaken in uneasy alliance with Philip Augustus of France, who learned to fear Richard's military prowess and who profited from Richard's captivity in Germany by seizing castles and lands on the Norman borders. Once Richard had returned in 1194 he was forced to expend most of his energies and the profits of taxation in a long campaign to recover these lands. England he hardly visited, but drained off its silver. He had only just recovered the ground lost when he died in 1199.

Richard I left the borders of the Plantagenet lands much as he had found them in 1189, except that he had granted Quercy and the Agenais to the count of Toulouse as the dowry of his sister.

GEORGIA

QUERCY
AGENAIS

KEY:

Richard I's dominions

Granted by Richard in 1196

Black Sea

Constantinople

EASTERN EMPIRE

Tigris

Mosul

SELJUK SULTANATE OF RUM

EDESSA

Edessa

Euphrates

Antioch

PRINCIPALITY
OF ANTIOCH

TRIPOLI

SELJUK EMPIRE

CYPRUS

Tripoli

Gibelet

Damascus

Tyre

Acre

Mediterranean Sea

Arsuf
Jaffa

Jericho

Jerusalem

KINGDOM OF JERUSALEM

Krak

CRETE

thens

Alexandria

FATIMITE CALIPHATE

Cairo

Nile

Red Sea

EGYPT

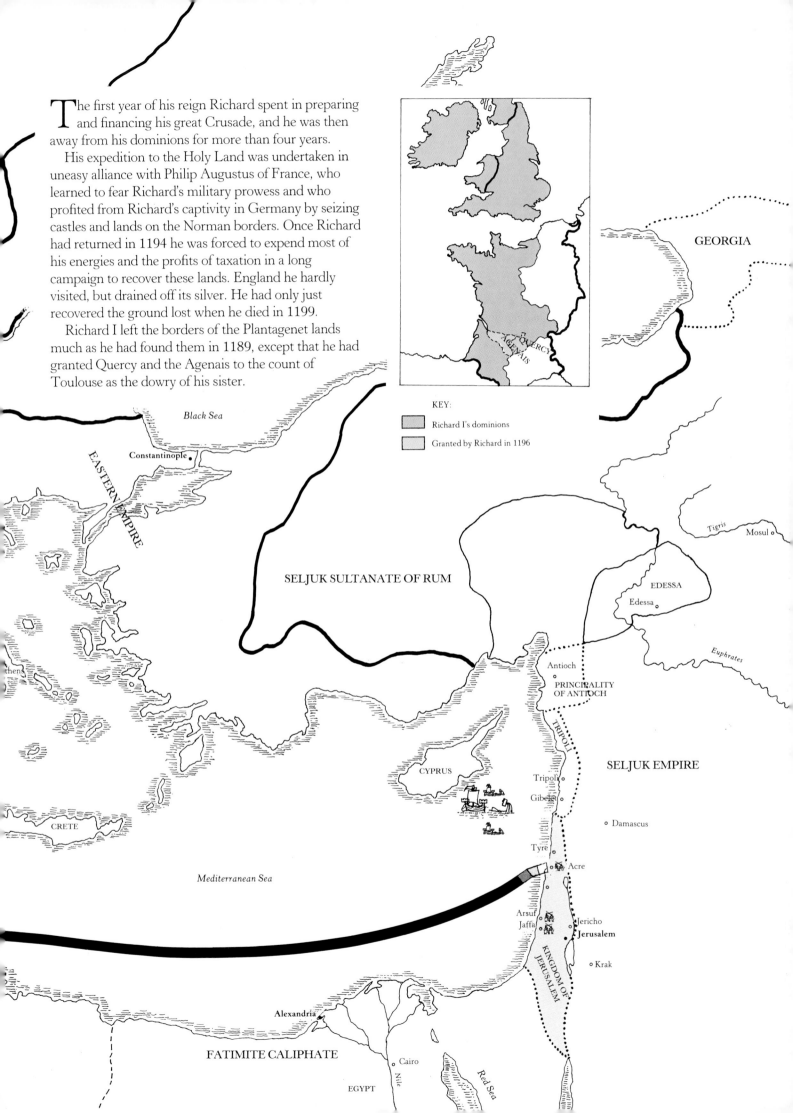

doing all he could to show honour to his mother. He hoped that his obedience to his mother would atone for his offence against his father.

These events revealed the truth of a prophecy which had puzzled all by its obscurity: 'The eagle of the broken bond shall rejoice in the third nestling.' They called the queen the eagle because she stretched out her wings, as it were, over two kingdoms – France and England. She had been separated from her French relatives through divorce, while the English had separated her from her marriage bed by confining her to prison (she was imprisoned for sixteen years altogether). Thus for both lands she was 'the eagle of the broken bond'. The second part of the prophecy, 'shall rejoice in the third nestling', you may understand as follows: Eleanor's first born son was William, who died while still a child. Henry, her second son, was raised to the estate of king but took up arms against his own father and paid his debt to nature. Richard, her third son – and thus the third nestling – was the one who would raise his mother's name to great glory. Queen Eleanor, learning that King Henry II's horses had been kept in the stables of the abbeys, distributed them as gifts with pious liberality. She contained the depredations of those sheriffs who were charged with the care of the forests, intimidating them with the threat of severe penalties.

On the summons of the archbishop of Canterbury the other bishops gathered at London on 3 September for the new king's coronation; the abbots and priors of the monasteries also came. Queen Eleanor, the count's mother, was asked at the request of the earls, barons and sheriffs. It is impossible to list all the bishops, but the archbishops of Canterbury, Trèves and Dublin were there.

The Deeds of King Richard *gives a vivid and detailed description of Richard I's coronation.*

Here begins the ceremony of the coronation of King Richard.

First came the bishops and abbots and many clerics dressed in purple copes, with the cross, candles, and thuribles going before them, up to the door of the inner chamber. And there they

The troubled lion

THERE are two Richard the Lionhearts: the Richard of legend, and the Richard of history. They are not easy to distinguish as the legend seems to have evolved naturally from the real man.

Always the first to attack, the last to retreat, he was described by an enemy as the 'most remarkable ruler of his times'. A typical picture is of Richard wading ashore at Jaffa to relieve the hard-pressed Christian garrison, calling 'shame on him who lags behind'. Richard took the 'impregnable' Taillebourg in Saintonge in three days; and raised Château Gaillard within two years.

Reckless in skirmishes, he was once saved only by the bravery of William of Préaux who diverted the enemy by pretending to be Richard. In Cyprus, Richard told a clerk who dared to urge caution on him to stick to his writing 'and leave matters of chivalry to us'.

Less flatteringly, one historian describes him as 'a bad son, a bad husband, a selfish ruler, and a vicious man', while another recalls his cold-blooded slaughter of the 'infidel' garrison of Acre. On another occasion, he hurled three prisoners to their deaths from a rock at Andelys, and blinded 15 others. Selfish and violent he once seized a valuable falcon in Sicily while threatening the owner with his sword; and became almost insanely angered when William of Barres bested him in a mock joust with canes. Richard was speaking what he believed to be the truth when he told the Holy Roman Emperor: 'I am born of a rank which recognizes no superior but God.'

He was undoubtedly a leader men could follow, just as his severity made him a king to be feared. When John's castellan of Mont St Michel heard that the king had returned to England after his captivity he dropped dead from fright.

Richard confessed his sins publicly on more than one occasion. At Messina in Sicily he threw himself almost naked before bishops to confess to the 'foulness of his past life'. A chronicler acidly commented: 'Happy is he who after repentance has not slipped back into sin.' The evidence for the recently fashionable view that he was a homosexual is slim; indeed, it suggests rather that he was a womanizer: he had a bastard son, Philip of Cognac.

Richard's generous spirit is shown in his forgiveness of both John for his treachery and plotting against him in his absence and, with less reason, of William of Barres for beating him in a mock tournament; and in his eventually giving the kiss of peace to St Hugh after the saint had first defied then shaken him. An educated man, he could joke in Latin at the expense of an archbishop of Canterbury, and while away the hours in his German prison writing songs.

Above *The great abbey at Chertsey has disappeared, but some of its remarkable pictorial tiles survive, including this picture of Richard Coeur de Lion.*

received the aforementioned Richard who was to be crowned and led him into the church of Westminster in this manner up to the altar with a solemn procession and hymnody.

In front went the clerics dressed in white, carrying the holy water and the cross and the candles and the thuribles, next came the abbots, then the bishops. In the middle of those men, however, went four barons carrying candelabra with candles.

After them came John Marshal, carrying in his hands two large and heavy spurs from the king's treasure. Next to him went Godfrey de Luci carrying the royal cope.

After them came two earls, namely William Marshal, earl of Pembroke and William earl of Salisbury. William Marshal was carrying the royal sceptre, on the top of which was a golden design of the cross; William earl of Salisbury was carrying the royal rod, which had a dove on the top.

And after them came three earls, namely David, the brother of the king of Scotland, earl of Huntingdon, and Robert earl of Leicester, and between them went John, count of Mortain and earl of Gloucester, Richard's brother. They were carrying three swords with splendid golden sheaths from the king's treasure.

And after them came six earls and barons carrying a single board on which were placed the royal accoutrements and clothes.

And after them went William de Mandeville, count of Aumâle and earl of Essex, carrying the golden crown in his hands. Next came Richard duke of Normandy, count of Poitou. Hugh, bishop of Durham went on his right, and Reginald bishop of Bath went on his left, and a silk coverlet was carried over them. And the entire crowd of earls and barons and knights and others, both clerics and laymen, followed up into the nave of the church, and so through the church up to the altar.

Then after he had arrived at the altar, Duke Richard made three oaths to the aforesaid arch-bishops and bishops, earls, barons, clergy and people. Accordingly he swore and promised on the most holy Gospels and on the relics of many saints, that he would bear peace and honour and reverence towards God and the holy Church and her ministers all the days of his life. Next he swore that he would administer fair justice to the people committed to him. Then he swore that if there were any bad laws or corrupt customs in his kingdom he would destroy them, and uphold good ones.

Then they stripped him of the clothes which he had been wearing, except for his shirt and breeches. That shirt was unstitched at the shoulder.

Then they shod him with sandals woven from gold.

Then the archbishop put the sceptre in his right hand and the royal rod in his left.

Then Baldwin, archbishop of Canterbury, pouring holy oil over him on three parts of his body, namely on his head, on his shoulders and on his right arm, with the appointed prayers for this act, anointed him as king.

Then he placed on his head a consecrated linen cloth and the cope over it. Then they dressed him in the royal garments: first a tunic, then a dalmatic.

Then the archbishop entrusted to him the sword for constraining those who do wrong to the Church.

Then the two earls put on him the splendid golden spurs from the king's treasure.

Then he was dressed in the cloak. Then he was led to the altar, and warned by the archbishop and forbidden by the authority of God that as a man he should not assume this honour for himself, unless he kept it in mind to maintain the oaths and promises which he had made earlier. And he answered that with God's help everything he had said before would be upheld in good faith.

Then he took the crown from the altar, and gave it to the archbishop and the archbishop placed it on the head of the king.

And so the crowned king was led to his throne. Hugh bishop of Durham on his right and Reginald bishop of Bath on his left were leading him, the candles and the aforementioned three swords going before them.

Then the Lord's Mass was begun. And when it reached the point of the offertory, the two aforesaid bishops led him to the offering, and then led him back to his throne.

After Mass had been celebrated and everything had been carried out according to the service, the two aforesaid bishops, one on his right and one on his left, led back the crowned king, carrying the sceptre in his right hand and the royal rod in his left; properly advancing from the church to the king's own dwelling by procession. Then the procession returned into the choir.

Meanwhile the king took off his crown and royal vestments, and put on a lighter crown and clothes, and thus the crowned man came to the banquet. And the archbishops and the bishops and the abbots and the other clergy were seated with him on his own table, each one according to his rank and worthiness. The earls and the barons and the knights were sitting at other tables and they feasted magnificently.

After they had banqueted, however, the leaders of the Jews arrived against the express decree of the king. And since the previous day the king had forbidden by public notice that any Jew or Jewess could come to his coronation, the courtiers laid hands on the Jews and stripped them and flogged them and having inflicted blows, threw them out of the king's court. Some they killed, others they let go half dead. One of those Jews was so badly injured with slashes and wounds that he despaired of his life; and so terrified was he by the fear of death that he accepted baptism from William, prior of the Church of St Mary at York, and was christened William. And in this way he avoided the danger of death and the hands of his persecutors.

However, the people of the city of London, hearing that the courtiers had raged thus against the Jews, turned on the Jews of the city and robbed them and killed many of both sexes; they set light to their houses and razed them to ashes and embers. Yet a few of the Jews escaped that massacre, shutting themselves up in the Tower of London or hiding in the houses of their friends.

On the following day, the king, having heard of this event, had some of those criminals arrested and brought before him. By the judgement of the court three of them were hanged on the gibbet: one because he had stolen something from a certain Christian, the other two because they had started a fire in the city, on account of which the houses of Christians had been burnt. Then the king sent for that man who had now been made a Christian from being a Jew, with those attending who had seen him baptized. And the king asked him if he was now become a Christian. The man replied that he was not, but since he wanted to avoid death he had allowed the Christians to do as they wished with him. Then the king asked the archbishop of Canterbury and the many archbishops and bishops who were present, what he should do about him. The archbishop replied with rather less tact than he should have shown, saying that: 'If he himself does not wish to be a man of God, let him be a man of the Devil.' And so the man who had been a Christian was returned to the law of Judaism.

The next day the king received the homage and fealty of the archbishops, bishops, abbots, earls and barons of his country.

Diceto shows what arrangements Richard made in his English Kingdom.

Richard, king of England, wishing to begin his rule by making an offering to the Lord, granted to the Cistercians an annuity of a hundred marks to be drawn from various of his properties and contributed it to their funds — his first act as king. He sent a letter bearing his own seal to communicate his decision.

On the instructions of the king and the

archbishop, a general council gathered at Pipewell on 15 September to discuss appointments to England's vacant sees. And so Richard bishop of Ely, treasurer to the king, was made bishop of London, and William Longchamp, the king's chancellor, was made bishop of Ely.

The dean and canons of London, on the instructions of Henry II, had crossed the Channel so that they might take part in the election of the bishops. On their return to England, they received forty marks from the treasury to cover their expenses.

As a last ditch attempt to withstand Saladin's encroaching army, Guy of Lusignan, king of Jerusalem, with a small Christian army, laid siege to Acre, held by the Muslims since 1187. Diceto quotes this newsletter to the pope which explains how his bold move eventually succeeded.

"The king of Jerusalem, the Knights Templar and Hospitaller, the archbishop of Pisa and many of the men of Pisa besieged Acre on 28 August despite Conrad, marquis of Montserrat, the archbishop of Ravenna and many other Christians who had advised them against such a plan. On arriving there, they surrounded the city with such a mighty force that none of the Saracens could enter or leave. On the third day, Saladin came with a great army, and attacked the king's brother, Geoffrey of Lusignan, and the Hospitallers. He compelled them to draw in their line of battle so that a way was opened for those wishing to enter or leave the town. Our Christians were overcome with terror and at once drew back, retreating towards some high ground nearby. But they were unable to escape Saladin, who, with a hundred thousand knights, surrounded them near the bottom of the mountain. However, the king of Jerusalem, seeing that he was surrounded, sent messengers to Tyre to the marquis, the archbishop and the other knights who had been against his plan. He besought them not to blame him, inexperienced as he was, but to come and lend them aid in their difficult position. The marquis of Montserrat, distressed to see Christians in such difficulties, crossed the water from Tyre and came to their aid with the archbishop, a thousand knights and twenty thousand foot soldiers, on 24 September.

The massacre of the Jews

IN THE years immediately after the Norman Conquest, the English kings encouraged Jews to cross the Channel from Normandy to London, and by the mid-12th century, in most of the larger county towns, small groups were acting as money-lenders to their Christian neighbours. Richard's preparations for the Third Crusade against the Moslems provoked widespread popular hostility towards the Jews who were set apart as the only significant religious and racial minority in England. The anti-Jewish riots which accompanied Richard's coronation at Westminster on 3 September 1189 sparked off a long series of nationwide assaults on Jewish areas in the provincial towns during the following winter and spring. These reached their climax in the notorious massacre and mass-suicide of some 150 Jews within the royal castle of York on *Shabbat ha-Gadol*, the night of 16 March 1190. Richard himself took immediate steps to avoid the repetition of such an outrageous act of mob violence.

After the 1190s the lives and money-lending activities of English Jews, who had long enjoyed royal protection but were already reduced to being serfs of the royal chamber, were more highly regulated than before – to ensure that they could be subjected to ferociously heavy royal taxation. King John apparently despised them, but insisted that, since they were useful as a source of money, they should be protected. As he remarked, 'If I give my peace even to a dog, that peace must be kept inviolate,' but so heavily did John fine the Jews that many fled from England to escape his rapaciousness. In 1290 that precarious royal peace was withdrawn completely by Edward I and the Jews were expelled from England for the rest of the Middle Ages and indeed beyond.

Right *The Jew's House in Lincoln, where a thriving community lived in the 12th century. The occupations a Jew could follow were restricted; money-lending was allowed, indeed encouraged, and made use of by barons as well as the king.*

Below *Jews are attacked by a soldier.*

Saladin was filled with fear at the prospect of their arrival and retreated a mile up the mountain.

On 4 October, we joined battle with the Saracens. The king led the Knights Hospitaller and the French in one battle line. The marquis took the second battle line together with the archbishop of Ravenna – and we too were with them. The Landgrave led the third line with the Pisans and the Germans. In the fourth were the Knights Templar, the Catalans and some of the Germans. The king's brother and James of Avesnes stayed in the camp. Altogether we were four thousand knights and one hundred thousand foot soldiers. However, our enemy Saladin had one hundred thousand knights. Nevertheless, we were armed with the sign of the holy cross and, when we joined battle at the third hour of the day, God favoured our side. They fled before our swords and we pursued them up to their very tents. The seventh line of Saracens was much depleted by our endeavours. We killed Saladin's son Baldwin, and his brother Takieddin was stricken with a fatal wound – we are now certain of his death also. We managed to kill five hundred of Saladin's knights – far more than we had hoped. While we were engaged in battle with Saladin, five thousand knights left the city and made a sudden attack on us. Saladin, when he saw his allies thus attacking us, used the full strength of his own forces against us. Nevertheless, we still managed to hold up against Saladin on one side and offer courageous resistance on the other, before retreating to our camp. However, the master of the Knights Templar and many more of our men were killed on that day."

"Philip, king of France by the grace of God, greets with sincere love his brother king and faithful man, Richard, king of England.

You will learn with pleasure that our efforts to lend aid to the city of Jerusalem are progressing well. We beseech God with frequent prayers to make manifest his reward for our devotion to his service in the land of Jerusalem. We understand from your words and from the information brought just lately by your messengers, that you desire and intend to journey to Jerusalem. Through the agency of these messengers, we convey to you our approval of your wish and plan in this matter. We shall confirm this through our letters patent. Indeed, our messengers shall tender you security in this matter and shall hand over to you our own letters patent. This business was executed in the month of October in the one thousand one hundred and eighty-ninth year of our Lord."

John of Anagni, cardinal of St Mark, came to England as legate of the Holy See, landing at Dover on 20 November. On the following day, Queen Eleanor issued instructions that he should travel no further as he had come to England without the king's knowledge. He thus spent a tedious thirteen days in Dover at the archbishop's expense.

King William of Scotland came to Canterbury accompanied on his journey by the archbishop of York and the bishop of Lincoln. He did homage to the king and found favour with him, paying him ten thousand marks to redeem all his feudal holdings. The allegiances of his men by which they had bound themselves to our king were transferred back to King William.

John count of Mortain, the king's brother, presented an important suit in the presence of the king, the legate and the bishops. He complained that, after he had appealed to the pope, the archbishop had laid an interdict on all his lands because he had married the daughter of William, earl of Gloucester. When the legate John of Anagni heard this, he granted his appeal and released his lands from the interdict.

Richard, king of England, would have outdone all his predecessors in respect of his immense wealth if the promises of money made within the first four months of the new reign and confirmed with sureties had been equalled by his income even in the following year.

After discussing a few matters concerning the disposition of the kingdom with certain officials at Dover, he crossed the Channel on 14 December and landed that day near Gravelines.

At around that time, William king of Sicily, brother-in-law to the king of England, died without a direct heir and was succeeded by Tancred, his closest kinsman.

Above *Contemporary fresco of Philip II.*

Left *Statue of Philip in Reims Cathedral.*

Philip Augustus

WHEN Richard and Philip II of France met at
Vézelay, the French king was by far the least
impressive of the two men. Short, fat and rarely in good
health, he had lost his hair on the Third Crusade;
moreover, he tended to be a hypochondriac. In battle too
he compared badly with the English king. Often forced
into flight, he lost his artillery at Verneuil, his wagon-train
at Fréteval, and fell into the water at Gisors. Even in his
great victory against John and his allies at Bouvines in
1214, he was unhorsed.

Yet even if Philip was not built in the heroic mould, he
was nonetheless a most capable ruler. When he was
young, he was found dreaming under a tree – wondering
whether he would be as great as Charlemagne. The
French historian Fawtier describes him as 'the great king
of the Capetian dynasty', while a chronicler said he 'greatly
enlarged the rights and the power of the realm of the
French and enriched the royal treasure'. He increased the
possessions of the monarchy fourfold, defeated John's ally
Otto IV, the Holy Roman Emperor, at Bouvines, and
brought about the collapse of the Plantagenet dominions.
Under him, France was administered effectively by local
officials and Paris became a great capital.

Philip was married three times. He found his second
wife, Ingeborg of Denmark, unsatisfactory after only one
night of marriage, and his repudiation of her and
subsequent nuptials with Agnes of Meran led to
considerable papal hostility and his excommunication. In
1213, after the birth of his grandson, he took Ingeborg
back as his wife.

When the crusade was launched, a tithe was imposed throughout England on all movable goods so that help might be sent to Jerusalem. The tax was collected with such violence that both clergy and laymen were frightened when they saw that charity was merely serving as a mask for rapacity.

"Philip, king of France by the grace of God, and Richard, king of England by that same grace, duke of Normandy and Aquitaine, count of Anjou, tender their greetings in the name of the Lord to all who shall read this letter.

Let it be known amongst you that we have firmly conceived a plan with the advice of the prelates of the Church and the noblemen of our countries, that we shall make the journey to Jerusalem together, with the Lord God as our guide, each promising to serve the other with good faith and love. I, Philip king of France, shall hold Richard, king of England, as my friend and faithful man; I, Richard, king of England, shall hold Philip, king of France, as my friend and lord. And so, we have decided that all those in our lands who have taken up the sign of the holy cross, shall either precede us a week before Easter or come with us in our company, unless they have our permission to remain. If any one should presume to stay behind us without our knowledge and permission, he shall be excommunicated and our prelates shall lay an interdict on his lands. It is our wish, our plan and our recommendation that all the noblemen of our lands, if they have the means, shall support each other from their wealth. However, the property of those who travel to Jerusalem, whether with us or in anticipation of our expedition, shall remain unharmed and intact as if it were our own. If anyone should harm the interests of those persons, our judges and bailiffs will take action, as the law allows, according to the custom of our lands. If anyone shall presume to make war against our lands or any part thereof in our absence and evades justice, he shall be excommunicated. And if he does not make good the injury within forty days, we declare that he and his heirs shall be disinherited in perpetuity. These arrangements were made on 30 December at Nonancourt."

However, this general treaty between the two kings could not be confirmed at once, so they say, because the day on which it was drawn up was a

The long arm of kingship

THE success of the Third Crusade, from 1189–1192, was limited. It proved impossible to regain Jerusalem, but Saladin was fought to a standstill on his own ground and the Christian kingdom, which had in 1187 seemed on the verge of extinction, was re-established as a coastal strip which endured for another century. Moreover, when Richard conquered the strategic island of Cyprus in 1191, on his way to the Holy Land, an offshore supply basé was acquired.

Most of the credit for the crusader success belongs to Richard, whose abilities as a politician and organizer were as important as his more familiar military skills. The arrangements he made for the government of the Plantagenet dominions in his absence were practical. His subjects were already accustomed to an absentee ruler, for his father Henry had passed only a short time in each province. But on this occasion the distance involved meant that although Richard and his officials remained in touch through messengers, the king would only have been able to react to events two months after they occurred.

In England, Normandy, Anjou, Poitou and Gascony he appointed loyal, experienced men to represent him. To protect his interests in the turbulent duchy of Aquitaine he married Berengaria and secured the support of her father King Sancho VI of Navarre against Count Raymond of Toulouse. Eleanor, with other officials, was also at hand to protect the royal authority.

The arrangement generally worked well, despite minor difficulties that were inevitable in an age where the absence or illness of a monarch could pose severe problems. The main threats came from Richard's enemies – Philip II of France, Raymond of Toulouse and, of course, his brother John – in the year before his return. If he had come back to England when he expected to, rather than spending a year in a German prison, his arrangements for governing his lands while on crusade would have been remarkably successful.

Right *The defence of Jerusalem was a matter of honour amongst the monarchs of Western Europe. The plan of the city, c. 1170, shows a kneeling saint on the left, looking towards Jerusalem, the symbol of the birth of Christianity. Making 'the journey to Jerusalem', as the chronicles say over and over again, was a rallying cry to make people put aside all other differences and quarrels and unite in defeating the hated infidel.*

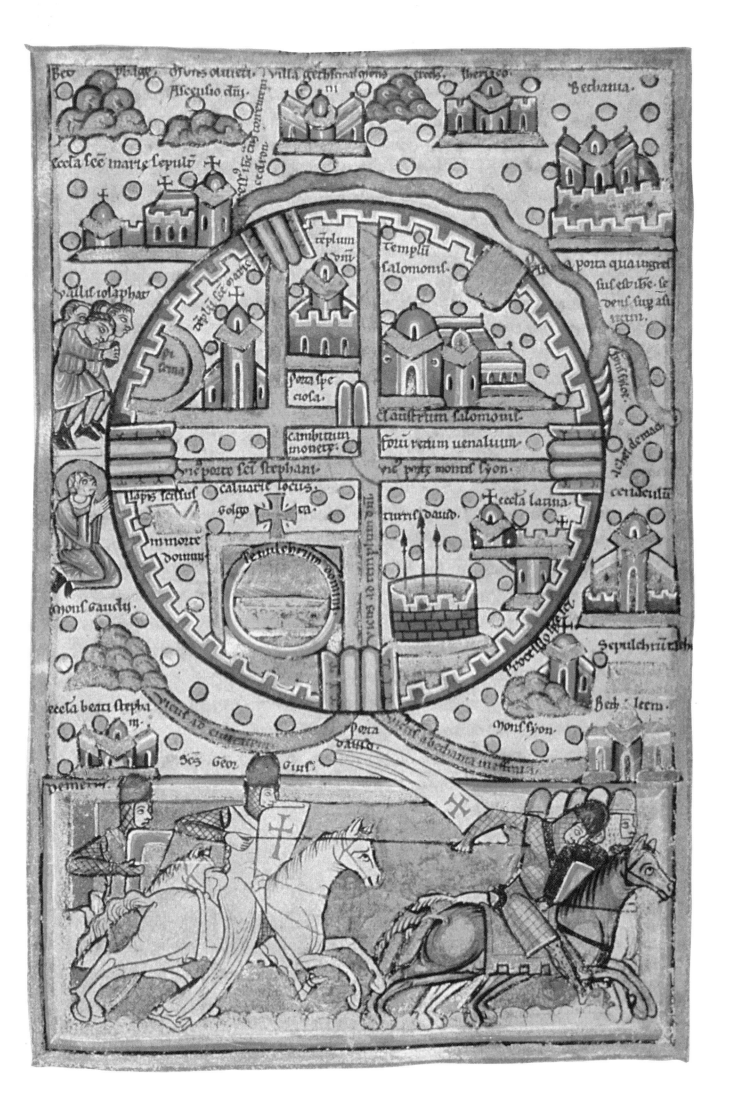

Saturday. It was put off until the following feast of St John the Baptist, a Sunday, 24 June, when they began the crusade. On that same day, Margaret queen of France died in childbirth at Paris, and was buried in the great church of Notre-Dame, the first queen of France to be so.

1190

Throughout England, many of those preparing to join the crusade to Jerusalem decided they would first rise up against the Jews before they attacked the Saracens. And so, on 6 February in Norwich, all those Jews who were found in their homes were slaughtered. On 7 March many were killed in Stamford during the fair. And they say that at York, on 16 March, about fifty were killed, many of them inflicting wounds on each other. For they preferred to meet death at the hands of their own people rather than to perish at the hands of the uncircumcised. On 18 April, Palm Sunday, they say that fifty-seven were massacred at Bury St Edmunds. Wherever Jews were found they were slaughtered by the crusaders, unless the burgesses managed to rescue them. However, let no one believe that wise men rejoiced at the dire and dreadful slaughter of the Jews, for it is written in the Psalms of David which come frequently to our ears. 'Slay them not'.

About this time, when Acre was first besieged, a certain Englishman called William, a chaplain of Ralph of Diceto dean of St Paul's, took a vow when going to Jerusalem that if he came safely to the port of Acre he would found a chapel as far as his resources would permit, to be dedicated to the holy martyr Thomas Becket, and would also have a cemetery there in his honour. Which duly came to pass. A lot of people came from all around to the chapel, and by common consent William was called 'prior'. Since he was a devoted knight of Christ, he took especial care of the poor, and worked extremely hard to bury the bodies of the dead, both those killed by the sword and those who died in their beds. There is also another cemetery, called the German hospital, and a third one, older than the rest and named after St Nicholas, in which a hundred and thirty-four thousand men were buried in one year.

Queen Eleanor, King Richard's mother, on her journey to Rome declined the perils of the sea and went via Mont-Genèvre and the plains of Italy.

"Pope Clement to William bishop of Ely, greeting.
Acceding to the laudable wishes and beneficent request of our dearest son in the Lord Richard, illustrious king of the English, we commit by apostolic authority to you, our brother, the office of legate in all England and Wales, in the provinces of both Canterbury and York, and in those parts of Ireland where John count of Mortain, the king's brother, has jurisdiction and lordship. Given at the Lateran, 7 July, in the third year of our pontificate."

"Richard king of the English to all his faithful men, greeting.
We enjoin and command that, as you are faithful to us and as you love yourselves and your property, you obey our dear and faithful chancellor the bishop of Ely in all our affairs, and that you do for him just what you would do for ourselves in all matters in which he gives you our instructions. Witness myself at Bayonne, 6 June."

The two kings, of England and France, agreed to meet at Vézelay on about 24 June, to go to Jerusalem. The king of France set out towards Genoa, the king of England towards Marseille.

King Richard embarked at Marseille on 9 August 1190. After ploughing through the foaming brine they came to the port of Rome and were received by the bishop of Ostia and many other messengers from the pope. The king declined the pope's invitation to visit him, and went to the south, via Capua.

Richard I and Philip II of France reached Sicily in September 1190 and decided to winter there. During his stay, Richard heard about the visionary prophesyings of Joachim of Fiore and asked to hear them himself. The author of The Deeds of King Richard *describes what Joachim said to the king.*

At that time there was a certain Cistercian abbot in Calabria, by name Joachim, abbot of Corazzo who, filled with the spirit of prophecy, preached to the people about the future. The English king listened freely to these prophecies and to his wisdom and doctrine. For Joachim was erudite in the scriptures and interpreted the visions of blessed John the Evangelist which are written in the Apocalypse, just as if he had written this book with his own hand. The king and many of his people were pleased when they heard him.

This then was the passage: 'A woman clothed with the sun and with the moon under her feet and on her head a crown of twelve stars, who, being in the pangs of childbirth cried out as she delivered. And behold there was also a great red dragon with seven heads and ten horns and seven crowns on his heads and his tail dragged a third of the stars from heaven and sent them to the earth. And the dragon stood before the woman who was in labour so that when she had delivered he might devour her child. And the woman gave birth to a male child who was to rule all the people with a rod of iron. And the child was taken up to God and to his throne. The woman, however, fled into the wilderness into a place which had been prepared by God in order that she might be fed there for one thousand two hundred and sixty days.' [Revelation xii, 1–6.]

This vision was interpreted by Joachim, abbot of Corazzo, in the following way: 'The woman clothed with the sun and with the moon under her feet', signifies the holy Church, sheltered and clothed by the sun of justice who is Christ the Lord, under whose feet this world, with its defects and eager desires, is always crushed. 'And upon her head a crown of twelve stars': the head of the Church is Christ, the crown the faithful of the Church, represented by the twelve apostles. And 'being in the pangs of childbirth she cried out as she delivered,' signifies the holy Church always joyful at new birth when, through the crucifixion, souls are saved through God's work. 'And behold there was a dragon with seven heads and ten horns', signifies the Devil, who can truly be said to have seven heads. The head of the Devil is the iniquity of all; reckoned as seven, as if a finite end could be placed on infinity. For the heads of the Devil are infinite, that is the persecutors of the Church and the iniquitous are infinite in number.

Joachim, however, enumerated seven principal persecutors in his exposition, namely Herod, Nero, Constantius, Mohammed, Melsemutus, Saladin and Antichrist; and of these the blessed Evangelist John says in the Apocalypse 'they are seven kings; five have died, one is, and the other is still to come.' This was interpreted by Joachim who said that the seven kings were the seven named above, of whom five are dead, namely Herod, Nero, Constantius, Mohammed and Melsemutus; one is alive, namely Saladin, who at the present time oppresses the Church of God, and casts into servitude the city of Jerusalem together with the burial place of the Lord and the land in which the feet of the Lord have stood. It was said that he would soon lose the kingdom of Jerusalem and would be killed, perishing through the rapacity of greed. There would be a great slaughter such as has not been seen since the beginning of the world, the infidels' habitation would become wasted, their cities would be desolated and Christians would then return to the Lord's pastures and would make a home in them.

Going to Richard, the abbot said: 'God has revealed all this and through you it is going to happen that He will give you victory over your enemies and He will glorify your name in eternity; and you will glorify Him and in you He will be glorified if you persevere in the work which He has begun. And one will soon come who is the Antichrist.' Concerning the Antichrist, the abbot said that he had discovered that the Antichrist had already been born; and that fifteen years had passed since his nativity, but that he had not yet come into the fullness of his power.

After many had exclaimed about these things which they had heard, the king said to the abbot, 'Where has the Antichrist been born? And where is he to reign?' Joachim replied that he believed the Antichrist had been born in the city of Rome and would hold the Apostolic See there.

To this the king replied, 'If the Antichrist has been born in Rome and is to occupy the Apostolic See then I believe he must be that Clement who is now pope.' He said this because he hated the pope. The king said furthermore: 'I believed that the Antichrist was to be born in Babylon or in Antioch of the root of Dan and that he would rule in the Temple of God.' And when the abbot of Corazzo offered the aforementioned explanation concerning the coming of the Antichrist many, including nearly all those ecclesiastics who were learned in the Scriptures strove to prove him wrong.

1191

Richard and Philip were meanwhile quarrelling with one another and involving themselves in local politics.

On 1 March 1191, a Friday, Richard the English king went to the city of Messina to speak with Tancred king of Sicily on the advice of Philip king of France. And on the third day following the English king came to the city of Catania where lay the most holy body of the blessed Agatha, virgin and martyr.

And when Tancred king of Sicily heard of Richard's arrival he went almost five miles outside the city to meet him. And when he saw him coming from afar, before they actually came together, both dismounted and, running one to the other, they hurried to embrace one another with salutations and kisses. Then, remounting their horses, they entered the city and the clerics and people welcomed them with hymns and songs in praise of God. They prayed before the tomb of the blessed Agatha, and the king then entered the palace of King Tancred and stayed with him for three days in suitable state.

On the fourth day the king of Sicily offered the king of England many vessels of gold and silver and presented him with horses and precious clothing; but the king of England did not wish to accept anything, except a certain small ring which he took as a token of mutual affection. The English king, however, did give Tancred the sword of the famous Arthur, once king of the Britons, which the Britons called Excalibur. Tancred also gave four great ships and fifteen galleys.

When King Richard returned, Tancred escorted him in person for two full days' journey through

The Sicilian connection

SICILY and Norman England had close connections long before the marriage of Henry II's daughter Joanna to William II of Sicily in 1177 drew them closer still. A hundred years earlier, when William the Conqueror and his barons were establishing their rule in England, Roger I led the Norman Conquest of Sicily. Throughout the 12th century, Anglo-Norman barons and churchmen were welcome on the island, which must have struck them as a marvellously exotic place. Sicily's Norman kings had absorbed rather than suppressed its rich Mediterranean cultures, and their churches were a wonderful mixture of Norman architecture, Moorish patterns and golden Byzantine mosaics. The cathedral and the palace chapel, both at Palermo and both built by Roger II towards the middle of the 12th century, are examples.

Sicily's elegant Byzantine styles seem to have made an enormous impression on visitors from north of the Alps. Archbishop William of York, nephew of Henry of Blois, and a distant cousin of Roger II, visited the country in *c.*1150, and returned to Winchester and then York loaded with precious gifts. A York sculptor probably copied a Byzantine ivory to produce the famous Virgin and Child, now in the crypt of York Minster.

Monreale, near Palermo, was to be William's burial church, and a capital in the cloister shows him presenting a model of the building to the Virgin. Founded by the

Below **The cloister at Monreale, Sicily.**

king in 1177 it is one of the richest churches built in the Middle Ages. The cloisters have twisted marble columns encrusted with glittering mosaics, and seem more suited to a harem than to a monastery. The exterior of the church is entirely covered with multicoloured patterns made from intersecting arcading in the Arabic style; the interior glimmers with the soft gold of Byzantine mosaic.

Above *William II, king of Sicily, giving the cathedral of Monreale to the Virgin Mary. This mosaic panel shows how the Byzantine effect of gold and richly coloured mosaics created a very Eastern atmosphere.*

211

Taormina. Then, when he was ready to depart, King Tancred said to him, 'Now I truly believe and can prove that what the French king told me about you in his letters came rather from jealousy than out of any love for me. For he told me that you would serve me neither with peace nor in faith, that the agreement which had been made between us had been transgressed and that you would not come into this kingdom except in violence against me.

The king of England replied to this no less firmly in words than in his heart: 'Let all evil doers be confounded. I cannot believe he said this when he is my lord and my sworn companion on this pilgrimage.'

To which King Tancred replied: 'So that you will believe I speak the truth I will show you those letters which the French king sent me.'

And when the English king had received the letters from the hand of King Tancred, the French king came to Taormina to speak with King Tancred.

The English king, on the other hand, returned to Messina. The French king stayed for one night in Taormina and then returned on the morrow to Messina. The English king was greatly moved to anger against him and would not be merry or make peace, but sought an opportunity to go away from there with his men. The French king then diligently enquired as to the matter and the English king, through the mediation of Philip Count of Flanders and others of his familiars, told the French king what the king of Sicily had said to him, and showed him the letters which he had received from King Tancred as proof. When the French king heard this he fell silent, knowing himself guilty, and did not know how to answer. But recovering, he declared: 'These words are fictitious and newly invented. For I believe and am certain that he seeks excuses to enable him to malign me. Is it possible that through such falsehoods he is rejecting my sister whom he has sworn to marry?'

To this the English king replied, 'I do not despise your sister but I will never take her as my wife because my father knew her and had a son by her.' King Richard stood firm against the king of France who, after much evasion, freed the English king from his engagement to his sister Alice, and as part of the agreement received ten thousand marks from the king of England on her behalf. Once the French king returned to France his sister would be given back to him, together with Gisors and all those other things which the French king had settled on her as a marriage portion.

The French king then gave licence to the English king to marry whomsoever he wished. He also conceded that the duke of Brittany should be a vassal of the English king and his heirs for Brittany in perpetuity and that the king of England and his heirs should then be answerable to the French king and to his heirs. On that day the king of England and the king of France became friends and they faithfully confirmed all their agreements with oaths, and in writing under their seals.

Having been released from his oath to Alice, Richard was now free to marry Berengaria of Navarre. Diceto relates that Eleanor of Aquitaine brought her to Sicily.

Queen Eleanor, after staying with her son for four days in Messina, returned to England leaving behind Berengaria, daughter of the king of Navarre, whom Richard was to marry. On 10 April King Richard and his army sailed away in a fleet of one hundred and fifty-six ships, twenty-four transports and thirty-nine galleys, taking with them his sister Joanna and Berengaria. The king of the French sailed from Messina on 29 March.

On about the twentieth day of his voyage King Richard came to the island of Rhodes. He stayed for five days in the town, and after a further five days' voyage landed on Cyprus at a place called Limassol. Cursac [Isaac Ducas Comnenus], lord of that country, who called himself 'emperor', went with a strong force to contest the king of England's landing, and did much damage to the king's men, plundering those who were shipwrecked and shutting them up in prison to die of hunger. King Richard was enraged and hastened to avenge such injuries, fighting the enemy and winning a quick victory. He kept the

The alternative queen

ON 12 May 1191, Richard the Lionheart married Berengaria, daughter of Sancho VI of Navarre, and she was crowned queen of England. Little is known about Berengaria, but it seems agreed that she was more prudent than beautiful and that the marriage was arranged for political reasons. Richard had three motives in choosing Berengaria: as an alternative to his betrothed, Alice of France, whom he had rejected in 1190; to make an ally of Navarre; and to get a son. Only in the last case was he to be disappointed.

Eleanor, Richard's mother, took Berengaria to Richard while he was *en route* for the Holy Land and left her with him in Sicily in February 1191 even before Philip II had agreed to free Richard from his 20-year-old vow to marry Alice. It was Lent, a season when marriages could not take place, and Richard resolved to sail on for the Holy Land. But the ship containing Berengaria was separated from his main fleet in a storm and was found sheltering near Limassol in Cyprus. The plight of Berengaria, who was threatened by the island's ruler Isaac Comnenus, led Richard to attack Comnenus and to conquer Cyprus. The wedding of Richard and Berengaria then took place at Limassol.

The marriage was a political success – for Berengaria's brother Sancho the Bold helped to defend Aquitaine against the French during Richard's captivity – but it was not happy. Richard spent little time with his wife, they had no children and Berengaria played no great political role. After Richard's death, she lived on at Le Mans where she was famed and respected for her generous almsgiving.

Above *Detail from Berengaria's splendid effigy, below, in l'Epau Abbey near Le Mans. She died in 1230.*

conquered man in chains, capturing his only daughter and subjugating the whole island of Cyprus with all its castles. Cursac struck a bargain with the king not to be kept in irons. This was duly observed: the king had silver chains made for him, and had him imprisoned in a castle near Tripoli, called Markyab. Cursac's daughter was kept in honourable custody by the two queens in the royal chamber.

Meanwhile Guy of Lusignan, king of Jerusalem, and his army waited outside Acre for help to come, as Diceto shows in what follows.

"To the venerable lord and father in Christ Richard bishop of London, Hubert by the same grace bishop of Salisbury, greetings in continuing and devoted friendship.
The city of Acre is strongly resisting our attacks, and we cannot capture it because it is well supplied with men, defences and engines of war; and Saladin on the other side of us has surrounded us. The Christians hope to be able to bear the burdens and distresses of the siege until our kings arrive. That is, if they come around next Easter. If they delay longer we will not be able to afford to continue, and our hope of early consolation will vanish. This is how it is with the siege of Acre."

The French king landed at Acre on Easter Saturday, 20 April 1191. What the Christian army then achieved in assaulting the city for seven weeks, all those who were present know and remember.

King Richard, accompanied by thirteen great ships called *buccas* each with three sets of sails, one hundred transport ships and fifty trireme galleys, set sail from Cyprus and, while skimming across the vast deep, espied the sails of a great ship fitted out at huge expense by Safadin, lord of Babylon and brother of Saladin, to come to the aid of the Saracens besieged in Acre. It was packed with victuals, and with armaments apt for any kind of warfare, Greek fire, and containers full of explosives, and the crew was said to number one thousand five hundred.

Quickly snatching up everything necessary for a naval battle, the galleys surrounded the great ship, which was becalmed, and began a fierce attack on it.

Travellers' tales

IT is wrong to think of the Middle Ages as a time of poor communication and little movement. Traders and merchants travelled regularly, by land, river and sea, within Europe and between the continent and England. Overland, the Great St Bernard pass was the most frequently used route across the Alps at this time, although bridges and roads opened up the St Gotthard pass, soon afterwards, in the early 13th century.

But people did not travel only because of commerce. Pilgrims and crusaders were inspired by religious motives as well as love of adventure, while many members of royal and aristocratic families journeyed from court to court or country to country for state or military reasons. Inns, hostels and monasteries all opened their doors to poor travellers, while the wealthy would stay in more luxurious monastic quarters, in castles or on their own manors. The visit of the royal household could be a ruinous event for an abbot or bailiff.

Road travel was by horse, or in a cart pulled by horses or sometimes, but increasingly less frequently, the slower oxen. Barges were used on rivers, sometimes in such numbers that canals and locks had to be built, as in Flanders and Holland in the later 12th century. Travel by river was indeed often far quicker than traversing the often rutted and muddy roads.

The round cog, with its single mast, square sail and raised castles at both ends was probably the most widely used ship in northern Europe, although the English may have continued to use craft more like Viking longships. In the Mediterranean, two-masted vessels with triangular sails were normal. But crossing the sea could be a dangerous business: Berengaria of Navarre narrowly escaped shipwreck in a storm off Cyprus shortly before her marriage to Richard I.

Above left *A galley, its oars staggered in two rows.*

Above *An illustration of the use of Greek fire, mentioned frequently in the chronicles, and a favourite weapon of the Byzantines. Bronze tubes were filled with a flammable mixture which was emitted in a stream of liquid fire.*

Right *On land, horses were the fastest means of transport for anyone with sufficient funds.*

Below *Crusaders embarking for the Holy Land.*

Then one of the rowers, copying the small bird called a diver, swam beneath the waves until he came to the ship, and pierced it with a bore. Perhaps he had heard how Eleazar in the time of the Maccabees had crept under the elephant which was surrounded by the press of battle, and killed it by striking its stomach. Eleazar was crushed while carrying out the deed for the Jews, but the rower, with Christ in his heart, returned safely to his galley and resumed his seat. After a little while, the water seeping in rose above the boards and cut off the escape of the crew, who previously had been so confident of their defences. King Richard ordered one thousand three hundred of them drowned, keeping two hundred of them. This occurred on 6 July.

The king continued on his course and soon approached the port for which he was making. The shore resounded to clarion calls, the braying of trumpets and the fearful din of horns, exciting the Christians to the fight and striking terror into the hearts of the besieged Saracens, announcing the arrival of a great prince. King Richard entered the port of Acre on 8 June.

Philip king of France and Richard king of England set up their siege engines around Acre and sited their stone-throwers near the walls, and when the size of the stones had begun to weaken the defences, the Saracens began to be afraid and lose hope of holding out. After they had consulted the other Saracens they began to treat for peace, making an agreement that Saladin would restore the holy cross on a stipulated day and release one and a half thousand Christian captives whom he was holding in chains. Thus the city was surrendered to the two kings on 12 July with all the arms and impedimenta of the Saracens, who saved only their lives.

But when the agreed day came Saladin did not keep his part of the bargain. In revenge for this about two thousand six hundred Saracens lost their heads, a few of the nobles being spared and put at the kings' mercy weighed down by chains.

Once the city had surrendered, the French king proposed to go home as if everything was now finished. When King Richard heard this he offered the French king as his lord half of everything he had brought, whether gold and silver, supplies, arms, horses and ships, and promised it to him on whatever security he liked to name if he would stay. But Philip was absolutely determined to leave, and against the objections of his own men and to the outrage of the whole Christian army he took ship with a few companions to sail home.

After he had left, the breaches in the walls of Acre were repaired and the city fortified with ditches, and King Richard, to advance the Christian cause and to fulfil his vow, set out towards Jaffa. With him were the duke of Burgundy with the French under him, Count Henry and his men, and many other counts and barons and innumerable common people. It is very far from Acre to Jaffa; and with great effort and serious losses the king got as far as Caesarea undaunted. Saladin also sustained losses on the same journey. The army paused there a little to draw breath, and then bravely resumed its march towards Jaffa.

When the advance guard had reached Arsuf, Saladin made a sudden attack on the rear, but by divine mercy he was put to flight by a counter attack of four squadrons of Christians, himself fleeing for a league chased by the crusaders, who in one day inflicted such a massacre on the Saracen nobles as Saladin had not received in forty years.

The following is an eyewitness account of the battle of Arsuf, written by Richard, canon of Holy Trinity, Aldgate, in London.

At first light on 7 September everyone carefully armed themselves with their weapons, as if the Turks were to be encountered at once.

There you could see the most able companies, standards of various kinds, and many patterned ensigns, as well as a most hardy people, keen, alert, very suitable for war.

King Richard and the duke of Burgundy, with a chosen company of knights, skirting roundabout, observed everywhere from right to left, carefully noting the disposition and condition of the Turks so that they could alter the arrangements of the army as they found advisable. Certainly their diligence was very necessary.

Now in mid-morning a great host of Turks, almost ten thousand, descended on us with a sudden attack. They threw javelins and shot arrows, yelling horribly with wild voices. After this a diabolical people ran forward, coloured very black, who take their name not inappropriately from the colour: since they are black, they are called Negroes; also the Saracens who live in the desert, who are commonly called the Bedouin, are frightening and as black as soot. They are most unruly foot soldiers, a swift and lightly-armed people, using bows with quivers and round bucklers. These were the men who resolutely, unswervingly threatened our army.

In front of the emirs some men went forward blowing a fanfare on horns and bugles, some holding trumpets, others with pipes, drums, rattles and cymbals, others again winding different instruments; all set about the task of producing an appalling wailing cacophony. By their harsh cries and jarring noises, everywhere the land resounded so that the din of thunder-claps could not be distinguished from the sound of trumpets. They were intended to encourage zeal and daring; for the noisier it became, so much was their spirit more ardent for battle.

The abominable Turks attacked our army so that for the space of two miles roundabout so much land was taken up with the fight that nothing was visible except the hostile Turks. Then the bolder and braver men, whom honour forbade to flee and whose keen spirit sought the crown [of martyrdom], persevering in the conflict, fought back with great constancy and struggled with unfailing valour.

When he saw the army thus aroused and engaged with the enemy, King Richard spurred his horse and swiftly flew there, nor did he draw rein from the gallop until he had first joined the fighting Hospitallers to bring them aid with his own followers. Thundering in from the right he came down on a most miserable gang of Turkish foot soldiers, who were compelled to die, amazed by his onslaught, falling beside him on right and left. There King Richard, alone, beserk, came on the Turks, attacked them and everywhere laid them low. There was not a man who could escape his swordplay. For wherever the king went he made a clear path far and wide, wielding his sword. The king advanced irresistibly with the switches of his sword through the evil people, as if mowing hay with a scythe. From the example of the other crowd of dying men, the living gave him a wider berth; for the space of half a mile the bodies of dead Turks lay on their faces on the ground.

Such great fury was directed against the Turks that day, the fatal strokes so increasing, that soon all the enemy turned from their relentless conflict and gave way to the advance of our army. So eventually our wounded came to the standard. And again regrouped by battle-line, they advanced in file up to Arsuf and pitched their tents outside the town.

On that day, according to the reports of those who saw them, you could find the tracks of the Turks fleeing through the mountains by their discarded spoil and the camels and horses lying about dead, which fell along the way in thousands and hundreds, laden with equipment.

While still in Sicily, Richard had sent Walter of Coutances, archbishop of Rouen, back to England to keep an eye on events there, and to give messages to William Longchamp, the chancellor. Diceto traces the growing hostility between John, count of Mortain, and William Longchamp.

Walter archbishop of Rouen came back to England from Sicily, landing at Shoreham on 27 June, bearing the following letter:

"Richard king of the English to William his chancellor, Geoffrey FitzPeter, William Marshal, Hugh Bardolf and William Brewer, greeting.
Since we bear a great love to the venerable father Walter archbishop of Rouen and have great trust in him, we send him to you for the safety and defence of our kingdom, releasing him from his pilgrimage with the consent of the pope; because we know him to be prudent, discreet and capable, and ever faithful

Above *Richard, Philip II and Conrad encamped in front of Acre in 1191.*

Right *The fall of Acre, with Richard, Philip and King Guy of Lusignan. The city had been besieged for two years when* Philip and Richard, uneasy allies, arrived at the gates. By July the city had fallen. It was given to the Knights Hospitaller and, known as St John of Acre, remained the centre of Christianity in the Middle East until 1291, when it was retaken and largely destroyed by Saracen troops.

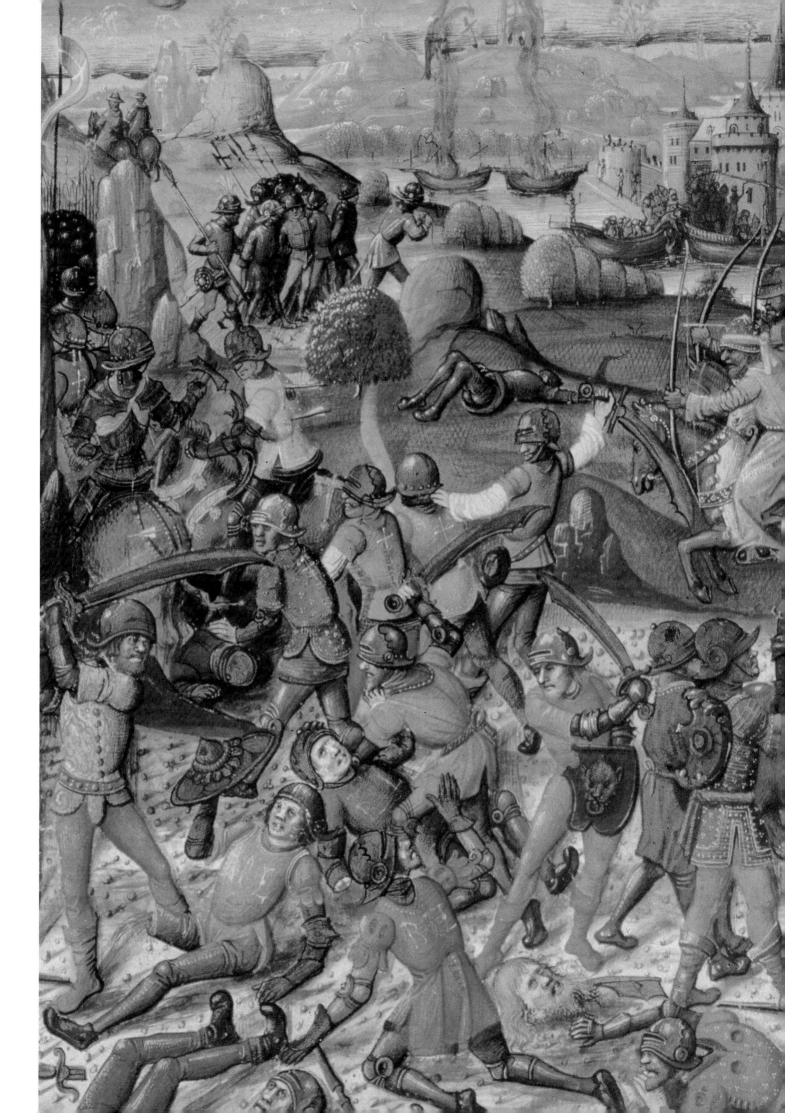

to ourselves. Wherefore we command and firmly order you to act on his counsel in all matters concerning us, you and he taking each other's advice in all things for as long as he is in England and we are on our pilgrimage. And we order you to do what we told him to tell you about the archbishopric of Canterbury. Witness myself, 23 February 1191, at Messina."

"Richard king of the English to William Marshal, Geoffrey FitzPeter, Hugh Bardolf and William Brewer.
If our chancellor does not act faithfully according to the advice of yourselves and others to whom we have committed the care of our kingdom, we order you to carry out your own dispositions in all the affairs of our kingdom, in castles and escheats, without any dispute."

"William Longchamp, by grace of God, bishop of Ely, to the sheriff of Sussex.
We order that if the archbishop-elect of York arrives at any of the ports of your bailiwick, or any of his envoys does, you retain him until you receive an order from us. Likewise we order that you retain any letters of the pope or any important man."

Geoffrey, the illegitimate son of Henry II, and archbishop-elect of York, had agreed to stay out of England for three years while Richard I was away on crusade – a promise which he was to break.

While the archbishop of York was journeying to England, he landed at a certain port by the name of Dover on 14 September. On his disembarkation, the sister of William Longchamp bishop of Ely, who was guarding the castle at the order, so it is said and believed, of her brother, wickedly had the archbishop and his clergy besieged by a multitude of armed men for six days, in the priory of St Martin. They confined him to such an extent that he could scarcely beg for food to be given while he was there. When the malice of the traitors took a turn for the worse, two knights of the bishop of Ely, Aubrey of Marney and Alexander Puintel, came armed to the aforementioned church, with unsheathed swords in their hands, charged into the church, rushed at the archbishop and firmly ordered him to leave the kingdom without delay or hesitation and go to

Flanders with his men. When he refused, he was dragged by the feet, legs and arms from the altar along a muddy road and through filthy places, wearing his stole and bearing his cross, his head knocking violently on the pavement. With his clergy and religious men who had gathered to see him from many parts, on 18 September, he was led into the castle where he was thrust into prison for eight days.

On hearing this, Richard bishop of London, acting almost as a go-between, hurried as fast as he could to the chancellor, William Longchamp, from whom after many entreaties he only just obtained the release of the archbishop by binding his whole diocese as a surety. Leaving the prison on 26 September, the archbishop of York hurried along the same muddy road and through the filthy places where he had been dragged with his insignia, stole and cross, until he got to the monastery of St Martin. Here, thanking God and St Martin, he was received with great exultation by people coming up from every side. On arrival at London, the archbishop was received in solemn procession at St Paul's, on 2 October, and Richard bishop of London showed all the kindess he was capable of in lavish expenditure both for him and his followers.

William Longchamp's treatment of Geoffrey archbishop of York shocked the English Church, thus providing a fruitful field for Count John's plots against the chancellor.

"John count of Mortain to Richard bishop of London, greetings.
As you love the honour of God and the Church and the king and kingdom and me, be present at the bridge over the Loddon on 5 October, between Reading and Windsor, because, God willing, I will meet you there to confer about certain important and serious matters concerning the king and kingdom."

The fact that a Sunday was fixed for the discussions gave many to understand that something unfortunate would come of it, since, as many people believe, an oath given on the Sabbath is very rarely effective.

So the chancellor, having Windsor castle in his

custody, gave as an excuse the denseness of the forest, the narrowness of the lanes and the large number of knights on foot and horseback who had gathered to Count John, the king's brother, from all quarters ready to fight, and also the secret plans of treachery of Henry de Vere, whose disinheritance he himself had occasioned, as well as the considerable distance of the said bridge from the castle, and so the meeting was postponed until Monday.

At midday on Sunday the archbishops of Rouen and York, as well as a number of bishops who had met at Reading so that they could be present at the conference, mounted the pulpit, once the candles were lit, anathematized all those who had given counsel, help or orders that the archbishop of York be dragged from the church, humiliated and thrust into prison, and excommunicated them, naming Aubrey of Marney and Alexander Puintel. On Monday, so as to remove all sinister suspicion, Count John proposed to go to the meeting in a very safe place near Windsor, as the chancellor had requested, promising in return every kind of security through the bishop of London. On the same day, since he had decided to stay at Staines, John's household rose in the morning and rushed around suspecting an attack in everything.

When he heard this, the chancellor fled before the face of the count whom he thought was following his track in great anger, and like someone who is somewhat afraid, distanced himself, I do not say fled, until he reached the Tower of London along with his arms and baggage and household. He stabled his horses in the ground floor of the Tower and in the old dining hall, and prepared himself for the siege which was imminent, so he believed.

The count, on hearing what the chancellor had done, came too and lodged at London with Richard FitzReiner. Roger de Planes, justiciar for the whole land of Count John, was seriously wounded by a certain Ralph Beauchamp whom the chancellor had knighted, and he died on 7 October. Next day, Tuesday, so as to dispel the hostility between himself and the chancellor, Count John, together with archbishops, bishops, earls and barons, met in the chapter house of St Paul's at London, and bells were rung which usually summon people to gather together. After they had all held long discussions together, Count John swore loyalty to King Richard.

On Thursday 10 October a conference was held at the eastern part of the Tower of London. Present were John count of Mortain, the chancellor, archbishops, bishops, earls and barons. By common assent it was decided that all the castles which the chancellor at his pleasure had entrusted to the custody of his relatives should be returned, especially the Tower of London. The chancellor promised with a sacred oath that he would do that. Three castles which he had received from the hand of King Richard — Dover, Cambridge and Hereford in Wales — would stay in the chancellor's custody, once hostages had been given by the castellans whom the chancellor had set there. Henry and Osbert, brothers of the chancellor, and Matthew the chamberlain were given as hostages until the castles were given up. For the chancellor had sworn that he would not leave the kingdom until the castles had been returned. On Saturday 12 October the chancellor went to Dover, led by Gilbert bishop of Rochester and Henry of Cornhill sheriff of Kent.

On the following Thursday William Longchamp, the chancellor put on female attire, but being unable to change the way he walked could not help showing that he was a man rather than a woman. So he was apprehended by sailors who recognized his face, and was seized and taken away, and was extracted with difficulty from the grasp of women. He was taken into custody until, by common decision of the justices of the kingdom who reside in London, he was given the freedom to go wherever he wished. However, warned and ordered to put into effect what he had sworn to do in the meeting near the Tower, the chancellor on 29 October embarked for Normandy and landed at Le Tréport.

A certain boy of the bishop of London's household who enjoyed playing with birds used to school his hawk, but found teals easier to train. At the sound of the instrument that falconers call a 'tabor', a teal would rush forward with a rowing motion of its wings. Once, deceived by this, his

cadauera mozuoz piciuntt i fluuio

Above *Corpses are removed from the field of battle.*

Below *A king goes on crusade.*

Right *The unglamorous face of war: a troop of foot soldiers. Whatever Richard's other failings he distinguished himself over and over again as a general, especially at Acre.*

222

hawk dived and caught a pike swimming just below the surface of the river, and carried it about forty feet onto dry land. The bishop sent both hawk and pike to Count John on 22 October as a memorial of such an unusual occurrence.

On the same day the election to the see of Canterbury was discussed as King Richard had ordered, but after long negotiations the matter was put off.

The king of the French came back from Jerusalem, and was received in Paris in solemn procession on 27 December. But whether his mission will be taken as honourable, or shortened by illness, or ignominious by those in the camps, those who know will say.

1192

Henry count of Champagne, King Richard's nephew, took to wife the daughter of King Amaury of Jerusalem [she was Amaury's heiress], whom the marquis had married in some way or other, and thus Henry gained control of the whole land as any king of Jerusalem had had it, in so far as the Christians will win it back.

A band of Saracens going from Babylon [Cairo] to Jerusalem carrying all kinds of supplies and arms was intercepted by the Christians. What the French took, they kept; what the Templars, Hospitallers and others took, they distributed by the king of England's judgement.

On 14 May the king of England came to Darum, which King Amaury had fortified to the damage and injury of the Saracens, and which Saladin had subsequently captured; King Richard besieged it and after four days took it with more than five thousand prisoners.

On 31 July the Saracens took Jaffa. The following day Richard, flying to arms, went to help the Christians and with three galleys and only ten knights, he landed before Jaffa, defeating the Saracens and capturing the town. The enemy, gathering courage when they heard he had come with very few men, charged in to try to take him

alive. He resisted manfully though, and killed many of them.

On 9 August a truce was made. The Christians were allowed to enter Jerusalem unarmed, but the archbishop of Tyre would excommunicate anyone who went there to fulfil his crusading vows with prayer conducted by the Saracens. The truce was to last from the following Easter for three years, three months, three weeks, three days and three hours, and nobody questioned the wisdom of the phrase 'a threefold rope is hard to break'. And to leave no doubt that the Saracens would keep their word they sent an arrow as a sign of peace, meaning that there need be no fear of the flying arrow during the day.

On 29 September the two queens, namely Berengaria of England and Joanna of Sicily, boarded ship at Acre; King Richard did so on 9 October. About 11 November he landed at a place called Corfu, in the territories of the emperor of Constantinople. Then he left the great ships and went on with two galleys, landing in Slavonia. When he had gone through Venice and Aquileia, he entered the lands of the duke of Austria.

He was captured in the city of Vienna on 20 December. Although the duke did not actually put the king's feet in shackles, the rudeness of his guards made his stay worse than if he had been in chains, for the men of that region stink of barbarism, are frightful in their speech, squalid in their habits and covered in filth, so that it was more like staying among animals than men.

1193

On 28 February Saladin died.

On 23 March the duke of Austria handed the king of England over to the emperor [Henry VI], having agreed on a sum of money. After the emperor had compelled King Richard with threats to pay an enormous ransom, he had him imprisoned in a castle called Trifels, on the borders of Germany and Lorraine. It is sited on the summit of a mountain higher than all the others around, and was built especially as a prison for notorious enemies of the Holy Roman empire.

The web of German politics

HENRY VI, the Hohenstaufen emperor, was ruler of Germany when Richard was imprisoned there in 1193–4. Henry's father, Frederick Barbarossa, among the greatest of all medieval emperors, had extended imperial interests in Italy and had married his son to Constance, the heiress of Norman Sicily. This was one cause of conflict between Henry VI and Richard. The latter's sister Joanna had been married to William II, king of Sicily, who died in 1189; Richard, who was on his way to the Holy Land, supported his successor, Tancred of Lecce, against Henry VI.

There was also cause for hostility in Germany. Henry the Lion, duke of Saxony and Bavaria, and an opponent of the Hohenstaufens, was married to another of Richard's sisters, Matilda. Barbarossa, with other princes, had overcome the duke, but his son, Henry VI, was far from secure. The Welfs, a powerful dynasty in the northeast, were hostile and a dispute over the bishopric of Liège had brought conflict with the princes in the northwest. Henry VI was sadly in need of the opportunities provided by the capture of the Lionheart.

Although it was not easy to select a route home from the crusade, Richard's final decision to return through Austria, ruled by his old crusading enemy, Leopold, seems reckless. He was captured, in 1192, pretending to be a kitchen servant turning a spit in an inn outside Vienna and Leopold handed him to Henry VI. He was imprisoned in Germany at Durnstein, and later at Trifels where in song he bemoaned his 'doleful plight'. He was released in 1194 only when he had paid a massive 100,000 marks ransom (with another 50,000 to come unless he persuaded Henry the Lion to make peace with the emperor), and agreed to recognize Henry VI as feudal overlord of England.

Henry's triumph was short-lived. He died three years later in 1197, and the empire passed to Richard's ally, Otto of Brunswick, son of Henry the Lion.

Below *Richard is arrested in Austria.*

Far below *Henry VI of Germany. Richard had to pay him a ransom and do homage for his lands before he could go free.*

This did not happen by chance, but it was wisely and beneficially ordained by divine vengeance, to bring Richard to penitence and reparation for the excesses he had perpetrated against his earthly father Henry II of England, when he was dying at Le Mans, in besieging the town with the aid of the French king, and although Richard had not actually struck his father himself, nonetheless he had forced his retreat by frequent and savage attacks.

When John count of Mortain heard that his brother was in prison, he was enticed by a great hope of becoming king. He won over many people all over the kingdom, promising much, and he quickly strengthened his castles. Crossing the sea, he made a pact with the king of the French that his nephew Arthur duke of Brittany should be excluded from the hopes the Bretons nourished for him.

While King Richard was in prison he was most concerned about the vacancy in the see of Canterbury, and wrote in the following terms:

"Richard by the grace of God king of the English to his dear and faithful Richard bishop of London, dean of the church of Canterbury, and to all the suffragan bishops, greeting.
We would like to discuss with you how we can, as far as in us lies, appoint to the church of Canterbury, which is the head and mother of you all, a suitable person, acceptable to us and you and all the realm, who will seek after the peace and tranquillity of the Holy Church and our kingdom."

When this letter had been read publicly, many bishops assembled on the summons of the bishop of London; some made reasonable excuses for their absence by letter or through messengers. Many heads of religious houses also answered his call. The election was to take place on 29 June.

Queen Eleanor the king's mother and Walter of Coutances archbishop of Rouen, chief justiciar of England, and other barons, did their utmost to conserve the peace of the kingdom, seeking to join together hearts which were permanently at loggerheads with each other. The justiciar decided that

Geoffrey prior of Canterbury, and the monks who had come to London with him, should go back to Canterbury where Thomas the glorious martyr acquired his crown with his own blood. To magnify his name throughout the world, on 29 May the monks anticipated the bishops and elected Hubert Walter, [bishop of Salisbury and] formerly dean of York who, some spirit had revealed to them, was about to be elected by the bishops. Certain men of middle rank, presiding as justices in the chapter house at Canterbury, gave their consent to the election.

On the Sunday as arranged, a holy day, Hubert bishop of Salisbury was elected archbishop of Canterbury by the bishops, and the result announced in public by the bishop of London at Westminster, the famous royal seat and the time-honoured place for electing archbishops. Walter archbishop of Rouen and chief justiciar of England gave the royal assent and confirmation.

There was a general meeting of all the magnates of Germany at Worms on 5 July, where the ransom of the king of England was discussed. There the price which the Emperor Henry had paid to Duke Leopold of Austria was made public, namely fifty thousand marks of silver. But the emperor was such an outstanding usurer that he was able to double his money in a day, and extorted one hundred thousand marks from the king. The actual sum for the king's ransom was one hundred thousand pounds of the money of Cologne, paid in instalments at certain times, and fifty hostages were given for payment.

As for how the money was raised, we shall now demonstrate the devotion which the king's faithful men showed, beginning with the Church: the greater churches came up with treasures hoarded from the distant past, and the parishes with their silver chalices. It was decided that the archbishops, bishops, abbots, priors, earls and barons should contribute a quarter of their annual income; the Cistercian monks and Premonstratensian canons their whole year's wool crop, and clerics living on tithes one-tenth of their income.

The Germans were amazed that there was such a constant stream of bishops, abbots, earls and barons

A king's ransom

RICHARD was only freed from his German captivity by an enormous ransom of £66,000 raised from his lands. The credit for this is due to his chancellor William Longchamp, to his mother Eleanor, and to a system developed by Richard and his predecessors which could function efficiently even in the king's absence.

Richard went on crusade in 1190 as a great and wealthy king. Although he had spent only a few months in England, he had used them well. In the words of a chronicler, 'he put up for sale everything he had: offices, lordships, earldoms, sheriffdoms, castles, towns, lands, the lot'. Richard himself confessed: 'I would sell London itself if I could find a buyer.' Even Longchamp had to pay £3000 for his chancellorship. As a result Richard impressed the Saracens more than Philip was able to. He had more ships, siege engines and men; he gave more valuable gifts.

In his absence, his lands were ruled well by loyal ministers – despite the troublemaking efforts of the king's ambitious brother John. In England William Longchamp 'oppressed the people with heavy exactions' to finance his master's campaigns, making himself unpopular, and John tried to exploit this. Scorn crackles in Roger Howden's description of Longchamp as a 'wretched man' who slept with boys, a 'man of low rank, exalted on high', and who, in trying to escape from John and his followers in 1191, dressed as a woman and was discovered when fumbled by an amorous fisherman.

In spite of paying the ransom – and this without Longchamp's skills to help – Richard was able to raise enough money between 1194 and 1199 to recover Philip's gains in Normandy, to build the magnificent Château Gaillard and keep his dominions intact.

Top *The castle of Trifels, where Richard was imprisoned.*

Right *The Lionheart is pictured at the feet of the German emperor. It is unlikely that he would have been treated quite so badly, or humiliated by such an extreme posture of submission. He was, rather, under a kind of house arrest which allowed him to send letters and give advice on political and financial matters which were concerning his supporters at home. The ransom itself was roughly twice England's gross income; in today's terms, something like a hundred billion pounds.*

227

and even lesser people from such various and distant countries who wanted to see the king, but almost everyone in all his lands despaired of his return. As different people brought back different instructions, the king wrote the following letter:

"Richard king of the English to Walter arch-bishop of Rouen.
However many times we send messages to you in England with orders for you, you are only to believe those which concern our own honour and advantage; those which do not affect our honour or profit are not to be believed."

Hugh bishop of Chester, summoned by the king, as he said, with great gifts which he had prepared very carefully, was ambushed before he even had to face the perils of Germany. While he was resting near Canterbury one night, he was captured and robbed. Matthew de Clere, castellan of Dover, lent his authority to the robbers; but although excom-municated by name by the archbishop and all the bishops with lighted candles, it is not known whether he made proper satisfaction for the outrage.

Philip king of the French married the sister of the king of Denmark. But they were then unexpec-tedly divorced, and that was more talked about than what happened at the wedding on 15 August at Amiens. The divorced queen preferred to live with the nuns at Soissons than to return to her Danish homeland.

The messengers the archbishop had sent to the pope to fetch his pallium came back, among them one called Episcopellus carrying the pallium itself. There was a general council of bishops at Canterbury on 5 November, also attended by some abbots, for the archbishop's reception and enthronement.

When everything needed for this kind of welcome had been made ready, he was solemnly enthroned and given the kiss of peace, with the bishop of London on his right and the bishop of Winchester on his left. They then went in procession to meet Episcopellus carrying the pallium, and coming to the high altar the archbishop was bound by the ancient triple oath, with the addition of a few new forms of words which we think superfluous to relate here.

Poets and patrons

ALTHOUGH Richard, more than his brothers, is known as a patron and artist, all the sons of Henry II followed in the footsteps of their maternal great-grandfather, Duke William IX of Aquitaine, famed as the first troubadour. Not all the minstrels of Languedoc were poor: poetic composition could be an aristocratic pastime, as well as a precarious livelihood for travelling professionals.

Troubadours might be performers, but they were primarily composers of lyric poetry, sung to the accompaniment of viol, rebec or tabor. It was essential to integrate words and melody and it is unfortunate that surviving manuscripts do not allow an accurate reconstruction of these poems as a musical performance.

These compositions, of great formal complexity, celebrate a sophisticated yet sublimated eroticism, 'courtly love', the imagery of which is like that of spiritual writings. The term reflects the importance of the aristocratic court as a forum for troubadours and as a source of patronage. Love-songs express adoration of a noble and idealized lady, to whom the troubadour rendered devoted obedience, mirroring the service due to a feudal lord. That the lady was married added exquisite complications; the ennobling experience of love was adulterous in spirit, even if it normally remained only spiritual.

It is impossible to judge whether these lyric arts of love were ever more than intellectual exercises for the relaxation of a leisured élite. Although it was a major cultural transformation to place the lady on a pedestal, in fact a whole social class was glorified. A code of 'courtliness' developed, in which skill in warfare was complemented by the social graces, gentility and generosity. The aristocracy, under attack from ecclesiastical reformers and prosperous merchants, was adamant that its literature should demonstrate its superiority.

The troubadours were not, however, uniformly servile, and the Plantagenets were often savagely criticized. Songs could plead the cause of rebels as well as rulers. They provided a vehicle for social comment and political analysis, and often fostered enthusiasm and encouraged recruitment for holy – and profane – wars.

Poetry was even employed as propaganda by Richard I himself. The song he composed during his captivity expresses the desolation of a prisoner and appeals urgently for his ransom to be paid: 'I have many friends', he says bitterly, 'but their gifts are few'. According to later legend, it was his minstrel who secured his deliverance. Blondel scoured Germany for his lord, and outside every castle wall sang verses which they had composed together until, one day, he heard the answering refrain.

There were obviously close connections between the Plantagenets and the troubadours, one of whom, the bellicose knight Bertran of Born, gave Richard his nickname 'Yea-and-Nay' (Oc-e-No) – reflecting his sometimes treacherous changes of heart. The death of the Lionheart, as of his brothers Henry and Geoffrey, inspired moving laments for the untimely disappearance of gifted princes who epitomized the troubadours' ideals of courtly and chivalric excellence.

Above Eleanor's grandfather had been a famous troubadour, and she always encouraged music and poetry. The song above was written by Bernart de Ventadorn, her devoted admirer and friend. Surrounded by such examples, Richard grew up to enjoy writing and performing.

Overleaf Two contemporary illustrations of troubadours; the left-hand picture is said to be of Bernart himself.

tella quen bernarz an
los que uos auzirez ai

uol ioi eamor auer. Qu

kesbaudeis.

La nö ectar dü ecioi n

Then for two and three-quarter years, Walter the archbishop of Rouen directed the affairs of the kingdom. As justiciar of England, he did not walk in the company of the nobles, keeping his hands from gifts, considering parties equally in the scales. This man, at King Richard's behest, went over to Germany. Eleanor, the king's mother, also made the journey, celebrating Epiphany along the way.

1194

"Walter archbishop of Rouen to Ralph of Diceto dean of London.
I know that since we came to our most dear, renowned lord, the king of the English, we have written to no one in England; until on 3 February we heard matters which were worthy of being told and which we ought to write to you about. For on that day the merciful Lord looked to his people at Mainz in bringing about the release of the lord king. That same day at the ninth hour, with ourselves attending the lord King, the archbishops of Mainz and Cologne went between the lord emperor and the lord king and the duke of Austria pleading for the king's liberty. After much toil and effort and with very great difficulty, the same archbishops obtained his release.

"The Queen, ourselves, and the bishops of Bath, Ely and Saintes, and many other nobles, approached the king in person, briefly telling him the happy news. Thus the lord emperor announced to him, that though he had held him in his custody for a long time, now would he set him free and at liberty, so that he might henceforth resume his own authority. His freedom is obtained and it is resolved according to his wish."

At about that time Henry, the first-born son of Henry duke of Saxony, the nephew of King Richard of England, married the only daughter and heiress of Conrad count of the Palatinate.

Many negotiations were undertaken between the emperor and the king, not merely to arrange how the ransom-money was to be paid, but to reduce the status of the king [by making him the emperor's vassal]. In those dealings something completely criminal was involved, that was most definitely contrived against the laws, against the

canons, and against good precedents. Yet even though the king and his vassals swore to observe it and gave letters patent, which were accepted everywhere in the world, the parties were absolved from their oath because it was extorted unlawfully, so the letters ought not to obtain any authority in the future, nor acquire power in the course of time.

Walter archbishop of Rouen, William Longchamp, the king's chancellor, and certain others were given over as hostages until such time as they were ransomed for ten thousand marks, which the king was charged to pay promptly. And they swore to observe this ruling themselves, and not leave Germany without the emperor's knowledge.

The king of the English, coming to Cologne at the urgent request of Archbishop Adolf was received with the utmost courtesy in his palace. With rich luxuries and splendid feasts, he stayed there for three days. Then on the third day, the archbishop took matters in hand so that the king might hear Mass in the church of St Peter. And the archbishop, laying aside his grandeur, assumed the position of precentor, and standing in the choir with the other choristers, solemnly began the holy Mass: 'Now I know truly that the Lord has sent his angel and has rescued me from the hand of Herod.'

Keeping to a sure course, King Richard landed in England at Sandwich on Sunday, 20 March. On 23 March, to the great acclaim of both clergy and people, he was received in procession through the decorated city into the church of St Paul's. Making then for Nottingham, he soon arrived there. After three days, he received in surrender all its defenders who were seeking his mercy.

The king celebrated Easter at Northampton. Eight days later he received the crown of the kingdom from Hubert Walter, the archbishop of Canterbury, at Winchester. William king of Scotland was also present.
On 12 May King Richard embarked in a ship at Portsmouth. Arriving in Normandy at Brix [actually at Lisieux], he met his brother John who, falling at his feet, sought and obtained his clemency. Advancing towards Verneuil, he heard that the king of the

French was besieging the castle, and that there had been no abatement for eight days either in the firing of catapults, nor the clashing together of great stones, nor the use of siege-engines, nor the mining by tunnels under the defences, nor the injuring of the bodies of the defenders. Then that great day of the calendar arrived, the day dedicated to the Highest Majesty, the most important day in all the world, the day of Whitsun, celebrated by Christian people everywhere throughout the globe of the earth.

Then the French heard how under the cover of night, the king of the English was preparing for a fight, and they heard that he was to attack the next day. Terrified by this report the frightened men preferred to flee rather than fight. To their own eternal shame and loss, they retreated from the fort.

Walter archbishop of Rouen, after the ten thousand marks had been paid, returned from Germany and was received on 19 May at the church of St Paul's, London, where he preached a sermon to the people. Having completed the rituals of the Mass, he was entertained courteously in the house of the bishop of London. On 30 May he embarked for Normandy.

The king of the French, retreating in some haste from Verneuil, lest he appeared to have been doing nothing, besieged a small town near Rouen, which is called Fontaine on account of its bubbling springs. Four knights were inside, together with twenty men-at-arms as guards, intending nothing less than to divert so great a prince with all his army to such a little place.

Then, having meted out the most fierce assaults, the king attacked the gate on the fourth day, overwhelmed the small garrison and destroyed everything. But he respected the men of Rouen itself, in case they were boldly inflamed with the same spirit and deeds as the men of Verneuil. So he retired into his own territories at least with some small victory.

About this time the Angevin army besieged the castle of William Gouet, built near La Ferté-Bernard, which is called Montmirail. They captured it and destroyed it completely.

After the king of the French had retreated from Verneuil, the king of the English, coming to Tours, where lay the blessed Martin, received two thousand marks as a free gift from the burghers of the city which had been collected without any compulsion. Richard advanced to Beaulieu, which is situated on the borders of Touraine, and then besieged and within a few days captured the castle of Loches. The king of the French had received Loches into his power from the bailiffs of the king of the English while he was in chains as a pledge not to break the agreement the two kings had made, and had garrisoned it with fifteen knights and eighty men-at-arms and enough provisions to defend the place.

Around that time the son of the king of Navarre, coming as an ally to the king of the English, gathered a large army including one hundred and fifty crossbowmen. He ravaged the land of Geoffrey of Rançon, lord of Taillebourg, and the land of the count of Angoulême.

The king of the French, encroaching on the borders of Touraine, pitched his tents near Vendôme. But when he saw the king of the English was coming, he struck camp very early in the morning and retired in haste to Fréteval. Richard followed after him and captured his baggage train, and the counts, barons and noble knights fighting for him, with all their equipment. The gold and silver kept in chests and in other places, as well as the tents, crossbows and countless other things, of which the value was immeasurable, Richard siezed and took away without any injury to himself.

From the feast of Whitsun when Philip, the king of the French sought flight, escaping from Verneuil by night, it was thirty-seven days to that day when, staying near Vendôme, he was surprised in the morning and with serious injury to his own men threw himself, terrified, into Châteaudun.

The king of the English, scenting victory, crossed over to Poitou and, after a few days, took over Taillebourg and all the land of Geoffrey of Rançon, and all the land of the count of Angoulême, so that from the castle of Verneuil to the cross of Charles [the pass of Roncevaux in the

Pyrenees, supposed scene of the battle in the Song of Roland], not one rebel remained against him.

"Pope Celestine to the bishop of Verona: We wish, and by apostolic writ we command and order that you take an oath from the duke of Austria with whatever pledge you think necessary, that he will obey without deception our orders transmitted to him by yourself, or by letters or messengers. Having received this oath, command him by virtue of it that all the hostages of the king of the English should be released, all the terms which he extracted from the king should be annulled, and everything taken from him should be returned to him and his own men; what he obtained wrongly by the ransom of the king should be completely restored, and henceforth he should venture no such action. You are to ordain a suitable reparation for the injury and damage he has inflicted.

"After these things have been completed and carried out, you are to confer the gift of absolution upon him and relax the interdict that was laid on his lands. Also you are to command the said duke and his men, having received their oath and granted them absolution, that as soon as they are able, they should go to the region of Jerusalem and spend the same amount of time there in the service of Christ as the aforementioned king is known to have stayed in captivity. But if they shall not observe these things, let you reinstate the same sentence of excommunication on him and his men, with no right of appeal. Given at Rome, at St Peter's, 6 June 1194."

By general decree the king of the English summoned all the nobles of his allegiance to Le Mans, where he loudly praised the loyalty of the English to him in his adversity.

A truce was made between the kings of France and England, but the passage of merchants through the battle lines was forbidden.

At about this time the king of England, imposing certain measures to improve the royal finances, announced that knights should come together from all over England to try out their strength in tournaments; thinking perhaps that if he should

declare war on the Saracens or his neighbours, or if outsiders presumptuously invaded the kingdom, he would find them more vigorous, better trained and readier for warfare.

At length on a certain day at a certain place he summoned to the tournament the devotees of knightly exercises: Englishmen well trained in military manoeuvres, skilled with swords, capable of inflicting blows and beatings. But wielding light lances rendered them not so much ready for battle as for sumptuous and luxurious feasts, and showed them to be best at obtaining and lighting candlesticks. Yet young knighthood, desirous of praise but not wealth, never crushed the men defeated in arms with the burden of imprisonment, nor forced them to an unreasonable ransom by special tortures, but having captured them by right of war, with a single promise of good faith, they allowed their captives to go away, to return when they were asked.

Four messengers came from King Philip to Richard the king of the English proffering peaceful words, to discuss the affairs of the two kingdoms. They feared that their subjects would desert many settlements on account of the exhaustion of their gold and silver, if they were not destroyed by warring swords and the shedding of blood. They constantly said it was their lord's wish that the uncertain outcome of the whole dispute between them might be settled by the single combat of five brave men, and the judgement of the gladiators should declare to the people of both kingdoms, expectant and waiting, which king's right was favoured in the sight of the eternal King.

At once the plan and the terms won much favour with the king of the English. The king of the French chose five of his men, the king of the English also five of his men, and having been carefully prepared with armour and weapons they closed together, equally matched.

During those same days a fish which is commonly called a 'fat fish' [i.e. a whale], by the blasts of the winds and the current of the sea was stranded on the Naze, a manor of the canons of St Paul's of London. When the question was raised as to whether the fish ought to belong to the king or

The tournament

TOURNAMENTS were splendid social occasions, and sometimes political gatherings where rebels mustered armies. But their real purpose was to serve as mock battles, where groups of knights learned to fight as disciplined units in co-ordination with their infantry, and where they established the tactics which brought victory in battle.

Competition was not confined to enclosed lists, but could range over wide areas of open countryside. Dirty tricks were employed on occasions. A shrewd ploy was for a group of knights to pretend that they were not competing and then to join the fray at the end of the day when the other participants were exhausted. In the tourney, as in war, captured knights had their harnesses taken and paid ransoms; a poor knight who was a skilled warrior could make his fortune from these competitions. The greatest example is William Marshal, whose rise from landless fourth son to regent of England began when his prowess at tournaments caught the attention of Henry II's queen, Eleanor.

Above *Two knights, their horses fully caparisoned. Although tournaments are generally thought of as a game played for an admiring audience, especially of women, they were often dangerous contests in which old scores could be settled and serious injury or even death occur. In this illustration, one of the knights has succeeded in putting his lance through the neck of the other. Skills in combat were not only lucrative, they also brought the troubadour myths and legends to life.*

Although knights practised assiduously for pitched battle it was rare in medieval warfare. That was not because commanders were incompetent, but because battles were generally considered too uncertain. On the whole there was far more to be achieved by taking or holding castles and towns, and reducing an enemy's economic resources by despoiling his land. Similarly, challenges to single combat made good propaganda but had no practical value to sensible generals.

235

the canons, the privileges of the church of London were inspected by the chief justiciar of the kingdom, and the decision was that the fish ought not to belong to the king but to the dean and chapter.

Richard king of England returned to the dean and canons of Tours and all the other clerics, both monks and others, all their possessions which he had seized. He generously bestowed these things into the hands of the lord legate. These things were carried out at Alençon on 11 November.

"Walter archbishop of Rouen to Ralph of Diceto, dean of London, greeting:
The lord legate and ourselves have achieved the recovery of all the ecclesiastical possessions which the king of the English had confiscated from the land of the lord king of the French; we are now working on the French king to restore to ourselves and other churchmen those things which he has taken from the land of the English king. Given at Sens."

The Emperor Henry, making his way to Palermo, was solemnly received in procession at the cathedral and crowned king of Sicily on 22 November.

On 26 December Leopold duke of Austria was taying at Graz and, demonstrating his knightly prowess with his fellow soldiers, fully armed after the manner of his country, he fell from his horse and his foot was crushed; he was wounded almost to the death. On the advice of the doctors urgent measures were taken and his foot amputated. Thus the man who bound the feet of King Richard when he was on his way back from Jerusalem, suffering the mortification of the cross on his own body and intending to return to the Holy Land, and who denied him permission to go where he wished, was deprived of his own foot in punishment for such a crime, just like the sentence of Peter of Ravenna, who, writing about the prodigal son, says amongst other things 'for luxury, gluttony and greed let the torture of hunger be apportioned, so that the punishment shall strike the place where the sin did rage.'

"Henry by the grace of God Roman emperor, ever Augustus, and king of Sicily, to his dear friend, Walter archbishop of Rouen, love and greeting.
We know that you rejoice greatly in our happiness and success, and so we let you know that by God's grace we possess the whole kingdom of Sicily and Apulia in peace. Certain great men of the kingdom, who were much opposed to us at first, recovered our good graces; but afterwards they plotted a monstrous betrayal against our person. However, as nothing is hidden which shall not be revealed, by God's grace the plot was uncovered and itself betrayed, wherefore we ordered them all to be taken and loaded with chains. Divine mercy has further augmented our happiness, in that our beloved consort Constance illustrious empress of the Romans and Augusta, on 26 December bore unto us a son. Joining with us in our pleasure, give us news of yourself and the state of your land. Given at San Marco, 20 January."

1195

With the favour of all the cardinals, Hubert archbishop of Canterbury [and chief justiciar] was made papal legate, enjoying a fullness of power unheard-of for centuries.

"William bishop of Ely to Ralph dean of London.
We send you the following letter which the Old Man of the Mountain sent to Duke Leopold of Austria about the death of the marquis [of Montferrat] in the following words:

Letter purporting to come from the leader of the ruthless Islam sect known as the Assassins, claiming that they rather than Richard I were responsible for the death of Conrad, marquis of Montferrat. Blatantly a forgery, its purpose was to clear the English king of the incident.

'To Leopold duke of Austria, the Old Man of the Mountain sends greeting.
Since many kings and princes beyond the sea blame Lord Richard, king of England, for the death of the marquis, I swear by the God who reigns for ever and by the law we hold, that he has no guilt for that death. The reason for the marquis's death is this. One of our brothers was coming back to our regions from Satalia, but the

The market places of Europe

Most communities developed specialist trades.
Top left Carrying bricks for building.
Above Weaving on a treadle loom.
Below A variety of everyday occupations including fishing and making shoes.

DURING the 12th century there was a rapid quickening in trade and commercial life. Italian merchants, particularly in Venice, Genoa and Pisa, imported commodities like spices, cotton, luxury fabrics and leather from Byzantium and Africa, and from the 1170s more and more of these goods began to reach England, Flanders, Germany and other parts of northern Europe.

The great theatre of exchange was Champagne, where fairs were held six times a year in the towns of Lagny, Bar, Provins and Troyes and where the Italians met Flemish cloth merchants from centres such as Ypres and Arras. Wine was shipped along the Atlantic coast from Gascony to England and English wool supplied to Flemish weavers.

In north Germany, Lubke, and the other towns which later co-operated to form the Hanseatic League and control trade in the Baltic, started to flourish from about the middle of the 12th century.

Although industry hardly existed by modern standards, the 12th century was a time of great development. Water was extensively used to drive fulling- and tanning-mills and hydraulic saws, all of which were probably invented during this period. Windmills also appeared for the first time, while weaving became an established craft in most English towns.

wind drove him to Tyre, where the marquis had him taken and killed, and robbed him of much money. We sent our messengers to the marquis, telling him to return our brother's money to us and come to terms with us about his death. But he did not wish to do so, and moreover showed contempt for our messenger, and even accused us of the death of Lord Reinald of Sidon – but we know from friends of ours that he himself had Reinald killed and robbed. Then we sent another messenger called Idris to him, whom he wanted to drown, but our friends helped the messenger escape from Tyre, and Idris then hurried to us and told us what had happened. From that moment we wanted to kill the marquis, and so we sent two brothers to Tyre, who killed him openly and before almost all the people of the city. This was the cause of the marquis's death, and we can tell you in truth that Richard king of England is not guilty of the death of the marquis, and anyone who does him harm on that account does so unjustly and without cause. And know for certain that we do not kill any man in this world for a fee or money of any kind unless he has first done us an injury. And this letter was made in our castle of Messiac in the middle of September before our brothers, and sealed with our seal, in the year since Alexander 1504.'

"We send a copy of this letter to you, of whose love we are well aware, so that you may put it in your chronicle."

1196

At about this time there was a sudden serious flood which swept away everything lying near the Seine, whether wood or stone. Philip king of France and Maurice bishop of Paris were staying in Paris at the time, and were not a little terrified.

Perhaps the king considered the line, 'Lest the tempest of water drown me and the depths swallow me up' [Psalm lxix, 16], and decided to take refuge on a hill. Leaving his palace, he took his son Louis and all his family to spend the night at Ste-Geneviève. The bishop said 'The waters have entered my soul' [Psalm lxix, 2], but he took himself and his people to stay at St Victor.

Omens and apparitions

MEDIEVAL man was fascinated by strange happenings of all kinds believing that freakish events were signs of God's will. And certainly there was a great variety of astronomical and meteorological phenomena. The most famous, Halley's Comet, appeared in 1066 and was widely interpreted as a harbinger of doom; the Bayeux Tapestry shows the comet overhead at Harold's coronation, with the king and his companions looking up at it in consternation. The Anglo-Saxon Chronicle for 1100 records that blood was seen bubbling from the earth in Berkshire at Whitsun, and that later in the same year William Rufus was killed in the New Forest.

The 1190s were notable for portents. William of Newburgh, who wrote his *History of English Affairs* in 1196–8 was probably an eye-witness to several. He tells how, in January 1193, for two hours part of the sky went so red that it seemed to be on fire. It happened again in

Below *Total solar eclipse with the brilliance of the sun ringing the black shape of the moon. An eclipse was seen as a sign of heavenly displeasure and warning, cutting off the earth from the heat and light of the sun.*

February and November and, on the second occasion, monks rushed from their church to see which buildings were burning. William thought it foretold Richard the Lionheart's imprisonment on his journey home from the Third Crusade. Today the phenomenon is known as *Aurora Borealis*. Three years later, in 1196, William saw a double sun which he interpreted as a sign that war was about to break out between Richard and Philip Augustus, an event which duly happened. But some people took a more sceptical view of such apparently hostile portents: Richard impatiently dismissed the rain of blood which fell while he was building Château Gaillard.

Above Scientific subjects were of some interest to medieval man, although phenomena were thought to be caused by supernatural powers, ordained by God. The phases of the moon were known to affect the tides, but whenever anything unusual occurred, such as an exceptionally high or low tide, it was usually regarded as a bad omen.

In these days I often saw how wickedness and discord spread in the city of London, about the distribution of the burden of the gifts to be made to the treasury, according to each one's ability to pay, which many said was unfairly arranged. The leader of this dissent was one William FitzOsbert, who often called assemblies and had people swear oaths contrary to the king's dignity. He persecuted his own brother and two others of sound opinions even to death. As his final act of sedition he incited a riot in the church of St Paul's. When he found that he had deservedly stirred the authorities to anger, he shut himself up in the tower of a church especially pertaining to the archbishop of Canterbury [St Mary le Bow], turning the sacred place into a castle. Then when he saw many armed men coming, in order to escape his approaching death he set fire to the church and thus burnt down part of the Lord's temple.

He was taken out of the church to the Tower of London to meet his fate, and so that one man's punishment might strike fear into many, he was sentenced by the nobles to be stripped, with his hands tied behind his back and his feet tied by a long rope, and dragged by a horse through the middle of the city to the gallows near Tyburn. There he was hanged, in iron chains so that he should not die too quickly. Nine of his companions in crime were hanged with him, so that those polluted with the same wickedness should suffer the same punishment. In order to secure and maintain the peace of the realm, by the chief justiciar's decree the sons or relatives of many men of middle rank were taken hostage and put into various prisons around the country. The poor made suitable satisfaction according to the judgement of their neighbours.

"Walter archbishop of Rouen to Ralph dean of London.
You know what trials and tribulations the church of Rouen has had to put up with for a long time now. We hoped to be able to persuade the king to be more gentle to us and our church, but preferring the bad advice of others he has occupied the patrimony of the church, namely Les Andelys, and ignoring our prohibition has started to build a castle, doing to the head damage which in the course of time can only redound to the harm of the limbs. Both we ourselves,

as was right, and others have warned the king, twice and three times, to desist from what he has begun and to make proper satisfaction to us for the various damages he and his men have caused, burning down our manors, and other enormities, and to return to us our chapelry of Blyth with its income which he has had in his own hands for a year or more. He has put forward various excuses, worthless and irrational ones, but has persisted in what he started and has not listened to our warnings. If he wished to be merciful and spare our lives, he would spare Les Andelys, which is the one relief for ourselves and for the needs of the poor.

"But what makes this enormity inexcusable is that not only does he retain our island in his occupation despite our warnings, but he is even fortifying more of our land with ditches and barbicans. Seeing this invasion becoming rapidly worse, we humbly went again to our lord the king, and lest we be thought to be acting tactlessly we took some of the seniors of our church with us and begged and entreated the king to show mercy towards us and return our island which he has usurped and make good the damage he has done to us and our church. We added that if he had not satisfied us within three days we would no longer be able to close our eyes to his obstinacy and leave it unpunished. Then, to pile sadness upon misery and to afflict our church with civil war, William bishop of Lisieux, driven by pride and other pests of hell, raised objections against his mother the Church, for which reason he has deservedly been excommunicated on the advice of his fellow bishops for his many excesses and contumacious disobedience.

"Since we have not been able in any way, by pleading or warning, to bring the king to reason, and the set term has elapsed with no satisfaction forthcoming, we find ourselves driven by necessity no longer to leave so many great injuries unpunished unless the king hastens to revoke his error. We shall set out for Rome on 7 November, where by God's grace we hope to cover the bishop of Lisieux in shame and confusion before the pope. His intolerable behaviour leaves us no alternative but to find a condign punishment for him. We request you by God's mercy to have fraternal compassion for us and to pray to God for us."

Paris

THE foundations of Paris's greatness were laid during the reign of Philip II when, despite setbacks like the flood of 1196, the first steps were taken towards making the city the capital of France. Helped by the king's initiative, the separate trading and educational communities which had grown up around the old settlement on the Ile-de-France, with its royal residence and the cathedral of Notre-Dame, became a single centre which was the heart of the great city of later centuries.

A near-contemporary chronicler describes how Philip, at the window of his palace, was nauseated by the stench from the insanitary streets and ordered that they be paved. A new wall enclosed an area of some 625 acres, instead of the previous 25, and in 1183 the town's markets were concentrated on the site now famous as Les Halles; two large buildings were specially constructed to contain them. From 1190 the royal archives and treasury were permanently sited in the city and Parisians were given prominent positions in the royal administration. Philip also encouraged the formal formation of the university of Paris and gave it his protection.

Although late 12th-century Paris seems absurdly small – the Louvre was at its western boundary and the eastern end of the modern Ile-Notre-Dame was near its eastern – Philip made it the largest walled settlement in France, the centre of French government and a community with a strong corporate identity.

Above left *A lecture in progress. Paris had one of the earliest and most renowned universities in western Europe.*

Below *Arriving by boat at the citadel of Paris. Rivers were an important route into the heart of any city, even though there was the risk of floods from time to time.*

Overleaf *Paris today, from the tower of Notre Dame; the city has spread far beyond its original site on the small islands of the Seine.*

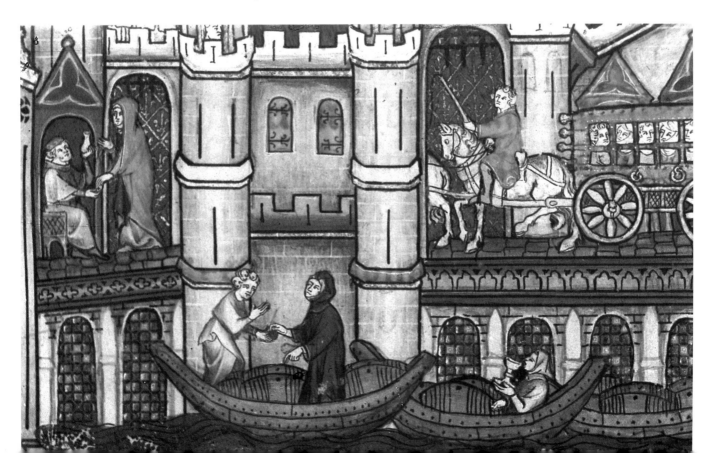

1197

The archbishop of Canterbury was taken gravely ill and was not able to celebrate Mass on Christmas Day, but fortunately he recovered, and spent the Christmas period at Canterbury. He entered the chapter house for discussions with the prior and monks, and it is said that he left all his household, even his cross-bearer, outside. One of the monks, John of Dover, went before him carrying his cross. What happened inside during the next three days is unknown to most people. Only this was divulged: the archbishop entered peacefully, and the king's justiciar emerged peacefully, and nothing was found in the whole gathering to deserve public condemnation either ecclesiastical or civil.

King Richard, with a large army, burnt the castle of St-Valéry and devastated the surrounding province. The captains of five ships bringing supplies to his enemies were hanged, and whatever was found in the ships he distributed to his men on 15 April.

It rained heavily for three days in England, which terrified many people.

"Let all who read this letter know that this is the agreement and treaty between Richard king of England and Baldwin count of Flanders and Haino his kinsman. The king of England will make no truce or peace with the king of France without the wish and assent of the count, nor will the count make truce or peace with the king of France without the wish and consent of the king of England. And if it should happen that both king and count make peace with the king of France, and that the king of France afterwards makes war on one of them, then the king of England and the count shall be bound to mutual assistance and aid, as far as they are able and as they were doing at the time this treaty was made. This agreement is not to last only during wartime but for ever between the parties and their heirs who shall hold their lands after them, in peace and in war.

"If the king of England does not keep the agreement, those who have sworn on his behalf that he will, shall deliver themselves up to the said count within one month of knowing of the breach, without waiting for the count's summons. Similarly if the count should break the agreement, those who have sworn on his behalf shall surrender themselves to the king of England within the month without awaiting summons. On the king's behalf there swears John count of Mortain the king's brother, and the count of Flanders swears on his own behalf to keep the treaty. There are very many witnesses on both sides, whom it would be too long to enumerate. Done at Les Andelys."

Hubert archbishop of Canterbury was ordered by the king of England to cross the sea and he left Lambeth, returning there on 8 November, twenty weeks and six days later.

While in Normandy he accomplished many useful acts. He heard that the bishop of Beauvais in his twin roles of bishop and count, found girded with knightly arms according to what he boasted were the customs of his ancestors, had been captured and was held in chains by Richard I. The archbishop managed to persuade the king to keep the bishop in easier confinement. He reconciled the church of Rouen, where divine service had been suspended. He added certain clauses to the peace treaty between the king of England and Baldwin count of Flanders and their successors. He worked hard, and in the event successfully, to restore peace between Richard and the archbishop of Rouen, as a permanent exchange was made to the church of Rouen for Les Andelys.

Richard's need for money was still so acute that Hubert called the English barons together to ask them for a further substantial contribution. Hugh, bishop of Lincoln, was among those who resisted the king, as his biographer relates.

1198

Almost a year and four months before his death, Richard king of the English became exceedingly angry with Hugh bishop of Lincoln. The king was across the sea, engaged in a bitter struggle with Philip king of the French, and a general council of all the barons of England was summoned at Oxford by Hubert archbishop of Canterbury. The archbishop, who presided in the king's stead, explained the king's serious position. With smaller resources and forces he was struggling against a

The Plantagenet harvest

CONTEMPORARIES did not doubt that Richard was a wealthier monarch than Philip. The biographer of Saladin and witness to the Third Crusade, Beha ed-Din, compared the two: Richard's 'kingdom and rank were inferior to those of the French king, but his wealth, reputation and valour were greater'. Other contemporaries drew the same conclusion. A chronicler from northeast France ascribed Philip's setbacks in the wars of 1194–8 to his enemy's superior wealth: 'in terms of land and money King Richard was richer than the king of France.'

These interpretations were probably correct. Philip ruled a compact kingdom which was far overshadowed by his rival's domains. The Plantagenet possessions were broad and generally fertile. They contained many prosperous towns and sat astride the arteries of commerce: the North Sea, Channel and Atlantic routes and the lower courses of the three great rivers Seine, Loire, and Garonne.

However, if the resources of the Plantagenets were greater than those of the Capetians, some reason must be found for John's lack of military success against Philip. The answer was obvious to 13th-century chroniclers: John's ineptitude as a ruler. In recent years, historians shifted some of the blame from John by arguing that the financial balance had tilted in favour of his opponent. The 'Great Inflation' of *c.*1180–*c.*1220 devalued his resources, Richard's heavy taxation impoverished England, the treasure-house of the Plantagenets, and Philip grew richer. The first and last arguments are undeniable. But Richard had had to cope with the same problems; and the evidence of John's taxation suggests that England's resources were far from exhausted when he came to the throne in 1199.

The use to which these resources were put is an important consideration. Unlike John, Richard seemed never to be short of money, which he employed to raise armies, build fortresses and secure allies. Between 1194 and 1198 he waged a series of successful campaigns against Philip, whose setbacks only increased the pressure upon French resources. John, on the other hand, fuelled sedition among his subjects and did not employ his revenues effectively. The resources of the Plantagenets were therefore almost certainly greater than those of the Capetians, but their usefulness hinged on the extent to which they could be translated into effective action.

Above *Canterbury Cathedral. Both Richard and John were crowned here by the archbishop, but their very different characters are shown by their relations with the primate during their reigns. Richard gave Hubert Walter very considerable political power, whereas John's quarrel with the pope over the appointment of Archbishop Langton resulted in an Interdict on England, and in continuing resentment and financial squabbles until John's death.*

very powerful king, who was straining every nerve to disinherit and ruin him. Finally, he asked them to decide as a body by what means they could best help their lord in his desperate situation. It was then suggested by those who, like him, believed that the king's every wish should be unhesitatingly obeyed, that the barons of England amongst whom the bishops were included should provide him with three hundred knights to fight for a whole year across the sea at their expense against his enemies.

When the bishop of Lincoln was publicly asked to consent to this, he remained silent and thoughtful for a short time until first the primate, the archbishop of Canterbury and then Richard bishop of London, who held the office of dean amongst the bishops, had declared their readiness to devote themselves and their men and property to the king in his need. He then immediately answered to this effect: 'I am well aware that the church of Lincoln is bound to serve the king in war, but only in this country, and it is a fact that no service is due beyond the frontiers of England. I should therefore prefer to return to my native land and resume my normal way of life rather than remain here as bishop and cause unprecedented burdens to be laid on the church under my charge by surrendering her ancient rights.'

The archbishop took this answer badly, and in a low voice and with lips trembling from anger he asked Herbert bishop of Salisbury for his opinion about the provision of aid to the king. He replied to this question shortly and as follows: 'It seems to me that without great damage to my church, I cannot say or do anything else than the bishop of Lincoln has just suggested be done.' The archbishop now completely lost control of himself, and stormed at the bishop of Lincoln. Having dismissed the council, he informed the king that the latter was responsible for the rejection of his proposal. When the king had received two or three messengers from the archbishop, in great wrath and indignation he ordered that all the bishop's possessions should be confiscated. The same instructions were sent about the bishop of Salisbury who had supported the bishop of Lincoln. What next? The bishop of Salisbury suffered confiscation

Poetry and romance

RICHARD had a great cultural inheritance from his parents, but although this was probably the mainspring of his well-known love of music and poetry, Henry and Eleanor were not solely responsible; the reigns of the early Plantagenets had seen the flowering of the troubadours' art, and a dazzling variety of vernacular court literature reflecting the aspirations, preoccupations and tastes of its aristocratic audience. This link between life and literature is nowhere better illustrated than in clerk Wace's verse narratives, dedicated to the glory of the new Plantagenet dynasty. The *Roman de Brut* (i.e. Brutus the Trojan) and the *Roman de Rou* (i.e. Rollo of Normandy) were the stories Richard grew up with. Wace's works trace the histories of the past kings of England and the dukes of Normandy and provide his royal patrons with a star-studded 'family history', demonstrating the continuity of power from Brutus the Trojan to the Plantagenet king.

This poet's highly successful *Roman de Brut* introduced the stories of King Arthur into vernacular literature and so to a wider public. The Anglo-Norman nobility of Britain developed an enthusiasm for things 'Breton' – the *matière de Bretagne*. Celtic folklore and legend, with its mythology, monsters and magic, was eagerly seized on by 12th-century authors and reworked to suit the public's taste: romances by Chrétien de Troyes, who was protected and encouraged by Eleanor's daughter Marie of Champagne, told of Arthur and the knights of *la rëonde table* 'of which', as Wace reminded his audience, 'the Bretons tell many tales'. This world of knights in shining armour, mysterious quests and adventures is in close contact with the other world of enchantment and the supernatural. Lancelot, in search of the abducted Queen Guenevere, performs deeds of chivalry for mysterious damsels, is threatened by magical flaming spears and crosses bridges of naked swords before liberating his beloved from an enchanted land. Arthurian themes are interwoven with values dear to the troubadours, and literary compositions often explore questions of philosophical importance. Entertainment could provide instruction in courtly matters.

Celtic tales had long been told by minstrels and were popular at the court of Poitiers. Poets illustrated their declarations of love with references to the tragic love of Tristan for Iseult, wife of his uncle King Mark of Cornwall. The house of Anjou took a particular interest in this legend. In the work by Thomas d'Angleterre, Tristan's shield bears Henry II's golden lion on a red field.

Tristan and Iseult also appear in the works of Marie de France, one of the few known female writers of the

Middle Ages. She too drew on Celtic legends – tales told in verse and set to music (*lais*) – which she transformed into verse narratives in the vernacular – *en romaunz*. Thought to be Henry II's half-sister, who ended her days as abbess of Shaftesbury, Marie dedicated her *lais* to the 'noble king' her kinsman. She uses stories dealing with the plight of the wife of a good-natured werewolf, fairy mistresses, twins separated at birth and the dilemma of a man in love with two women to investigate the conflict of love and loyalty.

The subject of love, within and without marriage, generated such interest that Andreas Capellanus compiled a codification of its 'rules' for the court circles of Champagne. His *De Amore*, generally thought to have been written in the 1180s, also records 'drawing-room' judgements supposedly made on points of courtly love by noble ladies, including Marie of Champagne and her mother Eleanor of Aquitaine. Even though love was in vogue, the public continued to demand epic *chansons de geste* in which legendary heroes of the past, depicted as contempory knights and lords, did battle with the Saracens or with treacherous or rebellious fellow-countrymen.

These anonymous works give some indication of the concerns and values of a feudal warrior society in transition. The hero of the famous *Chanson de Roland* embodies knightly valour, honour and loyalty to his lord Charlemagne, a loyalty which cannot in reality have always been so absolute and selfless.

Below A lai *by Marie de France. The translation reads, in part, that when a good thing is well known, it flowers for the first time, and when it is praised by many, its flowers have blossomed.*

immediately; only by going to the king, and enduring many insults and much rudeness and being put to great expense, was he able with great difficulty to buy back the king's favour and his own possessions by the payment of a large sum of money. No one, however, dared to lay hands on the lands and goods of the bishop of Lincoln, because they feared to offend him, and dreaded his excommunication as much as a death sentence. Nothing, therefore, was done almost from the feast of St Nicholas to the beginning of September, for the royal escheators dared not sequester the bishop's property in spite of the king's frequent peremptory orders.

At last, at the urgent request of the Exchequer officials, who were pressed by royal commands to confiscate his property, the bishop of Lincoln went overseas to the king. He approached the king himself, without making use of the services of an intermediary, and found him in the chapel of his new castle at Les Andelys hearing high Mass, on the feast of the great doctor St Augustine, 28 August, and immediately greeted him. The king was on a royal throne near the entrance, and the two bishops, Philip of Durham and Eustace of Ely, stood at his feet. When the bishop of Lincoln greeted him the king did not reply but, having frowned at him, after a little while turned his face away. The bishop said to him 'Lord king, kiss me.' But Richard turned his head even further and looked the other way. Then the bishop firmly gripped the king's tunic round his chest, and shook it violently, saying again, 'You owe me a kiss, because I have come a long way to see you.' The king answered 'You deserve no kiss from me.' He shook him more vigorously than before, this time by his cloak which he held firmly, and said boldly 'I have every right to one,' adding, 'Kiss me.' The other, overcome by his courage and determination, after a while kissed him with a smile.

The bishop of Lincoln remonstrated with the king in a few forcible words for his recent wholly undeserved anger, giving some very good reasons to show that he had never failed in his duty to the king. The king could not contradict him and laid all the blame on the archbishop of Canterbury, who had so often misrepresented him in his letters. The bishop by his ready explanations was easily able to convince

him that it was all completely untrue. He said: 'Except for the honour of God and the salvation of my soul and yours, I have never up till now opposed anything which was to your advantage.'

The king's indignation was thus dispelled. He made royal gifts to the bishop, and sent him to lodge as his guest at Château-Gaillard which he had recently constructed on a certain island [Les Andelys] not very far away. The king asked the bishop to come back to see him on the next day so that after another interview he might return home assured of his friendship. Hugh bishop of Lincoln heard this thankfully and promised to return on the morrow.

As the king's spiritual father, Hugh felt his responsibility for the welfare of Richard's soul, and so, taking his hand, made him get up from his chair and drew him apart to a place near the altar. Hugh asked Richard to sit down, and sitting down himself, spoke thus to him in private. 'You are our parishioner, Lord King, and because of our priestly office we shall have on the terrible Day of Judgement to answer for your soul, which the Lord of the world redeemed with his own blood. I ask you, therefore, to tell me the state of your conscience, so that I can give you effective help and counsel as the Holy Spirit shall direct me. At least a year has passed since I spoke to you about it on another occasion.

'Concerning you, indeed, and I speak in sorrow, it is generally reported that you are not faithful to your marriage bed, and do not keep inviolate the privileges of the Church, especially in the matter of the appointment or election of bishops. It is even said that you have been wont to promote people to the rule of souls from motives of friendship or because they have paid for it, and this is a very heinous sin. If it is true, undoubtedly God will not grant you peace.'

The king listened attentively to his exhortations and counsels, denying in some cases that he was guilty, and imploring the assistance of his prayers in others.

After receiving blessing the king sent him away, and Hugh thankfully set out for the lodging which the king had chosen and provided for him.

Accounting for England

THE word 'Exchequer' describes both a cloth divided into squares, a giant abacus on which counters were used to calculate sums of money, and the committee who worked at the table on which it lay. Twice a year the king's officials held sessions to examine the accounts of sheriffs responsible for collecting the king's revenues. A preliminary view was held after Easter, and final accounts after Michaelmas (late September).

The Exchequer was in existence in England in 1110, early in Henry I's reign, but the civil war of Stephen's reign so disrupted government that Richard FitzNeal, Henry II's treasurer, later wrote that the expertise of the Exchequer had almost perished. It recovered during Henry II's reign, and its workings in the late 1170s were described in detail in the *Dialogue Concerning the Exchequer*, the earliest English office manual.

The money brought in by the sheriffs and others was kept in a well-guarded area, the receipt, in the lower Exchequer, while, around the chequered cloth, the sheriff rendered his account to the treasurer and his colleagues of the upper Exchequer. Vouchers, in the form of parchment writs, were used to authorize expenditure made by the sheriff, and notched wooden tallies represented sums paid into the receipt. The account was recorded in the great roll of the Exchequer, or pipe roll – large strips of parchment called 'rotulets', sewn end to end and then rolled up. These were, initially at least, easy to transport, and much royal government was done on the move.

Although this twice-yearly event looked like a game of chess played between sheriff and officials, the purpose of the account was serious. As FitzNeal emphasized, the security of the realm depended on the Crown's wealth, in peace as well as war. Like any civil servant, he took pride in the importance of his department to his royal master. The procedures of the Exchequer ensured that the king received his income, but at the same time, by making the sheriffs account in detail for the money and resources in their charge, they went some way towards preserving the rights of his subjects.

Below *The Irish Exchequer in action, with its chequered cloth.*

The king in the meantime discussed the bishop with his attendants and commented with much appreciation on his holiness. 'Indeed,' he said, 'if the other bishops were such as he, no king or ruler would dare raise up his head against them.'

We resume Diceto's narrative of Richard's reign in 1198, which saw a crucially important event in European politics – the election of Pope Innocent III.

Pope Celestine III having been released from the business of life, the cardinal-deacon Lothario was elected pope on 9 January, taking the name Innocent III. On 21 February he was consecrated bishop and enthroned in St Peter's chair.

On 8 May there was a downpour of bloody rain on men building a tower at Les Andelys in the territory of Rouen.

Aachen, which Otto nephew of Richard king of the English had besieged, was surrendered to him on 10 July. On the following day he married the only daughter and heir to the duke of Brabant, aged seven years. On 12 July he was crowned by Adolf archbishop of Cologne, and ascended the throne of the Caesars.

On the Welsh Marches, near what is called 'Matilda's Castle' the principal defence forces of the area gathered with hostile intent, equipped for battle. In the first grouping of the Welsh were only foot soldiers; in the second, knights and infantry; in the third, knights only. In the first grouping of the [King's] army were placed foot soldiers, and knights in the second; but the whole strength of the army was in the third grouping. On the first engagement, the Welsh turned their backs and spoils were seized from them. Many were captured, and very many killed, amounting to as many as three thousand warriors, so it is said. Thus was the prophecy fulfilled, 'The roaring cubs shall cause great slaughter among any who oppose them.'

Richard bishop of London, of fond memory, having occupied his see for eight years, eight months and ten days, died on 10 September.

Baldwin count of Flanders came before the

Château Gaillard: Richard's 'fair daughter'

RICHARD'S response when the French breached the vital defences of the Seine valley was to construct a system of fortifications to protect Rouen, and more importantly, to provide a base from which to recover his lost possessions in eastern Normandy. At the core lay the remarkable 'castle of the Rock' or 'saucy castle' (Château Gaillard) with its concentric walls, rock-cut ditches and elliptical citadel whose curvilinear wall allowed the defenders' missiles to sweep any approach a besieger might take. A network of roads, bridges and forts radiated from this formidable fortress. It was distinguished by the hectic speed of its construction – a mere two years, the vast sum of £11,500 spent on the castle alone, and by Richard's close personal interest in the design and building. According to a contemporary, 'If an angel had descended from heaven and told him to abandon it, that angel would have been met by a volley of curses and the work would have gone on regardless.' The king boasted he would hold the castle even were the walls made of butter.

Château Gaillard was Richard's brainchild, the product of his mastery of siegecraft, and a rebuttal of the enduring myth of medieval warfare that western advances in fortification were learned from the more sophisticated Byzantines and Arabs, from crusader castles such as Krak des Chevaliers. In fact the ideals which were to be employed in the East in the 13th century had already been put into effect in Europe during the 12th century.

Above right Krak des Chevaliers was built by the Knights Hospitaller in approximately 1131–36, and it stood firm against all attempts until it was taken in 1188 by Saladin.

Right Richard built Château Gaillard in the 1190s for defensive purposes. It represented new and remarkable developments in castle building in western Europe, and stood firm against attackers until Philip II, facing not the redoubtable Richard the Lionheart but his weaker brother John, finally took it in 1204.

town of Saint-Omer with his army on 6 September, and laid siege to it for three weeks.

While the count was laying siege, a messenger came from the king of France, carrying a letter which said that if the castellan and townspeople could hold and defend their town against the count until 30 September, he would come to their aid with a large army on that day; if he did not come, the castellan and townsmen were to do the best they could. Thus the town was surrendered to the count.

Richard king of the English entered the territory of the king of the French with a large army on 27 September, and took the castles of Courcelles, Burriz and Sirefontaine. On the next day the king of France came from Mantes with four hundred knights and sergeants with their supplies to help the castle of Courcelles, which he did not think was captured. Therefore the king of the English, as soon as he saw him coming, pursued him as he turned back in flight, and placed him in such straits at the gates of Gisors that the bridge was broken under him, with twenty knights drowned. Meanwhile the king of England with his own lance laid low Matthew of Montmorency, Alan of Rusci and Fulk of Gilervalle, and took them captive along with up to one hundred knights with numerous sergeants. Two hundred warhorses were taken, one hundred and forty of which were armoured.

1199

Pope Innocent III was added as the one hundred and eighty-fourth pope to the catalogue of popes beginning with Peter the apostle, to whom Lord Jesus Christ said, 'You are Peter and on this rock I will build my church.'

William, by birth a Norman, canon of the church of London, at the demand of Ralph of Diceto, dean of London, received the gift of consecration at Westminster, in the chapel of St Catherine, from Hubert archbishop of Canterbury, in the presence of thirteen bishops on 23 May.

Richard, king of the English, after nine years, six months and nineteen days, on 26 April was wounded by an arrow from Peter Basilius at the castle of Châlus in the Limousin in the duchy of Aquitaine, and afterwards passed away at the castle, on a Tuesday, appropriately for a man dedicated to the work of Mars.

He was buried at Fontevrault, at the feet of his father, Henry II.

Adam of Eynsham gives a graphic description of Hugh bishop of Lincoln's hasty and perilous journey to attend Richard I's funeral at Fontevrault.

The venerable abbess of Fontevrault came to the bishop of Lincoln and privately informed him that the king had been wounded by a shaft from a crossbow, and had passed some days in great pain. His condition was critical and it was doubtful whether he would live or die. As far as I can remember, the king had received his fatal wound on the very day that the bishop had been so harassed by the importunity of his evil counsellors. During the time which elapsed between the wounding of the king and the messenger's arrival, to our amazement no one conferred with him as to how this affair should be conducted. He indeed quietly awaited 'the salvation of God.'

In the meantime, the dean and canons of Angers asked the bishop to officiate at Mass on Palm Sunday, as their bishop had not returned from the curia at Rome where he had recently been consecrated. He had consented when, on the Saturday before, while he was on his way to the city, a clerk named Gilbert de Lacy met him on his way, and put the king's death beyond a doubt, for he informed him that on the morrow he would be taken to be buried with his father at Fontevrault.

On hearing this news the bishop groaned aloud, and immediately told his attendants that he would go to the place I have mentioned to attend the funeral. Almost all of them tried to prevent his doing so. When, moreover, he came to the city, he heard rumours from all sides that everywhere travellers were being attacked and robbed. Some of his own people, who were bringing him money from England, fell into the hands of freebooters who took from them forty silver marks.

The Angevin abbey

Above *The abbey church at Fontevrault, with its slender columns and tall windows, is an appropriate burial place for the handsome Plantagenet family.*

FONTEVRAULT was founded in the early 12th century on the wave of reformist enthusiasm which gave rise to the Cistercians and Carthusians among other religious orders. It was a double abbey, with priests and lay brothers serving Benedictine nuns and, as usual, this caused some scandal. Nevertheless, it eventually became, in effect, the Plantagenet mausoleum or burial church: Henry II, Richard the Lionheart, Eleanor of Aquitaine and John's wife, Isabella of Angoulême, are buried here, and Isabella and Eleanor retired to the abbey at the end of their lives.

The tombs show the Plantagenets, crowned and dressed in their finest clothes, lying on draped funeral biers. All are in stone, except Isabella whose effigy is in wood. Originally they were painted, to look yet more life-like. The figures of Henry and Richard date from *c*.1200,

and were probably commissioned as a pair by Eleanor. Her effigy, the only one of the four which depicts its subject alive, shows her reading the bible. It is of a much higher quality than the others and was probably carved by a sculptor who had been working on the transepts at Chartres.

Fontevrault was not built as a burial place and seems to have become the Plantagenet mausoleum by accident rather than design: Henry and Richard both happened to die near the abbey. A Romanesque building, dating from *c*.1130, the abbey received generous grants from Eleanor of Aquitaine and its unaisled nave is covered by the distinctive Aquitaine domes.

Overleaf *The exterior of Fontevrault.*

253

His friends and servants both urged him not to expose himself and his companions to these risks, and to stay in the city until the dead king's rightful successor had succeeded in repressing the violence of wicked men. Many of them alleged that their wickedness was so great that they had no more respect for a bishop than for a layman. 'What', they said, 'would you do, which way would you turn, if, which God forbid, in some lonely spot you should be despoiled of your horses and garments?'

He, who like the just man was as brave and confident as a lion, and who indeed became more fearless in the face of danger, replied to this as follows: 'It is abundantly clear how many things there are to alarm nervous travellers on this journey. What, however, seems to me much more to be feared is that I, like a coward, should deny my attendance to my former lord and king on this occasion, and fail to pay to the dead the honour and homage I always faithfully rendered to the living. Suppose he did injure me, because he was not sufficiently on his guard against evil counsellors and their flattery? To be sure he did; but when I was with him he always treated me with the utmost respect, and granted my requests whenever I approached him personally about any matter concerning myself. If he treated me badly in any way when I was absent this should be put down to the malice of my traducers and not to any ill-will of his own. I will therefore do my best to make some return for his frequent unsolicited acts of kindness, nor will it be my fault if I do not render my services at his funeral. If I encounter robbers on my way, and if they take away my horses and my garments, my feet will get me there all the more quickly, if they have been relieved of the weight of my clothes. If they also tie my feet together and

deprive me of any power of motion, then and then only will my bodily absence be excusable, being due not to my own fault but to the obstacles imposed by other people.'

After he had said this, he left most of his companions and almost all his baggage in the city and set out, taking with him only one of his least important clerks, a monk and a few of his servants. Hearing, however, that Queen Berengaria was staying in the castle of Beaufort, he left the highroad and journeyed through a wild forest region to that town, in order to comfort her for the death of her husband. His words went straight to the soul of the sorrowing and almost heart-broken widow, and calmed her grief in a wonderful way. He spoke to her most beautifully on the need for fortitude in misfortune and for prudence in happier times, and after celebrating Mass, and giving the queen and those with her his solemn blessing most devoutly, he at once departed. That day he reached a town called Saumur, where the townsfolk came joyously to meet him. He yielded to the earnest entreaties of the Gilbert de Lacy I have already mentioned, who was attending the schools there and stayed with him, where he was most hospitably entertained. At dawn the following day, which was Palm Sunday, he came to the monastery of Fontevrault, and met at the very door of the church the bearers of the king's coffin. When he had been most honourably buried with royal pomp, the bishop at last retired to the lodging assigned to him. From there for three whole days he used to go to the monastery and by the repetition of masses and psalms, prayed for pardon and the bliss of everlasting light for the souls of the kings buried there and of all the faithful who had fallen asleep in Christ.

The greatness of valour

IN just ten years Richard earned a place in the history of England, France, Europe and the Crusades. His military achievements are widely acknowledged. He was skilled in siege warfare, in battle, and in castle-building, and England and his French lands were relatively well governed even in his absences. He will always be best remembered for his crusading exploits, when his courage and military skill earned him a reputation shared by no other English king. Although his failure to recapture Jerusalem was a disappointment, not least to himself, Richard did as much and more than could have been expected when he was in Palestine.

Richard was killed, not in a major battle to defend his inheritance, but when besieging the castle of Chalus-Chabrol, held by the rebellious *vicomte* of Limoges. On 26 March 1199 the king was inspecting the progress made by his own troops, armed only with a helmet and shield. A lone crossbowman on the castle wall shot at him; Richard admired this brave gesture but was too late in getting out of the way. The bolt entered his shoulder, and was removed only with difficulty. Richard stayed in his tent to recuperate – but his wound turned gangrenous and the infection spread. His mother, Eleanor of Aquitaine, hastened to his bedside, but the powerful king's strength ebbed away, and on 7 April he died. Like his father, Henry II, he was buried at Fontevrault Abbey, at the heart of his mighty Angevin dominions.

Below *The tombs of the Plantagenets at Fontevrault, with Henry on the right, Eleanor next to him and Richard on her other side. Although John was buried in Worcester Cathedral, his wife, Isabella of Angoulême, is buried in this French abbey.*

Part V

John
1199–1216

The reign of King John marked a watershed in English history. All the vast Plantagenet dominions in France, except Gascony, were lost to the French king, Philip II, severing the house of Anjou's links with its homeland. In addition, the increasingly ruinous expense of fighting the French, and John's frequently maladroit handling of his subjects, resulted in a concerted baronial resistance which, in 1215, forced John to concede much — temporarily — in Magna Carta. He died suddenly in 1216, leaving his infant son Henry III as his heir. Ralph of Diceto begins the narrative of John's reign, but his Images of History *ends in 1201 and for the next four years the story is taken up by Ralph, abbot of Coggeshall, a monastic writer with a penchant for miraculous events. Gervase, a monk of Canterbury, describes events from 1205 to 1210, in his* Deeds of Kings. *A devoted son of his cathedral priory, his writings show the art of the monastic chronicler at its best. Finally, for the last six years of John's reign, the anonymous Barnwell chronicler gives a relatively balanced and sophisticated, but lively, account of those crucial years in the history of England.*

(Opposite: King John)

JOHN, lord of Ireland, lawful heir to his brother Richard I, was invested as duke of Normandy at Rouen by Walter, archbishop of Rouen, on 25 April, 1199. When he arrived in England, he was solemnly anointed king of Westminster by Hubert, archbishop of Canterbury, on Ascension Day, 27 May.

King John of England visited St Thomas (Canterbury) just after his coronation and afterwards Bury St Edmund's and spent Whitsun at Northampton. After that, on 19 June, he crossed the Channel with a multitude of knights, foot soldiers and ships, from Shoreham.

The king's divorce from the daughter of the earl of Gloucester was executed in Normandy by the bishops of Lisieux, Bayeux, and Avranches and other bishops present. King John had married her with the permission of the pope, receiving the counties of Gloucester, Somerset, Devon and Cornwall, and many other honours throughout England. However, seized by the hope of a more elevated marriage, he acted on wicked counsel and rejected his wife, thereby incurring the great wrath of the pope, Innocent III, and the whole of the curia of Rome, by rashly presuming contrary to the laws and canons to dissolve what had been bound by their authority.

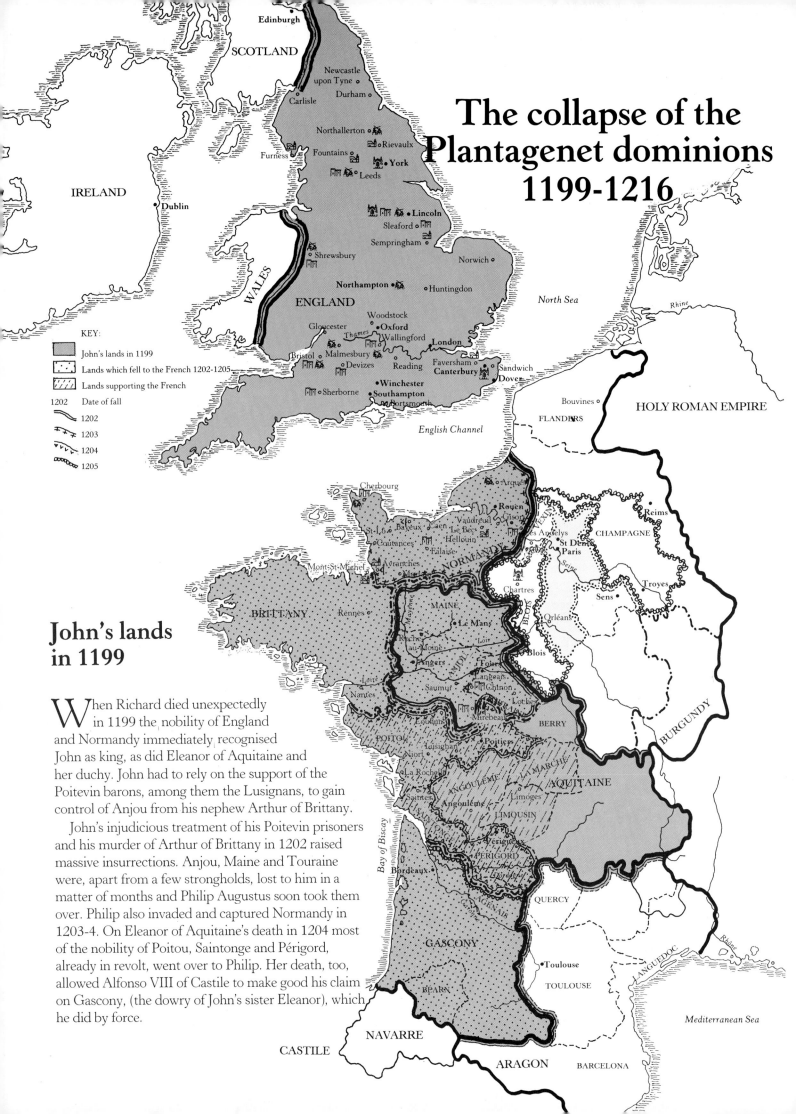

The collapse of the Plantagenet dominions 1199-1216

John's lands in 1199

When Richard died unexpectedly in 1199 the nobility of England and Normandy immediately recognised John as king, as did Eleanor of Aquitaine and her duchy. John had to rely on the support of the Poitevin barons, among them the Lusignans, to gain control of Anjou from his nephew Arthur of Brittany.

John's injudicious treatment of his Poitevin prisoners and his murder of Arthur of Brittany in 1202 raised massive insurrections. Anjou, Maine and Touraine were, apart from a few strongholds, lost to him in a matter of months and Philip Augustus soon took them over. Philip also invaded and captured Normandy in 1203-4. On Eleanor of Aquitaine's death in 1204 most of the nobility of Poitou, Saintonge and Périgord, already in revolt, went over to Philip. Her death, too, allowed Alfonso VIII of Castile to make good his claim on Gascony, (the dowry of John's sister Eleanor), which he did by force.

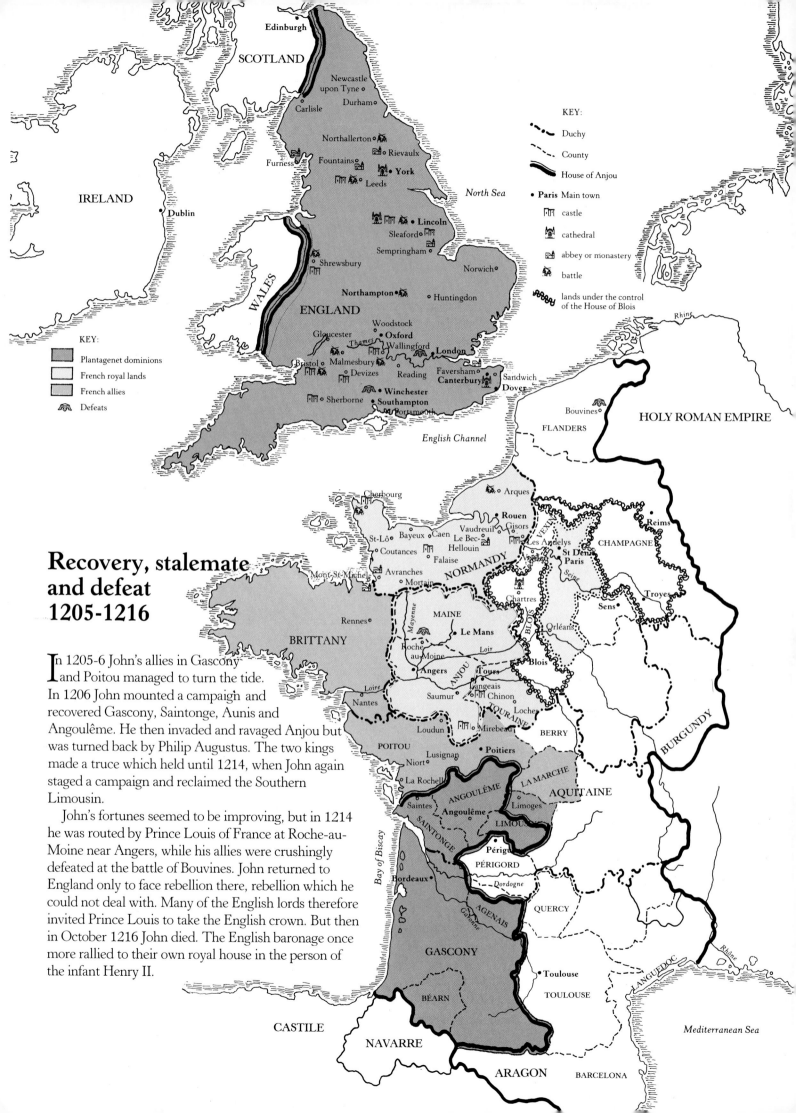

Recovery, stalemate and defeat 1205-1216

In 1205-6 John's allies in Gascony and Poitou managed to turn the tide. In 1206 John mounted a campaign and recovered Gascony, Saintonge, Aunis and Angoulême. He then invaded and ravaged Anjou but was turned back by Philip Augustus. The two kings made a truce which held until 1214, when John again staged a campaign and reclaimed the Southern Limousin.

John's fortunes seemed to be improving, but in 1214 he was routed by Prince Louis of France at Roche-au-Moine near Angers, while his allies were crushingly defeated at the battle of Bouvines. John returned to England only to face rebellion there, rebellion which he could not deal with. Many of the English lords therefore invited Prince Louis to take the English crown. But then in October 1216 John died. The English baronage once more rallied to their own royal house in the person of the infant Henry II.

KEY:
- Plantagenet dominions
- French royal lands
- French allies
- Defeats

KEY:
- Duchy
- County
- House of Anjou
- Paris Main town
- castle
- cathedral
- abbey or monastery
- battle
- lands under the control of the House of Blois

SCOTLAND
Edinburgh
IRELAND
Dublin
Newcastle upon Tyne
Durham
Carlisle
Northallerton
Rievaulx
Furness
Fountains
York
Leeds
North Sea
Lincoln
Sleaford
Sempringham
Norwich
Shrewsbury
WALES
Northampton
Huntingdon
ENGLAND
Woodstock
Gloucester
Oxford
Thames
Wallingford
London
Bristol
Malmesbury
Devizes
Reading
Faversham
Canterbury
Sandwich
Dover
Winchester
Sherborne
Southampton
Portsmouth
English Channel
HOLY ROMAN EMPIRE
Bouvines
FLANDERS
Rhine

Cherbourg
Arques
Rouen
Gisors
St-Lô
Bayeux
Caen
Vaudreuil
Le Bec-Hellouin
Les Andelys
Reims
CHAMPAGNE
Coutances
Falaise
NORMANDY
St Denis
Paris
Avranches
Mortain
Mont-St-Michel
Chartres
Troyes
Sens
Rennes
MAINE
Le Mans
Mayenne
Loir
Orléans
BLOIS
BRITTANY
Roche au Moine
Angers
ANJOU
Tours
Blois
Loire
Nantes
Saumur
Langeais
Chinon
TOURAINE
Loches
BERRY
Loudun
Mirebeau
POITOU
Lusignan
Poitiers
LA MARCHE
Niort
La Rochelle
AQUITAINE
BURGUNDY
Saintes
ANGOULÊME
Angoulême
Limoges
SAINTONGE
LIMOUSIN
Bay of Biscay
Périgu
PÉRIGORD
Dordogne
QUERCY
Bordeaux
AGENAIS
Garonne
Rhône
LANGUEDOC
GASCONY
Toulouse
BÉARN
TOULOUSE
CASTILE
NAVARRE
ARAGON
BARCELONA
Mediterranean Sea

Arthur, the son of John's brother Count Geoffrey of Brittany, came to the king and obeyed his every wish, but John somewhat incautiously dismissed him. Arthur then went to the king of France who, with an avid eye on his wealth, had him brought up with his own son at Paris.

John and Arthur of Brittany were in 1199 rival claimants to the Plantagenet lands. Arthur had substantial support in Anjou, but the lords of Poitou stood by Eleanor of Aquitaine in accepting John and this tipped the balance against Arthur. Then Arthur gained the protection of Philip II of France and was to remain a major threat to John's control of his lands.

1200

An eclipse of the moon occurred on 3 January in the middle of the night, for a duration of three hours. Presently it turned the colour of blood and emitted rays like fire.

This year peace was made between Philip II, king of France and John, king of England. Louis, son of the king of France, married the daughter of the king of Spain, niece to the king of England. On his marriage King John gave him the whole of his lands of Berry and Auvergne, and also castles and many honours in Normandy, Gascony and many other places.

Ralph of Diceto's chronicle now ends, and we continue the story with the colourful account of Ralph, abbot of Coggeshall. He, like Diceto, tells of the peace made between John and Philip II of France in 1200 and gives more details. John, he says, conceded lands and castles and granted Philip 30,000 marks (£20,000). He also did homage for his French lands. To raise the money he imposed a heavy tax on England of 3s on each carucate of land.

King John, coming to the province of York, demanded money from certain Cistercian abbots who met him there, and from the other abbots of the order. He wished to oppress the order with the obligation of the tax, since until now it had been held free from payments of this kind. Not yet having communicated with their fellow abbots, and fearing that if they agreed to the royal exaction, servile obligations would afterwards be imposed on the order, the abbots simply replied that they never paid any money without the common consent of the general chapter.

The king was greatly irritated by their response. In anger and in fury he ordered his sheriffs (those present by word of mouth, those absent by letter) that they should injure the men of that order by whatever means they could. They should persecute them, show them no justice in their injuries and law-suits and not help them in their disputes, but refer everything to the king.

At this harsh edict those men of virtue were not a little sorrowful and fearful, and referred the king's mandate to Hubert, archbishop of Canterbury, begging him to meet the king to discuss this cruel command, and to soften his animosity in any way possible, with prayers and gifts. Being compassionate towards their troubles, Hubert reproached the king openly for his great harshness, pronouncing him a persecutor of the Holy Church who presumed to impose such great and so many injustices on these most worthy sons of the Church, whom the whole Church praised and venerated on account of the merit of their life and the austerity of their religious observances.

Until now kings and princes had always held these men in such veneration that they gave them lands and ample possessions and protected them all with a shield of defence.

King John favoured the arguments of the archbishop at the time, and in irritation recalled the priors with new letters, but he did not rid his mind of the animosity he bore towards them. As the king was about to cross the sea, the archbishop, to please him, promised 1,000 marks of silver on behalf of the order, on condition that he confirmed the liberties granted to them by King Richard. The king completely rejected this offering because it was so small. Then he crossed the sea, breathing threats and slanders against the disciples of Christ, complaining to the abbots overseas about the reply of the abbots living in England.

Marriage to Isabella

Above Lusignan, where the church tower still dominates the town, although the great castle no longer stands. The entire area was one of the French possessions lost by John.

JOHN had been married for ten years to his second cousin, Isabella of Gloucester, when he came to the throne in 1199. They had been betrothed since before he was ten. They had no children, although most of John's bastards seem to have been born during their marriage, and John did not have her crowned with him. As king, it suited him to be free to contract another marriage for political reasons. Because of their family relationship, John's marriage with Isabella had attracted strong opposition from the Church, and he had no difficulty in obtaining a divorce.

In 1200, during a visit to Aquitaine, he unexpectedly married a new wife, also called Isabella. Rumour had it that he was besotted with her – certainly this explains the haste. She was only about 12 years old, and the daughter of Audemar, count of Angoulême, one of the duchy's most prominent barons, who had earlier caused trouble by doing homage to Philip II of France as a way of asserting his independence from King Richard. There was much to be said for the marriage, since it secured the allegiance of the count and his strategically important

domains. Isabella had been engaged to Hugh the Brown, lord of neighbouring Lusignan, a courageous crusader from a turbulent and successful family. A friend of Richard, he was in dispute with Isabella's father over the county of La Marche. John not only took Hugh's bride, but in 1201 confiscated his county and gave it to his own new father-in-law, Audemar. To make matters worse, he seized the Norman lands held by Hugh's younger brother, Ralph.

The Lusignan brothers both appealed to the French king, Philip II, for justice, and Philip summoned John to the French royal court. John failed to appear, an omission which allowed Philip to pronounce all John's French fiefs confiscated in April 1202. (Philip later accepted Arthur's homage for all these lands and arranged for the young Breton count to marry his daughter Mary.) The sentence gave Philip's subsequent conquests their legal validity. Philip, Arthur and the Lusignan brothers all took up arms against John.

263

King John paid the king of France 30,000 marks as part of his peace with him, and with all his enemies pacified and subdued he returned to England at the time of the feast of St. Michael, 29 September. He came with his wife Isabella, the daughter of the count of Angoulême, whom he had married overseas with the consent of King Philip. He had put aside his first wife in the previous year on the basis of their consanguinity. The next day, John wore the crown at Westminster and his wife, who was about twelve years old, was crowned queen.

Early in the morning, before going to church, the king ordered Hugh de Neville, the master forester, and other powerful men to notify all the Cistercians that they must remove their stud-horses, pigs and flocks from the royal forests within the week, and at the end of this term any found within the forest were to be taken and sold for the king's use.

When, therefore, the harsh order of the king was announced to the monks everywhere, each house provided for its flocks as best it could. The monks patiently bore the great indignation of the king and in their hardship prayed to the Lord their champion to turn the spirit of the king to gentleness towards them, and to free His flock from their trials and sorrows. He, who heard them and had not abandoned those putting their hope in Him, quickly released them from their tribulation. Thus the archbishop, discovering the king's command, ordered and counselled the abbots to meet at Lincoln for the king's arrival on 19 November so that at this assembly they could with him more easily bring the boiling temper of the king round towards mercy and reconciliation. The abbots freely agreed to this exhortation and met at the said place on the said day, trusting more to the help of God than to their own ability. They assembled the next day, the feast of St. Edmund, and reverently greeted the archbishop as he came out of the city. They dismounted and fell to their knees, humbly begging the archbishop to deal kindly towards them in this dispute and by his care to incline the king, who was exasperated with them, towards generosity. The archbishop, however, was stunned by the humility of so many illustrious men; he got off his horse and similarly humbling himself, he wept. Then he promised to be their helper and adviser in all things and, having listened to their counsel, to attend to the peace and utility of the order as much as he could and try to placate the king in all ways.

The abbots then left the city without seeing the king and discussed the dispute with him among themselves. Some thought that they should pay him in full, others that they should refuse, the latter counsel in the end prevailing.

The first Wednesday after the feast of St Edmund, King John met with William, king of Scotland who, with Roland, prince of Galloway and many other lords had come to Lincoln to do his homage to the king, which until now he had withheld. The business of the abbots was, therefore, delayed. The next day, however, the archbishop wishing to intercede with the king about the abbots' business, heard him speak as if moved by anger, 'Archbishop, I pray you, do not make me angry today as I have proposed to be bled.' Therefore the archbishop was careful to advise the abbots not to come within sight of the king. On the following Sunday, when the king had heard mass with the archbishop and was leaving the church, the primate asked the king to deal mercifully with the business of the abbots, who were standing in his presence.

After a short delay, the king went to them and addressed them in a loud voice, 'And where is our lord and father the archbishop?' The archbishop hurried forward and soon there were secret discussions with him and the bishops while the abbots remained standing in the chamber. At length the abbots were called before the king who ordered the archbishop to tell them his plan and his will. The archbishop began thus: 'Firstly, we inform you, fathers, that the king has cast from his mind all the anger and indignation which he had appeared to bear towards you.' At these words the abbots prostrated themselves on the ground and gave thanks to the king. Then the archbishop continued, 'Similarly the king humbly asks you to forgive him whatever harm you have borne as a result of this disagreement.'

John as king

THE knowledge that John was ultimately a failure as a king has largely determined opinion concerning his character. Roger of Wendover and Matthew Paris, two monks of St Albans who wrote in the 13th century during the reign of Henry III, John's son, were especially responsible for this point of view. Other chroniclers, who died before John's fortunes seriously declined, are less hostile, and recent historians also recognize that he was an able administrator, and appreciate the difficulties he encountered in trying to hold his unwieldly dominions together in the face of French pressure.

Many contemporary writers emphasized his ruthlessness, cruelty, greed and lust. John's father, Henry II, had also been accused of these faults, but he was far more successful as a king. John's lack of more than momentary military success, from his first military expedition to Ireland in 1185 to his war against the rebel barons at the end of his reign, was a severe drawback in the eyes of his subjects. Although many called him John 'Softsword', he was dilatory rather than cowardly. He occasionally took decisive military action in a manner reminiscent of his father, but was sometimes let down by others at crucial moments. John's desertion of his father in 1189 and his intrigues against Richard in 1192–4 do not show him in a good light; but Richard had not encouraged his loyalty when he recognized Arthur as his heir in 1190. John retained the support of some important barons as well as families entirely dependent on him for their position, but many nobles and landholders did not trust him and he could maintain their allegiance only by taking hostages and keeping them in debt to him. He could be generous to people who could not harm him, but vicious to people in his power. In 1206 he stripped William Braose of his office of bailiff of Glamorgan and in 1208 tried to take his sons hostage. William Braose refused and John sent men to arrest his family, who managed to escape to Ireland in the nick of time. The king's anger could often be bought off with a fine; even some of his closest supporters occasionally had to resort to this means of regaining his favour.

John's poor relations with barons like the northerner, Eustace of Vesci, may have been because he lusted after their wives and daughters. He had at least five bastards, and kept mistresses during both his marriages. Although, like his predecessors, he founded his own religious house at Beaulieu in Hampshire, and was buried at the shrine of his favourite saint, St Wulfstan, at Worcester, he showed no spiritual side to his character. His quarrel with the pope over Stephen Langton's appointment as archbishop of Canterbury resulted in an interdict on England from 1208 to 1213 and cost him the support of some churchmen. John was feared by many and some gave him their loyalty; few gave him their love. As the Barnwell chronicler wrote, 'at his end few mourned for him'.

Above left *King John was a difficult man who found more enjoyment in the company of animals than in his tangled relationships with people. This illustration shows him hunting.*

Below *John playing with his dogs.*

265

The archbishop began again, 'The king asks that at the Cistercian chapter you should intercede for him, that he should be received into the brotherhood and community of the order and that in their letters each house should pray for him. Moreover, the king has decided, following your advice, to build a monastery in England so that he shall be especially remembered while he is alive and where, after his death, if God favours it, he shall be honourably buried. And he promises hereafter to be the patron and defender of your order, and the protector of all your things.' When the abbots heard these words, they were filled with great joy and gave many thanks to Almighty God who had thus turned the spirit of the king to gentleness and reverence for the order.

When these things were agreed in the usual way and everyone was given the kiss of peace by the king, the abbots suggested that the king should send letters to each of his sheriffs, lest they presume to do the order any further harm. The king freely agreed to this suggestion and gave the archbishop the task of sending letters in the king's name to the sheriffs of each province. The tenor of the letters was thus:

"John, by the grace of God, king of England, lord of Ireland, duke of Normandy and Aquitaine, count of Anjou, to the sheriffs of Essex and Hertford, greeting. Know that we have received the abbots of the Cistercian order into full grace and all their goods and possessions into our hand, keeping and pro-tection. And therefore I strictly enjoin you to protect, maintain and defend these men and all their possessions, just as if they were our own royal goods; and do them no injury or harm, nor permit them to suffer any harm or injury within your bailiwick. And if any crime or harm has been caused by anyone on account of the indignation we are said to have borne towards them, then make amends without delay. Witnessed by myself, Lincoln, 26 November."

Earlier, on 1 November, sudden and dreadful thunder was heard, portending something of great note. Hugh, bishop of Lincoln, once prior of Witham, a Carthusian house in England, returned to England from a visit to Rome and was detained by a serious illness in London. As a result of this illness,

The surest road

E VEN before the first English Cistercian abbey was founded in 1128, at Waverley in Surrey, the chronicler William of Malmesbury reported that the order of the White Monks was widely regarded as possessing 'the surest road to heaven'. A century later there were 70 Cistercian abbeys in England and Wales.

In 1132, under the direct sponsorship of St Bernard of Clairvaux, a group of Cistercians settled in the little valley of the Rye, north of Helmsley in Yorkshire and founded the abbey of Rievaulx. By the time of the death of its most famous abbot, Ailred, 35 years later in 1167, Rievaulx had become the home of 140 monks and 500 lay brothers and abbey servants.

The slightly later Cistercian foundation of Fountains Abbey near Ripon, created by a group of dissident Benedictine monks from St Mary's Abbey, York, was even more successful. They had left their mother-house and their regulated but not very austere lifestyle in order to follow the purer and simpler form of religious life advocated by St Bernard. Fountains Abbey rapidly became – and remained – the richest Cistercian monastery in medieval England.

The early Cistercians were famed for their plain living and high thinking. A tightly regulated order with a system of visitations and strong discipline, its founders went back for their inspiration to the Rule of St Benedict, which prescribed manual labour as part of the daily round. Unlike the great Benedictine monasteries though, the Cistercian Order proscribed close ties to the lay community – patrons were encouraged to give money and land but were not permitted to interfere with the running of the abbeys. The fine, plain Cistercian churches and claustral buildings – with excellent drains – were constructed as far away as possible from habitation.

Thanks to a highly efficient system of estate management based on the labour of numerous lay brothers – uneducated men who lived the monastic life but followed a simplified version of the choir-monks' daily liturgical round – the Cistercians became renowned as England's leading sheep farmers: in 1193–4 the confiscation of their entire annual wool crop helped to pay for Richard I's ransom after his capture on returning from the Third Crusade.

Ten years later, the prestige of the Cistercian order was still enough to persuade King John to endow Beaulieu Abbey in Hampshire, his only monastic foundation. By then, however, the reputation of the White Monks in England was already under attack and their way of life increasingly worldly, like that of the older monastic orders they had once hoped to reform.

Above *Beaulieu Abbey, John's only*
monastic foundation.

Below *Rievaulx Abbey, founded in 1132*
under the direct sponsorship of St Bernard.

after occupying his see for 15 years and 15 days, he crossed from this light, as we believe, to the never failing light, on 1 December. His lifeless body was carried from London to Lincoln, his episcopal seat, where at that time, by God's will, the king of England was conferring with William, the king of Scotland, and where had gathered three archbishops and almost all the nobles of both kingdoms.

When it was announced that the body of the bishop was approaching the city, the people rushed out in a crowd to the funeral procession of their pastor. The kings themselves, the archbishops and all the clergy and princes reverently attended. John, putting aside royal pomp, with the archbishops, heads bowed, humbly put the coffin on their shoulders and carried the holy burden for some time, ignoring the mud of the streets for the funeral of such a man.

At length Hugh's body was borne into his episcopal church by the archbishops, bishops and clergy of the town, singing hymns and psalms. Lessons were read at the night service by the bishops and archbishops. They thought themselves lucky who could touch his coffin, kiss his feet or touch some of his vestments. Many offerings and donations were made to him while he lay in state, wearing his pontifical insignia, with his face uncovered according to custom and his head adorned with his mitre.

Bishop Hugh had begun in that town a new church in honour of God the Father, according to an elegant design, which would outshine all other churches in England by its beautiful construction, and which he ordered to be completed whether he was alive or dead. Indeed, he established a guild within his bishopric which paid 1,000 marks each year for this work.

The rumour spread that through Hugh's merits, God's grace had healed certain sick people. Nor is it any wonder that God revealed a miracle to men on earth to glorify his beloved Hugh, whose famous sanctity was already believed in by many who knew him to have led a life of unfailing virtue. Pre-eminent above all bishops in his religious observances, Hugh was held in the highest regard amongst religious men, because even after he was made bishop he always tried to live a humble and monastic life, as far as his pastoral cares permitted. He hated the plague of simony so much that he would never bestow an ecclesiastical benefice on anyone because of a favourable petition of the king or any powerful man, unless there was proof that he was worthy. There are many things which could usefully be written about his praiseworthy way of life, but we leave that to those who are more eloquent and have more knowledge of his deeds.

Our author here breaks his narrative to introduce several miraculous stories intended to instruct and entertain his readers. The events had happened some years earlier.

At the time of Henry II, when the knight Bartholomew of Glanville kept the castle at Orford, it happened that fishermen fishing in the sea there caught a wild creature in their nets; he was handed over to the castellan for inspection. He was naked all over and in all his limbs he looked like a human being. He had a long and pointed beard and his chest was hairy and rough.

The said knight had him kept in custody for a long time, day and night, lest he went back to the sea. He eagerly ate everything that was brought to him, raw as well as cooked fish, but he strongly crushed the raw fish in his hands until all the wateriness had gone before he ate it. He did not wish to speak or rather he could not, even when hanging by the feet and severely tortured. When he was taken to church, he showed no sign at all of veneration or belief, either by bending his knee or inclining his head, however many times he saw the sacrament. He always hurried to his bed at sunset, lying there until sunrise.

It happened also that they took this man to the sea, and put him in the sea having placed in front of him very strong nets in three rows. Seeking the very depths of the sea and crossing through all the nets, again and again he emerged and for a long time looked at those watching on the shore. Often he dived, and after a little time he emerged, as if taunting those watching that he had evaded their nets. And when he had played for a long time thus in the sea and all hope of his return had been abandoned, swimming in the waves of the sea he came again to them of his own free will and stayed with them for another two months.

Afterwards he was kept negligently and held in disgust, so he fled to the sea secretly and was never found again. Whether this was a mortal human, or some kind of fish appearing as a human being, or some evil spirit hiding in the body of a drowned man, as we read of someone in the life of St. Ouen, it is not easy to tell, especially because so many wondrous things are told of so many events like this.

Another similar wonder occurred in Suffolk, at Woolpit. A boy and his sister were found by the inhabitants next to the mouth of a pit which was there. They looked in appearance like other humans in the shape of their limbs, but differed from all normal humans in the colour of their skin, for its whole surface was tinged with green.

Nobody could understand their speech. Having been taken to the house of a certain knight, Sir Richard de Calne, at Wix, to be wondered at, they wept inconsolably. Bread and other food was put before them, but they did not want to eat anything they were offered even though they were tortured with a great hunger, having eaten nothing for a long time; this was because they believed this kind of food was inedible, as the girl later confessed. When at length some freshly cut beans on their stalks were brought into the house, they indicated with great eagerness that they should be given to them. When the beans were brought before them, they opened the stalks and not the bean pods, thinking that the beans were in the stalks. When they could not find the beans in the stalks they began to cry again. Those who were present opened the pods, they showed them the naked beans and these they ate with great happiness, and touched no other food for a long time.

The boy was always depressed as if by a great languor and died within a short time. The girl, however, thoroughly enjoying continuing health and growing accustomed to other food, lost that green colour and slowly gained a ruddy complexion over her whole body. Re-born by the sacrament of baptism, she stayed for many years in the service of that knight (as we have often heard from him and his household) and she was lively and pert.

Often asked about the people of her region, she asserted that all the inhabitants had green skin, and that they never saw the sun, but enjoyed a certain clear light like after the setting of the sun. When asked how she came to arrive in this land with her brother, she replied that when they were following their sheep they wandered into a cave. When they entered they heard the delectable sound of bells; captivated by the sweet sound they walked on, wandering through the cave for a long time, until they came to the exit. When they emerged they were stunned and made senseless by the sun's brightness and the unaccustomed temperature of the air, and they lay for a long time at the mouth of the cave. They were terrified by the enquiries of those who arrived and they wished to flee, but they could not find the entrance to the passage and were captured.

In the time of King Richard, at the seashore of Essex, at a village called *Edolfes Nesse*, two teeth from a giant were found. They were so huge that two hundred of a man's teeth could be cut from them. We saw these teeth at Coggeshall and agreed they were truly to be wondered at. A rib of this giant was also found there, of great size and length. And in the province of York, the head of a giant whose skull could hold a bushel of corn was found on the seashore.

In Wales a certain young man of immense height, who was five cubits tall and whose fingers were extremely long and thick, but he had somehow been deprived of his strength in adolescence. In the same year in that province there appeared human footprints of unusual length on a grassy plain, and wherever the prints had been made, the grass was as if scorched by fire.

Coggeshall resumes his chronological narrative and brings us back abruptly to the events of 1201.

1201

One of the nobles of Aquitaine, namely Hugh, known as the Brown, rebelling against King John, sought to invade many parts of the province with his allies. This was because the king had married the daughter of the count of Angoulême, who had previously been betrothed to him and in his keeping. On account of this the king crossed the sea and subjugated the rebels.

On the day after the nativity of St John, there arose a savage storm of thunder, lightning and hail, with violent rain, which caused great destruction of men, animals and fields, the burning of houses and the uprooting of trees in many places. After fifteen days again another storm arose, not unlike the first, so that the meadows could not be cut, for whatever had been cut was carried away by the swift floodwater. A great multitude of fish died from the pollution of the water caused by rotting hay. Indeed, there were such floods, on many days and so many areas that bridges were broken, harvests and hay wasted and everything submerged so that some feared that by this downpour God intended another Great Flood.

The abbot of Flay came to England to spread the word of God in diverse places. He exhorted the people about the observance of Sunday and the celebration of the solemnities of the saints, amongst other things; and he forbade them to go to any kind of market on a Sunday. Whereby it happened that throughout the province of Canterbury and in many places in England the people did not go to the markets on Sundays and went to divine services. Many astounding miracles have been reported, and in many places in England there was talk of divine punishment inflicted on those who, after his preaching, refused to leave their servile tasks on holy days and sabbaths after the nones had sounded.

In the time of Peter, the fourth abbot of Coggeshall, it happened that brother Robert, a lay brother of that house who had the keeping of the guest house, entering the guest hall one day before dinner as was his custom, found certain persons, venerable in their appearance and dress, sitting in

Liquid gold

ALE and beer were the staple drinks of northern Europe during the Middle Ages. Served in leather and pottery jugs, they were brewed and consumed in vast quantities – the standard daily allowance for a monk was up to two gallons.

Wine was used at Mass, but was otherwise for the tables of aristocrats, often in silver containers. England did produce some wine – *Domesday Book* in 1086 mentions about 45 vineyards – but it tended to be thin, and hard on the palate. Even late in the 12th century, a chronicler suggested that English wine could be drunk only with closed eyes and through clenched teeth.

This helped French wine to become popular in England, where its importation had been greatly encouraged by the marriage of Henry II and Eleanor. The fine wine of Poitou, produced in the St Jean d'Angély and Niort regions, was shipped north from La Rochelle. Bordeaux, the Rhine and Moselle also supplied wine to this ever-expanding market. A few observations by Alexander Neckham, an early 13th-century writer, reflect a delightful variety of drinks for both digestion and enjoyment: pure wine, cider, beer, unfermented wine, mixed wine, claret, nectar mead, pear wine, red wine, wine from Auvergne, clove-spiced wine. . . .

John's decision to keep the price of wines from Anjou and Poitou at a relatively low level was a popular move. (John and his entourage certainly benefited from the *prisage*, the tax in kind which the Crown levied on the incoming shipments.) But some people disapproved of the results of this form of price control; the chronicler Roger Howden said that England was subsequently 'filled with drink and drinkers'.

Left, below, right Grape picking and pressing. Although wine was considered an aristocratic drink, it was also becoming popular with the growing middle class and lesser nobility.

A description of a kitchen in the 12th century included a storeroom full of alcoholic beverages: '"pure" wine, cider, pear wine, red wine, wine from Auvergne, clove-spiced wine for gluttons whose thirst is unquenchable . . .' Grapes were

harvested very much as they are today, although a modern vintner might be horrified at the casual way the bunches were handled when they were cut.

Gerald of Wales was appalled by the over-indulgence of the clergy, especially when they preferred so many kinds of wine to 'beer, made at its best in England and above all, in Kent . . .'

the hall. They wore cloaks like those of the Templars, and each had a cap on his head. There were about nine of them, or more, because the brother had not sufficiently carefully observed how many had gathered there. Thinking them to be Templars he greeted them kindly. One of them who appeared to be in charge of the others said, 'Where are we to dine?', and he replied, 'You will eat in the chamber with the abbot.' The other immediately replied, 'It is not our custom to eat in private chambers but in the hall with the guests.' After this the brother came out of the hall and went to the abbot, announcing the arrival of the guests. The abbot ordered him to prepare everything necessary and to set the table, and promised that he would eat with them in the chamber. Therefore when the abbot came to the table, he ordered the brother to bring in the guests.

The brother went into the hall, but the guests, whom he had left there a short time before, could not be found. Going into the inner rooms and various other places he could find absolutely none of them. Soon he went out, running hither and thither through the courtyard hoping to meet the men. A man said he had seen them going towards the church and the brothers' cemetery. He quickly sent a messenger there, but the messenger found no one. The gatekeepers were questioned about the guests, but said that no such men had gone in or out of the gate that day. Indeed, who those men were, how they came and where they went remains a mystery today.

We do not doubt the story of the brother who saw them and talked with them because we know his life and his conscience. He has frequently told us this story, even in his greatest sickness which took him from this light, and he talked about it simply, for he was a simple storyteller, using few words and showing no ostentation in his words or his deeds.

1202

In the year 1202 peace was made between Philip, king of France and John, king of England. But King John immediately launched a bitter attack on the count of La Marche, namely Hugh known as the Brown and his brother the count of Eu, who had rebelled against him because of his marriage to Isabelle of Angoulême.

King Philip had many times ordered John to desist from harassing his men and to make a peace settlement with them. But as he refused to comply with Philip's orders and requests, the king of England, as count of Aquitaine and Anjou, was summoned by the nobles of the kingdom of France to come to the court of his lord, the king of France, at Paris. He was to submit to its judgement, answer for his wrongs and comply with the law, as determined by his peers.

The king of England, however, replied that he was the duke of Normandy and was in no way obliged to attend a court at Paris. He would only confer with the king on the subject of the frontier between the kingdom and the duchy. This had been agreed in ancient times between the duke and the king and confirmed in genuine documents. King Philip, however, argued that it was not at all just that, because the same man was count of Aquitaine and duke of Normandy, he should lose his rights over Aquitaine.

This argument dragged on and many other issues arose from day to day; gradually animosity increased on both sides, with the addition of cruel threats.

At length the French court assembled and judged that the king of England should be deprived of all the lands which he and his predecessors had held from the French king, because they had done scarcely any service owed for a long time, and had refused to obey their lord. King Philip, therefore, gladly accepted and approved of the judgement of his court; he gathered an army and immediately attacked the castle of Boutavant, which had been built by King Richard in Normandy, and razed it to the ground. Then he seized all the land of Hugh de Gournay and all the nearby castles. He took the county and castle of Aumâle, the county of Eu and the whole of that land as far as Arques and met with no resistance.

A multitude of dishes

THAT entertaining raconteur Gerald of Wales describes and gently criticizes the multitude of dishes served to the monks as he sat at the high table with the prior of Canterbury in 1179: '. . . you might see so many dishes contrived with eggs and pepper by dexterous cooks, so many flavourings and condiments, compounded with like dexterity to tickle gluttony and awaken appetite.' From this and other evidence it is clear that any idea that the wealthier sections of medieval society were frugally supplied with food, even during Lent or another meatless fast day, is quite wrong.

The rich lands of France and England were fruitful and fertile. Game and wild birds were there for the catching, meadows supplied herbs and other flavourings and trade with the East brought spices such as ginger, nutmeg, cloves and cinnamon. Cooks were endlessly inventive in creating banquet pieces of staggering complexity with pastry, sweetmeats and decorations. Even a simple *omelette aux fines herbes* used 16 eggs flavoured with 'chopped dittany, rue, tansy, mint, sage, marjoram, fennel, parsley, beets, violet leaves, spinach, lettuce and pounded ginger'.

Although ordinary people seldom ate like this, in years of plenty even poor homes were probably well supplied by the standards of many other European countries: bread, berries, fruits and vegetables with fish and, occasionally, bacon, fowl or game is a healthy diet. In years of famine, however, it was the peasants who suffered.

Pigs and cattle were the main sources of meat, but in addition people ate what was caught locally: hare, deer, wild boar – even bear. Strange birds also appeared on aristocratic menus: swans and peacocks are well known. Cranes, herons and gulls must have tasted strongly of fish despite all the spices. Every monastery and castle had its own fish pond. Fresh fish included carp, sturgeon and salmon; the sea produced lobster, whitefish and cod, herrings for salting, and even whale from the Bay of Biscay.

Pies and pâtés were convenient for both preserving and decorating food. Stews, stuffings and sauces, thickened with bread soaked in broth or milk, were often made with wine or verjuice.

Boeuf bourguignon and *coq au vin* are basically medieval dishes, as are stewed eel and a version of *bouillabaisse*. Garlic sauces were popular and were even sold ready-made on the streets. In the larger towns and cities there were shops selling pre-cooked food, including meat or fish on a 'plate' of bread – the forerunner of the sandwich. Sweets were important sources of pleasure and energy: they included dried fruits served alone or made into pastes

> *A priest or a soldier attached to the court has bread put before him which is not kneaded, nor leavened, made of the dregs of beer, bread like lead, full of bran and unbaked; wine spoiled either by being sour or mouldy – thick, greasy, rancid, tasting of pitch and vapid . . . The beer at court is horrid to taste and filthy to look at. On account of the great demand, meat is sold whether it be fresh or not. The fish one buys is four days old, yet the fact that it stinks does not lessen its price. The servants care nothing whatever whether the unlucky guests become ill or die provided they load their masters' tables with dishes. Indeed the tables are sometimes filled with putrid food, and were it not for the fact that those who eat it indulge in powerful exercise, many more deaths would result from it.*
>
> Peter of Blois, *Letters*

Above *Peter of Blois came from a noble Breton family to study in Paris. He was invited to England by Henry II, where he settled, holding many appointments until he became archdeacon of Bath and then of London. His letters are much prized for their information about the customs and politics of his time, and were generally written with a sharp and sometimes even bitter edge.*

and jellies, biscuits, tarts, waffles and fritters, gingerbread and macaroons.

It seems that most people had their main meal early in the morning, usually at about nine or ten o'clock when everybody had been up and working for three or four hours, although it might be delayed until eleven or twelve if there were special guests.

Dinner in the hall of a great lord was one of the main events of the day. Guests and household followed custom and etiquette, using ewers and towels to wash their hands ceremonially. There were knives and spoons and salt cellars on the table, along with wine cups and jugs. Servants brought in the various courses and a great deal of business was transacted with visitors and travellers. Troubadours and players were always welcome, but the best entertainment was the abundant food, elaborately prepared and lavishly served up in a hundred and one guises for the amusement as well as the sustenance of the household.

At the age of sixteen Arthur, King John's nephew was knighted by King Philip and betrothed to his small daughter. At the importune suggestion of some, he rebelled against his uncle and, following evil and rash advice, set out with Hugh the Brown and Geoffrey of Lusignan and two hundred and fifty soldiers to besiege the castle of Mirebeau, where his grandmother, Queen Eleanor, was staying with her men. The queen, fearing capture, ordered her son John to bring her aid as soon as possible.

The king immediately set out there with part of his army. The rebels had entered the town and had closed up with earth all the gates except one. Securely they awaited the king's arrival, confident in their multitude of proven knights and serjeants. After heavy fighting the king entered the city and immediately, by God's will, caught all his enemies who had flocked there. He captured his nephew, Arthur, Count Hugh and Geoffrey of Lusignan and two hundred and fifty-two of the worthiest knights. And so he freed his mother and her adherents from the besiegers.

King Philip had been besieging the castle of Arques for a long time and just when he hoped to take the castle, the news of the capture of Arthur and the others reached him and took him away from the siege. He returned to France, very upset by the misfortune which had befallen his men.

Afterwards King John took the town of Tours and King Philip's castle there by violence and set fire to almost the whole of that fine city. Because of this he incurred the hatred of the inhabitants of Tours and the nobles of that area. He also burned the city of Le Mans to capture his enemies.

He imprisoned those captured at Mirebeau, sending them to different places. Later, on his own defeat, and at the petition of certain nobles, he released Count Hugh the Brown, Geoffrey of Lusignan and certain others captured at Mirebeau, after they had surrendered their castles and hostages and had given their oath not to rebel against him. They did not keep this oath for long, however, and they began to attack the king more

The hollow victory: Mirebeau

ON 1 August, 1202 John won a stunning victory over his rivals and wrote exultantly to the English barons: 'know that by the grace of God we are safe and well and God's mercy has worked wonderfully with us . . . we heard that the lady our mother was closely besieged at Mirebeau, and we hurried there as fast as we could . . . And there we captured our nephew Arthur . . . and all our other Poitevin enemies who were there, being upward of 200 knights, and none escaped. Therefore God be praised for our happy success.'

His mother Eleanor of Aquitaine had been actively supporting John, but Arthur and the Lusignans, with French support, trapped her in Mirebeau castle in July 1202. John moved rapidly to try to free her. The campaign was a masterpiece of its kind. A rapid approach march of more than 80 miles in two days enabled John to fall on Arthur and the Lusignans who, thinking themselves safe, were fully committed to the siege.

The political dividends of this ought to have been immense. The movement in favour of Arthur, John's rival for the Angevin inheritance, was beheaded at one stroke. Each prisoner could have bought his freedom for the payment of a ransom, as the laws of war allowed, and John could have bartered their liberty for castles and political support. Instead, he succeeded in snatching defeat from the jaws of victory and sowed the seeds of his

Below **This detail from a psalter shows a typical confused battle scene of the same period as Mirebeau.**

destruction by his treatment of the prisoners. William des Roches, who had commanded the attack at Mirebeau, was in revolt before the year was out: John had promised him a say in Arthur's treatment and then refused it.

In an attempt to put down this renewed opposition in the pivotal Loire region John released the two most dangerous of his prisoners, the Lusignans Hugh the Brown and his brother Ralph, on the condition that they remained loyal to him. But they had no intention of keeping their word and soon they too were in arms against him. His treatment of the remaining prisoners was equally crass. Instead of honourable imprisonment under house arrest they were laden in chains and incarcerated in dungeons. Arthur was sent to Falaise castle, never to be seen in public again. Many others were shipped to England. Twenty-five of those incarcerated under heavy

Above Another illustration from the same psalter illustrates medieval weapons and armour: spears, swords, helmets, chain mail, cross bows, etc, as well as defensive tactics like stone throwing.

security at Corfe Castle planned a breakout and seized the keep, but, being besieged by the king's men, 22 of them preferred to starve to death rather than to surrender again to John. The great nobles in Poitou, Anjou, Maine and Touraine all turned against him, and with Eleanor's death in 1204 he seemed to have irrevocably lost her duchy as well as his Angevin patrimony.

From the greatest victory of his career, therefore, John conjured up the ruin of the Angevin empire in just two short years.

275

fiercely than before and were joined by many companies of his enemy.

William des Roches, a powerful member of the Angevin nobility, with other nobles from Brittany, petitioned the king to hand Arthur, whom he was diligently keeping in custody, over to them. When John refused, they conspired together and launched a rebellion against him, collecting a large army from provinces which should have been under the king's authority. They devastated the land, pillaging and burning, and they attacked many castles.

At this several powerful men left the king and joined their fellow nobles, amongst whom were: Robert, count of Alençon, the viscount of Beaumont, William of Fougères and other Bretons. They held the castle of Angers with all the town and in a short time took many other fortified places.

The counsellors of the king, realizing that the Bretons were causing much destruction and sedition everywhere on behalf of their lord Arthur, and that no firm peace could be made while Arthur lived, suggested to the king that he order Arthur to be blinded and castrated, thus rendering him incapable of rule, so that the opposition would cease from their insane programme of destruction and submit themselves to the king.

Enraged by the ceaseless attacks of his enemies, hurt by their threats and misdeeds, at length in a rage and fury, King John ordered three of his servants to go to Falaise and perform this detestable act. Two of the servants, hating to do so evil a deed on such a noble young man, fled from the king's court. The third, however, wearing three rings on his foot, went to the castle in which the royal youth was being carefully kept by the royal chamberlain, Hubert de Burgh. When he took the king's order to Hubert, great grief and sorrow arose among those guarding him and they were moved with great pity for the noble youth.

Arthur, realizing the dire sentence which his uncle had pronounced on him and fearful for his own safety, burst into tears and pitiful complaints.

The man sent by the king to execute this task appeared and made himself known to the weeping and moaning youth. Suddenly Arthur stopped sobbing; he stood up and violently laid avenging hands on the man, calling to the knights there in a tearful voice, 'O my dearest lords! For the love of God let me be a little avenged on this villain, for he is the last of all that I shall see in this world.'

In order to quieten this tumult the knights quickly got up and restrained both his hands, and on Hubert's order, the young man who had come from the chamber was thrown out. From this expulsion and from the consoling words of those around him Arthur, with a sad heart, took a little comfort.

Hubert, the king's chamberlain, having regard for the king's honesty and reputation and expecting his forgiveness, kept the youth unharmed. He thought that the king would immediately repent of such an order and that ever afterwards would hate anyone who presumed to obey such a cruel mandate, which Hubert believed was the result more of a sudden anger than calm consideration.

Wishing to mollify King John's anger and at the same time stop the savagery of the Bretons, Hubert had it announced through the castle and the whole region that the sentence had been carried out and that Arthur had died from a broken heart and from the bitter pain of his wounds. This news circulated round both kingdoms over the following fortnight. Then bells rang out as if for his soul and his clothes were distributed to leper houses. It was also announced that Arthur's body had been taken to the Cistercian abbey of St André-en-Gouffern, in Normandy, and buried there.

At this news the Bretons were not subdued, but more and more enraged. Wherever possible they were even more destructive than before, swearing that henceforth they would never cease from attacking the English king who had performed such a detestable deed on their lord, his own nephew. This made it necessary to announce that Arthur, who everywhere was said to be dead, was still alive and well. So the enraged ferocity of the Bretons was somewhat pacified.

Eleanor's youngest son

SEVEN of Eleanor of Aquitaine's children by Henry II reached adulthood, and John was the youngest of these by eight years. Although Richard was her favourite, like her a Poitevin by nature, she also helped John's interests when she could. When Richard set off on his crusade in 1190, she persuaded him to allow his brother to remain in England. In 1192 she prevented John from allying with Philip II of France against Richard, but could not stop his intrigues in England. His elder brother forgave him for these two years later, patronizingly likening him to a child who knew no better.

When Richard died in 1199 Eleanor strongly supported John against her grandson, Arthur, duke of Brittany, and brought Richard's mercenary troops to his aid. She held her duchy of Aquitaine for John when Anjou, Maine and Touraine decided in favour of Arthur, and later that year made it over to him. In 1201, virtually bedridden, she used her remaining arts of persuasion on John's behalf in an attempt to calm the turbulent barons of Poitou. She was besieged by Arthur at Mirebeau in 1202 before John rescued her and captured Arthur.

Eleanor died in April 1204 soon after hearing of the fall of Château Gaillard to Philip II. This left her son's Norman patrimony open to the invader, and by her own death she left her beloved Poitou also vulnerable to French interference.

Below *Lincoln Cathedral. John was far more interested in England than Richard had been, and in 1200, while his mother was holding his lands for him in France, he took time to travel through the Midlands, stopping to see the new cathedral at Lincoln, then in construction. The elderly Bishop Hugh died during the visit; Hugh had been loved and admired by Henry II, and John's respect for him was made clear when, in spite of overwhelming political problems abroad, he stayed for the funeral and even helped to carry the coffin.*

When John was told, he was not displeased for the moment that his order had not been carried out. Some knights even said to him that he would find no more troops to guard his castles if he carried out his sentence on Arthur, for if any knight should by chance be captured by the king of France, he would immediately receive the same treatment without mercy.

In this year there was a great earthquake in the land of Jerusalem, such as had not been seen since the Passion of our Lord. The splendid city of Tyre with many of its inhabitants was almost completely destroyed by the tremors, as was one third of Acre with its castles and towers and many other castles among the Christians and the Saracens alike. The earthquakes affected many places in England. There was awful thunder, lightning and frequent hail and strong winds throughout August.

1203

In the year 1203 in April there was a sudden unexpected flood, which caused much damage throughout England. This occurred miraculously since only a little rain had preceded this great inundation.

Arthur was taken from Falaise to Rouen, and shut up in the castle, under the keeping of Robert de Vieuxpont. King Philip of France, with the Bretons, instantly ordered King John of England to release Arthur to them. They took many hostages for him and added fierce threats to these commands.

When John refused, Philip again attacked the castles of Normandy. Among others, he took the island of Les Andelys with its castle, and Vaudreuil, where many nobles had been stationed for its keeping, namely Robert FitzWalter with his knights and Saer de Quincy with his men, and with a great amount of military equipment. These men, disregarding their usual valiant soldierly behaviour because they did not expect to receive any help from the king, with no attempt at defence, as if powerless, surrendered themselves with their castle to the king of the French; they were ransomed with a great sum of money, namely five thousand

marks sterling. They were held up to derision and shame by the people of both kingdoms because of this, and they had disgraced their honour.

Afterwards, King Philip took Château Gaillard, which had seemed impregnable. It had been constructed by King Richard I of England at great expense near Les Andelys on the Seine, against the will of the archbishop of Rouen for that land belonged to him. The constable of Chester was in the castle with many famous knights and serjeants, who for a long time strenuously held the castle against the force of the whole army of the French king. But when they urgently needed food supplies they could resist the enemy no longer. King John, indeed, was unwilling to send troops to the besieged because he always feared the treachery of his men, and in winter in the month of December he crossed to England leaving all the Normans in great worry and fear.

Then he truly oppressed England with many demands for money, hoping to raise a great army and exterminate the forces of King Philip.

1204

In the year 1204 Queen Eleanor died. The daughter of the count of Poitou, her first husband had been King Louis VII of France and then she had married Henry II of England.

Eleanor's death lost John a formidable and influential supporter and advisor.

In this year in the middle of Lent King John, having held a council, sent ambassadors to the king of France, namely: the archbishop of Canterbury, the bishop of Norwich, the bishop of Ely, Earl William Marshal and the earl of Leicester. They were to find out the French king's intentions and negotiate a peace treaty with him. But King Philip would make a peace settlement only if Arthur were released to him alive. For if Arthur was now discovered to be dead, Philip hoped to marry his sister and thus to gain all her continental possessions. King Philip was unwilling to make peace because he was confident that he would soon possess all the lands of the English king.

The loss of Normandy

THE years from 1202 to 1204 seem an almost unbroken catalogue of disasters in John's attempts to defend his lands against the ever-growing tide of French success. By the middle of 1203, Philip II had gained the loyalty of most of Anjou, Maine and Touraine, and the French king then set his sights on Normandy. Here, John was dogged by the treachery of the Norman barons, and his use of rapacious mercenary soldiers further alienated the inhabitants of the countryside. The most effective resistance to Philip was put up by English commanders of castles, especially Robert de Lacy, who resolutely defended Château Gaillard for six months. Its loss opened the route to the main town, Rouen, which was a stronghold of loyalty to John, but Philip wisely decided to secure the rest of Normandy first, linking up with John's bitter enemies, the Bretons, who were attacking the duchy from the west, at Caen. Resistance having collapsed in the rest of the duchy, the citizens of Rouen could no longer hold out alone, and they surrendered their key town to the French king, coming to an arrangement with him which preserved their trading privileges. John who had fled to England by the end of 1203, and had acted indecisively throughout the campaign, was unable to raise an English relief army quickly enough. Although in 1205–6 John's supporters in southern Poitou and in Gascony managed to turn the tide once more in his favour in these regions,

Top *Rouen is still dominated by its cathedral, begun in the 11th century.*

Below *The 12th-century doorway of St Jean.*

John had lost Anjou, Maine and Touraine, the fatherland of the Plantagenets, as well as Poitiers, ancient capital of Aquitaine and the whole of the wealthy duchy of Normandy. The last loss was felt the most in England. Ties between John's English kingdom and the Norman duchy had become so close over more than a century that it was to prove harmful and difficult to break them.

At this stage John had no children, and in the event of his death Arthur's sister would have inherited his lands.

So he always suggested something awkward or impossible at the negotiations so as to bring shame and humiliation on King John, and to undermine his royal dignity. He always raged about the death of Arthur, whom he had heard had been drowned in the Seine. Therefore he swore that he would never desist from making war on John until he had deprived him of his entire kingdom.

At Easter, Philip gathered an army and besieged the castle of Falaise, which he soon took without resistance. Then he arrived at Caen and was peacefully received by the citizens there, for they had no one who might defend them. After that he took the whole province as far as Barfleur, Cherbourg and Domfront. The citizens of Rouen and Verneuil and those guarding the castle of Arques bought forty days, respite from the king of France so that they could send messengers to the English king to learn his will. For if their lord was unable or unwilling to help them they could surrender to King Philip's lordship without a violent conflict.

They immediately sent messengers to England with a miserable enough mission: to explain the wretched state of Normandy and to ask him to rescue them. King John, however, gave them no help, because he feared the treachery of some of his own men. The legates returned, sad and anxious, and thus the city of Rouen, hitherto unconquered and the citizens of Verneuil together with those at Arques surrendered to King Philip.

And so within a short time, stubborn Normandy, Anjou, Brittany, Maine and the province of Tours had been subjugated to the lordship of King Philip. This went according to Merlin's prophecy that in this year 'The sword shall be divided from the sceptre', that is Normandy from the kingdom of England. Kings of England had been dukes of Normandy for one hundred and thirty-nine years, from Duke William, who had conquered England, down to King John, who lost the duchy and many overseas lands.

For all this time, there had been a great conflict between the Poitevins and the Aquitanians. The former were loyal to King John, under Robert Thornham. With the latter were William des Roches and Count Hugh, who invaded the territory of King John. King Philip, with their support, was able to overrun almost all of Poitou, except La Rochelle, which bravely held out against everyone for a year. Likewise the castle of Chinon, with Hubert de Burgh in it, did not surrender to its enemies for all that time. Gerard d'Athée, keeper of the castle of Loches, bravely resisted the rebels.

The Gascons supported the English king, and King John gave Moreve, a certain Gascon, twenty-eight thousand marks to raise an army of thirty thousand men, who should arrive on command when John crossed the sea. The archbishop of Bordeaux, Moreve's brother, was in England to negotiate this business and was to act as a hostage for the money.

King John built an abbey in the New Forest, known as Beaulieu, and brought there thirty monks of Cîteaux.

Alexius, puppet emperor of Constantinople, was deposed and his cousin Muzuphulus emerged as emperor. He attacked the Western army on several occasions. In retaliation the crusaders sacked Constantinople.

The city of Constantinople was triangular, six miles wide, they say, and the perimeter of the city was eighteen miles, so that from corner to corner was six miles. The walls were fifty feet high and there were towers along the walls every twenty feet. In the city was the famous imperial palace called Blachernae, and the palace of Constantine and the palace of Bohemond. The city contained an incomparable church, called St. Sophia, built by Justinian. The scale of its construction and the beauty of its decoration are always said to be unbelievably wonderful. The emperor had endowed the church with abundant rents and established there nine hundred and fifty canons. They say for certain, those who know the city, that it has more inhabitants than live between the city of York and the River Thames.

When the city was taken and the Emperor Muzuphulus had fled, by common consent Baldwin, count of Flanders, was made emperor. Immediately he generously distributed a third of the imperial treasure, which amounted to one million, eight hundred thousand silver marks, between the Latin princes and the army. This huge sum of money, like everything else that is related to the wealth of the Greeks, and like the buildings of the city and St Sophia, seems incredible. For those who have returned from the city say that the emperor's daily income is thirty thousand *perpres* — a *perpres* is a golden penny and is worth three shillings in silver. He also generously endowed the princes and others with him with dignities and honours and many outstanding gifts. To King Philip, once his lord, he sent a certain carbuncle, a most precious stone, which could light up the whole palace with a red glowing brilliance, and two royal robes wonderfully woven with gold and precious stones.

In Constantinople there is a column, erected in ancient times by a certain churchman, using the mechanical arts, it is said. Its base is always in motion and on its capital are the images of three emperors: one looking to Asia, one to Europe and one to Africa. Above the images is a circle on which it is written in Greek that after three emperors named Alexius have ruled in Greece, the kingdom of the Greeks will come to an end and the empire will pass to a foreign people. On top of the circle stands a fourth image over the rest, more striking and sublime than the other images, which looks towards the western world and stretches her hand out to the West.

1205

In the year 1205 there was a harsh winter and the rivers froze so that you could cross the Thames on foot. The ground was so hard that it could not be ploughed from the feast of the Circumcision, 1 January, to the Annunciation, 25 March. Indeed, the winter crops were almost destroyed by the force of the cold and people quickly dug up the growing vegetables. A great famine arose throughout England, so that one mark was paid for a bushel of corn, which often in King Henry II's time had

only cost 12d. Measures of beans and peas now cost half a mark, and a bushel of oats cost 40d which you used to be able to buy for 4d. The money became so debased and corrupt through clipping that it became necessary to renew it this year.

Robert Thornham, who had held out so strongly against the Poitevin rebels, was now captured by the army of the French king. Gerard d'Athée was captured with the castle of Loches which he had so bravely defended for so long.

King John, who was very worried although he appeared to hide his sorrow, decided to cross the sea with a large army to recover his lost lands. He had won over the Poitevin and Gascon nobles with secret promises and was being constantly urged on by some of the Norman nobility, who complained bitterly of the tyranny of the French king.

So after Easter, having held a council at Northampton, King John made for the sea at Porchester with a great and noble army. He was joined there by a great multitude of ships from many ports. When the ships which had reached the port had been allocated to each of the nobles, and the food, supplies, and various types of arms had been loaded, and the day had arrived when the ships were ready, behold! the archbishop of Canterbury and Earl William Marshal, who had just returned from overseas, came to the king to persuade him at all costs to abandon the expedition.

They put forward the many dangers which could come from his crossing: that it would be very dangerous to land troops amongst the enemy without a secure base; that the French king could lead a much greater army against him, so that he could invade almost the entire land; that it was not safe to rely on the guile and fickleness of the Poitevins who were always planning something deceitful against their princes; that the count of Boulogne with his accomplices would quickly invade England if he heard it was empty of its leaders and famous army; that it was greatly to be feared that he would lose what he held in trying to recover what he had lost, especially since he left behind him no obvious heir to the kingdom who could take over the government of the realm if anything unfortunate happened to him overseas. Although he had heard these and other arguments the king could not be persuaded to give up his plan of going overseas. The archbishop and Earl William, seizing him by the knees, clung on to him lest he should escape from them, insisting that if he would not listen to their entreaties, they would detain him by force lest the whole kingdom be thrown into confusion by his departure.

The king was being pressed on all sides: on the one hand there was the shame of abandoning his plan, on the other there were urgent pleas to stay. Weeping and lamenting he asked the archbishop for advice which would be more useful for the kingdom and his royal reputation, and as to how to expediate his assistance to those waiting for him overseas. The archbishop having held council they decreed that some of the English nobles should be sent with some powerful knights as a force in advance of the king's coming.

At length the king was reluctantly persuaded to stay and told his lords and knights to return home and to account for the money they had been paid for the crossing. These men, who had borne many difficulties and incurred many expenses on this occasion, returned home with great indignation and with the burden of the victuals they had collected. They cursed the archbishop and other counsellors who had given the king such bad advice, as it seemed to many. This was especially true of the sailors, of whom there was said to have been fourteen thousand. They had brought their ships from remote parts and for some time had waited in vain, with great fatigue and at great expense, for the crossing. For they said that never had so many ships sailed to an English port for a crossing, and that never had a bigger army of strong knights assembled in England, eager to cross with the king. News of their arrival overseas had so terrified the French knights in Normandy, that some of them had abandoned the castles and towns near the sea and sought safety in flight.

The king, however, set out for Winchester from the coast with great sadness. He was touched by

Crusade against Christians

THE Fourth Crusade of 1202–4 is the most important and surprising turning-point in the long and tortuous history of the crusading movement: thousands of French barons and knights embarked from Venice in the autumn of 1202 and – despite the religious idealism that had inspired their journey – sacked Constantinople, the largest Christian capital in the world.

The ambitious and powerful Pope Innocent III was anxious to turn the tide against the infidel forces, and he exerted himself to the full to promote a new crusade. In 1200, the original intention of Theobald of Champagne, Baldwin of Flanders and their armies was to attack Egypt, which had become the principal centre of Islamic power. To do so, they needed to travel by sea, and Venice was well able to supply them with the ships they needed. But Venice's trading interests had suffered from Byzantine hostility, and the political interests of Boniface, marquis of Montferrat, the leader of the crusading forces from 1201 would be equally served by diverting the army to Constantinople. The port of Zara, claimed by the Venetians from the king of Hungary, was the only place given overt mention in the changed plans; but that city, having been taken in 1202, was only a short step to the great capital city of the Eastern Empire. Here, after much deliberation, the crusaders went. They deposed the emperor, replacing him with Alexius, a rival claimant who had helped to persuade the army to leave Zara in order to act on his behalf. Alexius had made promises (of men and money for the Holy Land), but these he was unable to keep, and after spending many months encamped outside Constantinople, the crusaders found the glittering prizes

offered by the Byzantine Empire too great to resist. In March 1204, the city was stormed and ruthlessly pillaged; many of its incomparable collection of Christian relics found their way to the churches of western Europe. A few weeks later Baldwin of Flanders became the first ruler of the new Latin empire of Constantinople. This precarious political entity, established in the south Balkan peninsula and the Greek archipelago, lasted for less than 60 years – it was recaptured by Emperor Michael VIII, the first of the Greek Palaeologus dynasty, in 1261. Except for the Venetians, who retained most of the Greek islands, no one gained from the crusade. It did nothing to halt the growing power of Islam – and much to increase the gulf between the Roman and Greek Christian Churches.

Left Fulk of Neuilly (d.1201) was a popular preacher in northern France, and Pope Innocent appointed him in 1199 to help convince the population of the need for the Fourth Crusade. It was said that tremendous crowds gathered at his meetings. However, a good deal of the money which he collected never found its way to the crusaders' fund, and his followers deserted him.

Below Distrust and bitterness were all too familiar during the entire crusade. This illustration shows clearly that the battle for Constantinople was between the Eastern and Western Churches rather than Christian and Islamic soldiers.

such a great sorrow and heaviness of heart that the next day he immediately returned to the coast. He rowed to the Isle of Wight and sailed here and there for two days, while his friends tried to dissuade him from crossing the sea without the army which he had disbanded.

Those who remained on land thought it very likely that the king had crossed and this news spread throughout the kingdom. The earl of Salisbury, the brother of the king, then crossed at this time with many knights and reached La Rochelle. A little before him Geoffrey, son of King John by a mistress, had arrived with many knights. What huge amount of money, what great amount of supplies were needed in the preparation of the ships and in the collection of food and stores cannot easily be reckoned.

Throughout the night of the feast of St John the Baptist, 24 June, there was horrible thunder and lightning coming from the heavens through-out England. A monster was struck by lightning in Kent, near Maidstone, with the sound of a great crack. It was found to have the head of an ass, a human belly and its other monstrous limbs were unlike those of any other species of animal. Scarcely anyone dared go near its blackened body, scorched by the lightning, on account of the intolerable smell.

On the night of 29 July there was such a great outbreak of horrible thunder, and such a chorus of crashing lightning from the collision of the clouds all over England, that many thought the Day of Judgement had come. Men and animals were almost senseless with the fear, dread and foreboding which filled the whole kingdom. Both men and women in many places perished through being struck by lightning. Animals were struck too, houses were overturned and burnt, crops were destroyed by hailstones which in some places were as big as goose eggs. Trees were ripped up by the roots and carried away, some were twisted like rope and some were snapped in half.

The next day some monstrous footprints were visible in many places of a type never before seen. People said they were the prints of devils who had

been forced to flee hither and thither by the thunderbolts of the good angels, as Jerome says in the *Ethics*. The good angels vented their rage on the ancient foe with blows and bolts, protecting the heavens with thunder and crashing lightning, and in a hail of arrows they destroyed the enemy and forced them into the yawning abyss of the earth. For the angels have such fiery power at their fingertips that they can scorch stone to tiny pieces and pull up trees. If the anger of rebellious man erupts, thousands of people can be slaughtered at the blow of one angel. This the Philosopher has argued more than anyone else.

The venerable Hubert, archbishop of Canterbury, left Canterbury with his company for Boxley, to make peace between the monks of Rochester and their bishop. On his journey he was gravely troubled by the double sicknesses of fever and ulcers, so that he made for his manor of Teynham, and there after four days, on 13 July he ended his life. The disease broke out on his back, on the third vertebra of his spine, which he was ashamed to show those in his chamber since his private parts could be seen.

A lesson may be learned from this dangerous ulcer. If the patient feels pains in the chest or starts to sweat, he is in mortal danger. This type of plague can be cured though, by a mixture of equal quantities of the yolks of raw eggs and salt, applied to the disease and frequently renewed. The sick person should eat only bread and water until the body is purified. Take care when letting blood lest the infection be drawn between the veins. If the archbishop had quickly recognized the disease he could have taken this remedy, which is infallible, so doctors tell me.

Coggeshall next describes the death of the archbishop in detail, but his chronicle then tails off into a series of annalistic entries. The story is taken up by Gervase, a monk of Canterbury, whose drama-tic and lively chronicle is permeated with devotion to his monastic cathedral.

On 12 July Archbishop Hubert died and three days later King John hurried to Canterbury. He talked kindly enough with the monks about

The fight against disease

MEDIEVAL medicine in Europe was crude and unsystematic. Diagnosis was haphazard and the causes of disease scarcely understood. The 12th century was, however, important in medical history. At Salerno in southern Italy the medical school established in the 9th century was at its apogee, and, through it, the much higher standards of ancient Greek and Arabic medicine, and the professionalism which is today associated with the Hippocratic Oath, were introduced to the West. A contemporary Syrian writer gruesomely illustrated the distinction between Arabic and Christian medicine in his description of how an Arab physician treated an abscess on a knight's leg with a dressing which opened up the sore, while a Christian recommended amputation – and carried it out with an axe, killing his patient.

Contemporary medical texts contain exotic herbal remedies. For headache and pains in the joints: 'Take helenium and radish, wormwood and bishopwort, cropleek and garlic and hollowleek, of each an equal amount. Pound up. Boil in butter and with celandine and red nettle. Put in a brazen vessel and leave therein until it be dark coloured. Strain through cloth. Smear the head therewith and the limbs where they are sore.'

Top A mother nurses her child.

Above A woman is revived with a burnt feather and herbal tea.

Inevitably many medieval remedies were based on common sense and proven success. Then as now, for example, feverfew could cure headaches and migraine. And as long ago as the 12th century, the doctors of Salerno recommended exercise and baths for good health.

Above *Friars* tended sick men as part of their religious vocation.

Below *Monks* used herbs and roots to make most of the common medicines.

Above right *Consultations* are held in one room while remedies are prepared next door.

Right *A nose operation*, using primitive scalpels and tubes.

fungus de nare sic inci
ditur;

replacing their pastor and gave them some hope that they could have someone from their own church. When he heard that the noble and outstanding archbishop had left them a portable chapel in his will worth three hundred marks [£200], he calmly asked to see it. When he saw it he was filled with wonder and ordered it to be carried off to Winchester, and he gave to the bishop of Winchester what he had taken from Christchurch. Next, he asked the prior and monks of Canterbury not to make an election before the feast of St Andrew, 30 November, and they agreed to his request.

Meanwhile the king secretly sent messengers to Rome. When the monks heard this they sent some of their number with their sub-prior to Rome also, lest the royal emissaries should ask for anything against the dignity and rights of Canterbury. Soon the royal messengers wrote to the king saying that the monks of Canterbury had elected their sub-prior and sent him to Rome. At this the king was astounded and went to Canterbury after the feast of St Andrew asking the monks whether they had elected their sub-prior or anyone else. They maintained that they had made no election and to prove what they had said and done, with the common advice and consent of the chapter they elected the bishop of Norwich and, singing, led him into the church, put him into the archbishop's seat and took the kiss of peace.

Since the king approved of their election, the monks sent messengers to Rome for the pallium. But the monks who had already gone to Rome, despite the prohibition of the monastery on pain of anathema, opposed the election, saying that the bishop of Norwich had not been elected by the monks but had been imposed by the king using force and that the election was void.

1206

At length monks who had been given the approval of the monastery of Canterbury to make an election on the pope's authority, after due consideration and with the pope's consent elected the venerable master Stephen Langton, a cardinal. The pope, out of reverence for the king, sent letters asking for the king's consent. The king, led on by evil counsellors, refused. He asked, however, whether all the monks agreed to the election of Stephen Langton. The monastery replied that they would never desert him. Whereupon the furious king swore that not one of them would remain in the church at Canterbury, nor even in England.

1207

[Stephen Langton was consecrated archbishop of Canterbury at Rome on 17 June.] Therefore, on 15 July, all the monks were expelled from Canterbury and were honourably received overseas by the monastery of St Bertin. The king, elated by his glorious victory, in vain sent letters to the abbot there trying to have the monks expelled.

In this year Henry, the first child of King John by his queen Isabella, the daughter of the count of Angoulême, was born. That was a vitally important event – John now had a male heir.

The bishop of London, the bishop of Ely, the bishop of Hereford, the bishop of Chester, the archbishop of York, who was the king's own brother, and numerous others, rich as well as poor, left England unable to bear the king's tyranny. There was not one man in the land who could oppose his will. The bishops of Durham, Lincoln and Chichester had died. Only the bishop of Winchester remained in the king's favour. The bishop of Norwich was in Ireland and those of Rochester and Salisbury sustained many injuries and then left for Scotland.

1208

The king himself was the only power in the land and feared neither God nor man. The pope was angry about the harassment of the church at Canterbury and he sent letters ordering the king to receive the archbishop and monks of the church of Canterbury and restore their confiscated goods. The king sent to Rome and promised that he would make amends for everything to God, the Holy Church and the pope. When the pope heard that the king had repented he was overjoyed and sent him a letter of indulgence. When the

The first income tax

IN THE years following the loss of Normandy, Anjou and his other French lands, John used every means open to him to finance the major military effort needed to recover his inheritance. Most dramatic in its impact on his people was the tax of one thirteenth – 1s. on each mark (13s. 4d.) – levied in 1207 on income from rents and moveable property. This was done with the reluctant consent of the baronage, but with opposition from the Church.

The amount due was assessed by different groups of justices in each county, was collected very rapidly by the sheriff and was accounted for at a special 'Exchequer of the thirteenth'. It was a model for further taxes on income which were to be regularly levied in the 13th century and which gradually replaced earlier ones on land.

There was much opposition to the 1207 tax. Some people hid their goods in monasteries. At Swineshead Abbey an official of the countess of Aumâle concealed his funds, which were, however, discovered when the royal officials carried out a raid. Elsewhere in Lincolnshire one of the county assessors, Fulk Doiry, hid his own goods. Such was the rapaciousness of the king's servants that the

Above The English people had paid their geld taxes in silver coins for many centuries, since the time of the Danish invasions. While Domesday Book, *in 1086, still recorded many kinds of manorial dues paid in wheat, honey and so on, the shift to coinage which it clearly showed ('in 1066 two loads of iron, now 6d') eventually made accounting much easier.*

bishop of Durham paid £100 to prevent them from searching out defaulters on his lands. The king's illegitimate half-brother, Geoffrey, archbishop of York, was forced into exile because he opposed the tax being levied on his tenants.

Financially the tax was a great success, however. Sixty thousand pounds was raised, about double the king's normal income each year, making it easily John's most profitable tax, but as his political fortunes declined later in his reign he was unable to repeat it.

Fines were a further method of taxation. In 1207–8 sheriffs had to pay large sums to keep John's good will. The king also accepted large sums for judicial favours, and from officials anxious to avoid giving a full account of their activities in office; the highest figure was 10,000 marks. The overt corruption of this approach to royal fundraising left a growing legacy of bitterness and mistrust.

messengers returned to England, the archbishop sent with them two bishops and two monks, to receive the possessions of the church of Canterbury. The king, when he heard what his emissaries had brought from Rome, was angry and swore that he had not sent them for that purpose. The royal chancellor who had drawn up the original promise under the royal seal was summoned, but the king denied having agreed to it.

Therefore the king withdrew from the negotiations and so did the bishops and everyone else and, on 24 March by papal mandate, divine services were suspended throughout England. Great sorrow and anxiety spread throughout the country. Neither Good Friday nor Easter Sunday could be celebrated, but an unheard-of silence was imposed on all the clergy and monks by laymen. The bodies of the dead, whether of the ordinary folk or the religious, could not be buried in consecrated cemeteries, but only in vile and profane places.

The king ordered the few monks who remained at Canterbury, the blind and crippled, also to be expelled, and the monks to be regarded as public enemies. Some fled from England, some were imprisoned, some were saved by money, others suffered many afflictions; their woods were cut down and their men were fined and taxed heavily. The whole of England suffered this burden. The people were forced to pay at first a quarter of their money, then a third, then a half. Even the rents of the cardinals and whatever they had in England were taken away from them and Peter's Pence, which the Roman Church had had since the time of Cnut, were withheld by the king. He especially imposed great afflictions on this occasion on the men of the Cinque Ports who defended the coast against hostile invasion. For he hanged some of them and put others to the sword; he imprisoned many, bound them in irons and at length released them only in return for pledges and money. Therefore the rich and poor left England, countless men and women; theirs was a thankless pilgrimage to avoid the enormous cruelty of the king rather than a devoted one. John even imprisoned the queen, his wife, in strict custody at Corfe castle.

'Christ's vicar on earth'

OF all King John's many political adversaries, none was more formidable than Innocent III, pope from 1198 to 1216 and the first supreme pontiff to style himself 'vicar of Christ'.

The conflict between pope and king escalated from a dispute about who should control the appointment to the most important ecclesiastical position in the country, that of archbishop of Canterbury. When John refused to accept the pope's candidate, an Englishman active in the papal court called Stephen Langton, Innocent imposed an Interdict in 1208. For the next five years the English clergy were prohibited from administering the sacraments and even burying the dead; most of their bishops left the country. However, in 1213, when he was facing the increasingly open hostility of his barons, John made his submission to Innocent III, accepted Stephen Langton as his archbishop and placed his kingdom under the direct overlordship of the papacy.

Ironically enough, John's final surrender to Innocent's demands for papal authority over England, more than his responsibility for the Interdict itself, damaged his political credibility and his posthumous reputation. This was despite the fact that the Interdict was the lowest point in the history of relations between England and the papacy in the entire Middle Ages.

Above *Innocent gives St Francis of Assisi permission to establish his order; by Giotto.*

Right *Mosaic portrait of the pope.*

1209

On hearing of these and other calamities, the pope, the consoling parent of the English Church, sent the king of England admonitory letters, warning him to desist from his evil deeds and restore the church of Canterbury to its original state, otherwise for certain he would suffer excommunication announced publicly by the pope himself, who would openly excommunicate the king not only in England but in other regions as well. John, however, thought little of the papal admonition and ignored the warning.

The king sent letters to King William of Scotland, a man of outstanding sanctity, ordering him to hand over either three castles on the border, or his son as a hostage. When the Scots king was unwilling to fulfil this command, the king of England wanted to seize with a great force what he could not obtain by petition, and to restore the three castles to his dominion.

When the king of England made for Scotland with his great force, his soldiers began to murmur, saying, 'Where are we going? What are we doing? We are like pagans, outside God's laws and Christianity. Why should we attack the holy king of Scotland? For surely God will fight for him and against us, and will perform a miracle for him.'

When these and other tales of his fellow soldiers were told to the king, lest by chance the whole army deserted him and left him in the battle itself, he ordered Geoffrey FitzPeter, the justiciar, and certain other earls to negotiate a peace with the church at Canterbury and in England, and to recall peacefully to England the archbishop of Canterbury, and other bishops and monks. For the pope had ordered these bishops to pronounce the sentence of excommunication on the king.

Therefore Geoffrey FitzPeter urgently sent letters to the bishop of London asking him to come to England as quickly as possible with his bishops, as he loved the honour of God and the Church and the peace of the king and the kingdom. For the king had given the bishops full power to make peace with the Church of God.

As the bishops were preparing to return to England, and as the king was on his way to Scotland with an army, the king of Scotland, fearing for the safety of his kingdom, much preferring to have peace than the sword and to provide for his people by wisdom rather than iron therefore sent his two daughters with faithful messengers to the king of England. One was to be married to the king's son and the other to an English noble. He also sent his son, not as a hostage but to make due fealty for the said castles and other lands which he held. And thus the peace of the kingdom of Scotland was restored and all returned home.

Now the bishops all arrived at Dover fully empowered to make peace. After much discussion they agreed to a form of peace, which was written down and sealed: and thus the sentence of excommunication imposed on the king was postponed for five weeks.

At the order of the king all the rich, poor and middling men of England over the age of fifteen met at Marlborough, there to swear fealty to the king and to his young three-year-old son, Henry, as his heir. When the king saw and heard the form of the peace treaty made with the agreement of so many people, he sent messengers with letters asking the archbishop of Canterbury to have a conference with him at Dover.

The archbishop, therefore, crossed the sea and waited for the king to arrive at Dover. When the king heard this he came to the castle of Chilham not far from Dover with all speed and fully armed.

He waited for the archbishop there, while the archbishop waited for him at Dover. The king, however, influenced by the tongues of evil detractors, changed his mind about his proposal and suddenly left. The archbishop, on the advice of the nobility, crossed the sea and returned to France, and the king of England was excommunicated by many churchmen on the pope's orders. He was excommunicated in France too.

In this year Richard, second son of King John, was born.

1210

The king, in a new plan, exacted an unheard-of amount of money from the English Jews, for he ordered some to be hanged and others to be blinded.

The Jews had long enjoyed an uneasy royal protection in return for making a part of their profits available to the Exchequer. John's cruel attempts to milk them dry of funds drove many to leave England altogether.

John did not exclude the clergy from his search for money. When the Cistercian abbots met together he asked them to help him not with their prayers but with their money. When his request was rejected quite humbly, he left enraged, and he led the army and the fleet, which it is believed he had prepared to go to Poitou, into Ireland and quickly subdued it either by force or fraud. There, though many opposed it, they could not resist; he instituted English laws and customs and ordered them to be observed and then he returned to England.

Many hoped that because of this victory the king would make amends for the bad deeds he had done towards the Church of God and would correct his errors. But a new anger inflamed him, especially towards the Cistercians, from whom he could exact no money either by force or prayer, so that, dispersed through various churches in England, they were forced to beg for food. Nor would he allow his abbots to cross the sea to the general chapter; he would not even give licence to cross to the abbot of Beaulieu, to whom he had given a wide and beautiful site in the New Forest on which to build an abbey.

John sent letters and messengers to the archbishop of Canterbury asking him to come to England so that they could discuss peace together at Dover. When everything was ready for the crossing, the archbishop received letters from certain English nobles who were loyal to him, telling him not to be deceived into coming to England and to avoid the ambushes prepared for him, and so he returned to France. For the king of England was so full of guile that he could scarcely keep faith with anything he wrote or said, for he upheld neither his promises nor his charters.

The king sent a great army into Wales under William, his brother, and the earl of Chester, who laid waste that land all around and killed many different men. And many said that Merlin's prophecy had come about saying. 'The sixth shall pull down the walls of Ireland' and 'his beginning shall succumb to his own unstable nature'. William I, William II, Henry I, Henry II, afterwards Richard. The sixth is John who acquired Ireland but in all other things was vain and useless.

Gervase of Canterbury's chronicle ends in 1210, the year he died. However, the well-informed but anonymous chronicler known as the Barnwell annalist provides a valuable account of the dramatic last years of John's reign.

1211

The king of England led an army into Wales against Llewellyn, but returned very quickly because the Welsh, fearing his advance, withdrew with their property into the mountains, so that the English army was beset with hunger. But after gathering a large quantity of provisions, the king was soon able to make another expedition into Wales, and now with a large force and with plenty of supplies he was able to force hostilities upon the Welsh. After having conducted matters as he wished he emerged with glory.

There was now no one in Ireland, Scotland or Wales who did not bow to his nod, a situation which, as is well known, none of his predecessors had achieved. He would thus have seemed successful and overflowing with promise for his successors except that he had been despoiled of his foreign lands and subjected to the sentence of excommunication.

Two nuncios were sent to England from Rome in order to reconcile the English Church, but, leaving before they had achieved any peace, they brought no profit to the wretched.

A large number of deer which were gathered together in the English forest which is called Cannock, after a terrible disorder of the bowels and much moaning, threw themselves into the sea at the mouth of the Severn. Amongst the deer they found a fawn with two heads and eight feet.

There was a total eclipse of the moon on 18 October. Samson, abbot of Bury St Edmunds, and Roger, constable of Chester, died.

1212

The power of the Moors, who had arisen in Spain with much pride and force, was ended. For their army having been ground down by the Christian princes, was dissuaded by confusion and fear from its impudent undertaking.

Throughout the cities of France boys gathered together, to the great amazement of onlookers. For wherever they went boys gathered as if they could not remain by themselves but rather must join together in groups. And although one was reckoned as a Parisian citizen at fifteen, none of those who gathered was over twelve years old. When asked what they were going to do, the boys said they were going to take up the cross of Christ.

This strange and spontaneous movement, the Children's Crusade, ended in tragedy. The 'army' was captured by slave-dealers and sold to the Egyptians.

A shower of blood was seen at Caen in Normandy on Saturday, 10 July. On the same day, at Falaise, three crosses were seen together in the sky as if in combat.

Throughout England it was permitted that those of the faithful who were nearing their end should be able to receive the sacred viaticum of the body of our Lord; this had been requested by the priests in the monasteries, to whom permission to celebrate the divine office once a week had already been given.

In the city of London an extraordinary and terrible fire occurred on the southern bank of the

Lord of Ireland

JOHN'S first encounter with the Irish was not propitious. In 1185, his father, Henry II, intent on bringing the warring Irish chieftains and independent Norman settlers to heel, sent him there with a substantial army and gave him the title 'Lord of Ireland'. But John's expedition was a fiasco. The Irish chieftains were so incensed by the ridicule with which John and his courtiers reacted to their beards that for once they united. Henry's mercenaries, unpaid, resorted to looting and plundering, while John retired discomfited, to his father's fury. Much of Ireland lapsed into anarchical and bloody wars.

John's campaign of 1210 was a remarkable contrast and one of the few great successes of his reign. A number of

Above *Trim castle was re-built in 1212
on the site of Hugh de Lacy's original stronghold.*

Right *Carrickfergus castle still stands.*

Anglo-Norman lords, including Walter and Hugh de
Lacy, had pacified and consolidated major landholdings
and John needed to re-establish and increase royal
authority. As before, he took a substantial force of English
knights and Flemish mercenaries. But this time he
showed great favour to the Irish chiefs, who sent their
own men to join his army. Walter de Lacy was
dispossessed and Hugh de Lacy put to flight. The royal
justiciar, whose authority had previously been nominal,
now exercised real powers in the king's name. Work
started on new castles at Carrickfergus and at Dublin –
castles which symbolized the beginning of effective
English rule over Ireland.

River Thames, near the church of the canons of Our Lady of Southwark. When a large crowd had crossed the river, either to put out the fire or to watch, suddenly the northern part also caught fire as the south wind was blowing, so that those crossing the bridge to go back were obstructed by the flames. And so it happened that when the other part of the bridge was affected by fire they were trapped. And then, placed as they were between the two fires, they were pressed by each in turn, until they expected only death.

Then some ships came to their aid, but so many foolishly rushed into them that the ships were sunk and everyone perished. This was regarded as a great disaster by the people and it was said that three thousand men had died either in the fire or in the shipwreck. It appeared that the misfortune which it had been predicted would befall England had brought great destruction upon the capital.

At the same time, something else happened so that all sane people were astonished. For suddenly, and for no identifiable reason, as if they had taken leave of their senses, certain people went about from town to town throughout England blowing horns, which in English is known as *the Hue*. And when it was said that this should only be done when following malefactors, and that they were following no man, they foretold that there would be a much greater disturbance in the near future.

In the autumn, right up until 8 September, the feast of the Nativity of Our Lady, the sky was clear and the weather bright. Then suddenly unceasing rain arrived which unexpectedly inflicted great damage upon the English. For the winter wind was so strong that even stone towers were thrown to the ground.

When William, king of the Scots, came of age, he could not pacify the innermost parts of his kingdom, which were disturbed by civil discord. He and his queen and their only son fled to the English king to ask for his aid. He did homage to John, who knighted him. Going with an army into the innermost parts of the kingdom, he captured Cuthred, called MacWilliam, the leader of the rebels, and hanged him. MacWilliam was a member of the ancient line of Scottish kings, who, like his father Donald, had fought for a long time against the present kings, sometimes secretly and sometimes openly, but always with enmity, trusting to the aid of the Scots and Irish. For the more recent Scottish kings were greatly influenced by the French and it happened that only the French were treated with friendliness and reverence after the language and culture of the Scots had been reduced to subjection.

The Welsh princes, encouraged by the pope who had absolved them both from the agreement which they had made in the previous year with the English king and from the allegiance and oaths which they had taken upon themselves, attacked the English king in return for the interdict being relaxed throughout their lands. King John, stirred up to violent anger, hanged the hostages and gathered an army against them from all parts of the kingdom. And then, when he had gathered such a multitude as had never before been seen in our times, God put his forces to flight.

Then King John's heart was troubled, since it was being said, without authority, that rumours had been heard that the barons who had gathered together were conspiring against him, and that in many ears there were tales of letters absolving the barons from John's allegiance; it was said that another king should be elected in his place and that John should be expelled from the kingdom. If on the other hand the king captured them, they would suffer death or perpetual imprisonment.

Having announced his return, the king began to have misgivings and would go nowhere without either being armed or accompanied by a great force of armed men. Having taken captive some who seemed to be too intimate with the rebels, he quickly seized the castles of the earls and barons, so that there was unrest for some time. Then the nobles of the country, fearing either the king's anger or the scruples of conscience, left England secretly. Eustace de Vesci was received in Scotland and Robert FitzWalter departed to the French. Their goods were confiscated and Robert's castle in London, which was called Castle Baynard, was demolished, together with other fortresses. Then

The growth of London

LONDON in the 12th century was by far the largest town in England, and merchandise from all over Europe was unloaded onto its wharves. Some of its citizens were rich, with splendid houses in the city. Although the sources of their wealth are not always clear – many must have been merchants – they dominated London's political life.

By 1200 (when the first stone London Bridge was being built) London was the home of the chief offices of the royal administration. Royal assemblies were often held there, attended by the king's chief noblemen, and Westminster had replaced Winchester as the location of the Exchequer, the centre of royal financial and judicial administration.

A system of city government, built around the court of the husting (the equivalent of the shire court) and the office of alderman (the leading officials of London's 24 wards), was discernible from the 11th century onwards. This was the basis of the commune, i.e., the right to municipal self-government, granted by John in 1191 while his brother King Richard was away on Crusade. Shortly afterwards, Henry FitzAilwin, an Englishman, emerged as the first mayor of London, a position he was to hold until his death in 1212.

William FitzStephen, Thomas Becket's 12th-century biographer, described London as beautiful and splendid, whereas the dramatic and florid chronicle by Richard of Devizes depicts it as a place of great evil, terror and

Above *In 1194 Richard confirmed London's liberties and customs for a fee.*

Below *Westminster Hall; originally built, 1097–99, as part of the royal palace, it now forms part of the Houses of Parliament.*

cynicism. It could be dangerous. Street gangs made it risky to walk out after dark and in 1180 a relative of the earl of Derby was killed on the streets. The low-life district, however, was not within the walls; it grew up in Lambeth, near the archbishop of Canterbury's palace.

the king began to have more consideration for his people and the land was silent.

Even amid such adversity King John set in motion a deed of great and laudable memory. For when the foresters harassed many in all parts of England with new exactions, the king, seeing the misery of the afflicted, revoked them entirely and forced the forest officials to swear that they would only exact the amount which they had been accustomed to collect in the days of his father.

He restrained those who had imposed new exactions and those who, under pretext of guarding the ports, had molested citizens, travellers and merchants, and repealed the new exactions, so that he would be said to be merciful and concerned to keep to the terms of the peace. Preparing to make peace with the pope, he exacted from all the prelates of the Church a confirmation of all that he had taken from them, on whatever occasion, since the beginning of the reign, so that in this way they would greatly modify their claims concerning what he had taken away. They confirmed the donations to him in charters with seals attached, and messengers were then sent to placate the pope in whatever way they were able.

It was said by certain men who testified to having seen a vision that, having been warned to correct his ways, the king would feel the divine vengeance before the year was out.

There was a certain man called Peter of Wakefield. He was a simple and rustic man supporting his life on bread and water and proclaiming to the people that he could foretell the future. He preached that King John's reign would not last beyond the next Ascension Day, because it had been revealed to him that King John would reign for fourteen years, and that those things which had been begun during those fourteen years would reach a happy conclusion. When Peter was asked whether the king would die or be expelled or yield, it is said that he replied that he did not know, but that he knew only one thing, which was that he would not reign any longer, neither he nor any of his people for him, unless God so willed it. And he did not hide this from the king.

The myth of Robin Hood

THE outlaw who lived in the greenwood, dined on the king's deer, robbed the rich to help the poor and engaged in a constant battle with the sheriff of Nottingham, is fundamental to the popular picture of medieval England. However, it is uncertain that there ever was a real Robin Hood and, even if there was, scholars disagree about when he lived.

The popular belief, that he was active in 1193–4 when Richard was in captivity in Germany and John was plotting against him at home, comes from the *History of Greater Britain* by the Scottish writer John Major, published in 1521. The use of 'Robinhood' surnames in 13th-century England indicates that the legend was known in 1262 so it is certainly possible that a Robin was alive in the late 12th century. However, the first direct reference to the legend is as late as 1377, and the earliest texts of Robin Hood stories date from the late 15th century. The most likely candidate for the original Robin Hood is a fugitive of that name, who failed to appear before royal justices at York in 1225; nothing else is known about him. The tales tell of Robin operating in Barnsdale in southern Yorkshire as well as in Sherwood Forest in Nottinghamshire.

Below *Sherwood Forest, mysterious and evocative even today. The legends of Robin Hood have persisted even though historians have found no proof that he did battle with the sheriff of Nottingham in defence of his liege, King Richard.*

At first he was regarded as an idiot and derided by his captors as insane. For indeed, as he was going about the countryside spreading his ideas, he was captured by the king's supporters and kept in custody. He seemed to have a very high opinion of himself, believing that his name, which a little while before had been unknown and despised, was now made famous by his capture and spoken by all. Every day false words of the common people were added to his falsehoods; every day new sayings were ascribed to him and lies which this Peter was said to have spoken in his heart.

There was a total eclipse of the moon on the Feast of Saint Martin, 11 November, during the first part of the night. John Cumin, first archbishop of Dublin, died, as a result of which the city came to be a possession of the English kingdom. Mauger, bishop of Worcester, also died, and Geoffrey, King John's brother who was archbishop of York in exile in France.

1213

The English bishops who were in exile in France petitioned the pope on behalf of the English Church. Moved by their pleas, he agreed to bring about an end to the evil. For he wrote to Philip, the king of France, and to the princes of those parts that unless the king of England capitulated, they should liberate England from his rule with a strong army. Neither was there any need for lengthy pleading and admonishing since King Philip and the princes had been inclined to this course of action for some time, both because of their hatred for John and because of their love of money and gold, since it was believed that the land abounded in such riches.

They encouraged each other and prepared themselves with all necessary things, building some ships and gathering others from all around the shore, deciding that the fleet should set out together from one port. The French king himself awaited the gathering of the ships not far from the sea. Having assessed the size of his army it was believed that it comprised no less than fifteen thousand men. Every day ships converged on the ports and knights on the castles.

The king of England heard this and had a large fleet gathered from all the English ports; and he appointed strong men skilled in arms to his galleys. With a large force they resisted the enemy's attack, and with great endeavour opposed them and injured the enemy's cause. He even offered to free serfs so that all should defend the kingdom and protect the person of the king, and they came to him armed. There gathered such a multitude as has never been seen in our times and he divided them between the port, where danger was feared, and the ships. All the army he kept with him near Dover. The remainder of the fleet was by the shore not far away. The galleys similarly prepared for war.

But the heart of the people was wavering, and was easily swayed first towards one side and then the other as if men's courage had been dried up by fear and anticipation of the enemy whom they believed to be arriving on the next tide. Peter's words terrified many, but on Ascension Day, which he had said would be fatal for the king, many began to doubt.

And whilst they were thus suspended in anticipation, behold, certain of the king's messengers who had departed for Rome in the previous year came back to him in great haste. A papal nuncio was sent with them whose name was Pandulph; he applied himself to the task of carrying out those things which had been ordered.

This was the most important part of his orders: that before 1 June four of the most important men in the kingdom should swear, on the king's behalf, he being present and ordering it, that if the pope sent the king a signed letter of agreement then the king would promise the same in his letters patent and seal the agreement with the archbishop and bishops. Otherwise the time of severest punishment had not yet come.

What need for many words? Inspired, it is said, by Him in whose hand are the hearts of kings, he acquiesced in peace. And those who swore to the aforesaid written agreement of the pope were Renaud, count of Boulogne, William, earl of Warenne, William, earl of Ferrers, and William, earl of Salisbury, the king's brother. And when this

A moneyed economy

MONEY was widely used in 12th and early 13th-century England. Surviving records of royal finance, for example, show that royal revenue was paid in money; the last vestiges of the old system of food-rents disappeared soon after the Norman Conquest. Although barter was undoubtedly still a major element in the peasant economy, little is known about it and peasant rents were usually paid in coin.

There were two new issues of coin during Henry II's reign: in 1158 and 1180. As under previous monarchs, the only coin minted was a silver penny. The first issue showed the king's crowned bust with his sceptre held over his right shoulder on one side, and a large cross surrounded by smaller crosses on the other.

This issue was a major turning-point in the history of English coinage: new coins had previously been issued every few years, while now the same one was kept in circulation for longer – the second issue of 1180 was not replaced until 1247 – probably reflecting an increasing use of money which made reminting irksome. Defined rates of international exchange also appeared at this time. The English pound sterling was accepted as being worth four times the Angevin pound, which was the regular currency in Normandy and Greater Anjou.

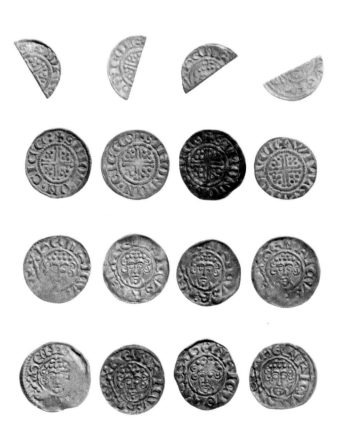

The Cost of Living
in the 13th Century

The prices and earnings given here are based on original 13th-century bailiffs' rolls, and farm and estate accounts. A shilling is worth 12 pennies.

Building a house

The following expenses are based on a daily rate paid to each person for a specified number of days' work:

> 2 masons .... 2½ pennies a day for 6 days' work
> 2 carpenters .... 3 pennies a day for 4 days' work
> Thatcher .... 2 pennies a day for 4 days' work
> Plumber .... 3 pennies a day

Running the home

On a miller's stipend of 5 shillings a year the candles are worth 2½ per cent of his income, and the silver spoons almost 50 per cent. On a chaplain's stipend of 40 shillings and two pence a year, the carpet – which was bought for 20 shillings by the earl of Clare – is worth nearly half the chaplain's income:

> 1 lb soap .... 1 penny
> 1 lb candles .... 1½ pennies
> 12 silver spoons .... 2 shillings, 4 pennies
> 1 yd linen .... 3¼ pennies
> Carpet with
> the arms of England .... 20 shillings

Food and drink account

Eggs and butter are within the budget of a carpenter who earns 3 pennies a day for 4 days' work, and someone as wealthy as the earl of Clare could easily afford luxuries such as cloves:

> 1 lb cloves .... 10 shillings
> 1 lb pepper .... 9 pennies
> 120 eggs .... 2½ pennies
> 1 gallon butter .... 4½ pennies
> 1 gallon cider .... ½ penny

Left *The silver penny of John's reign. The coins in the top row have been clipped in half – a simple way of achieving lower values. They could also be clipped into quarters for smaller amounts. The remaining rows show the reverse with the cross and the obverse with the king's head.*

had been completed the king promised the same in his letters according to the form which these four had sworn on his behalf.

On his own initiative the king added this: that the whole of his kingdom, that is England and Ireland, should be subject to God and to the holy apostles Peter and Paul and that, according to his own free will and in order to complete the agreement, he and his heirs should pay one thousand marks a year to the popes as a token of their subjection, that is seven hundred marks for England and three hundred for Ireland, not counting the payment of Peter's Pence. At the same time he swore liege homage and fealty to Pope Innocent III and to his successors. And all this was publicly proclaimed by letters patent published in the manner of charters.

The annalist then assesses John's submission to the pope as a prudent move, because it made him more difficult to attack for fear of papal reprisals.

Matters now began to improve for John. He allied with the count of Flanders against Philip II of France and his ships defeated the French navy in a sea battle. But still he lingered at Boulogne, fearful that Peter of Wakefield's prophecy of his death would come true.

Then came Ascension Day, 23 May, on which so many hopes had been placed. By the king's order his tent was erected in the camp at Boulogne and left wide open, and a general summons made to spend the feast day in solemn fashion with the king. It was a beautiful day, to the exhilaration and delight of the king himself, together with the bishops and barons who were gathered there. The day having passed in all health and happiness, those who had put their faith in Peter now believed him to be an idiot, deceived by a simple mind. He had predicted the end of the king on 23 May when, in fact, according to what he had been shown in his vision, the fourteen year-reign of the king ought to end on 27 May; and they now were less inclined to believe him.

When 27 May arrived, the day on which the king had been crowned fourteen years before, the

Followers of the Church

MEN and women in 12th-century England totally accepted the main tenets of the Christian faith. On all the available evidence, admittedly written by the clergy themselves, the Church had been completely successful in suppressing, or adapting to its own purposes, residual superstitions from the pre-Christian, pagan, English past. The shrines, relics and wells of Christian saints were the most important centres of popular devotion, while traditional pagan festivals had been thoroughly assimilated into the rhythms of an increasingly elaborate Church calendar. Throughout the Middle Ages, New Year's Day fell not on 1 January, but on 25 March, the feast of the Annunciation of the Blessed Virgin Mary.

The extent to which the villagers and townspeople of Plantagenet England understood the moral and theological content of the Christian religion depended above all on the quality of the priests who served the

Below *A scratch sundial, held by a monk, on the wall of a Norman church.*

country's 9,000 or so parishes. Although they were regularly criticized by contemporaries for their gross immorality and their inability to know enough Latin to repeat the church services correctly, there were important developments in their status during the 12th century. By the reign of King John, and after a campaign of more than a century, the practice of clerical marriage had more or less completely disappeared. According to Gerald of Wales, the parish priest was now most likely to maintain not a wife but 'a hearth-girl (*focaria*) in his house, who kindled his fire even if she extinguished his virtue'. As the local clergy ceased to be a hereditary caste (ie, no longer passing offices from father to son) their parishes were increasingly subject to the authority of the English

Above *Parish priests had to deal with many old superstitions which were still believed by the population. This illustration shows the Caladrius, a prophetic bird which was supposed to appear to those who were sick.*

bishops, who regarded the parishes as the central agencies for disseminating the Christian gospel.

Four generations after the Norman Conquest, most parish churches in England had been thoroughly rebuilt and extended – usually in massive Romanesque style – to cater for the growing needs of a more highly organized religious age.

day passed in peace and it was too late for those who had believed in visions to repent of their easy faith. These people were not only from among the ordinary folk but also from amongst the nobles and the wise of the world.

Meanwhile it was suggested to the king that Peter had disturbed the land, spread alarm and despondency among the people and had encouraged the king's enemies. For his words had even been carried to the farthest part of France and had been regarded as an incitement for the invasion of England. All this enraged the king so that he ordered that Peter should be hanged and furthermore that his son, who was imprisoned with him, should also be hanged in case he was either a participant in, or the author of, his father's prophecies.

The king then, seeing that the kingdom was peaceful and that he had nothing to fear from the French, endeavoured to transport all his accoutrements of war to Poitou. But many of the nobles listened less than eagerly to this proposal, annoyed at the prospect of a long expedition which they could not easily undertake since their purses were exhausted. The king's intention was thus frustrated and, regarding the barons as the instigators of this, he would have afterwards taken revenge, had he not been prevented by the intervention of the bishops and archbishop.

In the month of June, Stephen, archbishop of Canterbury, and the bishops William of London, Eustace of Ely, Giles of Hereford and John of Bath returned from the Continent, where they had been exiled, together with all the clerics and lay people who had been in exile with them. And all their possessions were restored to each one individually in full, together with the king's friendship. After a little while the king was publicly and solemnly absolved by the archbishop of Canterbury according to the customs of the Church, and after he had received the kiss of peace from the same archbishop and from the rest of the bishops he was led into the church to take part in the Mass; this was done to the great joy of all the people.

At this time God inspired Pope Innocent III to conduct a Crusade for the assistance of the land of Jerusalem and for the advancement of the Roman Church. For certain of his predecessors had at some time given aid to the Holy Land and it would have seemed incongruous if he, who was not their inferior in power and hard work, should seem to be less industrious in his undertakings. However, he realized that in these days heresy was rearing its head, that many princes had been excommunicated and many lands placed under interdict, so that he was scarcely able to bring the Crusade to pass, since there was much growing in the Lord's vineyard which, to secure the Gospel, should of necessity be amputated. The pope therefore called a General Council to perform this task and sent many industrious men from his side who preached the word concerning the release of the Holy Land to all parts of the Roman world and to discover what faults should be corrected.

The heretical Cathar sect had become very strong in the Languedoc. Pope Innocent III preached a Crusade which was, aimed in particular against Raymond, count of Toulouse, who was believed to support the heretics. The two most important figures in the Crusading forces were Simon de Montfort and Prince Louis, son of Philip II of France. The violent and savage struggle lasted sporadically until 1229, caused severe devastation in the Languedoc, and brought the area under the control of the French Crown.

Then it happened that a legate, Nicholas, bishop of Tusculum, came to England. There were special reasons for his legation, namely that in his presence the king should fulfil the promise which he had made to the Holy Roman Church. And this was done. Then, around 29 September, the king performed liege homage to Nicholas as the representative of the pope, giving him also a charter sealed with gold and one thousand marks, that is the annual payment, as a sign of his subjection. The king then received him and freely listened to him.

When this was done John began to eliminate evil customs from the kingdom with the advice and exhortation of the bishops, restraining the violations and hurtful exactions of his sheriffs and officials. This was because the sheriffs and lesser officials, when collecting the annual levy which alone they should have procured, elicited further moneys from the poor of the provinces. Removing those who practised cupidity, he appointed others who would handle the people carefully, who would make use of the advice of prudent men and who would work for their fellow countrymen in peace and quiet and not by cheating with money. He even instituted a thorough inquiry on this matter so that it should be known how much from the exactions of his ministers he actually received. But this was never completed because terror and tumult intervened when all men were called to arms because of invasion by the French.

The legate deposed the abbot of Westminster and the abbot of Evesham.

There were frequent meetings between the king and the bishops concerning a council of the Church, but when this was unable to convene, the interdict was continued into the following year. The king of Aragon, called by certain of his men to give them aid against Simon de Montfort, the conqueror of the heretics, was killed in battle by the Crusaders together with many of his own men and many infamous heretics. Geoffrey FitzPeter, justiciar of England, died.

1214

The king of the English crossed over to Poitou with his army at the beginning of February and stayed there until September and recovered a large part of that land which Philip, the French king, had confiscated earlier. He had reconciled many great men to himself and many of these he led with him in the army.

Ferrand, count of Flanders, after he had been expelled from his province by King Philip of France, sought aid from Otto IV, emperor of the Germans, and King John, and made a treaty with them. Confident of their aid, he returned to Flanders with the intention of taking everything back from the hands of the French king through the power and help of these illustrious men, and especially with the assistance of William, earl of Salisbury, the English king's brother and Renaud, count of Boulogne. These men came to Ferrand's aid together with a large army.

The French king then sent his son Louis against the English king whilst he himself collected an army against Flanders in which innumerable men were gathered together. Then when the borders of Flanders had been surrounded and the troops organized, a battle took place at the bridge of Bouvines between Mortain and Tournai on 27 July, a Sunday, and having killed many in the conflict the French king held the palm of victory. In the battle these distinguished fighters were captured: Pluto the German, Ferrand, count of Flanders, William of Salisbury, Renaud of Boulogne, the seneschal of Otto and one hundred and fifty other knights of illustrious status.

After this King Philip raised an army against the king of England, but after the legate had intervened, a five-year truce was established between them for the benefit of those who proposed to undertake a journey to Jerusalem. King Philip then returned to France and King John went back to England.

Meanwhile the bishop of Tusculum, who was acting as papal legate amongst the English people, treated the king with excessive leniency and governed the affairs of the Church in a lax manner. For, postponing the accomplishment of peace between the king and bishops, he came to an agreement with the king's ministers concerning the vacant sees and monasteries. The nuncios elected to these sees received letters concerning the debt which the king owed to the churches in compensation for their exile, namely that he should make compensation a little at a time throughout the following year and that if the king made an undertaking in this matter then the interdict should be lifted from England. And this was done; the interdict was lifted at the Council of London after the king had given satisfaction in this matter on 2 July, six years, three months and sixteen days after the interdict.

Soon after the return of the English king from Poitou, Nicholas, bishop of Tusculum, was recalled from his office as legate by the pope since it was said that the office should be exercised in England with less vigour. Then the king, having realized that he upon whom he had relied had been withdrawn, was more pacifying and conciliatory towards the bishops. Soon having satisfied them in the matter of all their hurts and injuries, he gave them in compensation many liberties, honours and manors. At this time he conceded the bishopric of Rochester to the archbishop of Canterbury and the abbey of Thorney to the bishop of Ely, that is to say their lands, as far as the king had the right to do so.

Fish of an unusual appearance were caught in England. It was as if they were helmeted and carrying shields and they looked extremely like an army of knights, though they were much more numerous.

Gilbert, bishop of Rochester, died, and also John, bishop of Norwich, on returning from Rome where he had negotiated for the king. William, king of the Scots, also died.

Around 8 September, the feast of the Nativity of the Blessed Virgin Mary, a flood of rising seas invaded the shore and caused great damage in England.

There arose a dissension between King John and some of the nobles concerning a scutage which he sought from them and which they would not give; nor would they follow him into Poitou. For although many had given, some of the northern barons – those nobles who during the previous year had hindered the king's crossing to Poitou – refused, saying that they ought not to follow the king outside the country in return for the lands which they held of him within England, nor should they help him with scutage. On the other hand the king demanded the aid which had been given to the Crown in the days of his father and brother and which would have continued to be paid if the legate had not intervened. The barons brought forward a certain charter of liberties granted by Henry I which they demanded should be confirmed to them by the king.

Bouvines: disaster and defeat

IN 1214 Philip II of France's victory against John's nephew and ally Otto IV, the Holy Roman Emperor and German king, at Bouvines, a village near Valenciennes in Flanders, brought an end to John's efforts to recover his lost lands in France. It also left him vulnerable to the baronial rebellion which followed in England.

Although many English barons objected to serving on the Continent, John gathered an army, filled a large treasure chest and in February 1214 sailed to Poitou. The earl of Salisbury was sent to Flanders with more troops and money for John's allies. Reinforced by some of his Poitevin barons, John set out from La Rochelle on campaign. He was successful in preliminary moves to secure Anjou, but when the French army approached the crucial fortress of la Roche au Moine, which John was besieging, and a pitched battle loomed, the Poitevin barons refused to fight. John, who had relied on their active support, had to retreat to La Rochelle. His ally, Otto IV, had meanwhile assembled in Flanders with the counts of Flanders and Boulogne, intending to march south and attack the French from the north. However, Philip, relieved of pressure from John in the south, was able to concentrate his might against this northern threat and defeated John's allies at Bouvines on 27 July, 1214.

fucor de tam inopinata uictoria letus: grāt deo et
soluit q̄ sibi talem gcessit ab aduisariis portare triū
phum. Tres q̄ comites supdem cū militū z aliozum
numiosa multitudie uinctis gstricti abducti sunt:
carcerali custodie mancipandi. In aduentu aū reg
tota ciuitas parisiaca facib; z latius cantrib; z plau
sib; classicis z laudib; die z nocte septite series z uia
riis ornata pannis sollent gritabatr. facta ÷ autē
h belli egresso mense iulio vi. kł. augusti——————.

Rex francoz philippus

Left *The continual battles of John's reign were exhausting to both sides, whether victors or losers. Men and horses like those shown in this psalter were expensive, and kings depended heavily on their armies as there were so many disputed borders and fortified towns.*

Above *The battle at Bouvines consolidated the power of the French monarchy, even though this illustration by Matthew Paris shows a moment of despair, when Hugo de Bouve is forced to flee as his king, Philip, lies momentarily helpless before his final victory.*

1215

At London there gathered those barons who had demanded the charter together with their accomplices including, as it is said, some of the bishops; and they met the king.

When he sought a termination of hostilities in this new quarrel he was not kindly heard because, amongst other reasons, so much time had passed when he had had a completely different intention in his heart. After certain persons had intervened, a day was set for the king's final answer, namely 26 April. The king assured the nobles in writing that if he did not give his answer on that day then one by one they might leave him and return to their own lands. And when this charter had been made public everyone agreed with those who had proposed it and they were all of one heart and will: namely that they were pledged to the defence of the house of the Lord and stood for the liberty of the Church and kingdom.

The king for his part resolved that now this had been done everyone throughout England should swear to him that they stood with him against all men and against this charter, and this in addition to the usual oath. And when he was not freely heard and excuses began to be made, he ceased what he had begun, not allowing time for a rising to be stirred up amongst the people. He then sent messengers to the pope complaining that the people had prepared to rise up against him contrary to their oath of fidelity. It was known through certain accomplices of the messengers that this had been determined many days previously. The barons on their part complained against his unjust exactions and tyranny.

At that time Eustace, bishop of Ely, died, a man of great authority upon whose advice a major part of these negotiations was said to depend.

The king took the cross at London from William, bishop of London. With the king and after him many of his own followers did likewise, some even at his instigation, and he gave them a white cross as had been the custom in the days of his father and brother. For it was an ancient custom that the English were marked with white crosses and the French were marked with red. Some barons interpreted his act wrongly, saying that he had not done this out of piety or love of Christ but in order to deprive them of a decision; and hearing that he had called foreigners to his aid they gathered together not waiting for the day, 26 April, which had been appointed.

When the king replied rudely to the barons through his messengers they determined that they would not deal civilly with him again. Each returned with haste to his own lands in order to fortify his castles and to seek aid, and began to prepare horses and arms.

Therefore in Easter week they gathered in a strong force according to the agreement which they had made. They came for the great part from the northern regions, and were therefore called the Northerners. Then they advanced to Northampton, not, however, doing anything hostile, except appearing ready for war. They were joined there by Giles, bishop of Hereford, Geoffrey de Mandeville, Robert FitzWalter, and many others who chiefly had something against the king.

Meanwhile the king tried to win them back through many emissaries and there was much discussion amongst them, the archbishop, bishops and other barons acting as intermediaries, the king himself staying near Oxford.

At the end of this conference, which took place not far from Brackley, sending defiant messages to the king, the barons left with their men and went back to Northampton and, with standards going before, prepared themselves for battle. Having closed the gates and placed guards around the walls they began to attack the fortress which was in the town; but they were frustrated because they had no siege engines. They therefore sent to their supporters both near and far that they should bring their forces with them.

They gathered to themselves a great number especially of younger men, that is sons and nephews of the barons, who wished to make a name for themselves in war. Houses were divided

The Chancery rolls

FROM the beginning of John's reign, the king's Chancery, the secretariat responsible for writing his charters and letters and attaching or appending seals as authentication, began to record their contents in long rolls not unlike the pipe rolls of the Exchequer. Archbishop Hubert Walter of Canterbury was chancellor, keeper of the seal, from 1199 to 1205 and this development is associated with him; as justiciar under Richard I, he had begun the systematic keeping of legal records.

The Chancery rolls may have been started to aid the efficient levying of the clerks' fees, but it seems more likely that the royal administration needed them to record who authorized particular actions. Whatever the reason, the rolls provide historians with more detailed information about the king's movements and actions than is available for any earlier reign.

There were separate series of rolls for the three main types of royal instrument which had developed by the reign of Henry II: charters, which made permanent grants of lands and privileges; letters patent (ie, open), which made temporary grants of, for example, the office of sheriff; and letters close (ie, closed), which delivered secret instructions to royal officials, particularly sheriffs. It was necessary to break the seal to open letters close, whereas the seals of charters and letters patent hung from the documents on cords or parchment tags and did not need to be broken for their more public contents to be read.

Governments have continued to produce patent rolls up to the present day. Though their use is now largely ceremonial, for centuries they were of vital administrative importance.

Below *The patent rolls were kept to record royal letters patent; these are some of the earliest and date from John's reign.*

Far below *The parchment membranes, written horizontally, were sewn end to end to form continuous rolls which can be unrolled from top to bottom to find the reference needed.*

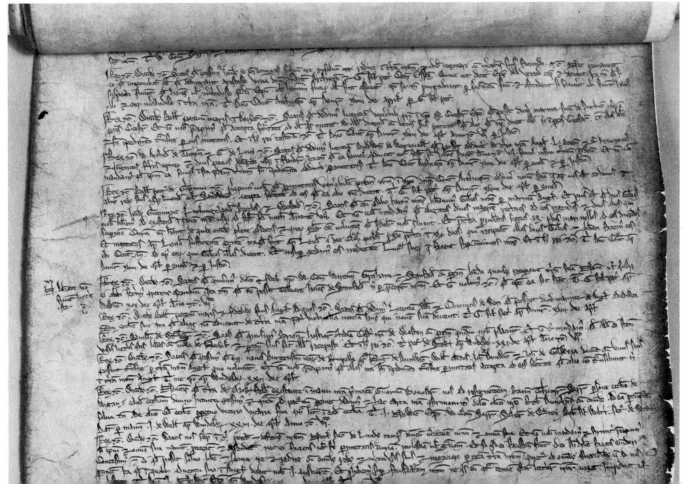

by the hostilities, for fathers and older men adhered to the king whilst sons and young men stood with his adversaries. We even knew some who crossed to the other side for love of their sons. There were those who did not join the rebels at first, but who did later either because they were friends of fortune, or lovers of new things. It was said that both Alexander, king of the Scots and Llewellyn, prince of North Wales, were in league with them.

In these days the archbishop of Canterbury called a provincial synod at Oxford. And when certain of the prelates had arrived, the deliberations being affected by the turbulence of the kingdom, they left.

Those who therefore gathered together in a strong force accused the king of many things, and, when he had been accused, condemned him saying that they should no longer have him for king, and their voices gathered strength, and a powerful conspiracy arose against him. Leaders of the army were appointed, called marshals of the army of God, and after a time about five hundred knights advanced towards London. It was a Sunday whilst the populace was in church, when some, together with certain accomplices from the city, preceded the rest and creeping towards the walls, climbed them. Then opening first one gate and then another, they admitted their own men, the king's men and also, it is said, the greater part of the citizens, being ignorant of what was happening.

What more is there to say?

Taking captive those who resisted, others joining them, they took the city into their hands and placed sentries on the walls.

At this time a number of people led by the same spirit gathered together in Devon, and having first occupied Exeter they afterwards hid in the forests. But when they learned that certain men had taken control of the capital of the kingdom, they went out in such force that they could scarcely be resisted, capturing the king's houses and laying waste his parks, and the thoughts of many hearts

Right In the 12th century Wharram Percy was a thriving village community. Sheep provided wool; cattle provided meat, hides and dairy products; horses were used for ploughing on the light chalk soils. Animals grazed in the valley and on the hillside.
Mill and pond (far right): The stream was dammed to build a series of water-mills. This one was used for grinding corn.
Church: The pastor's house is between the pond and the graveyard, in front of the Norman church which was built of stone.
Manor house (far left): Larger and more substantial than the peasants' houses, it was built of stone and had a thatched roof with a firm timber base.
Peasants' houses (alongside and behind the church): Although they were mud huts with crudely thatched roofs, they had solid wooden doors with locks, and the windows had shutters. Pigs and animals were housed in lean-to sheds, but cattle also lived in the home. Inside were caskets and chests for belongings, a hearth for warmth and for cooking on, and candles in candle holders. Excavations have found medieval cooking pots, serving bowls, sewing materials, and bone dice and counters for fireside games.

In the villages of England

FROM the 9th to the 13th century a village society gradually replaced that of hamlets and isolated farmsteads. The former were uprooted, often on the lord's command – though probably lords and peasants co-operated in many cases – and there were new, planned villages with open fields. The framework of the earlier society, however, still exists in regions such as southwest England and East Anglia.

In all these villages, life was dominated by agriculture. Peasants held land from their lord, but in exchange were

expected to work in his fields, sometimes as frequently as two days a week and often longer at harvest time. In the 12th century this duty was sometimes replaced by a cash payment similar to rent. Ostensibly that worked to the peasants' advantage, since they could devote more time to their own lands. But the arrangement might be for only a short period and peasants risked being unable to pay if their crops failed.

Chronic monetary inflation in the late 12th century led many landlords to try to use the manor courts to worsen the conditions on which peasants held their land.

Right *The 11th-century tower is all that remains of the church.*

having been revealed, everywhere they killed and committed acts of depredation. A riot took place in Northampton. Many of the king's men who had been stationed there were murdered by the townspeople, and after a few days a large part of the town was consumed by fire.

Then the king, gathering aid so that he might be able to hold his own in peace, fortified his garrisons and castles with men and supplies. He sent some messengers in secret to foreign parts in order to seek aid from other nations and sent other messengers to the pope, complaining bitterly of those who fought against him. Not trusting the king's men who were in London, who were still making up their minds, the barons began to build siege engines and to besiege the fortress known as the Tower of London. Having heard this, those who had remained in the northern parts began by force and by flattery to capture much there, and having gathered together a considerable army they occupied Lincoln in the week of Whitsun, and prepared even to besiege the castle, which held out.

The king, seeing them gather strength, then began through certain people and especially through the archbishop, whom they greatly respected, to ask them for peace, promising faithfully that there was nothing which he would not do in the interests of obtaining peace. Having agreed upon a place where the parties could conveniently gather, after many deliberations they made peace with the king, and he gave to them all that they wanted, and confirmed it in his charter.

This was Magna Carta, which despite the occasional gesture towards the lower orders was fundamentally intended to protect the barons against the rapacious tyranny of King John.

Those who had come were received there with the kiss of peace and they did fealty anew, and they ate and drank together. A day was fixed for the completion of the peace, when they would finally achieve what they had determined on. And the king satisfactorily restored justice everywhere, lifting the sieges which he had begun and giving up the houses and castles which he held in his own

hand, or which his brother Richard had taken — that is, the castles of Mountsorrel, Rockingham, Colchester and many more. A universal peace was soon proclaimed and those who were in London and those who were in Lincoln ceased hostilities.

Now matters were settled, but alas! a new problem worse than the first arose, caused by the enemy who is the hater of peace and the author of discords. From this colloquy certain barons from across the Humber went away and renewed hostilities on the pretext that they had not been present. To create discord they now seemed to seek opportunities for terminating the friendship which had been initiated. For the king did not believe them himself and they refused to come near him.

Other rebels were received by the Londoners and began to repair the communal fortifications, others fortified the castles which the king had only just resigned or which they had held as if by hereditary right for a long time. There were those who even constructed new fortifications.

Meanwhile a copy of the charter was circulated around the towns and villages and all who saw it agreed to it, the king himself having ordered this.

The king then sent his messengers into the provinces to call upon the sheriffs to keep the peace, it being their job to keep peace in the provinces, and to deal with royal business. But when the messengers arrived at those parts where the said nobles were powerful, some were captured, and others were expelled not without injury.

When the king heard this, he suspected that the oath to observe the charter was aimed at him, because the charter said that the king would be forced to observe its terms. He quickly sent other messengers to foreign parts and his chancellor Richard Marsh to the pope, who was constantly sitting in the curia endeavouring to promote his interests.

John pressed his case because the Lateran Council was now imminent and because he knew that certain nobles were conspiring for his expulsion. He tried with vast promises to win over the French king to his side but was frustrated. For others, to whom the French king made secret undertakings, anticipated him; because there had been enmity between him and the English king for a long time except when it had been assuaged by truces.

Again there was much plundering and many depredations, the king himself staying in fortified places whilst the barons ran freely to and fro across the region. But as yet they spared the people, seeing that the time of harvest was drawing near, so long as they could plunder all the royal manors and houses which were in the north and could depopulate the forests by selling the wood and killing large numbers of wild animals.

The archbishop and all the bishops therefore, seeing the land go to ruin, reminded now the king and now the barons of peace. Finding that both the rebels and the king confessed themselves to be ready to seek peace, it was decreed that on 15 August, the feast of the Assumption of the Blessed Virgin Mary, the king should gather with his men at Oxford and the barons with their men at Brackley so that when mediation had been completed in due form they would be able to put to sleep their quarrel and bury their enmity.

On the appointed day all the bishops and barons gathered near Oxford in battle array, and the king sent excuses by his men saying that when he had come to them, not refusing anything, after the first peace, grave injuries and enormous harm had come to him which should have been corrected; and that they had come on this day, when it was hoped to be able to construct peace, armed and with such a great multitude that it was not safe or advisable to allow access to the king.

The papal mandate was then displayed in which it was decreed that the archbishop and his suffragans should excommunicate the assailants and enemies of the king of England, and should come to the Lateran Council under pain of suspension. The bishop of Winchester, the abbot of Reading, and Pandulph, a sub-deacon of the Roman Church, who was a friend of the pope, were commissioned with the execution of this mandate. This was the same Pandulph who, two years previously, had reconciled the king to the Roman church. After he had exerted himself working for both sides in order to renew the payment of Peter's pence and in order to bring the king back into the Roman Church, he found a place amongst the English and was elected bishop of Norwich.

Since there was a rumour that the king should surrender the kingdom, because it seemed that there was no confidence in his rule, the discussion between the bishops and the barons lasted three days so that the sentence of deposition might at least be suspended; meanwhile the bishops came to the king seeking to bring him to a parley at London or in the town called Staines; and they agreed that they would gather there.

The barons then returned to London, where certain of their accomplices lived. The bishops on the other hand followed the king with all haste to Portsmouth. They were scarcely able to recall him from the ship on which he had embarked, and unable to achieve anything other than that he should send some of his own men to accompany the bishops. For the men protested in the hearing of the bishops and their followers that they would not stay with the king until the agreed peace was concluded.

Therefore, on 28 August the bishops and barons gathered together as one at Staines. After much deliberation, since danger threatened the bishops, sentence was passed upon the disturbers of the king and kingdom according to the papal mandate, even though many said that the sentence should be pronounced on the king himself and should fall on his head, since he had disturbed the kingdom and should be expelled.

The barons then returned to London, not without pride, and divided amongst themselves that part of the kingdom which now seemed to be in their power. Essex was given to Geoffrey de Mandeville, Northampton to Robert FitzWalter, Norfolk and Suffolk to Roger de Crescy, the counties of Cambridge and Huntingdon to Saher, earl of Winchester, the county of Lincoln to William d'Albini, the counties of York and Nottingham to John, the constable of Chester, and Northumberland to Robert de Ros. And each of them should show himself to be capable of providing justice and peace in the region assigned to his care.

After a few days, it was announced that the king, together with many foreigners who had come to his aid, had gathered an army near Dover. For it seemed to him to be convenient to wait there for the others whom he hoped would come.

The barons having deposed and rejected him, now began to discuss the election of a new lord; and because it was proper that this should be done with the consent of the whole kingdom, they sent a peremptory summons alleging serious danger and citing the oaths that had been sworn. They decreed that all the nobility should assemble at a predetermined time and place. It happened then, that those barons who had not given their consent at the outset, after many delays and deliberations, now replied that they had not agreed with the king's deposition and expulsion but had protested themselves to be ready to serve him in peace. Then the barons were divided into two camps and the evils in the land were multiplied.

Although numerous, the rebels lacked confidence; and turning to King Philip of France, elected his eldest son Louis as their king, begging that he come to England with a strong force in order to release them from the hand of the tyrant whom they now had as ruler. And then when they had made that agreement through go-betweens, they besieged the castle at Northampton with the aid of the skill of French artificers in constructing siege engines. Then, when his task had been completed, they besieged the fortress at Oxford.

King John, who had stayed near Dover for some days, now began to lift up his head. There came to him all the powerful forces which had been promised to him when he sought aid; Poitevins, Gascons, Brabançons and men from Flanders came to him in a large number. Many came to him, even though much had been suffered

from a gale during the crossing, and one ship carrying the king's messengers had sunk.

His forces having multiplied, the king sent out some who were to break up the sieges at both Oxford and Northampton whilst he himself occupied the city of Rochester, which the barons had stirred up against him, and laid siege to the castle. This was the castle of the archbishop and there were many great men in it: that is ninety-five from the best and strongest knights; others also promised to give speedy aid if the king should besiege them. The king was not deterred, but having destroyed the bridges over which the knights hoped to obtain aid and having erected siege engines, he began to attack the fortress on all sides. But the brave and strong men resisting caused much slaughter amongst their enemies.

Having called together all their allies, the barons left London on Monday, 26 October together with seven hundred knights. And in order to aid the besieged, came to the town of Dartford. Yet when they heard that the king intended to attack them, they returned with haste to London, agreeing that on 30 November they would gather with a stronger and better force, believing that the besieged would be able to resist until that time.

Then they sent Saher, the earl of Winchester, with many others in order to speed the arrival of Louis and, in order that he should not retain any doubts, they swore secret oaths that they did not hold their land from King John in perpetuity. Many returned to their own lands whilst others stayed in London.

Meanwhile the besieged, being closely pressed at Rochester, urged the king to negotiate with them, but he refused to grant this request and hurled stones against them unceasingly, both day and night, with five throwing machines. All the fortifications having been broken down, only the keep remained, and because it was an ancient and solid work it resisted the onslaught. Then the sappers were sent in, but when half the keep had collapsed the besieged continued to resist in the other half. Such was the structure of the keep that

Magna Carta

MAGNA CARTA, the 'Great Charter', granted by John at Runnymede in June 1215, was a treaty of peace between the king and his rebellious barons. As a treaty it was not successful: the war it sought to prevent broke out after a few months. Some of its terms, such as removing John's hated administrators and returning his mercenary troops to the continent, were the result of temporary political circumstances and did not last. Most of the precepts, however, proved more permanent: they were retained when the charter was re-issued after John's death by the supporters of his son Henry III in 1216 and 1217, and when it was confirmed as law in 1225 in return for a grant of taxation to the king by his subjects.

A complex document of 63 clauses, Magna Carta begins with a general guarantee of privileges to the Church and goes on to deal with the grievances of the baronage, whose opposition had been largely responsible for bringing the charter about. The amount a baron's heir had to pay to enter his inheritance was limited to £100; John and his predecessors had often charged many times that amount. The charter also protected from exploitation any heir who was under age when his father died and so fell into the king's wardship; it laid down that any widow should receive her marriage portion immediately on her husband's death and that she should be free to choose whether or not to remarry; and it prevented the unnecessary seizure of the lands of Jews or debtors to the king. The rights which the king granted to his barons were to be conceded by them to their tenants, so the charter's effects spread down from the upper levels of society. It also dealt with consent to taxation: taxes henceforth could not be levied except with the agreement of leading churchmen and barons at a meeting of which they had to be given 40 days' notice.

Provisions were made to ensure that the royal court was in a fixed place – in practice, Westminster – where the king's justice could always be obtained, and that royal judges would visit each county regularly. Restrictions were put on the powers of the king's local officials, particularly sheriffs, to prevent them from abusing their financial, administrative and judicial powers. The extent of the king's forests was to be reduced and the powers of his forest justices limited. Clauses regulated weights and measures, ensured the safety of merchants and confirmed the privileges of the citizens of London – people whose support the baronial party valued.

Some terms of Magna Carta enunciated principles which have since been a recurring theme in English history. The king undertook not to sell, deny or delay justice to anyone. No one was to be imprisoned, lose his lands or be outlawed unless by the judgement of his equals or the law of the land. Magna Carta, therefore, did not only assert baronial privilege (although that was its primary intent); an additional, underlying theme, which was to have a longer lasting significance, was the upholding of individual rights against arbitrary government.

Above left *John's seal on the Magna Carta.*

Below *The charter itself; it was frequently reissued by later English kings as a sign of good faith to their subjects.*

one part was divided from the other by a solid stone wall. In our age there had never been another siege so determinedly pursued or so vigorously resisted. For after many days, when nothing remained to them within the narrow confines of the keep, they suffered from hunger, and lacking all other things, ate the flesh of horses and drank water, which was very hard for those who had been delicately nurtured.

And then it came to the end. At first some were sent out from the castle who seemed less warlike, the king causing the hands and feet to be cut off. Not long afterwards all were taken into captivity, and were thrown into chains, with the exception of those who proved themselves to be clerics. The king kept the knights and nobles for himself but gave the less important prisoners into the hands of others. Only one did he order to be hanged, a crossbowman whom he had nurtured since childhood, although it was thought that all would die on account of the king's bitter rage. Hearing of the outcome of the siege the rest of the barons were dismayed and with rising panic gathered in London or stayed in religious houses. There were few indeed who felt secure behind fortifications.

As they had appealed to the Council, the barons of England sent some who represented their views, but because they had been labelled as excommunicates these men were not given audience. Not only they were excommunicated, but also all those who were hostile to the king, together with their helpers and supporters. And because it was revealed to the pope that the French king and his son had made a treaty with the aforesaid barons, he sent frequent letters warning them that they should attempt nothing against the sentence; but he was disappointed. For either because of hatred for John or because they were too proud to draw back, having received hostages from the English barons, Philip II sent the marshal of France to London with a strong force of armed men who should prepare with the Londoners for the coming of his son Louis who it was believed would arrive very shortly.

The king, as has been said, captured Rochester at the beginning of December, and then turned towards Winchester. Then, going through the middle of England towards the north, his presence strengthened the hearts of the people who had been wavering, and reassured his supporters, whom he had stationed in castles and other fortified places. Coming to Nottingham he celebrated Christmas there; and whatever castles there were in that region were either left waste or given to him.

1216

King John then proceeded further and came as far as the castle of Berwick, and having captured the town and depopulated the countryside he returned to his own lands. In his going and in his coming back he wasted the land and took fortified places, and there were none who resisted him. For the king of Scotland, who was still a minor, fled into remote regions with all his followers.

At that time the Isle of Ely was invaded by some of the king's allies under the earl of Salisbury. Now, either because it was a religious place or because it was well fortified, a large number of women and infants had gathered there together with many knights and some nobles. They had closed off the entrances and had prepared to resist by placing guards in suitable places, but the earl took the opportunity of a harsh frost to cross the swamp, and they were captured by a mass of troops. Some of the knights were saved by fleeing across the ice and many of the women by being given the earl's protection. Having heard this, many who had sought refuge in religious places were terrified, and as many as were able fled to London.

The king then set out for Essex because it was said that many fortifications were being prepared for its defence. Yet when he arrived there, none resisted him except the castle of Colchester and this he besieged with a powerful force and captured it in the first week of March; and then there only remained London, where the French were gathering with the king's enemies. Although it was reported that the king had directed his army there, he went to Dover instead, feeling that in this way he would be able to impede the invasion of Louis. The pope, as well as sending very frequent letters, also sent a cardinal called Gualo who was to conduct business in person and perform the office of legate in England. But neither the king's preparations, nor the letters of the pope, nor the persuasions of the legate were able to impede Louis; and now he was not even halted by the wind which had been against him for so long.

On 14 May, Louis and his men landed on the Isle of Thanet, the king seeing them as they arrived. He had many foreigners and mercenaries with him who had taken the part of the French leader, and he did not even try to prevent their landing nor to assail them when they had taken possession of the shore. Troubled in mind and sad of face, he retired to Winchester in the company of the legate Gualo, who had landed in England.

Louis, having taken possession of the shore, went to Canterbury and there awaited his men whom he had called from London; so that having gathered his forces there he might progress with greater security. Both French and English gathered to his cause, and after his arrival had been reported they began to stir up the capital, and those who had awaited his coming for so long came out of their hiding places.

Then there began to desert the king many from amongst the English who had stood by him. Several castles were captured on the march and Louis came to London on the Thursday before Whitsun. He was accepted with all alacrity and happiness and they performed homage and swore an oath of fidelity to him there; so that it was thought that soon the whole island would be captured, and this was everywhere proclaimed. The king was believed to be desperate, since a little while beforehand he had ordered many castles throughout England to be demolished.

The legate gathered to himself the bishops and prelates of the Church and called them to the aid of the king and kingdom. In the presence of the king the legate excommunicated Prince Louis of France by name, and also his lieutenants and supporters, on Whit Sunday, 29 May; their lands were placed under interdict together with the city of London.

Louis, undeterred by this, pursued the king and captured Winchester and its surrounding fortifications which he then gave to the count of Nevers who had come with him. Then with many men he besieged Dover castle, which was defended by both natural and man-made fortifications. Sending some of the English barons with the count of Nevers he besieged the castle of Windsor. The Northern barons, however, were defeated in their attempts to take Lincoln. A certain lady called Nicola, who was the custodian's wife, freed herself from this siege with a money payment. The Northern barons, with the Scottish king, then went to Louis and did fealty and homage to him.

At that time many close friends deserted the king, namely the earl of Warenne, a kinsman of the king, the earl of Salisbury, the king's brother, the earl of Arundel, Earl Robert de Vere and also many others who, as it afterwards appeared, sided with Louis out of fear rather than conscience. John, after having considered for a long time what Louis had done, and believing him to be prospering less than at first, since he had been detained at the siege of Dover for a long time, now moved his camp into Norfolk, occupying the place that the king of the Scots had left.

Having heard this, those who were encamped at Windsor pursued him, and so that siege was lifted. John then went to the Isle of Axholme. And when he had wasted it with fire and sword he moved his forces through Lindsey, crossed Holland and arrived at Lincoln, where a few days before the king of Scotland had been encamped.

Throughout this journey he took his enemies' lands, plundered them and burnt them so that there had never been a time when there had been such fires in the land. Then, when all those who had gathered at Lincoln had fled before his face, he retreated rapidly, worn out by an attack of dysentery.

It was on this journey that John lost his baggage train in the Wash. Ralph of Coggeshall tells us that 'he lost on these travels, at the Wellstream, his portable chapel with his relics, and some of his packhorses with many household supplies. And

many members of his entourage were submerged in the waters of the sea and sucked into the quicksand because they had set out foolishly and in haste before the tide had receded.'

When John came to the castle of Sleaford, which he had taken from the bishop of Lincoln during the war, his illness grew worse and he was carried on a litter to Newark, another castle of the bishop of Lincoln, but which had been in the king's possession for some time.

Here therefore, laid low by illness, he ended his days on 19 October after he had ruled for seventeen years, five months and four days.

John was indeed a great prince but scarcely a happy one and, like Marius, he experienced the ups and downs of fortune. He was munificent and liberal to outsiders but a plunderer of his own people, trusting strangers rather than his subjects, wherefore he was eventually deserted by his own men and, in the end, little mourned. And since most of his forces were either hired men or foreigners, they quickly gathered at that place and, as if armed for war, carried his body as far as Worcester. This was not because he had asked to be buried there but because that place at that time seemed a safe one where his supporters could gather to deliberate on what was to be done next. His intestines, however, since he was rather fat, were interred in Croxton Abbey.

Above and opposite *The effigy of John in Worcester Cathedral; the monks were determined to mark their first royal burial with an appropriate monument. The tomb is made of Purbeck marble, a shell-like limestone that has been polished to a dark, gleaming finish. John's head is supported by two bishops, St Oswald and St Wulfstan – ironically perhaps, since his strained relationship with the Church was one of the problems of his reign.*

Previous pages *The Wash, an inlet that divides Norfolk from Lincolnshire. Four rivers and their estuaries create an area of shallow sandbars and marshy shores. The legend that John lost all his baggage and his treasure trying to cross the Wash is part of English folklore. Now, dredged channels make it safe for ships to sail to King's Lynn and Boston.*

1216: death of an English king

JOHN'S struggle with the barons, briefly interrupted by Magna Carta, continued until his death. Within five months of Magna Carta, war had broken out between him and his barons once more and in May 1216, a year after he had set his seal to the charter, Prince Louis of France, son of Philip II, crossed to England to seize John's throne. This was at the invitation of a number of leading English barons, who were angry because John had shown no signs of keeping the promises he had made in the charter. Having begun well, by the end of the summer Louis was losing support, and John took the initiative by advancing from his strongholds in the West Midlands to help his beleaguered followers at Windsor. In September, he drove back the Scottish king (Alexander, son of William the Lion), who had reached Cambridge, and temporarily relieved Lincoln. Soon afterwards he fell ill, possibly with dysentery or as a result of over-indulgence.

On 11 October John and his entourage tried to return from Norfolk to Lincolnshire by the quickest and shortest route, across the Wellstream estuary. However, they set out before the tide had properly receded and as a result, the king lost some of his chapel goods, some pack animals and some members of his household. The event was later exaggerated by the St Albans chroniclers according to whom John lost all his treasure, his household effects, and his foot-soldiers in whirlpools and quicksands.

John, increasingly ill, pressed on to Newark in Nottinghamshire, where he was attended by a doctor, the abbot of Croxton. He died in Newark castle on 19 October, after making a will appointing executors to secure the rights of his sons. Immediately, his household servants robbed him of his personal goods. His intestines were taken by the abbot and entombed at Croxton Abbey, but in accordance with his will his body was buried in Worcester Cathedral before the altar of St Wulfstan, the 11th-century English bishop, who had been canonized in 1203. The claims of John's own foundation, Beaulieu Abbey, were ignored. Henry II and Richard I had been buried at Fontevrault in Anjou. John, who had lost the heartlands of the Plantagenet dominions, and had spent so much of his reign in his English kingdom, was appropriately buried in an English cathedral near an English saint.

Epilogue

So died King John, and was—as Matthew Paris, writing some 50 years later, tells us—'released from much bitterness of mind, and a life of many disturbances and vain labours'. His unexpected demise almost certainly saved England for the Plantagenet line, for his young heir, Henry III, a mere nine years old, had no enemies of his own, and was soon given protection and help by the more chivalrous barons. Pope Innocent III was a formidable, vigilant and determined guardian of the new king, and support for Louis of France gradually slipped away as the English nobles came to recognize the avantages of having a malleable child on the throne rather than the strong and competent French king-in-waiting.

Henry III, who ruled for 56 years, grew into a pious, gentle man, a patron of the religious arts, shrewd rather than subtle, imbued with concern for the image of monarchy, but, even as an adult, unable to transmute that concern into the effective political action which was essential to successful medieval kingship. Like his father, he found it hard to gain or keep the trust of his barons, and, also like his father, became involved in bitter conflict with them. His problems were compounded by the English failure to recapture the lost Plantagenet dominions, despite immense financial outlay. Some or all of these factors—royal incompetence, lack of trust between crown and barons, overstretched government resources and failure in war with France—continued to recur in later centuries from time to time. But those monarchs who were, like Henry II at once able administrators, powerful leaders, and effective military commanders, were for the most part idolized by their subjects and have gained the admiration of posterity.

"By God's sword, if all abandoned the king, do
you know what I would do? I would carry him on my
shoulders step by step, from island to island, from
country to country, and I would not fail him not
even if it meant begging my bread."

William Marshal, guardian and protector of the
young Henry III, *The History of William the Marshal* (c. 1226).

Glossary

Advowson: The patronage of an ecclesiastical office or benefice; the right of presentation to a benefice.

Amercement: A financial penalty inflicted at the 'mercy' of the king or his justices (q.v.) for various misdemeanours and defaults. The offender was said to be 'in mercy', or 'amerced', and paid an 'amercement'; to be distinguished from fine (q.v.).

Assart: To clear land; to turn woodland into arable or pastureland. To assart in the royal forest without a licence was a grave offence. Land assarted with licence was subject to annual payments to the exchequer.

Assize: A rule, regulation or law, enforced on the authority of the Crown, though with the assent of the barons, which modified or changed the customary law. The term came to be applied to legal procedures under assize law (e.g., the 'assize' of *novel disseisin*), and eventually to the courts which entertained such actions and the justices (q.v.) who administered them.

Benedictine: Monks following the *Rule of St Benedict*, written in the 6th century by St Benedict of Nursia. Known also as black monks from the colour of their habit.

Burgess: Holder either of land or a house in a borough, with special judicial privileges and a part to play in running the borough.

Carthusian: Member of the Carthusian Order founded at La Grande Chartreuse in the 1080s by Bruno of Reims.

Castellan: A governor or holder of a castle.

Castellany: A lordship consisting of a castle and its surrounding lands.

Chancery: The king's writing office, headed by the Chancellor.

Cistercian: Belonging to the reformed Benedictine Order of Cîteaux founded by Robert of Molesme in 1098. Known also as white monks from the colour of their habit.

Custodian: The person responsible for collecting revenues and accounting for them all to the owner.

Customary due: A regular fixed rent or service, or percentage of a tax.

Disseisin: The act of wrongfully depriving a person of the possession – seisin (q.v.) – of lands, rents or other rights.

Escheat: The reversion of property to a lord of a fief (q.v.) for default of heirs or the outlawry of the holder.

Essoin: An excuse made by or on behalf of someone who is summoned to appear in court to perform suit or answer to an action, by reason of, e.g., sickness or infirmity.

Exchequer: The king's financial office and court, hearing pleas affecting the financial interests of the Crown.

Eyre: A visitation by the king or his justices (q.v.) acting in his name, carried out periodically, usually at intervals of a few years.

Farm: A fixed sum or rent, usually annual. The sheriff's farm was the fixed sum payable annually by the sheriff as composition for all the regular royal revenues coming in from the shire, i.e., the sheriff farmed the revenues – contracting in advance to pay a fixed amount and deriving his profit from whatever he could collect above this sum. A custodian (q.v.), on the other hand, directly accounted for all the revenues.

Fealty: An oath of fidelity. Sometimes confused with homage since both were commonly performed together when a vassal received a fief from a lord. An oath of fealty, however, could be performed to one from whom no land was held. Fealty to the Crown overrode all other obligations, even that of homage to another great lord.

Fief: A landed estate, normally heritable, held on condition of homage and of the performance of services to a superior lord, by whom it is granted. The services were principally to give military aid, later commuted to scutage (q.v.).

Fine: 1. In the 12th century a fine was not necessarily or even usually a financial penalty. It was, rather, a sum of money which an applicant to the Crown agreed to pay for having some grant, concession or privilege. The word most closely approaches its modern connotation when referring to payments made to escape the consequences of the king's displeasure. *To make fine:* to make one's peace, settle a matter or obtain exemption from punishment. 2. A final agreement. The agreement was embodied in a document known as a 'fine' or 'final concord'.

Forest: Not necessarily woodland, but land reserved for the king's hunting; usually under Forest Law controlled by the forester instead of the sheriff.

Franchise: A privilege or exceptional right (typically, rights of jurisdiction) granted by the sovereign power to a person or body of persons (such as a monastery).

Frankalmoign (or Free alms): The tenure of lands or tenements granted to those who had devoted themselves to the service of God, 'for pure and perpetual alms'. The service rendered by the grantee was the service of prayer, particularly for the souls of the grantor and his kin.

Gilbertine: Belonging to the order of Sempringham, founded by St Gilbert in the 1140s.

Grandmontine: Belonging to the ascetic monastic order of Grandmont, founded in about 1110 by Stephen of Muret.

Holding: (or **Fief**): the land of a tenant-in-chief, or an under-tenant.

Honor (or Honour): A technical term for the group of estates from which the greater tenants-in-chief of the Crown derived their prestige and status. A superior lordship upon which inferior lordships were dependent.

Hundred: An administrative sub-division of the shire, embracing several vills (q.v.), and having a court to which men of the hundred owed suit at regular intervals.

Jurisdiction: The right to administer justice, and keep the resulting fines.

Justice: Judge appointed by or on behalf of the Crown.

Justiciar: The chief legal and political advisor in England, who deputized for the king in his absence.

Knight's fee: A fief (q.v.) owing the service of one knight; notionally an estate providing sufficient revenue for the maintenance of one knight, although the size varied widely.

Lordship: Land held and farmed by the tenant-in-chief or by the under-tenant themselves.

Man: To be someone's man was to owe obligation to a lord, usually in the form of labour or service. A woman could also be someone's man in this sense.

Manor: The basic unit of landholding, with its own court and probably its own hall. Some consisted of one village, others of fractions of villages, others still of several villages.

Mark: A sum of money amounting to two-thirds of a pound sterling, i.e., 13s 4d; a gold mark = £6.

Moneyer: Coiner; a person licensed to strike coins.

Ordeal: A form of proof in a court of law, by which a divine sign of guilt or innocence was invoked. The person who was required to undertake the ordeal (usually the accused but sometimes the accuser) performed some feat such as carrying hot iron or plunging a hand into boiling water, and innocence was demonstrated if the wounds healed cleanly. The ordeal of cold water was customarily reserved for the unfree, but was the required ordeal for all those prosecuted under the Assize of Clarendon (1166).

Pipe roll: The record of the annual audit of the accounts of sheriffs and of other debtors to the Crown; properly known as The Great Roll of the Exchequer.

Pleas of the crown: The more serious crimes – breaches of the king's peace, and specially designated offences such as concealment of treasure trove, for example – jurisdiction over which could be exercised by no one except officers of the Crown.

Premonstratensian: A member of the order of regular canons founded by St Norbert at Prémontré, near Laon, in 1119. Also, a member of a corresponding order of nuns.

Reeve: A royal official. Also a manorial official, appointed by the lord, or sometimes elected by the peasants.

Relief: Money or kind paid to a lord by relatives after a man's death in order for them to inherit.

Scutage: Literally 'shield money'; a payment in lieu of military service, paid in respect of the knights which a tenant-in-chief owed to the Crown. The personal obligation of the tenant-in-chief himself to serve could not be discharged by scutage, but only by fine (q.v.).

Seat: The principal manor of a lord, still used today.

Seisin: Feudal possession. To be 'in seisin' was to be 'siezed of' control of an estate. *Livery of seisin* (i.e., delivery of seisin by a grantor) was usually done by some symbolic act. To be 'disseised' was to be ousted from seisin.

Sheriff: The royal officer of a shire, managing its judicial and financial affairs.

Tenant-in-chief: Lord (or institution, such as a church) holding land directly from the king.

Under-tenant: Tenant holding land from a main land-holder or tenant-in-chief.

Vill: The smallest administrative unit of the realm, a subdivision of the hundred, corresponding roughly to the administrative 'parish'. Usually identifiable with a village or township but including the area up to the bounds of neighbouring vills.

Bibliography

This is not intended as a comprehensive bibliography of all relevant works, but is a selection of books relating to the topics discussed in the notes and the chronicles. Articles have not been included because they are more difficult for the general reader to obtain; most of the works cited here contain bibliographies which are a good starting point for more detailed reading on individual subjects.

Politics, Law and Finance

Appleby, J. T., *England without Richard*, London, 1965

Appleby, J. T., *Henry II, the Vanquished King*, London, 1962

Baker, J. H., *An Introduction to English Legal History*, 2nd edn., London, 1979

Barber, R., *Henry Plantagenet, a Biography*, London, 1964

Barlow, F., *The Feudal Kingdom of England, 1042–1216*, 3rd edn., London, 1972

Barraclough, G., ed. and trans., *Medieval Germany, 911–1250*, 2 vols., Oxford, 1938

Barrow, G. W. S., *Feudal Britain: The Completion of the Medieval Kingdoms, 1066–1314*, London, 1956

Barrow, G. W. S., *The Kingdom of the Scots: government, church and society from the eleventh to the fourteenth century*, London, 1973

Barrow, G. W. S., *Kingship and Unity: Scotland 1000–1306*, London, 1981

Bates, D., *Normandy before 1066*, London, 1982

Bautier, R. H., ed., *La France de Philippe Auguste: le temps des mutations*, Paris, 1982

Brékilien, Y., *Histoire de la Bretagne*, Paris, 1979

Brooke, C. N. L., *Europe in the Central Middle Ages, 962–1154*, London, 1964

Brooke, C. N. L., *From Alfred to Henry III, 871–1272*, London, 1961

Brooke, Z. N., *A History of Europe, 911–1198*, London, 1938

Brooks, F. W., *The English Naval Forces, 1199–1272*, London, 1933

Brown, R. A., *The Normans and the Norman Conquest*, London, 1969

Brundage, J., *Richard Lion Heart*, New York, 1973

Boussard, J., *Le gouvernement d'Henri II Plantagenêt*, Paris, 1956

Boussard, J., *Le comté d'Anjou sous Henri Plantagenêt et ses fils, 1151–1204*, Paris, 1938

Bur, M., *La formation du comté de Champagne, v.950–v.1150*, Nancy, 1977

Cartellieri, A., *Philipp August König von Frankreich*, 4 vols, Leipzig, 1899–1922

Chartrou, J., *L'Anjou de 1109 à 1151*, Paris, 1928

Chrimes, S. B., *An Introduction to the Administrative History of Medieval England*, 2nd edn., Oxford, 1959

Clanchy, M. T., *England and its Rulers, 1066–1272*, London, 1983

Clanchy, M. T., *From Memory to Written Record, England, 1066–1307*, London, 1979

Cox, J. C., *The Royal Forests of Medieval England*, London, 1905

Cronne, H. A., *The Reign of Stephen, Anarchy in England, 1135–54*, London, 1970

Left *Boethius, a Roman consul, wrote an essay on music that was admired by medieval chroniclers.*

Davis, R. H. C., *A History of Medieval Europe from Constantine to Saint Louis*, London, 1957

Davis, R. H. C., *King Stephen*, London, 1977

Davis, R. H. C., *The Normans and their Myth*, London, 1976

Duby, G., *Le dimanche de Bouvines*, Paris, 1973

Duggan, A., *Devil's Brood: The Angevin Family*, London, 1957

Dunbabin, J., *France in the Making, 843–1100*, Oxford, 1985

Duncan, A. A. M., *Scotland: the Making of the Nation*, Edinburgh, 1975

Eyton, R. W., *The Court, Household and Itinerary of Henry II*, London, 1878

Fawtier, R., *The Capetian Kings of France, Monarchy and Nation, 987–1328*, trans. Butler, L., and Adam, R. J., London, 1966

Galbraith, V. H., *Studies in the Public Records*, London, 1948

Gillingham, J., *The Angevin Empire*, London, 1984

Gillingham, J., *Richard the Lionheart*, London, 1978

Gillingham, J., and Holt, J. C., eds., *War and Government in the Middle Ages*, Woodbridge, 1984

Gonzalez, J., *El Reino de Castilla en la epoca de Alfonso VIII*, Madrid, 1960

Guillot, O., *Le comte d'Anjou et son entourage au XIᵉ siècle*, 2 vols, Paris, 1972

Hall, H., *Court Life under the Plantagenets*, London, 1890

Hallam, E. M., *Capetian France, 987–1328*, London, 1980

Hallam, E. M., *Domesday Book through Nine Centuries*, London, 1986

Halphen, L., *Le comté d'Anjou au XIᵉ siècle*, Paris, 1906

Harding, A., *The Law Courts of Medieval England*, London, 1973

Hardy, T. D., *The Itinerary of John, King of England*, London, 1829

Harvey, J. H., *The Plantagenets*, London, 1948

Haskins, C. H., *Norman Institutions*, Cambridge, Mass., 1918

Heer, F., *The Holy Roman Empire*, trans. Sondheimer, J., London, 1968

Hodgson, C. E., *Jung Heinrich, König von England, Sohn König Heinrichs II, 1155–83*, Jena, 1906

Holdsworth, W., *A History of English Law*, 7th edn., London, 1956

Holt, J. C., *King John*, London, 1963

Holt, J. C., *Magna Carta*, Cambridge, 1965

Holt, J. C., *The Northerners*, Oxford, 1961

Hoyt, R. S., *The Royal Demesne in English Constitutional History, 1066–1272*, New York, 1950

Joliffe, J. E. A., *Angevin Kingship*, 2nd ed., London, 1963

Kibler, W. W., ed., *Eleanor of Aquitaine, Patron and Politician*, Austin, 1977

Knowles, M. D., *The Historian and Character and Other Essays*, Cambridge, 1963

Landon, L., *The Itinerary of Richard I*, Pipe Roll Society, 1935

Lemarignier, J. F., *La France médiévale, institutions et sociétés*, Paris, 1970

Lemarignier, J. F., *Le gouvernement royal aux premiers temps capétiens*, Paris, 1965

Lloyd, J. E., *A History of Wales, from the earliest times to the Edwardian Conquest*, 3rd edn., London, 1939

Luchaire, A., *Louis VI le Gros, annales de sa vie et de son règne, 1081–1137*, Paris, 1890

Madox, T., *The History and Antiquities of the Exchequer of England*, London, 1769

Malden, H. E., ed., *Magna Carta Commemoration Essays*, London, 1917

Marsh, F. B., *English Rule in Gascony, 1199–1259*, Ann Arbor, 1912

Mitchell, S. K., *Studies in Taxation under John and Henry III*, New Haven, 1914

Mitchell, S. K., *Taxation in Medieval England*, ed. Painter, S., New Haven, 1951

Moore, O. H., *The Young King Henry Plantagenet, 1155–83*, Columbus, Ohio, 1925

Morris, W. A., *The Medieval English Sheriff to 1300*, Manchester, 1927

Munz, P., *Frederick Barbarossa*, London, 1969

McKitterick, R., *The Frankish Kingdoms under the Carolingians, 751–987*, London, 1983

Norgate, K., *England under the Angevin Kings*, 2 vols, London, 1887

Norgate, K., *John Lackland*, London, 1902

Norgate, K., *Richard the Lionheart*, London, 1924

Oman, C. W. C., *The Coinage of England*, Oxford, 1931

Otway-Ruthven, A. J., *A History of Medieval Ireland*, 2nd edn., London, 1980

Pacaut, M., *Louis VII et son royaume*, Paris, 1967

Painter, S., *The Reign of King John*, Baltimore, 1949

Painter, S., *William Marshall*, Baltimore, 1933

Patourel, J. le, *The Norman Empire*, Oxford, 1976

Pernoud, R., *Eleanor of Aquitaine*, London, 1967

Petit-Dutaillis, C., *Le déshéritement de Jean-sans-terre et le meurtre d'Arthur de Bretagne*, Paris, 1925

Petit-Dutaillis, C., *The Feudal Monarchy in France and England from the Tenth to the Thirteenth Century*, trans. Hunt, E. D., London, 1935

Pollock, F., and Maitland, F. W., *The History of English Law before the Time of Edward I*, 2 vols, 2nd edn., Cambridge, 1898

Poole, A. L., *From Domesday Book to Magna Carta*, 2nd edn., Oxford, 1955

Poole, R. L., *The Exchequer in the Twelfth Century*, Oxford, 1912

Powicke, F. M., *The Loss of Normandy*, 2nd edn., Manchester, 1961

Ramsay, J. H., *The Angevin Empire, 1154–1216*, London, 1903

Ramsay, J. H., *The Revenues of the Kings of England*, 2 vols, Oxford, 1925.

Richard, A., *Histoire des comtes de Poitou, 778–1204*, 2 vols, Paris, 1903.

Richardson, H. G., and Sayles, G. O., *The Governance of Medieval England from the Conquest to Magna Carta*, Edinburgh, 1963

Rössler, O., *Kaiserin Mathilde*, Berlin, 1897

Round, J. H., *Geoffrey de Mandeville*, London, 1892

Sanders, I. J., *English Baronies: A Study of their Origin and Descent, 1086–1327*, Oxford, 1960

Saul, N., *The Batsford Companion to Medieval England*, London, 1983

Sayles, G. O., *The Governance of Medieval England*, Edinburgh, 1963

Schramm, P. E., *A History of the English Coronation*, trans. Wickham Legg, G., Oxford, 1937

Smith, L. M., ed., *The Making of Britain: the Middle Ages*, London, 1985

Southern, R. W., *The Making of the Middle Ages*, London, 1953

Stenton, D. M., *English Justice between the Norman Conquest and the Great Charter*, London, 1965

Stenton, F. M., *The First Century of English Feudalism*, 2nd edn., Oxford, 1961

Trautz, F., *Die Könige von England und das Reich*, Heidelberg, 1961

Ullmann, W., *Principles of Government and Politics in the Middle Ages*, London, 1961

Valin, R., *Le duc de Normandie et sa cour, 912–1204*, Paris, 1909

Waquet, H., *Histoire de Bretagne*, 3rd edn., Paris, 1958

Warren, W. L., *Henry II*, London, 1973

Warren, W. L., *King John*, London, 1961

Warren Hollister, C., *The Military Organisation of Norman England*, Oxford, 1965

West, F. J., *The Justiciarship in England, 1066–1232*, Cambridge, 1936

Wightman, W. E., *The Lacy Family in England and Normandy, 1066–1194*, Oxford, 1966

Young, C. R., *The Royal Forests of Medieval England*, Leicester, 1979

Aubert, M., *Suger*, Saint Wandrille, 1950

Barlow, F., *The English Church, 1066–1154*, London, 1979

Blair, P. H., ed. and trans., *The Rule of St Benedict*, 5th edn., Fort Augustus, 1948

Bolton, B., *The Medieval Reformation*, London, 1983

Brooke, C. N. L., and Swaan, W., *The Monastic World, 1000–1300*, London, 1979

Brooke, Z. N., *The English Church and the Papacy from the Conquest to the Reign of John*, Cambridge, 1931

Cheney, C. R., *From Becket to Langton: English Church Government, 1170–1213*, Manchester, 1956

Cheney, C. R., *Hubert Walter*, London, 1967

Colvin, H. M., *The White Canons in England*, London, 1951

Cowdrey, H. E. J., *The Cluniacs and The Gregorian Reform*, Oxford, 1970

Dickinson, J. C., *The Origins of the Austin Canons and their introduction into England*, London, 1950

Douie, D. L., *Archbishop Geoffrey Plantagenet*, York, 1960

Finucane, R. C., *Miracles and Pilgrims: Popular Beliefs in Medieval England*, London, 1977

Foreville, R., *L'église et la royauté en Angleterre sous Henri II Plantagenêt*, Paris, 1943

Formigé, J., *L'Abbaye Royale de Saint-Denis*, Paris, 1960

Gibson, M., *Lanfranc of Bec*, Oxford, 1978

Graham, R., *St Gilbert of Sempringham and the Gilbertines*, London, 1901

Hell, V. and H., *The Road to Compostella*, London, 1966

Hill, B. D., *English Cistercian Monasteries and their Patrons in the Twelfth Century*, Chicago, 1968

Kemp, E. W., *Canonisation and Authority in the Western Church*, Oxford, 1948

Knowles, M. D., *Christian Monasticism*, London, 1969

Knowles, M. D., *The Episcopal Colleagues of Archbishop Thomas Becket*, Cambridge, 1951

Knowles, M. D., *The Monastic Order in England, 940–1216*, 2nd edn., Cambridge, 1966

Knowles, D., *Thomas Becket*, London, 1970

Krehbiel, E. B., *The Interdict, its History and Operation*, Washington, 1909

Lambert, M., *Medieval Heresy*, London, 1977

Lawrence, C. H., *Medieval Monasticism*, London, 1984

Lekai, D. J., *Les Moines Blancs*, Paris, 1957

Moore, R. I., *The Origins of European Dissent*, London, 1977

Morey, A., and Brooke, C. N. L., *The Letters and Charters of Gilbert Foliot*, Cambridge, 1967

Power, E., *Medieval English Nunneries*, Cambridge, 1922

Robertston, J. C., *Becket, Archbishop of Canterbury. A Biography*, London, 1859

Saltman, A., *Theobald Archbishop of Canterbury*, London, 1956

Scott James, B., ed. and trans., *St Bernard of Clairvaux seen through his Selected Letters*, Chicago, 1953

Southern, R. W., *St Anselm and his Biographer*, Cambridge, 1963

Southern, R. W., *Western Society and the Church in the Middle Ages*, Harmondsworth, 1970

Tierney, B., *The Crisis of Church and State, 1050–1300*, New York, 1964

Vielliard, J., *Guide du pèlerin de Saint-Jacques-de-Compostelle*, c. 1163

Left *Ecclesiastical book covers often reflected a well-developed tradition of beautiful metalwork and encrusted jewels.*

Voss, L., *Heinrich von Blois, Bischof von Winchester*, Berlin, 1932

Webb, C. C. J., *John of Salisbury*, London, 1932

Williams, W., *St Bernard of Clairvaux*, Manchester, 1935

Zarnecki, G., *The Monastic Achievement*, London, 1972

Social and Economic

Baker, D., ed., *Medieval Women*, Oxford, 1978

Bautier, R. H., *The Economic Development of Medieval Europe*, London, 1971

Bennet, H. S., *Life on the English Manor*, 2nd edn., Cambridge, 1965

Beresford, M. W., and St Joseph, J. K. S., *Medieval England: an Aerial Survey*, Cambridge, 1958

Bloch, M., *Feudal Society*, trans. Manyon, L. A., 2nd edn., London, 1962

Boussard, J., *Nouvelle Histoire de Paris, I, Paris de la fin du siège de 885–886 à la mort de Philippe Auguste*, Paris, 1970

Brooke, C. N. L., and Keir, G., *London, 800–1216: the Shaping of a City*, London, 1975

Cazel, F. A., ed., *Feudalism and Liberty: the Articles and Addresses of Sydney Painter*, Baltimore, 1961

Chapin, E., *Les villes de foires de Champagne*, Geneva, 1937, reprinted, 1976

Dhondt, J., *Etudes sur la naissance des principautés territoriales en France, IXe–Xe siècle*, Bruges, 1948

Dion, R., *Histoire de la vigne et du vin en France des origines au XIXe siècle*, Paris, 1959

Duby, G., *The Chivralous Society*, ed. and trans. Postan, C., London 1977

Duby, G., *Medieval Marriage: two models from twelfth-century France*, trans. Forster, E., Baltimore, London, 1978

Duby, G., *Rural Economy and Country Life in the Medieval West*, trans. Postan, C., London, 1968

Evans, J., *Life in Medieval France*, London, 1957

Fourquin, G., *Lordship and Feudalism in the Middle Ages*, trans. Lytton-Sells, I. and A., London, 1976

Ganshof, F., *Feudalism*, trans. Grierson, P., 3rd edn., London, 1964

Hinde, T., ed., *The Domesday Book*, London and Markham, Ont., 1985

Lemarignier, J. F., *Recherches sur l'hommage en marche et les frontières féodales*, Lille, 1945

Lot, F., *Fidèles ou vassaux? Essai sur la nature juridique du lien qui unissait les grands vassaux à la royauté depuis le milieu du IXe jusqu'à la fin du XIIe siècle*, Paris, 1904

Mollat, M., *Histoire de l'Ile-de-France et de Paris*, Toulouse, 1971

Pirenne, H., *Les villes du moyen age*, Paris, 1971

Platt, C., *The English Medieval Town*, London, 1976

Poole, A. L., *The Obligations of Society in the Twelfth and Thirteenth Centuries*, Oxford, 1946

Postan, M. M., *The Medieval Economy and Society*, London, 1972

Power, E., *Medieval Women*, Cambridge, 1975

Pullar, P., *Consuming Passions*, 2nd edn., London, 1972

Reuter, T., ed. and trans., *The Medieval Nobility*, Amsterdam, New York, London, 1979

Richardson, H. G., *The English Jewry under the Angevin Kings*, London, 1960

Stenton, D. M., *English Society in the Early Middle Ages*, London, 1951

Tait, J., *The Medieval English Borough*, Manchester, 1936

White, L. T., *Medieval Technology and Social Change*, Oxford, 1962

Wilson, A., *Food and Drink in Britain*, 3rd edn., London, 1984

Anderson, M. D., *The Medieval Carver*, Cambridge, 1935

Arts Council of Great Britain, *English Romanesque Art 1066–1200*, London, 1984

Barber, R. W., *The Knight and Chivalry*, London, 1970

Boase, T. S. R., *Death in the Middle Ages*, London, 1972

Boase, T. S. R., *English Art, 1100–1216*, Oxford, 1953

Bony, J., *French Gothic Architecture*, Berkeley, 1983

Borenius, T., *St Thomas of Canterbury in Art*, London, 1932

Bottineau, Y., *Les chemins de Saint-Jacques*, Paris, 1964

Bradford, C. A., *Heart Burials*, London, 1933

Brooke, C. N. L., *The Twelfth Century Renaissance*, London, 1969

Broughton, B. B., *The Legends of Richard I*, The Hague, 1966

Catto, J. I., ed., *The History of the University of Oxford, I, The Early Oxford Schools*, Oxford, 1984

Chailley, J., *Histoire musicale du Moyen Age*, Paris, 1969

Chaytor, H., *From Script to Print: an introduction to medieval literature*, London, 1966

Clapham, A. W., *English Romanesque Architecture after the Conquest*, Oxford, 1934

Crosland, J., *Medieval French Literature*, Oxford, 1956

Davis, R. H. C., and Wallace Hadrill, J. M., ed., *The Writing of History in the Middle Ages … Essays to R. W. Southern*, Oxford, 1981

Delaborde, H. F., ed. and trans., *Oeuvres de Rigord et de Guillaume le Breton*, 2 vols, Paris, 1882–5

Dodwell, C. R., *Painting in Europe, 800–1200*, Harmondsworth, 1971

Erlande-Brandenburg, A., *Le roi est mort*, Geneva, 1975

Evans, G., *The Mind of St Bernard of Clairvaux*, Oxford, 1983

Evans, J., *Art in Medieval France*, Oxford, 1948

Evans, J., ed., *The Flowering of the Middle Ages*, London, 1966

Fino, F. F., *Fortresses de la France Médiévale*, Paris, 1967

Grabar, A., and Nordenfalk, C., *Romanesque Painting from the Eleventh to the Thirteenth Century*, Lausanne, 1958

Gransden, A., *Historical Writing in England c. 550 to c. 1307*, London, 1974

Harvey, J. H., *Cathedrals of England and Wales*, London, 1974

Harvey, J. H., *The Medieval Architect*, Gloucester, 1972

Haskins, C. H., *The Renaissance of the 12th Century*, New York, 1927

Heltzel, V. B., *Fair Rosamund: a Study of the Development of a Literary Theme*, Evanstown, 1947

Holt, J. C., *Robin Hood*, London, 1982

James, M. R., ed. and trans., *De Nugis Curialium by Walter Map*, Oxford, 1914

Kelly, A., *Eleanor of Aquitaine and her Courts of Love*, London, 1952

Kidson, P., Murray, P. and Honour, H., *A History of English Architecture*, London, 1962

Kidson, P., *The Medieval World*, London, 1967

Lasko, P., *Ars Sacra, 800–1200*, Harmondsworth, 1972

Leff, G., *Medieval Thought: St Augustine to Ockham*, Harmondsworth, 1958

Legge, M. D., *Anglo-Norman Literature and its Background*, Oxford, 1963

Mâle, E., *Religious Art in France: The Twelfth Century*, Princeton, 1978

Meras, *Abbayes et Pélerinages de France*, Paris, 1964

Meyer, P., ed. and trans., *Histoire de Guillaume le Maréchal*, 3 vols, Paris, 1891–1901

Morris, C., *The Discovery of the Individual, 1050–1200*, London, 1972

Musset, L., *Angleterre romane, I, le sud de l'Angleterre*, Paris, 1983

O'Meara, J. J. ed., *The History and Topography of Ireland by Gerald of Wales*, Harmondsworth, 1982

Panofsky, E., *Abbot Suger and the Abbey Church of Saint-Denis*, Princeton, 1946

Press, A. R., *An Anthology of Troubadour Lyric Poetry*, Edinburgh, 1971

Radice, B., ed., *The Letters of Abelard and Heloise*, Harmondsworth, 1974

Rashdall, H., *The Universities of Europe in the Middle Ages*, ed. Powicke, F. M., and Emden, A. B., 3 vols, Oxford, 1936

Richter, M., *Giraldus Cambrensis*, Aberystwyth, 1972

Sauerlander, W., *Gothic Sculpture in France*, London, 1972

Savage, A., ed. and trans., *The Anglo-Saxon Chronicles*, London, 1983

Sayers, D. L., ed. and trans., *The Song of Roland*, Harmondsworth, 1957

Simpson, O. von, *The Gothic Cathedral*, London, 1956

Southern, R. W., *Medieval Humanism and Other Studies*, Oxford, 1970

Thorpe, L., ed., *The History of the Kings of Britain by Geoffrey of Monmouth*, Harmondsworth, 1966

Topsfield, L. T., *Troubadours and Love*, Cambridge, London, New York, 1975

Van der Werf, H., *The Chansons of the Troubadours and Trouvères: a study of their melodies and their relation to the poems*, Utrecht, 1972

Webb, G., *Architecture in England: the Middle Ages*, Harmondsworth, 1954

Whitelock, D. and others, eds., *The Anglo-Saxon Chron*, rev. edn., London, 1961

Zarnecki, G., *English Romanesque Sculpture, 1066–1140*, London, 1951

Zarnecki, G., *Later English Romanesque Sculpture, 1140–1210*, London, 1953

Zarnecki, G., *Romanesque Art*, London, 1971

Crusades and Warfare

Benevenisti, M., *The Crusaders in the Holy Land*, Jerusalem, 1970

Brown, R. A., *English Castles*, 4th edn., London, 1976

Ehrenkreutz, A. S., *Saladin*, New York, 1972

Godfrey, J., *1204: the Unholy Crusade*, London, 1980

Hill, G., *A History of Cyprus*, 2 vols, Cambridge, 1940

Koch, H. W., *Medieval Warfare*, London, 1978

Lewis, B., *The Assassins*, London, 1967

Mayer, H. E., *The Crusades* trans. Gillingham, J., Oxford, 1972

Norwich, J. J., *The Kingdom in the Sun*, London, 1970

Oman, C., *A History of the Art of War in the Middle Ages, 378–1485*, 2 vols, 2nd edn., London, 1924

Prawer, J., *The Latin Kingdom of Jerusalem*, London, 1972

Riley-Smith, J., *The Knights of St John in Jerusalem and Cyprus, c. 1050–1310*, London, 1967

Runciman, S., *A History of the Crusades*, 3 vols, Cambridge, 1951–4

Setton, K. M. and others, *A History of the Crusades*, vols I–II, Madison, 1962

Right *The journey from London to Jerusalem.*

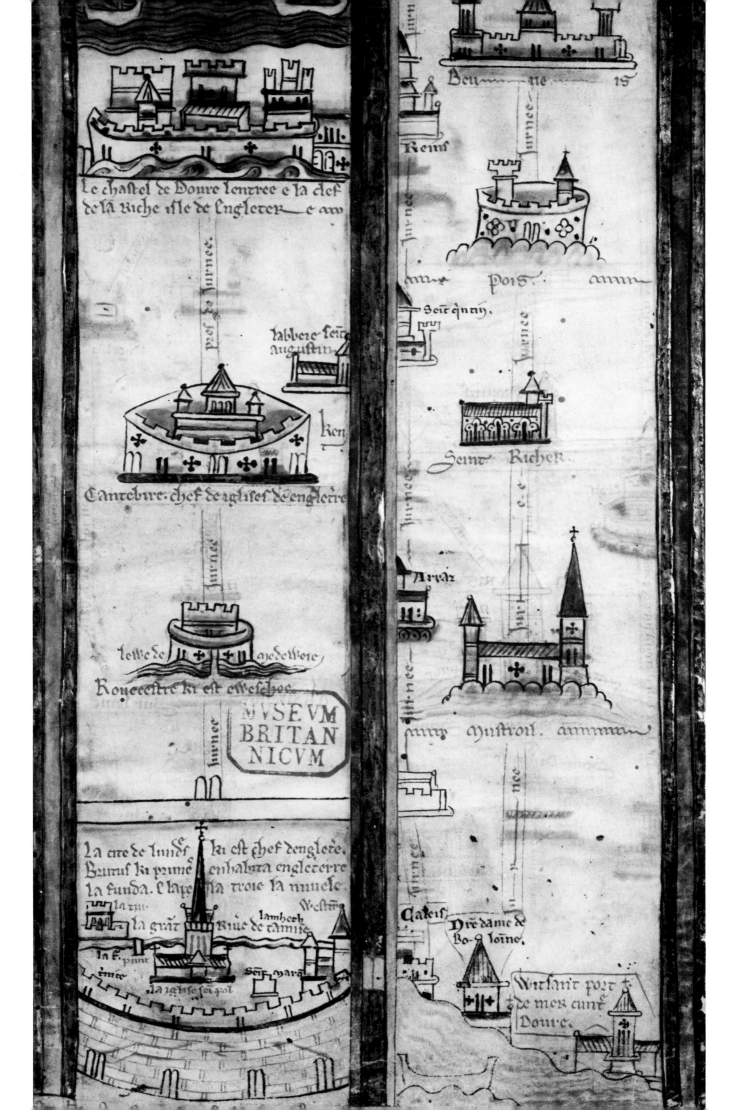

Le chastel de Doure lentree e la clef
de la riche isle de engleter. e au

labbeie seint
augustin

Cantebire chef de iglises de engletere

Kent

leuue de Rouecestre

Rouecestre ki est eueschee

MVSEVM
BRITAN
NICVM

La cite de lundres ki est chef denglere.
Brutus ki primer enhabita engleterre
la funda. e lapela troie la nuuele

Westm̃
lambeth
Riue de tamise

la rue

la grant

la F. punt

Seit mary

la iglise seint pol

Beuueie
15

Reins

Pois

Sei quatin

Seint Richer

Arraz

Hustroil

Cateis

Nredame de
Boloine

Wisant port
de mer cuntre
Doure

Smail, R. C., *Crusading Warfare, 1097–1193*, Cambridge, 1956

Sumption, J., *The Albigensian Crusade*, London, 1978

Verbruggen, J. F., *The Art of Warfare in Western Europe during the Middle Ages*, Oxford, 1977

Bibliographies, Atlases and Reference Works

Centre National de la Recherche Scientifique, *Bibliographie Annuelle de l'histoire de France*, Paris, 1953–

Douglas, D. C., and Greenaway, G. W., eds., *English Historical Documents II, 1042–1189*, London, 1953

Falkus, M., and Gillingham, J., *Historical Atlas of Britain*, London, 1981

Gross, C., and Graves, E. B., *A Bibliography of English History to 1485*, Oxford, 1975

Longnon, A., *Atlas Historique de la France*, 2 vols, Paris, 1885–9

Rothwell, H., ed., *English Historical Documents III, 1189–1327*, London, 1965

Royal Historical Society, *Annual Bibliography of British and Irish History*, London, 1976–

Chronicles

Part I

John of Marmoutier, *The Chronicles of the counts of Anjou,* ed. L. Halphen & R. Poupardin in *Chroniques des comtes d'Anjou et des seigneurs d'Amboise,* Collection des Textes, Paris 1913; pp 29–31, 37–44, 143–51, 161–2. Extracts.

Part II

John of Marmoutier, *The History of Duke Geoffrey,* in *The Chronicles of the counts of Anjou,* ibid.; pp 176–231. Extracts.

Henry of Huntingdon, *The History of the English,* ed. T. Arnold in Rolls Series 1879; pp 259–92. Extracts.

The Deeds of Stephen, (anon.), trans. and ed. Thomas Forester in *Henry of Huntingdon,* Henry G. Bohn, London 1853. Extracts.

Part III

Ralph of Diceto, *Images of History,* ed. W. Stubbs in *The Historical Works of Master Ralph of Diceto,* Rolls Series 1876; I, 291–439; II, 3–66. Extracts.

William of Newburgh, *The History of English Affairs,* ed. D.C. Douglas and G.W. Greenaway in *English Historical Documents 1042–1189,* London 1953; pp 322–3, 325, 329–30. Extracts.

The Deeds of King Henry II, in *English Historical Documents,* op. cit.; pp 377–9. Extracts.

William FitzStephen, *The Life of St Thomas Becket,* ed. and trans. G.W. Greenaway in *The life and Death of Thomas Becket, Chancellor of England and Archbishop of Canterbury,* The Folio Society, London 1961; pp 35–44, 55–8, 156–7. Extracts.

William FitzStephen, *Description of the city of London (1170–1183),* given as a preamble to his *Life of St Thomas Becket,* ibid. Extracts.

Adam of Eynsham, *The Life of St Hugh of Lincoln,* ed. the late Decima L. Douie & David Hugh Farmer in *Magna Vita Sancta Hugonis,* Oxford University Press, 2nd edn. 1985; I, 60–3, 85–6, 115–9; II, 93–4, 104–9, 125–30, 169–70. Extracts.

Jordan Fantosme, *Chronicle of the War between the English and the Scots,* in *English Historical Documents,* op. cit.

Part IV

Ralph of Diceto, op. cit.; II, 66–166. Extracts.

Rigord, *The Deeds of Philip Augustus,* ed. H.-F. Delaborde in *Oeuvres de Rigord et de Guillaume le Breton,* Société de l'Histoire de France 1882–5; pp 106–9. Extracts.

Richard, canon of Holy Trinity, Aldgate, *The Itinerary of the Pilgrims,* ed. W. Stubbs in Rolls Series 1864; pp 259–78. Extracts. Also *The Deeds of King Richard,* ed. W. Stubbs in Rolls Series 1867; II, 80–4, 151–5, 158–61. Extracts.

Adam of Eynsham, *The Life of St Hugh of Lincoln,* op. cit.; II, 98–105, 134–7. Extracts.

Gerald of Wales, *The Description of Wales,* trans. Lewis Thorpe in *Journey through Wales/Description of Wales,* Penguin, London 1978 (copyright: the Estate of Lewis Thorpe 1978). Extracts.

Part V

Ralph of Diceto, op.cit.; II, 166–75. Extracts.

Ralph of Coggeshall, *The English Chronicle,* ed. J. Stevenson in *Chronicon Anglicanum,* Rolls Series 1875; pp 101–62. Extracts.

The 'Barnwell' Annals (anon.), ed. W. Stubbs in *The Historical collections of Walter of Coventry,* Rolls Series 1873; II, 201–32. Extracts.

Gervase of Canterbury, *The Deeds of Kings,* ed. W. Stubbs in *The Historical Works of Gervase of Canterbury,* Rolls Series 1880; II, 96–106. Extracts.

Acknowledgements

Our grateful thanks to the many museums, libraries and individuals, including those listed below, who provided us with illustrations.

(b. = bottom; t. = top; t.l. = top left; t.r. = top right; c. = centre; r. = right; l. = left)

Aerofilms: 267b.
Agen, Bibliothèque Municipale: 145b; 289.
Aldus Archives, London: 223 (Paris, Bibliothèque Nationale); 237 t.l. (Dublin, Trinity College); 274, 275 (New York, Pierpont Morgan Library); 286t., 287b. (Oxford, Bodleian Library); 303 (London, British Library); (New York, Pierpont Morgan Library).
Archivo Mas: 77; 115b.; 177t
Avranches, Bibliothèque Municipale: 163.

Terry Ball: 310-311
Besançon, Bibliothèque Municipale: 147t.l., t.r., 271l.
J. Bethell, St Albans: 138; 143t.; 245.
Bibliothèque Nationale, Paris: 215b.; 229.
Bildarchiv Foto Marburg: 113.
Bodleian Library, Oxford: 6; 75; 145t.; 239; 285b.
Janet & Colin Bord: 294/295.
Boulogne, Bibliothèque Municipale: 187t.
Bridgeman Art Library, London: 265t.
British Library, London: 29; 69; 90; 103; 117t.; 194; 202; 247; 258; 265; 315b.
British Museum, London: 301.
British Rail Fund: 119.

Cambridge University Library: 89; 137.
J. Allan Cash: 50; 71; 115t.; 277.
Conway Library; London: 122; 123t., b.; 213t.; 320; 321.

Edimage, Paris: 41 (Châteauroux, Bibliothèque Municipale); 218; 230; 231.
Edimedia, Paris: 23 (Chantilly, Musée Condé); 25; 55; (Paris, Musée du Louvre); 167b. (Rome, Vatican Library); 199 (British Library); 215t., 241t.

Fotobank: 77

Giraudon, Paris: 47 (Rouen, Musée); 55; 205l.; 211; 222b. (Paris, Bibliothèque Nationale); 235.
Glasgow University Library: 146; 147b.l.; 147b.r.; 270; 271r.; 273.
G. Goldner, Paris: 241b.

The Hague, Royal Library: 207.

Sonia Halliday: 26/27; 38; 39; 131; 169; 170; 171; 219 (Paris, Bibliothèque Nationale); 251t.
Clive Hicks, London: 139.

Lyon, Bibliothèque Municipale: 78/79.

Marianne Majerus: 30; 31; 35; 51; 57; 58; 59; 62/63; 66; 67; 71; 75; 81; 82; 83; 87; 88; 95b.; 107t.; 126/127; 131t.; 135; 143b.; 151; 173; 174; 175; 176; 181; 182/183; 190; 191; 193; 203; 242/243; 251b.; 253; 254/255; 257; 263; 267t.; 279; 298; 311b.; 318/319.
Mansell Collection, London: 95t.; 125; 213b.

Newbury/Jarrold Publications: 297b.
Northern Ireland Tourist Board: 295.

Österreischiche National Bibliothek, Vienna: 237b.

Phoebe Phillips Archives: 2; 105; 249.
Public Record Office: 309t.; 309b.

St. John's College Library, Oxford: 187b.
Scala, Florence: 179; 291.
Science Photo Library, London: 238.
R. Sheridan, Harrow: 49t.,b.; 79; 99t.; 178; 205r.; 210; 302; 315t.
Sotheby's, London: 111, all.

Visual Arts Library: 10; 40; 42; 61 (Bibliothèque Nationale); 63; 86 (British Library); 87 (British Musuem); 97 (Vannes, cathedral); 99b. (Guildhall, London); 117b.; 149; 153 (Bodleian Library); 155t., 155b. (Vannes, cathedral); 158b. (Bodleian Library); 159 (British Library); 161; 215m.; 222t., 225t.,b., 227b. (Bern, Burgherbibliothek); 283, 285t. (Bodleian Library); 290 (Musée du Louvre); 297t. (London Records Corporation); 306 (Bodleian Library).

Washington, National Art Gallery: 58.
Winchester Cathedral: 158t.

Zefa, London: 227t.

Index

Manuscripts

6 Scribe at his lectern. (English, early 13th century. Bodleian Library, Oxford, MS Bodley 602, f.36.)

23 The Mouth of Hell. (Vincent de Beauvais: le Miroir Historial. French, 1463. Musée Condé, Chantilly, France.)

29 Monks and nuns in stocks. (The Smithfields Decretals, English, 14th century. British Library, London, MS Royal 10 E IV, f.187.)

38 The crusaders taking Jerusalem in 1099. (Guillaume de Tyr: Histoire de Jérusalem, French, c.1250. Bibliothèque Nationale, Paris, MS Fr.9081)

39 Pope Urban II preaching the First Crusade at the Council of Clermont. (Livre des passages d'Outre-Mer, French, 15th century. Bibliothèque Nationale, Paris.)

40 A king gives a sword to a young knight. (Latin Bible, French, 13th century. Bibliothèque Municipale, Le Mans, France, MS 262.)

41 Richard Lionheart does homage to Philip Augustus of France. (Chroniques de France, French, 15th century. Bibliothèque Municipale, Châteauroux, France.)

42 Tomb-lid of Geoffrey Plantagenet, 1150–60. (Musée, Le Mans, France.)

47 Reliquary cross from the Abbey of Valasse, 12th century. (Musée Départemental, Rouen, France.)

49 Wall paintings from the chapel of Pritz, near Laval, France.

55 Rock crystal vase. (Musée du Louvre, Paris.)

55 Musician at court. (Cantigas de Sta Maria, Spanish, 13th century. Madrid, Monastery of the Escorial.)

58 Chalice made of sardonyx, gold, silver, gilt, gems and pearls, 19 cm high. (National Gallery of Art, Washington, U.S.A.)

61 t. The crusaders assault Antioch. (Guillaume de Tyr: Histoire de Jérusalem, French, c.1250. Bibliothèque Nationale, Paris, MS Fr.9081, f.44)

61 b. The Patriarch of Antioch receives the Emperor of Constantinople (top). The Patriarch of Antioch with Renaud de Châtillon, comte de Foix (bottom). (Guillaume de Tyr: Histoire de Jérusalem, French, c.1250. Bibliothèque Nationale, Paris, MS Fr.9081, f.174.)

69 t. King Stephen holding a falcon. (Matthew Paris: Historia Major, English, c.1240. British Library, London, MS Roy.20AII, f.7.)

69 b. Seal of King Stephen: second seal, used in 1137–39. 9.5 cm in diameter. (Private collection)

75 Empress Matilda's writ. (Christ Church College, Cambridge, c.21,879/Bodleian Library, Oxford.)

77 Altarpiece of St. Bernard of Clairvaux, 12th century. (Museo archeologico, Palma de Majorca, Spain.)

79 t. Crusader. (Detail of a wall painting in the church of Areines, France.)

79 b. The siege of Damascus. (Guillaume de Tyr: Histoire d'Outre-Mer, French, c.1280. Bibliothèque Municipale de Lyon, MS828, f.189r.)

86 t. Henry of Blois. (1135–54, British Library, London, MS Nero DVII, f.87v.)

87 t. Henry of Blois, enamel plaques in copper, hammered, champlevé, engraved, enamelled and gilded by a Mosan goldsmith before 1171. (British Museum, London.)

90 Henry II. (Matthew Paris: Historia Major, English, c.1240. British Library, London, MS Roy.20AII.)

97 Detail of a marriage casket. Leather on wood, 12th century. (Cathedral of Vannes, France.)

99b. Deed of sale of land and a house, witnessed by the Mayor of London, two sheriffs and about twelve other witnesses in 1204. (Guildhall, London, Records of St. Paul's cathedral.)

103 Map of England. (Matthew Paris: Historia Major, English, c.1240. British Library, London, MS Cotton Claudius DVI, f.12v.)

111 Life of St. Thomas of Canterbury. (English, c.1230–40, Private collection.)

113 Tomb effigies of Henry the Lion and his wife Matilda. (Braunschweig cathedral, Germany.)

115 b. Tomb of Alfonso of Castile and his wife Eleanor. (Monastery of Las Huelgas, Burgos, Spain.)

117 t. Henry II and Eleanor sailing. (Matthew Paris: Historia Major, English, c.1240. British Library, London, MS Royal 14CVII, f.134v.)

125 Life of St. Thomas of Canterbury. (English, c.1230–40. Private collection.)

131 The penance of Henry II at the tomb of Thomas Becket. (Stained-glass, English, 12th century. Canterbury Cathedral, Trinity chapel.)

137 Plan of the waterworks of Canterbury Cathedral. (The Eadwine Psalter, English, c.1150–60. Cambridge, Trinity College Library, MS R17.I, ff.286v–287.)

145 t. A wedding. (Decretals of Pope Gregory IX, Italian, c.1241. Bodleian Library, MS Lat.th.b.4, f.151v.)

145 b. Adultery punished. (Livre juratoire d'Agen, 13th century. Bibliothèque Municipale, Agen, France, MS 41, f.42v.)

146 Harvesting. (The Hunterian Psalter, English, 12th century. Glasgow University Library, MS Hunter 229, f.4v.)

147 t.l. & r. Tilling the land. (Cistercian Psalter, French, early 13th century. Bibliothèque Municipale, Besançon, France, MS 54.)

147 b.l. & r. Same as p.146.

149 The Court Chancellery of Palermo, Sicily. (Petro d'Eboli: De Rebus siculis carmen, Italian, c.1200. Burghersbibliothek, Bern, Switzerland, Codex 120.)

153 Saladin defeats the Christians in 1187. (Matthew Paris: Historia Major, English, c.1240. Corpus Christi College, Cambridge, MS 16, p.279.)

155 b. Detail of a marriage casket (Cathedral of Vannes, France)

158 t. The Dream of Ezechiel. (Winchester Bible, English, 12th century. Winchester Cathedral.)

158 b. Ivory book cover. (12th century. Bodleian Library, Oxford, MS Douce 176.)

159 Hell. (Psalter of Henry of Blois, English, 12th century. British Library, London, MS Nero C.IV., f.39.)

161 Letter from 1190. William Longchamp was also bishop of Ely. (Guildhall, London, St. Paul's cathedral records, 25121/770)

163 A sentence. (Decretals of St. Gregory IX on trials.) (French, 13th century. Bibliothèque Municipale d'Avranches, France, MS 150, f.61v. Formerly in the monastery of Mont-St-Michel.)

167 t. Reliquary-portrait of Frederick Barbarossa. (Church of St. Johannes, Coppenberg, Germany.)

167 b. Frederick Barbarossa. (Robert de St. Rémy: Histoire de la 3ème croisade, French, 13th century. Vatican Library, Rome.)

177 b. Pilgrims at a city gate. (Cantigas of Sta Maria, Spanish, 13th century. Monastery of the Escorial, Spain.)

187 t. Horoscope. (Phénomènes of Aratus, French, 11th century. Bibliothèque Municipale de Boulogne, France, MS 188.)

187 b. Cosmological diagram. (The Byrhtferth Manual, English, c.1110. St. John's College Library, Oxford, MS 17, f.7v.)

189 Writ, 15 cm long, 12th century. (Public Record Office, London.)

194 Richard I. (Matthew Paris: Historia Major, English, c.1240. British Library, London, MS Royal 20.A.II.)

199 Richard Lionheart. (Title from Chertsey Abbey. British Museum, London.)

202 Jews persecuted. (Flores Historianum, 14th century. British Library, London, MS Cotton Nero D.ii, f.183v.)

207 Plan of Jerusalem. (c.1170. The Hague, Koninklijke Bibliothek, MS 69.)

214 t. Greek Fire (Byzantine MS. Prado, Madrid, Spain.)

215 t. Queen Constance leaves Salerno in a boat. (Petro d'Eboli: De Rebus siculis carmen, Italian, c.1200. Burghersbibliothek, Bern, Switzerland, Codex 120.)

215 c. Travellers. (Same as p.215 t.)

215 b. Crusaders sailing to the Holy Land in 1099. (Roman of Godefroy de Bouillon, French, 14th century. Bibliothèque Nationale, Paris, MS Fr. 22495, f.21.)

218 Philip Augustus, Richard I and Conrad III (Bibliothèque Nationale, Paris, MS Fr. 2824, f.80v.)

219 The fall of Acre. (Bibliothèque Nationale, Paris, MS Fr.)

222 t. Corpses removed from the battlefield. (ibid.215 t.)

222 b. Going to the crusade. (Guillaume de Tyr: Histoire de Jérusalem, French, c.1250. Bibliothèque Nationale, MS. Fr. 9081, f.99v.)

223 Foot soldiers. (c.1200. Bibliothèque Nationale, MS NAL.1390, f.57v.)

225 t. Richard disguised, arrested. (Petro d'Eboli: De Rebus siculis carmen, Italian, c.1200. Burghersbibliothek, Bern, Switzerland, Codex 120.)

227 b. Richard brought before Emperor Henry VI. He is now identified by his crown, while a servant holds his disguise. (ibid.225 t.)

229 Bernart de Ventadorn's song. (French, 13th century. Bibliothèque Nationale, Paris, MS Fr.854, f.26v.)

230 Bernart de Ventadorn. (French, 13th century. Bibliothèque Nationale, Paris, MS Fr.854, f.49.)

231 Ibid.230.

235 A joust between a knight from Anjou and Manfred. (French, 13th century. Wall painting in the Tour ferrande, Pernes-les-Fontaines, France.)

237 t.l. Building. (Matthew Paris, English, c.1240. Trinity College, Dublin, Ireland.)

237 t.r. Treadle loom. (Romance of Alexander, English, 12th century. Trinity College, Cambridge, MS 0.934.)

237 b. Work. (Reuner Musterbuch, German, c.1208–1218. Osterreichische Nationalbibliothek, Vienna, Austria, Codex 507, f.2r.)

239 t. Using an astrolabe. (Marvels of the East, English, c.1120–

1140. Bodleian Library, Oxford, MS Bodley 614, f.35v.)

241 b. Paris. (Vie de St Denis, French, 14th century. Bibliothèque Nationale, Paris.)

247 Lais de Marie de France. (French, 13th century. British Library, London, MS Harley 978, f.118r.)

258 King John. (Matthew Paris: Historia Major; c.1240. British Library, MS Royal 14.C.VII, f.9.)

265 t. King John. (Matthew Paris: Historia Major, English, c.1240. British Library, MS Royal 20.A.II)

265 b. King John hunting. (English, 13th century. British Library, MS Cotton Claudius D.2., f.113.)

270 Wine making. (Hunterian Psalter, English, 12th century, Glasgow University Library, MS Hunter 229.)

271 t. Grape picking. (Cistercian Psalter, French, early 13th century. Bibliothèque Municipale. Besançon, MS 54.)

271 r. Same as p.270.

273 Same as pp.270 & 271 r.

274 A battle. (The Maciejowski Psalter, French, 14th century. Pierpont Morgan Library, New York, MS 638.)

275 Ibid.274.

283 t. Foulques de Neuilly. (French, c.1330. Bodleian Library, MS Laud.Misc.587, f.1.)

283 b. The Fourth Crusade. (French, c.1330. Bodleian Library, MS Laud.Misc.587, f.1.)

285 t. Mother and child. (Caedmon Genesis, English, c.1000. Bodleian Library, MS Junius II, f.53.)

285 b. A swooning lady. (English, early 13th century. Bodleian Library, Oxford.)

286 t. Friars with sick patients. (English, 13th century. Bodleian Library, Oxford.)

286 b. Preparing herbal remedies. (Medica, English, early 13th century. Trinity College, Cambridge, MS 0.1.20, f.240r.)

287 t. Doctor and patient. (Jerome: De Nominibus Hebraicis, Medical treatise, 12th century. Trinity College, Cambridge, MS 0.1.20, f.241v.)

287 b. Doctor operates on a patient. (English, early 13th century. Bodleian Library, Oxford. MS Ashmole 1462 f.10 lower picture)

289 Paying taxes. (Livre juratoire d'Agen, French, 13th century. Bibliothèque Municipale d'Agen, MS 41, f.82v.)

297 t. Charter of Richard I. (Dated 23rd of April 1194. London, Records Corporation.)

303 Superstitions. (English, 13th century. British Library, London.)

306 Men and horses. (The Maciejowski Psalter, French, 14th century. Pierpont Morgan Library, New York, MS 638.)

307 Battle of Bouvines. (Matthew Paris: Historia Major, English, c.1240. (Corpus Christi College, Cambridge, MS 16, vol.2, f.37/Bodleian Library.)

315 b. Magna Carta. (English, 1215. British Library, MS Cotton Augustus II.106.)

326 Cambridge University Library, MS Ii.III. 12 f. 61v

335 Crusaders map: from London to Jerusalem. (Matthew Paris, circa. 1250. British Museum. MS Royal 14C VII.)

 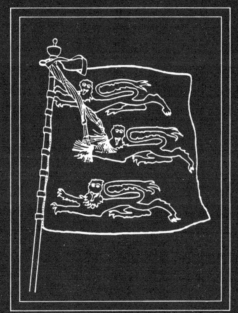 

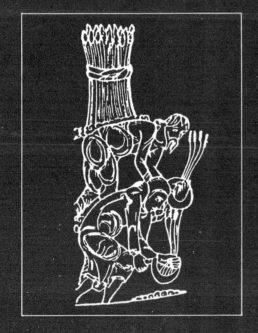